is a convenient presentation of election campaign issues in modern American political history. Each campaign, starting from 1928—when prosperity seemed assured and deserved—is highlighted in a mini-essay by the editor giving a succinct overview of the political, social, and economic climate of the time and a focus on the presidential candidates of the two major parties.

The selections themselves are the often hard-to-find nomination acceptance speech of each candidate and his most forceful or significant speech during the campaign for the nation's highest office. All speeches are reprinted in their entirety. Out of the hundreds of major and minor speeches delivered directly to the public, on radio, and later on television, the editor's choices allow an enlightening perspective on the parties' approach to issues and on the political personality of each candidate. The result is a striking re-creation of one important era of American history.

The general introduction by Mr. Singer deftly prepares the reader to experience the impact and excitement of the speeches as they were made to their contemporary audiences and increases his understanding of the progress—or lack of it—achieved toward resolving issues raised and argued in the 1976 presidential campaign. This volume is thus both a refresher for the student and the voter and a very useful guide to present and future campaigning.

ABOUT THE EDITOR

AARON SINGER teaches history at Manhattan College. He recently collaborated with

continued on back flap

continued from front flap

Robert L. Heilbroner on forthcoming books
on United States economic history.

Campaign Speeches of American Presidential Candidates 1928–1972

—— ☆ ——

Selected and Introduced by Aaron Singer

FREDERICK UNGAR PUBLISHING CO.

NEW YORK

To Audrey

Library of Congress Cataloging in Publication Data
Main entry under title:

Campaign speeches of American Presidential candidates,
1928-1972.

1. Campaign speeches—United States. 2. United
States—Politics and government—20th century—
Addresses, essays, lectures. I. Singer, Aaron.
E743.C235   309.1′73′09   75-39941
ISBN 0-8044-1301-0

PREFACE

This book has several purposes. The most important is to provide the reader with a convenient collection of the acceptance addresses and significant campaign speeches of the presidential candidates of the two major political parties for all the elections between 1928 and 1972. Each election is preceded by an introduction which places the campaign and the speeches in historical context in such a manner as to enable a reader with only a modest acquaintance with American history to read the speeches with profit. Collectively the speeches provide the reader with an overview of recent American political history.

Another aim of this book is to include speeches that captured the imagination of the American electorate by raising important issues. Furthermore, many of the speeches are sure to strike a responsive chord in the minds of today's readers, who will see mirrored in the past problems and issues of our own time.

Of necessity, this work must be selective, for to include all the campaign speeches of the candidates would require enough volumes to start a modest library. As a result, I have been faced with two procedural choices: either to include extracts from many campaign speeches, or to reproduce fewer in their entirety. I have chosen the latter course. I have tried to select one speech representative of each campaign; I believe that the reader can attain a clearer understanding of the issues, and a better insight into the overall campaign strategy of the candidates, from in-depth speeches. As a matter of form, the speeches of the winning candidates are presented first.

It is a pleasure to acknowledge here my indebtedness to John A. Garraty and Robert L. Heilbroner. The responsibility for the selection of the texts, and for the introductory material, is my own.

A. S.

CONTENTS

1940

1944

1948

1952

1956

1960

1964

1968

1972

INTRODUCTION

In 1831 an affluent young Frenchman named Alexis de Tocqueville set sail from Le Havre for America to discover the essence of democracy. While touring the United States Tocqueville witnessed a presidential campaign—an event which the prescient young visitor described in his classic analysis of American society, *Democracy in America*:

> For a long while before the appointed time has come, the election becomes the important and, so to speak, the all-engrossing topic of discussion. Factional ardor is redoubled, and all the artificial passions which the imagination can create in a happy and peaceful land are agitated and brought to light. . . . As the election draws near, the activity of intrigue and the agitation of the populace increase; the citizens are divided into hostile camps, each of which assumes the names of its favorite candidate; the whole nation glows with feverish excitement; the election is the daily theme of the press, the subject of every private conversation, the end of every thought and every action, the sole interest of the present.

Nor have Americans modulated their predilection for presidential elections. Indeed, with the advent of radio, television, and public opinion polls, presidential elections have acquired an even more compelling intensity.

Anyone who would be President of the United States must run in, and win, two major elections. First he must be nominated at his party's national convention. Then he must receive a majority of the country's electoral votes. But victory at the national convention is predicated on past conquests, especially triumphs in the preconvention primaries. Hence, the campaign for the presidency begins long before the convention.

Although the delegates at the national convention represent state and local interests, they must be sensitive to public opinion, for their function is to select a candidate who may occupy the most powerful and prestigious office in the world. Consequently, the possibilities of a "dark horse" emerging with the nomination are not very great. Not since Adlai Stevenson's nomination in 1952 has a candidate been "drafted" for the presidency.

Fundamentally, then, the delegates at the convention are there to ratify a decision that has already been made by the voters of their party. Perhaps the clearest indication of this lies in the fact that between 1956 and 1972 every presidential candidate has been nominated on the first ballot.

After winning the nomination the candidate is ready to wage his campaign. The trials and tribulations of the campaign odyssey were brilliantly summarized by Adlai Stevenson:

You must emerge, bright and bubbling with wisdom and well-being, every morning at 8 o'clock, just in time for a charming and profound breakfast talk, shake hands with hundreds, often literally thousands, of people, make several inspiring, "newsworthy" speeches during the day, confer with political leaders along the way and with your staff all the time, write at every chance, think if possible, read mail and newspapers, talk on the telephone, talk to everybody, dictate, receive delegations, eat, with decorum—and discretion!—and ride through city after city on the back of an open car, smiling until your mouth is dehydrated by the wind, waving until the blood runs out of your arms, and then bounce gaily, confidently, masterfully into great howling halls, shaved and all made up for television with the right color shirt and tie—I always forgot—an a manuscript so defaced with chicken tracks and last-minute jottings that you couldn't follow it, even if the spotlight weren't blinding and even if the still photographers didn't shoot you in the eye every time you looked at them. (I've often wondered what happened to all those pictures.) Then all you have to do is make a great, imperishable speech, get out through the pressing crowds with a few score autographs, your clothes intact, your hands bruised, and back to the hotel—in time to see a few important people.

But the real work has just commenced—two or three, sometimes four hours of frenzied writing and editing of the next day's immortal mouthings so you can get something to the stenographers, so they can get something to the mimeograph machines, so they can get something to the reporters, so they can get something to their papers by deadline time. (And I quickly concluded that all deadlines were yesterday!) Finally sleep, sweet sleep, steals you away, unless you worry—which I do.

The next day is the same.*

Essentially, the candidate's function during a campaign is to organize his party's campaign workers and to motivate the electorate. Because no candidate can presuppose that all the members of his own party will board his bandwagon, he must rely on party symbols: for Republicans this means invoking the name of Abraham Lincoln and extolling the virtues of economic individualism; for Democrats it means calling up memories of Jefferson and Jackson, and waving the banner of the New Deal. Most important, the candidate must go out and meet the electorate. It is no longer possible to win an election by conducting a "front-porch" campaign.

Thus, campaign oratory is an integral part of the election. The pace of the campaign, however, does not allow a candidate constantly to formulate new ideas. He therefore selects campaign themes which he constantly plays on, with minor variations to suit the audience and hour. On occasion external events will cause him to alter the course of his campaign; or he may decide to modify or broaden his themes because of public opinion polls—polls which allow the electorate to present itself to the candidate.

Yet candidates are not elected solely on the content of their speeches or their oratorical skills. Herbert Hoover's 1928 addresses sounded more like dull state papers than campaign speeches, but Hoover won the election. On the other hand, Adlai Stevenson's ability to edify as well as entertain an audience did not help him much in 1952 and 1956.

Clearly, parties and candidates wax and wane for reasons more complicated than campaign oratory. Candidates must penetrate the hearts as well as the minds of the voters if they are to be successful. Candidates and issues are indissoluble.

Of the many factors that have influenced the conduct of presidential campaigns in recent years, none has had the ubiquitous effect of radio and television. By 1928 one out of every three homes in America had a radio. People who were once distances removed from the centers of communication were brought into the mainstream of American political life.

But in the 1950s radio gave way to television. Because television is a visual medium, it must rely on images to sustain interest. Images, therefore, are frequently more important than content. In 1952 and 1956, for

* *Major Campaign Speeches, 1952* (New York: Random House, 1953).

example, Stevenson's eloquence was no match for Eisenhower's fatherly image.

Nevertheless, television has provided all candidates with a forum whence they could enter the homes of the American electorate to deliver their messages. "The people," observed Tocqueville, "reign in the American political world as the Deity does in the universe."

1928

— ☆ —

In the 1920s Americans were experiencing the greatest period of prosperity in their history. To most contemporary observers, these were the halcyon days of American civilization, the ineluctable culmination of the American dream of peace and prosperity.

Although Americans measured progress in terms of material success in these years, the nation's prosperity was based on more than just the entrance of radios, cars, and household gadgets into ordinary life. For in the 1920s Americans were earning more money, working shorter hours, enjoying better health, and spending more money on education than any other people in the world. By any standard, the American economy in the 1920s was an enormous success.

In these years, moreover, the Republican party came to be regarded as both the symbol and the guardian of prosperity. "The business of America is business," declared President Coolidge in 1925. Coolidge's renomination appeared certain, but in August, 1927, the President announced that he did "not choose to run for President in 1928."

Coolidge's enigmatic statement cleared the way for Secretary of Commerce Herbert Hoover to succeed to the presidency. At their presidential nominating convention in Kansas City, Missouri, the Republicans selected Hoover as their party's standard bearer on the first ballot.

Hoover reflected the image that Americans had of themselves and embodied the virtues that they most esteemed: industry, prosperity, respectability. Born on a farm in West Branch, Iowa, and orphaned at an early age, Hoover worked his way through Stanford University to become a highly successful mining engineer. His efforts on behalf of European relief both during and after World War I, coupled with his service as head of President Woodrow Wilson's wartime Food Administration Board, earned for Hoover an international reputation for efficiency and humaneness.

The Democrats opened their convention at Houston, Texas on June 26th. They, too, were able to nominate a candidate after one roll call: Alfred E. Smith, the governor of New York. Not only was Smith the first Catholic to run for the presidency, but he was also the first patently identified "city man" to run for national office.

Like Hoover, Al Smith too was a self-made man. Forced to leave school at the age of 11 to help support his family, his "universities" (as he called them) were the sidewalks of New York, the Tammany clubs, and the state assembly at Albany, in which he served from 1903-15. Although he supported many social reforms as governor, Smith was essentially a conservative. In fact, he chose John J. Raskob, a former Republican and the chairman of the finance committee of General Motors, to serve as his campaign manager.

While there were no discernible differences between the platforms of the two parties, Smith tried to outline his own position on the major issues of the day in his acceptance speech. To the consternation of his party, he also addressed himself to the most avidly discussed topic of the day: prohibition. As one of the country's most outspoken critics of prohibition, Smith—despite the fact that the Democratic platform pledged itself "to an honest effort to enforce the eighteenth amendment"—announced that he would recommend modification of the prohibition amendment and the Volstead Act if elected.

Hoover's acceptance speech, on the other hand, avoided controversial issues, reiterated the Republican platform, and assured the American people that they were on the threshold of eradicating poverty.

Smith failed to disassociate himself from his party's conservative platform and to establish a progressive position pointedly different from Hoover's. As a result, other issues, such as Smith's religion, were injected into the campaign. In a speech delivered before a hostile Protestant audience in Oklahoma City, Smith delivered his most cogent attack against bigotry.

Hoover stood on the Republican platform in 1928. In his speeches he articulated his philosophy of "rugged individualism" and praised the "American system" of free enterprise. Among the many speeches he delivered in this vein, his address in New York on October 22nd represents the quintessential statement of economic individualism.

HERBERT C. HOOVER

Acceptance Speech

STANFORD UNIVERSITY STADIUM, PALO ALTO, CALIFORNIA

August 11, 1928

You bring, Mr. Chairman, formal notice of my nomination by the Republican Party to the Presidency of the United States. I accept. It is a great honor to be chosen for leadership in that party which has so largely made the history of our country in these last seventy years.

Mr. Chairman, you and your associates have in four days traveled three thousand miles across the continent to bring me this notice. I am reminded that in order to notify George Washington of his election, Charles Thompson, Secretary of the Congress, spent seven days on horseback to deliver that important intelligence two hundred and thirty miles from New York to Mount Vernon.

In another way, too, this occasion illuminates the milestones of progress. By the magic of the radio this nomination was heard by millions of our fellow-citizens not seven days after its occurrence, nor one day, nor even one minute. They were, to all intents and purposes, present in the hall, participants in the proceedings. Today these same millions have heard your voice and now are hearing mine. We stand in their unseen presence. It is fitting, however, that the forms of our national life, hallowed by generations of usage, should be jealously preserved, and for that reason you have come to me, as similar delegations have come to other candidates through the years.

Those invisible millions have already heard from Kansas City the reading of our party principles. They would wish to hear from me not a

4

discourse upon the platform—in which I fully concur—but something of the spirit and ideals with which it is proposed to carry it into administration.

Our problems of the past seven years have been problems of reconstruction; our problems of the future are problems of construction. They are problems of progress. New and gigantic forces have come into our national life. The Great War released ideas of government in conflict with our principles. We have grown to financial and physical power which compels us into a new setting among nations. Science has given us new tools and a thousand inventions. Through them have come to each of us wider relationships, more neighbors, more leisure, broader vision, higher ambitions, greater problems. To insure that these tools shall not be used to limit liberty has brought a vast array of questions in government.

The points of contact between the government and the people are constantly multiplying. Every year wise governmental policies become more vital in ordinary life. As our problems grow so do our temptations grow to venture away from those principles upon which our republic was founded and upon which it has grown to greatness. Moreover we must direct economic progress in support of moral and spiritual progress.

Our party platform deals mainly with economic problems, but our nation is not an agglomeration of railroads, of ships, of factories, of dynamos, or statistics. It is a nation of homes, a nation of men, of women, of children. Every man has a right to ask of us whether the United States is a better place for him, his wife, and his children to live in, because the Republican Party has conducted the government for nearly eight years. Every woman has a right to ask whether her life, her home, her man's job, her hopes, her happiness will be better assured by the continuance of the Republican Party in power. I propose to discuss the questions before me in that light.

With this occasion we inaugurate the campaign. It shall be an honest campaign; every penny will be publicly accounted for. It shall be a true campaign. We shall use words to convey our meaning, not to hide it.

The Republican Party came into authority nearly eight years ago. It is necessary to remind ourselves of the critical conditions of that time. We were confronted with an incompleted peace and involved in violent and dangerous disputes both at home and abroad. The Federal Government was spending at the rate of five and one-half billions per year; our national debt stood at the staggering total of twenty-four billions. The foreign debts were unsettled. The country was in a panic from overexpansion due to the war and the continued inflation of credit and currency after the Armistice, followed by a precipitant nation-wide deflation which in half a year crashed the prices of commodities by nearly one-half. Agriculture was prostrated; land was unsalable; commerce and industry were stagnated; our foreign trade ebbed away; five millions of unemployed walked the streets. Discontent and agitation against our democracy were rampant. Fear for the future haunted every heart.

No party ever accepted a more difficult task of reconstruction than did the Republican Party in 1921. The record of these seven and one-half years constitutes a period of rare courage in leadership and constructive action. Never has a political party been able to look back upon a similar period with more satisfaction. Never could it look forward with more confidence that its record would be approved by the electorate.

Peace has been made. The healing processes of good will have extinguished the fires of hate. Year by year in our relations with other nations we have advanced the ideals of law and of peace, in substitution for force. By rigorous economy federal expenses have been reduced by two billions per annum. The national debt has been reduced by six and a half billions. The foreign debts have been settled in large part and on terms which have regard for our debtors and for our taxpayers. Taxes have been reduced four successive times. These reductions have been made in the particular interest of the small taxpayers. For this purpose taxes upon articles of consumption and popular service have been removed. The income tax rolls today show a reduction of eighty percent in the total revenue collected on incomes under $10,000 per year, while they show a reduction of only twenty-five percent in revenues from incomes above that amount. Each successive reduction in taxes has brought a reduction in the cost of living to all our people.

Commerce and industry have revived. Although the agricultural, coal, and textile industries still lag in their recovery and still require our solicitude and assistance, yet they have made substantial progress. While other countries engaged in the war are only now regaining their pre-war level in foreign trade, our exports, even if we allow for the depreciated dollar, are fifty-eight percent greater than before the war. Constructive leadership and co-operation by the government have released and stimulated the energies of our people. Faith in the future has been restored. Confidence in our form of government has never been greater.

But it is not through the recitation of wise policies in government alone that we demonstrate our progress under Republican guidance. To me the test is the security, comfort, and opportunity that have been brought to the average American family. During this less than eight years our population has increased by eight percent. Yet our national income has increased by over thirty billions of dollars per year or more than forty-five percent. Our production—and therefore our consumption—of goods has increased by over twenty-five percent. It is easily demonstrated that these increases have been widely spread among our whole people. Home ownership has grown. While during this period the number of families has increased by about 2,300,000, we have built more than 3,500,000 new and better homes. In this short time we have equipped nearly nine million more homes with electricity, and through it drudgery has been lifted from the lives of women. The barriers of time and distance have been swept away and life made freer and larger by the installation of six million more telephones, seven million radio sets, and the service of an additional fourteen million automobiles. Our cities are growing magnificent with beautiful buildings, parks, and playgrounds. Our countryside has been knit together with splendid roads.

We have doubled the use of electrical power and with it we have taken sweat from the backs of men. The purchasing power of wages has steadily increased. The hours of labor have decreased. The twelve-hour day has been abolished. Great progress has been made in stabilization of commerce and industry. The job of every man has thus been made more secure. Unemployment in the sense of distress is widely disappearing.

Most of all, I like to remember what this progress has meant to America's children. The portal of their opportunity has been ever widening. While our population has grown but eight percent, we have increased by eleven percent the number of children in our grade schools, by sixty-six percent the number in our high schools, and by seventy-five percent the number in our institutions of higher learning.

With all our spending we have doubled savings deposits in our banks and building and loan associations. We have nearly doubled our life insurance. Nor have our people been selfish. They have met with a full hand the most sacred obligation of man—charity. The gifts of America to churches, to hospitals, and institutions for the care of the afflicted, and to relief from great disasters have surpassed by hundreds of millions any totals for any similar period in all human record.

One of the oldest and perhaps the noblest of human aspirations has been the abolition of poverty. By poverty I mean the grinding by undernourishment, cold, and ignorance, and fear of old age of those who have the will to work. We in America today are nearer to the final triumph over poverty than ever before in the history of any land. The poorhouse is vanishing from among us. We have not yet reached the goal, but, given a chance to go forward with the policies of the last eight years, we shall soon with the help of God be in sight of the day when poverty will be banished from this nation. There is no guarantee against poverty equal to a job for every man. That is the primary purpose of the economic policies we advocate.

I especially rejoice in the effect of our increased national efficiency upon the improvement of the American home. That is the sanctuary of our loftiest ideas, the source of the spiritual energy of our people. The bettered home surroundings, the expanded schools and playgrounds, and the enlarged leisure which have come with our economic progress have brought to the average family a fuller life, a wider outlook, a stirred imagination, and a lift in aspirations.

Economic advancement is not an end in itself. Successful democracy rests wholly upon the moral and spiritual quality of its people. Our growth in spiritual achievements must keep pace with our growth in physical accomplishments. Material prosperity and moral progress must march together if we would make the United States that commonwealth so grandly conceived by its founders. Our government, to match the expectations of our people, must have constant regard for those human values that give dignity and nobility to life. Generosity of impulse, cultivation of mind, willingness to sacrifice, spaciousness of spirit—those are the qualities whereby America, growing bigger and richer and more powerful, may become America great and noble. A people or government to which these values are not real, because they are not tangible, is in peril. Size, wealth, and power alone cannot fulfill the promise of America's opportunity.

The most urgent economic problem in our nation today is in agriculture. It must be solved if we are to bring prosperity and contentment to one-third of our people directly and to all of our people indirectly. We have pledged ourselves to find a solution.

To my mind most agricultural discussions go wrong because of two false premises. The first is that agriculture is one industry. It is a dozen distinct industries incapable of the same organization. The second false premise is that rehabilitation will be complete when it has reached a point comparable with pre-war. Agriculture was not upon a satisfactory basis before the war. The abandoned farms of the Northeast bear their own testimony. Generally there was but little profit in Midwest agriculture for many years except that derived from the slow increases in farm land values. Even of more importance is the great advance in standards of living of all occupations since the war. Some branches of agriculture have greatly recovered, but taken as a whole it is not keeping pace with the onward march in other industries.

There are many causes for failure of agriculture to win its full share of national prosperity. The after-war deflation of prices not only brought great direct losses to the farmer, but he was often left indebted in inflated dollars to be paid in deflated dollars. Prices are often demoralized through gluts in our markets during the harvest season. Local taxes have been increased to provide the improved roads and schools. The tariff on some products is proving inadequate to protect him from imports from abroad. The increases in transportation rates since the war have greatly affected the price which he receives for his products. Over six million farmers in times of surplus engage in destructive competition with one another in the sale of their product, often depressing prices below those levels that could be maintained.

The whole tendency of our civilization during the last fifty years has been toward an increase in the size of the units of production in order to secure lower costs and a more orderly adjustment of the flow of commodities to the demand. But the organization of agriculture into larger units must not be by enlarged farms. The farmer has shown he can increase the skill of his industry without large operations. He is today producing twenty percent more than eight years ago with about the same acreage and personnel. Farming is and must continue to be an individualistic business of small units and independent ownership. The farm is more than a business: it is a state of living. We do not wish it converted into a mass-production machine. Therefore, if the farmer's position is to be improved by larger operations it must be done not on the farm but in the field of distribution. Agriculture has partially advanced in this direction through co-operatives and pools. But the traditional co-operative is often not a complete solution.

Differences of opinion as to both causes and remedy have retarded the completion of a constructive program of relief. It is our plain duty to search out the common ground on which we may mobilize the sound forces of agricultural reconstruction. Our platform lays a solid basis upon which we can build. It offers an affirmative program.

An adequate tariff is the foundation of farm relief. Our consumers increase faster than our producers. The domestic market must be protected. Foreign products raised under lower standards of living are today competing in our home markets. I would use my office and influence to give the farmer the full benefit of our historic tariff policy.

A large portion of the spread between what the farmer receives for his products and what the ultimate consumer pays is due to increased transportation charges. Increase in railway rates has been one of the penalties of the war. These increases have been added to the cost to the farmer of reaching seaboard and foreign markets and result therefore in reduction of his prices. The farmers of foreign countries have thus been indirectly aided in their competition with the American farmer. Nature has endowed us with a great system of inland waterways. Their modernization will comprise a most substantial contribution to Midwest farm relief and to the development of twenty of our interior states. This modernization includes not only the great Mississippi system, with its joining of the Great Lakes and of the heart of Midwest agriculture to the Gulf, but also a shipway from the Great Lakes to the Atlantic. These improvements would mean so large an increment in farmers' prices as to warrant their construction many times over. There is no more vital method of farm relief.

But we must not stop here.

An outstanding proposal of the party program is the whole-hearted pledge to undertake the reorganization of the marketing system upon sounder and more economical lines. We have already contributed greatly to this purpose by the acts supporting farm co-operatives, the establishment of intermediate credit banks, the regulation of stockyards and public exchanges, and the expansion of the Department of Agriculture. The platform proposes to go much farther. It pledges the creation of a Federal Farm Board of representative farmers to be clothed with authority and resources with which not only to still further aid farmers' co-operatives and pools and to assist generally in solution of farm problems but especially to build up, with federal finance, farmer-owned and farmer-controlled stabilization corporations which will protect the farmer from the depressions and demoralization of seasonal gluts and periodical surpluses.

Objection has been made that this program, as laid down by the party platform, may require that several hundred millions of dollars of capital be advanced by the Federal Government without obligation upon the individual farmer. With that objection I have little patience. A nation which is spending ninety billions a year can well afford an expenditure of a few hundred millions for a workable program that will give to one-third of its population their fair share of the nation's prosperity. Nor does this proposal put the government into business except so far as it is called upon to furnish capital with which to build up the farmer to the control of his own destinies.

The program adapts itself to the variable problems of agriculture not only today but which will arise in the future. I do not believe that any single human being or any group of human beings can determine in advance all questions that will arise in so vast and complicated an industry over a term of years. The first step is to create an effective agency directly for these purposes and to give it authority and resources. These are solemn pledges and they will be fulfilled by the Republican Party. It is a definite plan of relief. It needs only the detailed elaboration of legislation and appropriations to put it into force.

During my term as Secretary of Commerce I have steadily endeavored to build up a system of co-operation between the government and business. Under these co-operative actions all elements interested in the problems of a particular industry such as manufacturer, distributor, worker, and consumer have been called into council together, not for a single occasion but for continuous work. These efforts have been successful beyond any expectation. They have been accomplished without interference or regulation by the government. They have secured progress in the industries, remedy for abuses, elimination of waste, reduction of cost in production and distribution, lower prices to the consumer, and more stable employment and profit. While the problem varies with every different commodity and with every different part of our great country, I should wish to apply the same method to agriculture so that the leaders of every phase of each group can advise and organize on policies and constructive measures. I am convinced that this form of action, as it has done in other industries, can greatly benefit farmer, distributor, and consumer.

The working out of agricultural relief constitutes the most important obligation of the next administration. I stand pledged to these proposals. The object of our policies is to establish for our farmers an income equal to those of other occupations; for the farmer's wife the same comforts in her home as women in other groups; for the farm boys and girls the same opportunities in life as other boys and girls. So far as my own abilities may be of service, I dedicate them to help secure prosperity and contentment in that industry where I and my forefathers were born and nearly all my family still obtain their livelihood.

The Republican Party has ever been the exponent of protection to all our people from competition with lower standards of living abroad. We have always fought for tariffs designed to establish this protection from imported goods. We also have enacted restrictions upon immigration for the protection of labor from the inflow of workers faster than we can absorb them without breaking down our wage levels.

The Republican principle of an effective control of imported goods and of immigration has contributed greatly to the prosperity of our country. There is no selfishness in this defense of our standards of living. Other countries gain nothing if the high standards of America are sunk and if we are prevented from building a civilization which sets the level of hope for the entire world. A general reduction in the tariff would admit a flood of goods from abroad. It would injure every home. It would fill our streets with idle workers. It would destroy the returns to our dairymen, our fruit, flax, and live-stock growers, and our other farmers.

No man will say that any immigration or tariff law is perfect. We welcome our new immigrant citizens and their great contribution to our nation; we seek only to protect them equally with those already here. We shall amend the immigration laws to relieve unnecessary hardships upon families. As a member of the commission whose duty it is to determine the quota basis under the national origins law I have found it is impossible to do so accurately and without hardship. The basis now in effect carries out the essential principle of the law and I favor repeal of that part of the act calling for a new basis of quotas.

We have pledged ourselves to make such revisions in the tariff laws as may be necessary to provide real protection against the shiftings of economic tides in our various industries. I am sure the American people would rather entrust the perfection of the tariff to the consistent friend of the tariff than to our opponents, who have always reduced our tariffs, who voted against our present protection to the worker and the farmer, and whose whole economic theory over generations has been the destruction of the protective principle.

Having earned my living with my own hands, I cannot have other than the greatest sympathy with the aspirations of those who toil. It has been my good fortune during the past twelve years to have received the co-operation of labor in many directions, and in promotion of many public purposes.

The trade union movement in our country has maintained two departures from such movements in all other countries. They have been staunch supporters of American individualism and American institutions. They have steadfastly opposed subversive doctrines from abroad. Our freedom from foreign social and economic diseases is in large degree due to this resistance by our own labor. Our trade unions, with few exceptions, have welcomed all basic improvement in industrial methods. This largeness of mind has contributed to the advancing standards of living of the whole of our people. They properly have sought to participate—by additions to wages—in the result of improvements and savings which they have helped to make.

During these past years we have grown greatly in the mutual understanding between employer and employee. We have seen a growing realization by the employer that the highest practicable wage is the road to increased consumption and prosperity, and we have seen a growing realization by labor that the maximum use of machines, of effort, and of skill is the road to lower production costs and in the end to higher real wages. Under these impulses and the Republican protective system our industrial output has increased as never before and our wages have grown steadily in buying power. Our workers with their average weekly wages can today buy two and often three times more bread and butter than any wage earner of Europe. At one time we demanded for our workers a "full dinner pail." We have now gone far beyond that conception. Today we demand larger comfort and greater participation in life and leisure.

The Republican platform gives the pledge of the party to the support of labor. It endorses the principle of collective bargaining and freedom in labor negotiations. We stand also pledged to the curtailment of excessive use of the injunction in labor disputes.

The war and the necessary curtailment of expenditure during the reconstruction years have suspended the construction of many needed public works. Moreover, the time has arrived when we must undertake a larger-visioned development of our water resources. Every drop which runs to the sea without yielding its full economic service is a waste.

Nearly all of our great drainages contain within themselves possibilities of cheapened transportation, irrigation, reclamation, domestic water supply, hydro-electric power, and frequently the necessities of flood control. But this development of our waters requires more definite national policies in the systematic co-ordination of those different works upon each drainage area. We have wasted scores of millions by projects undertaken not as a part of a whole but as the consequence of purely local demands. We cannot develop modernized water transportation by isolated projects. We must develop it as a definite and positive interconnected system of transportation. We must adjust reclamation and irrigation to our needs for more land. Where they lie together we must co-ordinate transportation with flood control, the development of hydro-electric power and of irrigation, else we shall as in the past commit errors that will take years and millions to remedy. The Congress has authorized and has in process of legislation great programs of public works. In addition to the works in development of water resources, we have in progress large undertakings in public roads and the construction of public buildings.

All these projects will probably require an expenditure of upward of one billion dollars within the next four years. It comprises the largest engineering construction ever undertaken by any government. It involves three times the expenditure laid out upon the Panama Canal. It is justified by the growth, need, and wealth of our country. The organization and administration of this construction is a responsibility of the first order. For it we must secure the utmost economy, honesty, and skill. These works, which will provide jobs for an army of men, should so far as practicable be adjusted to take up the slack of unemployment elsewhere.

I rejoice in the completion of legislation providing adequate flood control of the Mississippi. It marks not alone the undertaking of a great national task, but it constitutes a contribution to the development of the South. In encouragement of their economic growth lies one of the great national opportunities of the future.

I recently stated my position upon the Eighteenth Amendment, which I again repeat:

"I do not favor the repeal of the Eighteenth Amendment. I stand for the efficient enforcement of the laws enacted thereunder. Whoever is chosen President has under his oath the solemn duty to pursue this course.

"Our country has deliberately undertaken a great social and economic experiment, noble in motive and far-reaching in purpose. It must be worked out constructively."

Common sense compels us to realize that grave abuses have occurred —abuses which must be remedied. An organized searching investigation of fact and causes can alone determine the wise method of correcting them. Crime and disobedience of law cannot be permitted to break down the Constitution and laws of the United States.

Modification of the enforcement laws which would permit that which the Constitution forbids is nullification. This the American people will not countenance. Change in the Constitution can and must be brought about only by the straightforward methods provided in the Constitution itself. There are those who do not believe in the purposes of several provisions of the Constitution. No one denies their right to seek to amend it. They are not subject to criticism for asserting that right. But the Republican Party does deny the right of anyone to seek to destroy the purposes of the Constitution by indirection.

Whoever is elected President takes an oath not only to faithfully execute the office of the President, but that oath provides still further that he will, to the best of his ability, preserve, protect, and defend the Constitution of the United States. I should be untrue to these great traditions, untrue to my oath of office, were I to declare otherwise.

With impressive proof on all sides of magnificent progress, no one can rightly deny the fundamental correctness of our economic system. Our pre-eminent advance over nations in the last eight years has been due to distinctively American accomplishments. We do not owe these accomplishments to our vast natural resources. These we have always had. They have not increased. What has changed is our ability to utilize these resources more effectively. It is our human resources that have changed. Man for man and woman for woman, we are today more capable, whether in the work of farm, factory, or business, than ever before. It lies in our magnificent educational system, in the hard-working character of our people, in the capacity of far-sighted leadership in industry, the ingenuity, the daring of the pioneers of new inventions, in the abolition of the saloon, and the wisdom of our national policies.

With the growth and increasing complexity of our economic life the relations of government and business are multiplying daily. They are yearly more dependent upon each other. Where it is helpful and necessary, this relation should be encouraged. Beyond this it should not go. It is the duty of government to avoid regulation as long as equal opportunity to all citizens is not invaded and public rights violated. Government should not engage in business in competition with its citizens. Such actions extinguish the enterprise and initiative which has been the glory of America and which has been the root of its pre-eminence among the nations of the earth. On the other hand, it is the duty of business to conduct itself so that government regulation or government competition is unnecessary.

Business is practical, but it is founded upon faith—faith among our people in the integrity of business men, and faith that it will receive fair play from the government. It is the duty of government to maintain that faith. Our whole business system would break down in a day if there was not a high sense of moral responsibility in our business world. The whole practice and ethics of business has made great strides of improvement in the last quarter of a century, largely due to the effort of business and the professions themselves. One of the most helpful signs of recent years is the stronger growth of associations of workers, farmers, business men, and professional men with a desire to cure their own abuses and a purpose to serve public interest. Many problems can be solved through co-operation between government and these self-governing associations to improve methods and practices. When business cures its own abuses it is true self-government, which comprises more than political institutions.

One of the greatest difficulties of business with government is the multitude of unnecessary contacts with government bureaus, the uncertainty and inconsistency of government policies, and the duplication of governmental activities. A large part of this is due to the scattering of functions and the great confusion of responsibility in our federal organization. We have, for instance, fourteen different bureaus or agencies engaged in public works and construction, located in nine different departments of the government. It brings about competition between government agencies, inadequacy of control, and a total lack of co-ordinated policies in public works. We have eight different bureaus and agencies charged with conservation of our natural resources, located in five different departments of their government. These conditions exist in many other directions. Divided responsibility, with the absence of centralized authority, prevents constructive and consistent development of broad national policies.

Our Republican presidents have repeatedly recommended to Congress that it would not only greatly reduce expenses of business in its contacts with government but that a great reduction could be made in governmental expenditure and more consistent and continued national policies could be developed if we could secure the grouping of these agencies devoted to one major purpose under single responsibility and authority. I have had the good fortune to be able to carry out such reorganization in respect to the Department of Commerce. The results have amply justified its expansion to other departments and I should consider it an obligation to enlist the support of Congress to effect it.

The government can be of invaluable aid in the promotion of business. The ideal state of business is freedom from those fluctuations from boom to slump which bring on one hand the periods of unemployment and bankruptcy and, on the other, speculation and waste. Both are destructive to progress and fraught with great hardship to every home. By economy in expenditures, wise taxation, and sound fiscal finance it can relieve the burdens upon sound business and promote financial stability. By sound tariff policies it can protect our workmen, our farmers, and our manufacturers from lower standards of living abroad. By scientific research it can promote invention and improvement in methods. By economic research and statistical service it can promote the elimination of waste and contribute to stability in production and distribution. By promotion of foreign trade it can expand the markets for our manufacturers and farmers and thereby contribute greatly to stability and employment.

Our people know that the production and distribution of goods on a large scale is not wrong. Many of the most important comforts of our people are only possible by mass production and distribution. Both small and big business have their full place. The test of business is not its size—the test is whether there is honest competition, whether there is freedom from domination, whether there is integrity and usefulness of purpose. As Secretary of Commerce I have been greatly impressed by the fact that the foundation of American business is the independent business man. The Department by encouragement of his associations and by provision of special services has endeavored to place him in a position of equality in information and skill with larger operations. Alike with our farmers his is the stronghold of American individuality. It is here that our local communities receive their leadership. It is here that we refresh our leadership for larger enterprise. We must maintain his opportunity and his individual service. He and the public must be protected from any domination or from predatory business.

I have said that the problems before us are more than economic, that in a much greater degree they are moral and spiritual. I hold that there rests upon government many responsibilities which affect the moral and spiritual welfare of our people. The participation of women in politics means a keener realization of the importance of these questions. It means higher political standards.

One-half of our citizens fail to exercise the responsibilities of the ballot box. I would wish that the women of our country could embrace this problem in citizenship as peculiarly their own. If they could apply their higher sense of service and responsibility, their freshness of enthusiasm, their capacity for organization to this problem, it would become, as it should become, an issue of profound patriotism. The whole plane of political life would be lifted, the foundations of democracy made more secure.

In this land, dedicated to tolerance, we still find outbreaks of intolerance. I come of Quaker stock. My ancestors were persecuted for their beliefs. Here they sought and found religious freedom. By blood and conviction I stand for religious tolerance both in act and in spirit. The glory of our American ideals is the right of every man to worship God according to the dictates of his own conscience.

In the past years there has been corruption participated in by individual officials and members of both political parties in national, state, and municipal affairs. Too often this corruption has been viewed with indifference by a great number of our people. It would seem unnecessary to state the elemental requirement that government must inspire confidence not only in its ability but in its integrity. Dishonesty in government, whether national, state, or municipal, is a double wrong. It is treason to the state. It is destructive of self-government. Government in the United States rests not only upon the consent of the governed but upon the conscience of the nation. Government weakens the moment that its integrity is even doubted. Moral incompetency by those entrusted with government is a blighting wind upon private integrity. There must be no place for cynicism in the creed of America.

Our Civil Service has proved a great national boon. Appointive office, both North, South, East, and West, must be based solely on merit, character, and reputation in the community in which the appointee is to serve; as it is essential for the proper performance of their duties that officials shall enjoy the confidence and respect of the people with whom they serve.

For many years I have been associated with efforts to save life and health for our children. These experiences with millions of children both at home and abroad have left an indelible impression—that the greatness of any nation, its freedom from poverty and crime, its aspirations and ideals are the direct quotient of the care of its children. Racial progress marches upon the feet of healthy and instructed children. There should be no child in America that is not born and does not live under sound conditions of health; that does not have full opportunity of education from the beginning to the end of our institutions; that is not free from injurious labor; that does not have every stimulation to accomplish the fullest of its capacities. Nothing in development of child life will ever replace the solicitude of parents and the surroundings of home, but in many aspects both parents and children are dependent upon the vigilance of government— national, state, and local.

I especially value the contribution that the youth of the country can make to the success of our American experiment in democracy. Theirs is the precious gift of enthusiasm, without which no great deed can be accomplished. A government that does not constantly seek to live up to the ideals of its young men and women falls short of what the American people have a right to expect and demand from it. To interpret the spirit of the youth into the spirit of our government, to bring the warmth of their enthusiasm and the flame of their idealism into the affairs of the nation—is to make of American government a positive and living force, a factor for greatness and nobility in the life of the nation.

I think I may say that I have witnessed as much of the horror and suffering of war as any other American. From it I have derived a deep passion for peace. Our foreign policy has one primary object, and that is peace. We have no hates; we wish no further possessions; we harbor no military threats. The unspeakable experiences of the Great War, the narrow margin by which civilization survived its exhaustion, is still vivid in men's minds. There is no nation in the world today that does not earnestly wish for peace—that is not striving for peace.

There are two co-operating factors in the maintenance of peace— the building of good-will by wise and sympathetic handling of international relations, and the adequate preparedness for defense. We must not only be just; we must be respected. The experiences of the war afforded final proof that we cannot isolate ourselves from the world, that the safeguarding of peace cannot be attained by negative action. Our offer of treaties open to the signature of all, renouncing war as an instrument of national policy, proves that we have every desire to co-operate with other nations for peace. But our people have determined that we can give the greatest real help—both in times of tranquillity and in times of strain—if we maintain our independence from the political exigencies of the Old World. In pursuance of this, our country has refused membership in the League of Nations, but we are glad to co-operate with the League in its endeavors to further scientific, economic, and social welfare, and to secure limitation of armament.

We believe that the foundations of peace can be strengthened by the creation of methods and agencies by which a multitude of incidents may be transferred from the realm of prejudice and force to arbitration and the determination of right and wrong based upon international law.

We have been and we are particularly desirous of furthering the limitation of armaments. But in the meantime we know that in an armed world there is only one certain guarantee of freedom—and that is preparedness for defense. It is solely to defend ourselves, for the protection of our citizens, that we maintain armament. No clearer evidence of this can exist than the unique fact that we have fewer men in army uniform today than we have in police uniforms, and that we maintain a standing invitation to the world that we are always ready to limit our naval armament in proportion as the other naval nations will do likewise. We earnestly wish that the burdens and dangers of armament upon every home in the world might be lessened. But we must and shall maintain our naval defense and our merchant marine in the strength and efficiency which will yield to us at all times the primary assurance of liberty, that is, of national safety.

There is one of the ideals of America upon which I wish at this time to lay especial emphasis. For we should constantly test our economic, social, and governmental system by certain ideals which must control them. The founders of our republic propounded the revolutionary doctrine that all men are created equal and all should have equality before the law. This was the emancipation of the individual. And since these beginnings, slowly, surely, and almost imperceptibly, this nation has added a third ideal almost unique to America—the ideal of equal opportunity. This is the safeguard of the individual. The simple life of early days in our republic found but few limitations upon equal opportunity. By the crowding of our people and the intensity and complexity of their activities it takes today a new importance.

Equality of opportunity is the right of every American—rich or poor, foreign or native-born, irrespective of faith or color. It is the right of every individual to attain that position in life to which his ability and character entitle him. By its maintenance we will alone hold open the door of opportunity to every new generation, to every boy and girl. It tolerates no privileged classes or castes or groups who would hold opportunity as their prerogative. Only from confidence that this right will be upheld can flow that unbounded courage and hope which stimulate each individual man and woman to endeavor and to achievement. The sum of their achievement is the gigantic harvest of national progress.

This ideal of individualism based upon equal opportunity to every citizen is the negation of socialism. It is the negation of anarchy. It is the negation of despotism. It is as if we set a race. We, through free and universal education, provide the training of the runners; we give to them an equal start; we provide in the government the umpire of fairness in the race. The winner is he who shows the most conscientious training, the greatest ability, and the greatest character. Socialism bids all to end the race equally. It holds back the speedy to the pace of the slowest. Anarchy would provide neither training nor umpire. Despotism picks those who should run and those who should win.

Conservative, progressive, and liberal thought and action have their only real test in whether they contribute to equal opportunity, whether they hold open the door of opportunity. If they do not they are false in their premise no matter what their name may be.

It was Abraham Lincoln who firmly enunciated this idea as the equal chance. The Sherman Law was enacted in endeavor to hold open the door of equal opportunity in business. The commissions for regulation of public utilities were created to prevent discrimination in service and prevent extortion in rates—and thereby the destruction of equal opportunity.

Equality of opportunity is a fundamental principle of our nation. With it we must test all our policies. The success or failure of this principle is the test of our government.

Mr. Chairman, I regret that time does not permit the compass of many important questions. I hope at a later time to discuss the development of waterways, highways, aviation, irrigable lands, foreign trade and merchant marine, the promotion of education, more effective administration of our criminal laws, the relation of our government to public utilities and railways, the primary necessity of conservation of natural resources, measures for further economy in government and reduction of taxes— all of which afford problems of the first order.

I would violate my conscience and the gratitude I feel, did I not upon this occasion express appreciation of the great President who leads our party today. President Coolidge has not only given a memorable administration, he has left an imprint of rectitude and statesmanship upon the history of our country. His has been the burden of reconstruction of our country from the destruction of war. He has dignified economy to a principle of government. He has charted the course of our nation and our party over many years to come. It is not only a duty but it is the part of statesmanship that we adhere to this course.

No man who stands before the mighty forces which ramify American life has the right to promise solutions at his hand alone. All that an honest man can say is that within the extent of his abilities and his authority and in co-operation with the Congress and with leaders of every element in our people, these problems shall be courageously met and solution will be courageously attempted.

Our purpose is to build in this nation a human society, not an economic system. We wish to increase the efficiency and productivity of our country, but its final purpose is happier homes. We shall succeed through the faith, the loyalty, the self-sacrifice, the devotion to eternal ideals which live today in every American.

The matters which I have discussed directly and deeply affect the moral and spiritual welfare of our country. No one believes these aspirations and hopes can be realized in a day. Progress or remedy lie often enough in the hands of state and local government. But the awakening of the national conscience and the stimulation of every remedial agency is indeed a function of the national government. I want to see our government great both as an instrument and as a symbol of the nation's greatness.

The Presidency is more than an administrative office. It must be the symbol of American ideals. The high and the lowly must be seen with the same eyes, met in the same spirit. It must be the instrument by which national conscience is livened and it must under the guidance of the Almighty interpret and follow that conscience.

HERBERT C. HOOVER

Campaign Speech

NEW YORK CITY

October 22, 1928

This campaign now draws near a close. The platforms of the two parties defining principles and offering solutions of various national problems have been presented and are being earnestly considered by our people.

After four months' debate it is not the Republican Party which finds reason for abandonment of any of the principles it has laid down or of the views it has expressed for solution of the problems before the country. The principles to which it adheres are rooted deeply in the foundations of our national life. The solutions which it proposes are based on experience with government and on a consciousness that may have the responsibility for placing those solutions in action.

In my acceptance speech I endeavored to outline the spirit and ideals by which I would be guided in carrying that platform into administration. Tonight, I will not deal with the multitude of issues which have been already well canvassed. I intend rather to discuss some of those more fundamental principles and ideals upon which I believe the government of the United States should be conducted.

The Republican Party has ever been a party of progress. I do not need to review its seventy years of constructive history. It has always reflected the spirit of the American people. Never has it done more for the advancement of fundamental progress than during the past seven and one-half years since we took over the government amidst the ruin left by war.

It detracts nothing from the character and energy of the American people, it minimizes in no degree the quality of their accomplishments to say that the policies of the Republican Party have played a large part in recuperation from the war and the building of the magnificent progress which shows upon every hand today. I say with emphasis that without the wise policies which the Republican Party has brought into action during this period, no such progress would have been possible.

The first responsibility of the Republican administration was to renew the march of progress from its collapse by the war. That task involved the restoration of confidence in the future and the liberation and stimulation of the constructive energies of our people. It discharged that task. There is not a person within the sound of my voice who does not know the profound progress which our country has made in this period. Every man and woman knows that American comfort, hope, and confidence for the future are immeasurably higher this day than they were seven and one-half years ago.

It is not my purpose to enter upon a detailed recital of the great constructive measures of the past seven and one-half years by which this has been brought about. It is sufficient to remind you of the restoration of employment to the millions who walked your streets in idleness; to remind you of the creation of the budget system; the reduction of six billions of national debt which gave the powerful impulse of that vast sum returned to industry and commerce; the four sequent reductions of taxes and thereby the lift to the living of every family; the enactment of adequate protective tariff and immigration laws which have safeguarded our workers and farmers from floods of goods and labor from foreign countries; the creation of credit facilities and many other aids to agriculture; the building up of foreign trade; the care of veterans; the development of aviation, of radio, of our inland waterways, of our highways; the expansion of scientific research, of welfare activities; the making of safer highways, safer mines, better homes; the spread of outdoor recreation; the improvement in public health and the care of children; and a score of other progressive actions.

Nor do I need remind you that government today deals with an economic and social system vastly more intricate and delicately adjusted than ever before. That system now must be kept in perfect tune if we would maintain uninterrupted employment and the high standards of living of our people. The government has come to touch this delicate web at a thousand points. Yearly the relations of government to national prosperity become more and more intimate. Only through keen vision and helpful co-operation by the government has stability in business and stability in employment been maintained during this past seven and one-half years. There always are some localities, some industries, and some individuals who do not share the prevailing prosperity. The task of government is to lessen these inequalities.

Never has there been a period when the Federal Government has given such aid and impulse to the progress of our people, not alone to economic progress but to the development of those agencies which make for moral and spiritual progress.

But in addition to this great record of contributions of the Republican Party to progress, there has been a further fundamental contribution—a contribution underlying and sustaining all the others—and that is the resistance of the Republican Party to every attempt to inject the government into business in competition with its citizens.

After the war, when the Republican Party assumed administration of the country, we were faced with the problem of determination of the very nature of our national life. During one hundred and fifty years we have builded up a form of self-government and a social system which is peculiarly our own. It differs essentially from all others in the world. It is the American system. It is just as definite and positive a political and social system as has ever been developed on earth. It is founded upon a particular conception of self-government in which decentralized local responsibility is the very base. Further than this, it is founded upon the conception that only through ordered liberty, freedom, and equal opportunity to the individual will his initiative and enterprise spur on the march of progress. And in our insistence upon equality of opportunity has our system advanced beyond all the world.

During the war we necessarily turned to the government to solve every difficult economic problem. The government having absorbed every energy of our people for war, there was no other solution. For the preservation of the state the Federal Government became a centralized despotism which undertook unprecedented responsibilities, assumed autocratic powers, and took over the business of citizens. To a large degree we regimented our whole people temporarily into a socialistic state. However justified in time of war, if continued in peacetime it would destroy not only our American system but with it our progress and freedom as well.

When the war closed, the most vital of all issues both in our own country and throughout the world was whether governments should continue their wartime ownership and operation of many instrumentalities of production and distribution. We were challenged with a peace-time choice between the American system of rugged individualism and a European philosophy of diametrically opposed doctrines— doctrines of paternalism and state socialism. The acceptance of these ideas would have meant the destruction of self-government through centralization of government. It would have meant the undermining of the individual initiative and enterprise through which our people have grown to unparalleled greatness.

The Republican Party from the beginning resolutely turned its face away from these ideas and these war practices. A Republican Congress co-operated with the Democratic administration to demobilize many of our war activities. At that time the two parties were in accord upon that point. When the Republican Party came into full power it went at once resolutely back to our fundamental conception of the state and the rights and responsibilities of the individual. Thereby it restored confidence and hope in the American people, it freed and stimulated enterprise, it restored the government to its position as an umpire instead of a player in the economic game. For these reasons the American people have gone forward in progress while the rest of the world has halted, and some countries have even gone backwards. If anyone will study the causes of retarded recuperation in Europe, he will find much of it due to stifling of private initiative on one hand, and overloading of the government with business on the other.

There has been revived in this campaign, however, a series of proposals which, if adopted, would be a long step toward the abandonment of our American system and a surrender to the destructive operation of governmental conduct of commercial business. Because the country is faced with difficulty and doubt over certain national problems—that is, prohibition, farm relief, and electrical power—our opponents propose that we must thrust government a long way into the businesses which give rise to these problems. In effect, they abandon the tenets of their own party and turn to state socialism as a solution for the difficulties presented by all three. It is proposed that we shall change from prohibition to the state purchase and sale of liquor. If their agricultural relief program means anything, it means that the government shall directly or indirectly buy and sell and fix prices of agricultural products. And we are to go into the hydro-electric power business. In other words, we are confronted with a huge program of government in business.

There is, therefore, submitted to the American people a question of fundamental principle. That is: shall we depart from the principles of our American political and economic system, upon which we have advanced beyond all the rest of the world, in order to adopt methods based on principles destructive of its very foundations? And I wish to emphasize the seriousness of these proposals. I wish to make my position clear; for this goes to the very roots of American life and progress.

I should like to state to you the effect that this projection of government in business would have upon our system of self-government and our economic system. That effect would reach to the daily life of every man and woman. It would impair the very basis of liberty and freedom not only for those left outside the fold of expanded bureaucracy but for those embraced within it.

Let us first see the effect upon self-government. When the Federal Government undertakes to go into commercial business it must at once set up the organization and administration of that business, and it immediately finds itself in a labyrinth, every alley of which leads to the destruction of self-government.

Commercial business requires a concentration of responsibility. Self-government requires decentralization and many checks and balances to safeguard liberty. Our Government to succeed in business would need become in effect a despotism. There at once begins the destruction of self-government.

The first problem of the government about to adventure in commercial business is to determine a method of administration. It must secure leadership and direction. Shall this leadership be chosen by political agencies or shall we make it elective? The hard practical fact is that leadership in business must come through the sheer rise in ability and character. That rise can only take place in the free atmosphere of competition. Competition is closed by bureaucracy. Political agencies are feeble channels through which to select able leaders to conduct commercial business.

Government, in order to avoid the possible incompetence, corruption, and tyranny of too great authority in individuals entrusted with commercial business, inevitably turns to boards and commissions. To make sure that there are checks and balances, each member of such board and commission must have equal authority. Each has his separate responsibility to the public, and at once we have the conflict of ideas and the lack of decision which would ruin any commercial business. It has contributed greatly to the demoralization of our shipping business. Moreover, these commissions must be representative of different sections and different political parties, so that at once we have an entire blight upon co-ordinated action within their ranks which destroys any possibility of effective administration.

Moreover, our legislative bodies cannot in fact delegate their full authority to commissions or to individuals for the conduct of matters vital to the American people; for if we would preserve government by the people we must preserve the authority of our legislators in the activities of our government.

Thus every time the Federal Government goes into a commercial business, five hundred and thirty-one Senators and Congressmen become the actual board of directors of that business. Every time a state government goes into business one or two hundred state senators and legislators become the actual directors of that business. Even if they were supermen and if there were no politics in the United States, no body of such numbers could competently direct commercial activities; for that requires initiative, instant decision, and action. It took Congress six years of constant discussion to even decide what the method of administration of Muscle Shoals should be.

When the Federal Government undertakes to go into business, the state governments are at once deprived of control and taxation of that business; when a state government undertakes to go into business, it at once deprives the municipalities of taxation and control of that business. Municipalities, being local and close to the people, can, at times, succeed in business where federal and state governments must fail. We have trouble enough with log-rolling in legislative bodies today. It originates naturally from desires of citizens to advance their particular section or to secure some necessary service. It would be multiplied a thousandfold were the federal and state governments in these businesses.

The effect upon our economic progress would be even worse. Business progressiveness is dependent on competition. New methods and new ideas are the outgrowth of the spirit of adventure, of individual initiative, and of individual enterprise. Without adventure there is no progress. No government administration can rightly take chances with taxpayers' money.

There is no better example of the practical incompetence of government to conduct business than the history of our railways. During the war the government found it necessary to operate the railways. That operation continued until after the war. In the year before being freed from government operation they were not able to meet the demands for transportation. Eight years later we find them under private enterprise transporting fifteen percent more goods and meeting every demand for service. Rates have been reduced by fifteen percent and net earnings increased from less than one percent on their evaluation to about five percent. Wages of employees have improved by thirteen percent. The wages of railway employees are today one hundred and twenty-one percent above pre-war, while the wages of government employees are today only sixty-five percent above pre-war. That should be a sufficient commentary upon the efficiency of government operation.

Let us now examine this question from the point of view of the person who may get a government job and is admitted into the new bureaucracy. Upon that subject let me quote from a speech of that great leader of labor, Samuel Gompers, delivered in Montreal in 1920, a few years before his death. He said:

"I believe there is no man to whom I would take second position in my loyalty to the Republic of the United States, and yet I would not give it more power over the individual citizenship of our country. . . .

"It is a question of whether it shall be government ownership or private ownership under control. . . . If I were in the minority of one in this convention, I would want to cast my vote so that the men of labor shall not willingly enslave themselves to government authority in their industrial effort for freedom. . . .

"Let the future tell the story of who is right or who is wrong; who has stood for freedom and who has been willing to submit their fate industrially to the government."

I would amplify Mr. Gompers' statement. The great body of government employees which would be created by the proposals of our opponents would either comprise a political machine at the disposal of the party in power, or, alternatively, to prevent this, the government by stringent civil-service rules must debar its employees from their full political rights as free men. It must limit them in the liberty to bargain for their own wages, for no government employee can strike against his government and thus against the whole people. It makes a legislative body with all its political currents their final employer and master. Their bargaining does not rest upon economic need or economic strength but on political potence.

But what of those who are outside the bureaucracy? What is the effect upon their lives?

The area of enterprise and opportunity for them to strive and rise is at once limited.

The government in commercial business does not tolerate amongst its customers the freedom of competitive reprisals to which private business is subject. Bureaucracy does not tolerate the spirit of independence; it spreads the spirit of submission into our daily life and penetrates the temper of our people not with the habit of powerful resistance to wrong but with the habit of timid acceptance of irresistible might.

Bureaucracy is ever desirous of spreading its influence and its power. You cannot extend the mastery of the government over the daily working life of a people without at the same time making it the master of the people's souls and thoughts. Every expansion of government in business means that government in order to protect itself from the political consequences of its errors and wrongs is driven irresistibly without peace to greater and greater control of the nation's press and platform. Free speech does not live many hours after free industry and free commerce die.

It is false liberalism that interprets itself into the government operation of commercial business. Every step of bureaucratizing of the business of our country poisons the very roots of liberalism—that is, political equality, free speech, free assembly, free press, and equality of opportunity. It is the road not to more liberty, but to less liberty. Liberalism should be found not striving to spread bureaucracy but striving to set bounds to it. True liberalism seeks all legitimate freedom first in the confident belief that without such freedom the pursuit of all other blessings and benefits is vain. That belief is the foundation of all American progress, political as well as economic.

Liberalism is a force truly of the spirit, a force proceeding from the deep realization that economic freedom cannot be sacrificed if political freedom is to be preserved. Even if governmental conduct of business could give us more efficiency instead of less efficiency, the fundamental objection to it would remain unaltered and unabated. It would destroy political equality. It would increase rather than decrease abuse and corruption. It would stifle initiative and invention. It would undermine the development of leadership. It would cramp and cripple the mental and spiritual energies of our people. It would extinguish equality and opportunity. It would dry up the spirit of liberty and progress. For these reasons primarily it must be resisted. For a hundred and fifty years liberalism has found its true spirit in the American system, not in the European systems.

I do not wish to be misunderstood in this statement. I am defining a general policy. It does not mean that our government is to part with one iota of its national resources without complete protection to the public interest. I have already stated that where the government is engaged in public works for purposes of flood control, of navigation, of irrigation, of scientific research or national defense, or in pioneering a new art, it will at times necessarily produce power or commodities as a by-product. But they must be a by-product of the major purpose, not the major purpose itself.

Nor do I wish to be misinterpreted as believing that the United States is free-for-all and devil-take-the-hindmost. The very essence of equality of opportunity and of American individualism is that there shall be no domination by any group or combination in this republic, whether it be business or political. On the contrary, it demands economic justice as well as political and social justice. It is no system of laissez faire.

I feel deeply on this subject because during the war I had some practical experience with governmental operation and control. I have witnessed not only at home but abroad the many failures of government in business. I have seen its tyrannies, its injustices, its destructions of self-government, its undermining of the very instincts which carry our people forward to progress. I have witnessed the lack of advance, the lowered standards of living, the depressed spirits of people working under such a system. My objection is based not upon theory or upon a failure to recognize wrong or abuse, but I know the adoption of such methods would strike at the very roots of American life and would destroy the very basis of American progress.

Our people have the right to know whether we can continue to solve our great problems without abandonment of our American system. I know we can. We have demonstrated that our system is responsive enough to meet any new and intricate development in our economic and business life. We have demonstrated that we can meet any economic problem and still maintain our democracy as a master in its own house and that we can at the same time preserve equality of opportunity and individual freedom.

In the last fifty years we have discovered that mass production will produce articles for us at half the cost they required previously. We have seen the resultant growth of large units of production and distribution. This is big business. Many businesses must be bigger, for our tools are bigger, our country is bigger. We now build a single dynamo of a hundred thousand horsepower. Even fifteen years ago that would have been a big business all by itself. Yet today advance in production requires that we set ten of these units together in a row.

The American people from bitter experience have a rightful fear that great business units might be used to dominate our industrial life and by illegal and unethical practices destroy equality of opportunity.

Years ago the Republican administration established the principle that such evils could be corrected by regulation. It developed methods by which abuses could be prevented while the full value of industrial progress could be retained for the public. It insisted upon the principle that when great public utilities were clothed with the security of partial monopoly, whether it be railways, power plants, telephones, or what not, then there must be the fullest and most complete control of rates, services, and finances by government or local agencies. It declared that these businesses must be conducted with glass pockets.

As to our great manufacturing and distributing industries, the Republican Party insisted upon the enactment of laws that not only would maintain competition but would destroy conspiracies to destroy the smaller units or dominate and limit the equality of opportunity amongst our people.

One of the great problems of government is to determine to what extent the government shall regulate and control commerce and industry and how much it shall leave it alone. No system is perfect. We have had many abuses in the private conduct of business. That every good citizen resents. It is just as important that business keep out of government as that government keep out of business.

Nor am I setting up the contention that our institutions are perfect. No human ideal is ever perfectly attained, since humanity itself is not perfect.

That wisdom of our forefathers in their conception that progress can only be attained as the sum of the accomplishment of free individuals has been reinforced by all of the great leaders of the country since that day. Jackson, Lincoln, Cleveland, McKinley, Roosevelt, Wilson, and Coolidge have stood unalterably for these principles.

And what have been the results of our American system? Our country has become the land of opportunity to those born without inheritance, not merely because of the wealth of its resources and industry but because of this freedom of initiative and enterprise. Russia has natural resources to equal ours. Her people are equally industrious, but she has not had the blessings of one hundred and fifty years of our form of government and of our social system.

By adherence to the principles of decentralized self-government, ordered liberty, equal opportunity, and freedom to the individual, our American experiment in human welfare has yielded a degree of well-being unparalleled in all the world. It has come nearer to the abolition of poverty, to the abolition of fear of want, than humanity has ever reached before. Progress of the past seven years is the proof of it. This alone furnishes the answer to our opponents, who ask us to introduce destructive elements into the system by which this has been accomplished.

Let us see what this system has done for us in our recent years of difficult and trying reconstruction and then solemnly ask ourselves if we now wish to abandon it.

As a nation we came out of the war with great losses. We made no profits from it. The apparent increases in wages were at that time fictitious. We were poorer as a nation when we emerged from the war. Yet during these last eight years we have recovered from these losses and increased our national income by over one-third, even if we discount the inflation of the dollar. That there has been a wide diffusion of our gain in wealth and income is marked by a hundred proofs. I know of no better test of the improved conditions of the average family than the combined increase in assets of life and industrial insurance, building and loan associations, and savings deposits. These are the savings banks of the average man. These agencies alone have in seven years increased by nearly one hundred percent to the gigantic sum of over fifty billions of dollars, or nearly one-sixth of our whole national wealth. We have increased in home ownership, we have expanded the investments of the average man.

In addition to these evidences of large savings, our people are steadily increasing their spending for higher standards of living. Today there are almost nine automobiles for each ten families, where seven and one-half years ago only enough automobiles were running to average less than four for each ten families. The slogan of progress is changing from the full dinner pail to the full garage. Our people have more to eat, better things to wear, and better homes. We have even gained in elbow room, for the increase of residential floor space is over twenty-five percent with less than ten percent increase in our number of people. Wages have increased, the cost of living has decreased. The job of every man and woman has been made more secure. We have in this short period decreased the fear of poverty, the fear of unemployment, the fear of old age; and these are fears that are the greatest calamities of human kind.

All this progress means far more than greater creature comforts. It finds a thousand interpretations into a greater and fuller life. A score of new helps save the drudgery of the home. In seven years we have added seventy percent to the electric power at the elbows of our workers and further promoted them from carriers of burdens to directors of machines. We have steadily reduced the sweat in human labor. Our hours of labor are lessened; our leisure has increased. We have expanded our parks and playgrounds. We have nearly doubled our attendance at games. We pour into outdoor recreation in every direction. The visitors at our national parks have trebled and we have so increased the number of sportsmen fishing in our streams and lakes that the longer time between bites is becoming a political issue. In these seven and one-half years the radio has brought music and laughter, education and political discussion to almost every fireside.

Springing from our prosperity with its greater freedom, its vast endowment of scientific research, and the greater resources with which to care for public health, we have according to our insurance actuaries during this short period since the war lengthened the average span of life by nearly eight years. We have reduced infant mortality, we have vastly decreased the days of illness and suffering in the life of every man and woman. We have improved the facilities for the care of the crippled and helpless and deranged.

From our increasing resources we have expanded our educational system in eight years from an outlay of twelve hundred millions to twenty-seven hundred millions of dollars. The education of our youth has become almost our largest and certainly our most important activity. From our greater income and thus our ability to free youth from toil we have increased the attendance in our grade schools by fourteen percent, in our high schools by eighty percent, and in our institutions of higher learning by ninety-five percent. Today we have more youth in these institutions of higher learning twice over than all the rest of the world put together. We have made notable progress in literature, in art, and in public taste.

We have made progress in the leadership of every branch of American life. Never in our history was the leadership in our economic life more distinguished in its abilities than today, and it has grown greatly in its consciousness of public responsibility. Leadership in our professions and in moral and spiritual affairs of our country was never of a higher order. And our magnificent educational system is bringing forward a host of recruits for the succession to this leadership.

I do not need to recite more figures and more evidence. I cannot believe that the American people wish to abandon or in any way to weaken the principles of economic freedom and self-government which have been maintained by the Republican Party and which have produced results so amazing and so stimulating to the spiritual as well as to the material advance of the nation.

Your city has been an outstanding beneficiary of this great progress and of these safeguarded principles. With its suburbs it has, during the last seven and one-half years, grown by over a million and a half of people until it has become the largest metropolitan district of all the world. Here you have made abundant opportunity not only for the youth of the land but for the immigrant from foreign shores. This city is the commercial center of the United States. It is the commercial agent of the American people. It is a great organism of specialized skill and leadership in finance, industry, and commerce which reaches every spot in our country. Its progress and its beauty are the pride of the whole American people. It leads our nation in its benevolences to charity, to education, and to scientific research. It is the center of art, music, literature, and drama. It has come to have a more potent voice than any other city in the United States.

But when all is said and done, the very life, progress, and prosperity of this city is wholly dependent on the prosperity of the 115,000,000 people who dwell in our mountains and valleys across the three thousand miles to the Pacific Ocean. Every activity of this city is sensitive to every evil and every favorable tide that sweeps this great nation of ours. Be there a slackening of industry in any place, it affects New York far more than any other part of the country. In a time of depression one-quarter of all the unemployed in the United States can be numbered in this city. In a time of prosperity the citizens of the great interior of our country pour into your city for business and entertainment at the rate of one hundred and fifty thousand a day. In fact, so much is this city the reflex of the varied interests of our country that the concern of every one of your citizens for national stability, for national prosperity, for national progress, for preservation of our American system is far greater than that of any other single part of our country.

We still have great problems if we would achieve the full economic advancement of our country. In these past few years some groups in our country have lagged behind others in the march of progress. I refer more particularly to those engaged in the textile, coal, and agricultural industries. We can assist in solving these problems by co-operation of our government. To the agricultural industry we shall need to advance initial capital to assist them to stabilize their industry. But this proposal implies that they shall conduct it themselves, and not by the government. It is in the interest of our cities that we shall bring agriculture and all industries into full stability and prosperity. I know you will gladly co-operate in the faith that in the common prosperity of our country lies its future.

In bringing this address to a conclusion I should like to restate to you some of the fundamental things I have endeavored to bring out.

The foundations of progress and prosperity are dependent as never before upon the wise policies of government, for government now touches at a thousand points the intricate web of economic and social life.

Under administration by the Republican Party in the last seven and one-half years our country as a whole has made unparalleled progress and this has been in generous part reflected to this great city. Prosperity is no idle expression. It is a job for every worker; it is the safety and the safeguard of every business and every home. A continuation of the policies of the Republican Party is fundamentally necessary to the further advancement of this progress and to the further building up of this prosperity.

I have dwelt at some length on the principles of relationship between the government and business. I make no apologies for dealing with this subject. The first necessity of any nation is the smooth functioning of the vast business machinery for employment, feeding, clothing, housing, and providing luxuries and comforts to a people. Unless these basic elements are properly organized and function, there can be no progress in business, in education, literature, music, or art. There can be no advance in the fundamental ideals of a people. A people cannot make progress in poverty.

I have endeavored to present to you that the greatness of America has grown out of a political and social system and a method of control of economic forces distinctly its own—our American system—which has carried this great experiment in human welfare farther than ever before in all history. We are nearer today to the ideal of the abolition of poverty and fear from the lives of men and women than ever before in any land. And I again repeat that the departure from our American system by injecting principles destructive to it which our opponents propose, will jeopardize the very liberty and freedom of our people, and will destroy equality of opportunity not alone to ourselves but to our children.

To me the foundation of American life rests upon the home and the family. I read into these great economic forces, these intricate and delicate relations of the government with business and with our political and social life, but one supreme end—that we reinforce the ties that bind together the millions of our families, that we strengthen the security, the happiness, and the independence of every home.

My conception of America is a land where men and women may walk in ordered freedom in the independent conduct of their occupations; where they may enjoy the advantages of wealth, not concentrated in the hands of the few but spread through the lives of all; where they build and safeguard their homes, and give to their children the fullest advantages and opportunities of American life; where every man shall be respected in the faith that his conscience and his heart direct him to follow; where a contented and happy people, secure in their liberties, free from poverty and fear, shall have the leisure and impulse to seek a fuller life.

Some may ask where all this may lead beyond mere material progress. It leads to a release of the energies of men and women from the dull drudgery of life to a wider vision and a higher hope. It leads to the opportunity for greater and greater service, not alone from man to man in our own land, but from our country to the whole world. It leads to an America, healthy in body, healthy in spirit, unfettered, youthful, eager— with a vision searching beyond the farthest horizons, with an open mind, sympathetic and generous. It is to these higher ideals and for these purposes that I pledge myself and the Republican Party.

ALFRED E. SMITH

Acceptance Speech

ALBANY, NEW YORK

August 22, 1928

Upon the steps of this Capitol, where twenty-five years ago I first came into the service of the State, I received my party's summons to lead it in the nation. Within this building, I learned the principles, the purposes and the functions of government and to know that the greatest privilege that can come to any man is to give himself to a nation which has reared him and raised him from obscurity to be a contender for the highest office in the gift of its people.

Here I confirmed my faith in the principles of the Democratic Party so eloquently defined by Woodrow Wilson: "First, the people as the source and their interests and desires as the text of laws and institutions. Second, individual liberty as the objective of all law." With a gratitude too strong for words and with humble reliance upon the aid of Divine Providence, I accept your summons to the wider field of action.

Government should be constructive, not destructive; progressive, not reactionary. I am entirely unwilling to accept the old order of things as the best unless and until I become convinced that it cannot be made better.

It is our new world theory that government exists for the people as against the old world conception that the people exist for the government. A sharp line separates those who believe that an elect class should be the special object of the government's concern and those who believe that the government is the agent and servant of the people who create it. Dominant in the Republican Party today is the element which proclaims and executes the political theories against which the party liberals like Roosevelt and La Follette and their party insurgents have rebelled. This reactionary element seeks to vindicate the theory of benevolent oligarchy. It assumes that a material prosperity, the very existence of which is challenged, is an excuse for political inequality. It makes the concern of the government, not people, but material things.

I have fought this spirit in my own State. I have had to fight it and to beat it, in order to place upon the statute books every one of the progressive, humane laws for whose enactment I assumed responsibility in my legislative and executive career. I shall know how to fight it in the nation.

1909582

It is a fallacy that there is inconsistency between progressive measures protecting the rights of the people, including the poor and the weak, and a just regard for the rights of legitimate business, great or small. Therefore, while I emphasize my belief that legitimate business promotes the national welfare, let me warn the forces of corruption and favoritism, that Democratic victory means that they will be relegated to the rear and the front seats will be occupied by the friends of equal opportunity.

Likewise, government policy should spring from the deliberate action of an informed electorate. Of all men, I have reason to believe that the people can and do grasp the problems of the government. Against the opposition of the self-seeker and the partisan, again and again, I have seen legislation won by the pressure of popular demand, exerted after the people had had an honest, frank and complete explanation of the issues. Great questions of finance, the issuance of millions of dollars of bonds for public projects, the complete reconstruction of the machinery of the State government, the institution of an executive budget, these are but a few of the complicated questions which I, myself, have taken to the electorate. Every citizen has thus learned the nature of the business in hand and appreciated that the State's business is his business.

That direct contact with the people I propose to continue in this campaign and, if I am elected, in the conduct of the nation's affairs. I shall thereby strive to make the nation's policy the true reflection of the nation's ideals. Because I believe in the idealism of the party of Jefferson, Cleveland, and Wilson, my administration will be rooted in liberty under the law; liberty that means freedom to the individual to follow his own will so long as he does not harm his neighbor; the same high moral purpose in our conduct as a nation that actuates the conduct of the God-fearing man and woman; that equality of opportunity which lays the foundation for wholesome family life and opens up the outlook for the betterment of the lives of our children.

In the rugged honesty of Grover Cleveland there originated one of our party's greatest principles: "Public office is a public trust." That principle now takes on new meaning. Political parties are the vehicle for carrying out the popular will. We place responsibility upon the party. The Republican Party today stands responsible for the widespread dishonesty that has honeycombed its administration.

During the last presidential campaign the Republican managers were partially successful in leading the American people to believe that these sins should be charged against the individual rather than against the party. The question of personal guilt has now been thoroughly disposed of and in its place, challenging the wisdom and good judgment of the American people, is the unquestioned evidence of party guilt.

The Democratic Party asks the electorate to withdraw their confidence from the Republican Party and repose it with the Democratic Party pledged to continue those standards of unblemished integrity which characterized every act of the administration of Woodrow Wilson.

But I would not rest our claim for the confidence of the American people alone upon the misdeeds of the opposite party. Our must be a constructive campaign.

The Republican Party builds its case upon a myth. We are told that only under the benevolent administration of that party can the country enjoy prosperity. When four million men, desirous to work and support their families, are unable to secure employment there is very little in the picture of prosperity to attract them and the millions dependent upon them.

In the year 1926, the latest figures available show that one-twentieth of one percent of the 430,000 corporations in this country earned 40 percent of their profits; 40 percent of the corporations actually lost money; one-fourth of 1 percent of these corporations earned two-thirds of the profits of all of them. Specific industries are wholly prostrate and there is widespread business difficulty and discontent among the individual business men of the country.

Prosperity to the extent that we have it is unduly concentrated and has not equitably touched the lives of the farmer, the wage-earner and the individual business man. The claim of governmental economy is as baseless as the claim that general business prosperity exists and that it can exist only under Republican administration.

When the Republican Party came into power in 1921 it definitely promised reorganization of the machinery of government, and abolition or consolidation of unnecessary and overlapping agencies. A Committee was appointed. A representative of the President acted as Chairman. It prepared a plan of reorganization. The plan was filed in the archives. It still remains there. After seven years of Republican control the structure of government is worse than it was in 1921. It is fully as bad as the system which existed in New York State before we secured by constitutional amendment the legislation which consolidated more than one hundred offices, commissions and boards into eighteen coordinated departments, each responsible to the Governor. In contrast with this, the Republican Party in control at Washington when faced with the alternative of loss of patronage for faithful or more efficient and economical management of the government permitted the old order to continue for the benefit of the patronage seekers.

The appropriations for independent bureaus and offices not responsible to any cabinet officer increased from $3,400,000 in 1914 to $163,000,000 in 1921, and to $556,000,000 in 1928. No wonder that a cabinet officer of the Republican President of 1921 said "if you could visualize the government as a business or administrative unit, you would see something like one of those grotesque spectacles of a big oyster shell to which in the course of years, big and irregular masses of barnacles have attached themselves without symmetry or relevancy." And the Chamber of Commerce of the United States said in its annual report this year: "No progress has been made on the plan of reorganization of the government's departments as advocated by the Chamber." The administration spokesman answers only: "We have given an economical administration," and that has been repeated so often that some people begin to believe it without the slightest proof. I assert that there is no proof.

The appropriation bills signed by the President of the United States for the last year are just one-half a billion dollars more than they were for the first year of his administration. The appropriations for the Executive Department itself (The President and Vice-President) have increased more than 10 percent under President Coolidge.

The figures for expenditure as distinguished from appropriations tell the same story. Aside from interest on the public debt which has been reduced by retirement of bonds or by refinancing at lower interest rate, the actual expenditures for governmental activities during the fiscal year ending in 1928 were just $346,000,000 more than in President Coolidge's first year.

If the defenders of the administration answer that taxes have been reduced, they find themselves in a similar dilemma. The total taxes collected are $24,000,000 more than in the first year of the Coolidge administration. While tax rates have been reduced and some war-time taxes abandoned, the government actually took from the people in income taxes $383,000,000 more during the last fiscal year than during the first year of the Coolidge administration. And even these reductions in tax rates have been brought about primarily because the administration has committed the government to appropriations authorized but not made, amounting approximately to one billion dollars, which is an obligation that is being passed on to succeeding administrations. I wish to focus the public attention on these fundamental facts and figures when it is fed with picturesque trifles about petty economies, such as eliminating stripes from mail bags and extinguishing electric lights in the offices at night.

With this has gone a governmental policy of refusal to make necessary expenditures for purposes which would have effected a real economy. The Postmaster-General states that there was a large annual waste in the handling of mail, resulting from lack of modern facilities and equipment. Scarcely a large city in the country has adequate quarters for the transaction of Federal business. The government pays rent in the city of Washington alone of more than one million dollars annually. It is estimated that the government is paying rentals of twenty million dollars in the nation. True economy would be effected by the erection of Federal buildings, especially in the numerous instances where sites acquired many years ago have been left vacant because the administration did not desire to have these expenditures appear in the budget. It is not economy to refuse to spend money and to have our soldiers living in barracks which the Chief of Staff of the Army recently stated were indecent and below the standard for the meanest type of housing permitted anywhere. And the wise, properly timed construction of needed public improvements would substantially tend to lessen the evils of unemployment.

If the people commission me to do it, I shall with the aid of the Congress effect a real reorganization and consolidation of governmental activities upon a business basis and institute the real economy which comes from prudent expenditure. I shall aid programs for the relief of unemployment, recognizing its deep, human and social significance and shall strive to accomplish a national well-being resting upon the prosperity of the individual men and women who constitute the nation.

Acting upon the principle of "Equal opportunity for all, special privileges for none," I shall ask Congress to carry out the tariff declaration of our platform. To be sure the Republican Party will attempt in the campaign to misrepresent Democratic attitude to the tariff. The Democratic Party does not and under my leadership will not advocate any sudden or drastic revolution in our economic system which would cause business upheaval and popular distress. This principle was recognized as far back as the passage of the Underwood Tariff Bill. Our platform restates it in unmistakable language. The Democratic Party stands squarely for the maintenance of legitimate business and high standards of wages for American labor. Both can be maintained and at the same time the tariff can be taken out of the realm of politics and treated on a strictly business basis.

A leading Republican writing in criticism of the present tariff law, said: "It stands as one of the most ill drawn pieces of legislation in recent political history. It is probably near the actual truth to say that taking for granted some principle of protection of American business and industry, the country has prospered due to post-war conditions abroad and in spite of, rather than on account of, the Fordney-McCumber tariff." What I have just quoted is no part of a campaign document. It was written a few months ago by Professor William Starr Myers of Princeton University, writing the history of his own party.

Against the practice of legislative log-rolling, Woodrow Wilson pointed the way to a remedy. It provided for the creation and maintenance of a non-political, quasi-judicial, fact-finding commission which could investigate and advise the President and Congress as to the tariff duties really required to protect American industry and safeguard the high standard of American wages. In an administration anxious to meet political obligations, the Commission has ceased to function and it has been publicly stated by former members of it that the work of the Commission has been turned over to the advocates of special interests. To bring this about, it is a matter of record that the President demanded the undated resignation of one of its members before he signed his appointment.

I shall restore this Commission to the high level upon which President Wilson placed it, in order that, properly manned, it may produce the facts that will enable us to ascertain how we may increase the purchasing power of everybody's income or wages by the adjustment of those schedules which are now the result of log-rolling and which upon their face are extortionate and unnecessary.

Pay no attention to the Republican propaganda and accept my assurance as the leader of our Party that Democratic tariff legislation will be honest. It will play no favorites. It will do justice to every element in the Nation.

The Constitution provides that treaties with foreign powers must be ratified by a vote of two-thirds of the Senate. This is a legal recognition of the truth that in our foreign relations we must rise above party politics and act as a united nation. Any foreign policy must have its roots deep in the approval of a very large majority of our people. Therefore, no greater service was ever rendered by any President than by Woodrow Wilson when he struck at the methods of secret diplomacy. Today we have close relations, vital to our commercial and world standing, with every other nation. I regard it, therefore, as a paramount duty to keep alive the interest of our people in these questions, and to advise the electorate as to facts and policies.

Through a long line of distinguished Secretaries of State, Republican and Democratic alike, this country has assumed a position of world leadership in the endeavor to outlaw war and substitute reason for force. At the end of President Wilson's administration we enjoyed not only the friendship but the respectful admiration of the peoples of the world. Today we see unmistakable evidences of a widespread distrust of us and unfriendliness to us, particularly among our Latin American neighbors.

I especially stress the necessity for the restoration of cordial relations with Latin America and I take my text from a great Republican Secretary of State, Elihu Root, who said: "We consider that the independence and equal rights of the smallest and weakest member of the family of nations deserve as much respect as those of the great empires. We pretend to no right, privilege or power that we do not freely concede to each one of the American Republics."

The present administration has been false to that declaration of one of its greatest party leaders. The situation in Nicaragua fairly exemplifies our departure from this high standard. The administration has intervened in an election dispute between two conflicting factions, sent our troops into Nicaragua, maintained them there for years, and this without the consent of Congress. To settle this internal dispute, our marines have died and hundreds of Nicaraguans in turn have been killed by our marines. Without consultation with Congress, the administration entered on this long continued occupation of the territory of a supposedly friendly nation by our armed troops.

To no declaration of our platform do I more heartily commit myself than the one for the abolition of the practice of the President of entering into agreements for the settlement of internal disputes in Latin American countries, unless the agreements have been consented to by the Senate as provided for in the Constitution of the United States. I personally declare what the platform declares: "Interference in the purely internal affairs of Latin American countries must cease" and I specifically pledge myself to follow this declaration with regard to Mexico as well as the other Latin American countries.

The Monroe Doctrine must be maintained but not as a pretext for meddling with the purely local concerns of countries which even though they be small are sovereign and entitled to demand and receive respect for their sovereignty. And I shall certainly do all that lies in my power to bring about the fullest concerted action between this country and all the Latin American countries with respect to any step which it may ever be necessary to take to discharge such responsibilities to civilization as may be placed upon us by the Monroe Doctrine.

The evil effect of the administration's policy with respect to Latin America has extended to our relations with the rest of the world. I am not one of those who contend that everything Republican is bad and everything Democratic is good. I approve the effort to renew and extend the arbitration treaties negotiated under the administration of President Wilson. But the usefulness of those treaties as deterrents of war is materially impaired by the reservations asserted by various nations of the right to wage defensive wars as those reservations are interpreted in the light of President Coolidge's record. Defending his policies he announced on April 25, 1927, the doctrine that the person and property of a citizen are a part of the national domain, even when abroad. I do not think the American people would approve a doctrine which would give to Germany, or France, or England, or any other country, the right to regard a citizen of that country or the property of a citizen of that country situated within the borders of the United States as part of the national domain of the foreign country. Our unwarranted intervention in internal affairs in Latin America and this specious reason for it constitute the basis upon which other countries may seek to justify imperialistic policies which threaten world peace and materially lessen the effectiveness which might otherwise lie in the multilateral treaties.

The real outlawry of war must come from a more substantial endeavor to remove the causes of war and in this endeavor the Republican administration has signally failed. I am neither militarist nor jingo. I believe that the people of this country wish to live in peace and amity with the world. Freedom from entangling alliances is a fixed American policy. It does not mean, however, that great nations should not behave to one another with the same decent friendliness and fair play that self-respecting men and women show to one another.

In 1921 there was negotiated a treaty for the limitation of the construction of battleships and battle cruisers of over ten thousand tons. It was approved without party dispute as a start of the process of removing from the backs of the toiling masses of the world the staggering burden of the hundreds of millions of dollars that are wrung from them every year for wasteful transformation into engines of destruction. For seven years the Republican administration has followed it with nothing effective. No limitation has been placed upon land armaments, submarines, vessels of war of under ten thousand tons displacement, poisonous gases or any of the other machinery devised by man for the destruction of human life. In this respect our diplomacy has been futile.

I believe the American people desire to assume their fair share of responsibility for the administration of a world of which they are a part, without political alliance with any foreign nation. I pledge myself to a resumption of a real endeavor to make the outlawry of war effective by removing its causes and to substitute the methods of conciliation, conference, arbitration and judicial determination.

The President of the United States has two constitutional duties with respect to prohibition. The first is embodied in his oath of office. If, with one hand on the Bible and the other hand reaching up to Heaven, I promise the people of this country that "I will faithfully execute the office of President of the United States and to the best of my ability preserve, protect and defend the Constitution of the United States," you may be sure that I shall live up to that oath to the last degree. I shall to the very limit execute the pledge of our platform "to make an honest endeavor to enforce the 18th Amendment and all other provisions of the Federal Constitution and all laws enacted pursuant thereto."

The President does not make the laws. He does his best to execute them whether he likes them or not. The corruption in enforcement activities which caused a former Republican Prohibition Administrator to state that three-fourths of the dry agents were political ward heelers named by politicians without regard to Civil Service laws and that prohibition is the "new political pork barrel," I will ruthlessly stamp out. Such conditions can not and will not exist under any administration presided over by me.

The second constitutional duty imposed upon the President is "To recommend to the Congress such measures as he shall judge necessary and expedient." Opinion upon prohibition cuts squarely across the two great political parties. There are thousands of so-called "wets" and "drys" in each. The platform of my party is silent upon any question of change in the law. I personally believe that there should be change and I shall advise the Congress in accordance with my constitutional duty of whatever changes I deem "necessary or expedient." It will then be for the people and the representatives in the national and State legislatures to determine whether these changes shall be made.

I will state the reasons for my belief. In a book "Law and its Origin," recently called to my notice, James C. Carter, one of the leaders of the bar of this country, wrote of the conditions which exist "when a law is made declaring conduct widely practiced and widely regarded as innocent to be a crime." He points out that in the enforcement of such a law "trials become scenes of perjury and subornation of perjury; juries find abundant excuses for rendering acquittal or persisting in disagreement contrary to their oaths" and he concludes "Perhaps worst of all is that general regard and reverence for law are impaired, a consequence the mischief of which can scarcely be estimated." These words written years before the 18th Amendment or the Volstead Act were prophetic of our situation today.

I believe in temperance. We have not achieved temperance under the present system. The mothers and fathers of young men and women throughout this land know the anxiety and worry which has been brought to them by their children's use of liquor in a way which was unknown before prohibition. I believe in reverence for law. Today disregard of the prohibition laws is insidiously sapping respect for all law. I raise, therefore, what I profoundly believe to be a great moral issue involving the righteousness of our national conduct and the protection of our children's morals.

The remedy, as I have stated, is the fearless application of Jeffersonian principles. Jefferson and his followers foresaw the complex activities of this great, widespread country. They knew that in rural, sparsely settled districts people would develop different desires and customs from those in densely populated sections and that if we were to be a nation united on truly national matters, there had to be a differentiation in local laws to allow for different local habits. It was for this reason that the Democratic platform in 1884 announced "We oppose sumptuary laws which vex the citizens and interfere with individual liberty," and it was for this reason that Woodrow Wilson vetoed the Volstead Act.

In accordance with this Democratic principle, some immediate relief would come from an amendment to the Volstead Law giving a scientific definition of the alcoholic content of an intoxicating beverage. The present definition is admittedly inaccurate and unscientific. Each State would then be allowed to fix its own standard of alcoholic content, subject always to the proviso that that standard could not exceed the maximum fixed by the Congress.

I believe moreover that there should be submitted to the people the question of some change in the provisions of the 18th Amendment. Certainly, no one foresaw when the amendment was ratified the conditions which exist today of bootlegging, corruption and open violation of the law in all parts of the country. The people themselves should after this eight years of trial, be permitted to say whether existing conditions should be rectified. I personally believe in an amendment in the 18th Amendment which would give to each individual State itself only after approval by a referendum popular vote of its people the right wholly within its borders to import, manufacture or cause to be manufactured and sell alcoholic beverages, the sale to be made only by the State itself and not for consumption in any public place. We may well learn from the experience of other nations. Our Canadian neighbors have gone far in this manner to solve this problem by the method of sale made by the state itself and not by private individuals.

There is no question here of the return of the saloon. When I stated that the saloon "is and ought to be a defunct institution in this country" I meant it. I mean it today. I will never advocate nor approve any law which directly or indirectly permits the return of the saloon.

Such a change would preserve for the dry states the benefit of a national law that would continue to make interstate shipment of intoxicating beverages a crime. It would preserve for the dry states Federal enforcement of prohibition within their own borders. It would permit to citizens of other states a carefully limited and controlled method of effectuating the popular will wholly within the borders of those states without the old evil of the saloon.

Such a method would re-establish respect for law and terminate the agitation which has injected discord into the ranks of the great political parties which should be standing for the accomplishment of fundamental programs for the nation. I may fairly say even to those who disagree with me that the solution I offer is one based upon the historic policy of the Democratic Party, to assure to each State its complete right of local self-government. I believe it is a solution which would today be offered by Jefferson, or Jackson or Cleveland or Wilson, if those great leaders were with us.

Publicity agents of the Republican administration have written so many articles on our general prosperity, that they have prevented the average man from having a proper appreciation of the degree of distress existing today among farmers and stockraisers. From 1910 to the present time the farm debt has increased by the striking sum of ten billions of dollars, or from four billion to fourteen billion dollars. The value of farm property between 1920 and 1925 decreased by twenty billions of dollars. This depression made itself felt in an enormous increase of bank failures in the agricultural districts. In 1927 there were 830 bank failures, with total liabilities of over 270 millions of dollars, almost entirely in the agricultural sections, as against 49 such failures during the last year of President Wilson's administration.

The report of November 17, 1927, of a Special Committee of the Association of Land Grant Colleges and Universities states: "Incomes from farming since 1920 have not been sufficient to pay a fair return on the current value of capital used and a fair wage for the farmer's labor, or to permit farm people to maintain a standard of living comparable with other groups of like ability." The Business Men's Commission on Agriculture said in November, 1927, "Since the war, the prices of farm products have persisted in an uneconomic and unfavorable adjustment to the general scale of prices of other goods and services;" and "the disparity between urban and farm incomes has emphasized the disparity in standards of living in the rural and urban populations." "The value of farm land and farm property decreased heavily in the post-war deflation" and "large numbers of farmers have lost all their property in this process."

We have not merely a problem of helping the farmer. While agriculture is one of the most individualized and independent of enterprises, still as the report of the Business Men's Commission points out, "Agriculture is essentially a public function, affected with a clear and unquestionable public interest." The country is an economic whole. If the buying power of agriculture is impaired, the farmer makes fewer trips to Main street. The shop owner suffers because he has lost a large part of this trade. The manufacturer who supplies him likewise suffers as does the wage earner, because the manufacturer is compelled to curtail his production. And the banker cannot collect his debts or safely extend further credit. This country cannot be a healthy, strong economic body if one of its members, so fundamentally important as agriculture, is sick almost to the point of economic death.

The normal market among the farmers of this country for the products of industry is ten billions of dollars. Our export market according to latest available figures is, exclusive of agricultural products, approximately one billion, six hundred millions of dollars. These large figures furnish striking indication of the serious blow to national prosperity as a whole which is struck when the buying power of the farmer is paralyzed.

When, therefore, I say that I am in accord with our platform declaration that the solution of this problem must be a prime and immediate concern of the Democratic administration, I make no class appeal. I am stating a proposition as vital to the welfare of business as of agriculture.

With the exception of the administrations of Cleveland and Wilson, the government of this country has been in Republican hands for half a century. For nearly eight years the President and Congress have been Republican. What has been done to solve this problem? Many promises were made which have never been fulfilled. Certainly the promise of relief by tariff has not been fulfilled.

The tariff is ineffective on commodities of which there is exportable surplus without controlled sale of the surplus. Our platform points the way to make the tariff effective for crops of which we produce a surplus. There has been government interference with laws of supply and demand to benefit industry, commerce and finance. It has been one-sided because business, industry and finance would have been helped more if proper attention had been given to the condition of agriculture. Nothing of substance has been done to bring this basic part of our national life into conformity with the economic system that has been set up by law. Government should interfere as little as possible with business. But if it does interfere with one phase of economic life, be it by tariff, by assistance to merchant marine, by control of the flow of money and capital through the banking system, it is bad logic, bad economics and an abandonment of government responsibility to say that as to agriculture alone, the government should not aid.

Twice a Republican Congress has passed legislation only to have it vetoed by a President of their own party, and whether the veto of that specific measure was right or wrong, it is undisputed that no adequate substitute was ever recommended to the Congress by the President and that no constructive plan of relief was ever formulated by any leader of the Republican Party in place of the plan which its Congress passed and its President vetoed. Only caustic criticism and bitter denunciation were provoked in the minds of the Republican leaders in an answer to the nation-wide appeal for a sane endeavor to meet this crisis.

Cooperative, coordinated marketing and warehousing of surplus farm products is essential just as coordinated, cooperative control of the flow of capital was found necessary to the regulation of our country's finances. To accomplish financial stability, the Federal Reserve System was called into being by a Democratic administration. The question for agriculture is complex. Any plan devised must also be coordinated with the other phases of our business institutions. Our platform declares for the development of cooperative marketing and an earnest endeavor to solve the problem of the distribution of the cost of dealing with crop surpluses over the marketed unit of the crop whose producers are benefited by such assistance. Only the mechanics remain to be devised. I propose to substitute action for inaction and friendliness for hostility. In my administration of the government of my State, whenever I was confronted with a problem of this character, I called into conference those best equipped on the particular subject in hand. I shall follow that course with regard to agriculture. Farmers and farm leaders with such constructive aid as will come from sound economists and fair minded leaders of finance and business must work out the detail. There are varying plans for the attainment of the end which is to be accomplished. Such plans should be subjected at once to searching, able and fair minded analysis, because the interests of all require that the solution shall be economically sound.

If I am elected, I shall immediately after election ask leaders of the type I have named irrespective of party to enter upon this task. I shall join with them in the discharge of their duties during the coming winter and present to Congress immediately upon its convening, the solution recommended by the body of men best fitted to render this signal service to the nation. I shall support the activities of this body until a satisfactory law is placed upon the statute books.

Adequate distribution is necessary to bring a proper return to production. Increased efficiency of railroad transportation and terminal handling means lowering of cost which in turn reflects itself in the form of increased purchasing power through reduction in the cost of every-day necessities of life.

Nor do railroads exhaust means of transportation. I believe in encouraging the construction and use of modern highways to carry the short haul of small bulk commodities and to aid in effective marketing of farm products.

Of great importance and still in a highly undeveloped state are our transportation routes by waterways. Commodities of great bulk, where the freight cost is a large part of the cost to the ultimate consumer, are among the least profitable to railroads to carry and lend themselves most readily to water transportation.

Certain areas of our country are deeply interested in opening up a direct route from the middle west to the sea by way of the Great Lakes and adjacent waterways. Controversy has arisen over the relative merits of the St. Lawrence route or the All-American route. As Governor of New York, I have heretofore expressed a preference for the All-American route, basing my view on engineers' reports made to me. The correctness of these reports and also of those favoring the St. Lawrence route has been challenged. As President of the United States, therefore, it would be my clear duty to restudy this question impartially upon engineers' reports the accuracy of which must be above question. When the result of such a study are given to Congress, I am entirely willing to abide by the decision of Congress.

With the development of inland waterways goes the control of floods thereon. The Mississippi flood of last year brought home to the nation the imperative need for a national policy of flood control. The last two administrations waited for this calamity and for universal demand that something be done instead of taking leadership in this important work. Forethought, courage, and leadership and knowledge of what real ultimate economy means would have done much to prevent this calamity with its ensuing waste and misery. An ounce of prevention is worth a pound of first aid and relief. In the last Congress the Reid-Jones Bill laid down sound lines for the solution of this great problem. The policy thus initiated for the Mississippi must be carried through. The money actually appropriated for flood relief is too small to make even a start. Too much time has been spent in squabbling over who shall pay the bill.

The Mississippi river and its tributaries constitute a great network of waterways flowing through a large number of States. Much more than flood control is involved. Fullest development of the Mississippi river and its tributaries as arteries of commerce should be the goal.

Wide possibilities for public good are latent in what remains of our natural resources. I pledge myself to a progressive liberal conservation policy based upon the same principles to which I have given my support in the State of New York, and to fight against selfish aggression in this field wherever it appears and irrespective of whom it may involve. No nation in history has been more careless about the conservation of natural resources than has ours. We have denuded our forests. We have been slow to reclaim lands for development and have allowed to run to waste or have given to private exploitation our public waters with their great potential power for the development of electrical energy.

The value of this heritage can best be measured when we consider the recent disclosures of the methods employed by private monopolies to wrest our remaining water powers from public control.

No more dishonest or unpatriotic propaganda has ever been seen in this country than that disclosed by the investigation into the methods of certain utility corporations. Private corporations to gain control of public resources have procured the writing of textbooks for the public schools; have subsidized lecturers pretending to give the country their own honest and unbiased advice; have employed as their agents former public officials and have endeavored to mislead public opinion by the retention of the services of leaders of the community in various parts of the country. Highly paid lobbyists, penetrated into every State and into the legislative halls of the nation itself.

As against propaganda, it is the duty of the Democratic Party to set up truth. The ownership of some of these great water powers is in the nation, of others in the several states. These sources of water power must remain forever under public ownership and control. Where they are owned by the Federal Government, they should remain under Federal control. Where they are owned by an individual State, they should be under the control of that State, or where they are owned by States jointly, they should be under the control of those States.

Wherever the development, the government agency, State or Federal as the case may be, must retain through contractual agreement with the distributing companies the right to provide fair and reasonable rates to the ultimate consumer and the similiar right to insist upon fair and equal distribution of the power. This can be secured only by the absolute retention by the people of the ownership of the power by owning and controlling the site and plant at the place of generation. The government—Federal, State or the authority representing joint States—must control the switch that turns on or off the power so greedily sought by certain private groups without the least regard for the public good.

I shall carry into Federal administration the same policy which I have maintained against heavy odds in my own State. Under no circumstances should private monopoly be permitted to capitalize for rate-making purposes water power sites that are the property of the people themselves. It is to me unthinkable that the government of the United States or any State thereof will permit either direct or indirect alienation of water power sites.

Electrical energy generated from water power as an incident to the regulation of the flow of the Colorado river is the common heritage of all the States through which the river flows. The benefits growing from such development should be equitably distributed among the States having right of ownership. The duty of the Federal Government is confined to navigation. I am of the opinion that the best results would flow from the setting up of a Colorado River Authority, representative equally of all the States concerned. The development should be by the States through the agency of this authority by treaty ratified by Congress.

It will be the policy of my administration while retaining government ownership and control, to develop a method of operation for Muscle Shoals which will reclaim for the government some fair revenue from the enormous expenditure already made for its development and which is now a complete waste. In this way the original peace-time purpose of construction of this plant will be achieved. The nation will be reimbursed, agriculture will be benefited by the cheap production of nitrates for fertilizer and the surplus power will be distributed to the people.

The remaining public natural resources now under control of the Federal Government must be administered in the interests of all of the people.

Likewise a complete survey and study of the remaining undeveloped public resources of land, coal, oil and other minerals is greatly needed and should be undertaken.

The United States because its people use more wood than any other on earth is therefore more dependent on the forest than any other great nation. At the same time we are the most wasteful of all people in the destruction of our forest resources.

The use of our national forests for recreation should be greatly extended. I also pledge myself to give the same continuing interest and support to a national park, reforestation and recreation program as have brought about the establishment of a great Conservation and State Park System in the State of New York.

It was Grover Cleveland who first made our national forest and conservation policy into a great public question. Theodore Roosevelt followed in his footsteps. What these two men began must be continued and carried forward.

The American people constitute a structure of many component parts. One of its foundations is labor. The reasonable contentment of those who toil with the conditions under which they live and work is an essential basis of the nation's well-being. The welfare of our country therefore demands governmental concern for the legitimate interest of labor.

The Democratic Party has always recognized this fact and under the administration of Woodrow Wilson, a large body of progressive legislation for the protection of those laboring in industry, was enacted. Our platform continues that tradition of the party. We declare for the principle of collective bargaining which alone can put the laborer upon a basis of fair equality with the employer; for the human principle that labor is not a commodity; for fair treatment to government and Federal employees; and for specific and immediate attention to the serious problems of unemployment.

From these premises it was inevitable that our platform should further recognize grave abuses in the issuance of injunctions in labor disputes which threaten the very principle of collective bargaining. Chief Justice Taft in 1919 stated that government of the relations between capital and labor by injunction was an absurdity. Justice Holmes and Justice Brandeis of the United States Supreme Court unite in an opinion which describes the restraints on labor imposed by a Federal injunction as a reminder of involuntary servitude.

Dissatisfacton and social unrest have grown from these abuses and undoubtedly legislation must be framed to meet just causes for complaint in regard to the unwarranted issuance of injunctions.

The Judiciary Committee of the United States Senate has already in progress a careful study of this situation. I promise full cooperation to the end that a definite remedy by law be brought forth to end the existing evils and preserve the constitutional guarantees of individual liberty, free assemblage and speech and the rights of peaceful persuasion.

I shall continue my sympathetic interest in the advancement of progressive legislation for the protection and advancement of working men and women. Promotion of proper care of maternity, infancy and childhood and the encouragement of those scientific activities of the National Government which advance the safeguards of public health, are so fundamental as to need no expression from me other than my record as legislator and as Governor.

None can question my respect for and cooperation with the Civil Service nor my interest in proper compensation for government service. I believe in that true equality of women that opens to them without restriction all avenues of opportunity for which they can qualify in business, in government service and in politics.

I have a full appreciation of what this country owes to our veteran soldiers. I know that when the country called, the veteran came promptly. When the veteran in distress calls to the country, the country should be equally prompt. Red tape and technicalities and autocratic bureaucracy should be brushed aside when the time comes for a grateful American people to recognize its debt to the men who offered themselves in our hour of need.

During all of our national life the freedom of entry to the country has been extended to the millions who desired to take advantage of the freedom and the opportunities offered by America. The rugged qualities of our immigrants have helped to develop our country and their children have taken their places high in the annals of American history.

Every race has made its contribution to the betterment of America. While I stand squarely on our platform declaration that the laws which limit immigration must be preserved in full force and effect, I am heartily in favor of removing from the immigration law the harsh provision which separates families, and I am opposed to the principle of restriction based upon the figures of immigrant population contained in a census thirty-eight years old. I believe this is designed to discriminate against certain nationalities, and is an unwise policy. It is in no way essential to a continuance of the restriction advocated in our platform.

While this is a government of laws and not of men, laws do not execute themselves. We must have people of character and outstanding ability to serve the nation. To me one of the greatest elements of satisfaction in my nomination is the fact that I owe it to no one man or set of men. I can with complete honesty make the statement that my nomination was brought about by no promise given or implied by me or any one in my behalf. I will not be influenced in appointments by the question of a person's wet or dry attitude, by whether he is rich or poor, whether he comes from the north, south, east or west, or by what church he attends in the worship of God. The sole standard of my appointments will be the same as they have been in my governorship—integrity of the man or woman and his or her ability to give me the greatest possible aid in devoted service to the people.

In this spirit I enter upon the campaign. During its progress I shall talk at length on many of the issues to which I have referred in this acceptance address, as well as other important questions. I shall endeavor to conduct this campaign on the high plane that befits the intelligence of our citizens.

Victory, simply for the sake of achieving it, is empty. I am entirely satisfied of our success in November because I am sure we are right and therefore sure that our victory means progress for our nation. I am convinced of the wisdom of our platform. I pledge a complete devotion to the welfare of our country and our people. I place that welfare above every other consideration and I am satisfied that our party is in a position to promote it. To that end I here and now declare to my fellow countrymen from one end of the United States to the other, that I will dedicate myself with all the power and energy that I possess to the service of our great Republic.

☆

ALFRED E. SMITH

Campaign Speech

OKLAHOMA CITY, OKLA.

September 20, 1928

Our country has achieved its great growth and become a model for the nations of the world under a system of party government. It would be difficult to predict what might be the evil consequences if that system were changed. If it is to survive, campaigns for the presidency must be fought out on issues really affecting the welfare and well-being and future growth of the country. In a presidential campaign there should be but two considerations before the electorate: The platform of the party, and the ability of the candidate to make it effective.

In this campaign an effort has been made to distract the attention of the electorate from these two considerations and to fasten it on malicious and un-American propaganda.

I shall tonight discuss and denounce that wicked attempt. I shall speak openly on the things about which people have been whispering to you.

A former Senator from your own State, a member of my own party, has deserted the party which honored him, upon the pretense, as he states it, that because I am a member of Tammany Hall I am not entitled to your support for the high office to which I have been nominated. Here tonight I challenge both the truth and the sincerity of that pretense. I brand it as false in fact. I denounce it as a subterfuge to cover treason to the fundamentals of Jeffersonian Democracy and of American liberty.

What Mr. Owen personally thinks is of no account in this campaign. He has, however, raised an issue with respect to my record with which I shall deal tonight without mincing words. I know what lies behind this pretense of Senator Owen and his kind and I shall take that up later.

What he says, however, has been seized upon by the enemies of the Democratic Party and the foes of progressive government. They have thus made my record an issue in this campaign. I do not hesitate to meet that issue. My record is one of which I am justly proud and it needs no defense. It is one upon which I am justified in asking your support.

For the present, let us examine the record upon which has beaten the light of pitiless publicity for a quarter of a century. I am willing to submit it to you and to the people of this country with complete confidence.

Twenty-five years ago I began my active public career. I was then elected to the Assembly, representing the neighborhood in New York City where I was born, where my wife was born, where my five children were born and where my father and mother were born. I represented that district continuously for twelve years, until 1915, when I was elected Sheriff of New York county.

Two years later I was elected to the position of President of the Board of Aldermen, which is really that of Vice-Mayor of the City of New York.

In 1918 I was selected by the delegates to the State convention as the candidate of the Democratic Party for Governor and was elected.

Running for re-election in 1920, I was defeated in the Harding landslide. However, while Mr. Harding carried the State of New York by more than 1,100,000 plurality, I was defeated only by some 70,000 votes.

After this defeat I returned to private life, keeping up my interest in public affairs, and accepted appointment to an important State body at the hands of the man who had defeated me.

In 1922 the Democratic Convention, by unanimous vote, renominated me for the third time for Governor. I was elected by the record plurality of 387,000, and this in a State which had been normally Republican.

In 1924, at the earnest solicitation of the Democratic presidential candidate, I accepted renomination. The State of New York was carried by President Coolidge by close to 700,000 plurality, but I was elected Governor. On the morning after election I found myself the only Democrat elected on the State ticket, with both houses of the Legislature overwhelmingly Republican.

Renominated by the unanimous vote of the convention of 1926, I made my fifth State-wide run for the governorship and was again elected the Democratic Governor of a normally Republican State.

Consequently, I am in a position to come before you tonight as the Governor of New York finishing out his fourth term.

The record of accomplishment under my four administrations recommended me to the Democratic Party in the nation, and I was nominated for the presidency at the Houston convention on the first ballot.

To put the picture before you completely, it is necessary for me to refer briefly to this record of accomplishment:

In the face of bitter Republican opposition, I succeeded in bringing about a reorganization of the government of the State of New York, consolidating eighty or more scattered boards, bureaus and commissions into nineteen major departments and bringing about efficiency, economy and thoroughgoing coordination of all the State's activities.

Under it was set up for the first time the Cabinet of the Governor.

A drastic reform was secured in the manner and method of appropriating the public money, commonly referred to as the executive budget.

During my legislative career, as well as during my governorship, I sponsored and secured the enactment of the most forward-looking, progressive, humanitarian legislation in the interests of women and children ever passed in the history of the State. I appointed the first Commission on Child Welfare, while Speaker of the Assembly, as far back as 1913.

I had a large part in the enactment of the Workmen's Compensation Law and the rewriting of the factory code, which went as far as government possibly could to promote the welfare, the health and the comfort of the workers in the industrial establishment of our State.

I have stood behind the Department of Education with all the force and all the strength I could bring to my command.

The present Commissioner of Education is a Republican. Any one in Oklahoma, or in any other part of the United States, may write to Frank P. Graves, Department of Education, Albany, N. Y., and ask him the blunt question, "what Governor of that State rendered the greatest service to the cause of public education?" and I am confident he will write back a letter with my name in it.

Figures sometimes speak louder than words. In 1919, my first year in office, the State appropriated to the localities for the promotion of public education $11,500,000. Last year, for the same purpose, I signed bills totalling $86,000,000, an increase in appropriations for public education of $74,500,000 during the period of my governorship.

I have given of my time, my energy and my labor without stint to placing the Department of Public Health upon the highest level of efficiency and usefulness, to bettering the condition of the unfortunate wards of the State hospitals and institutions for the poor, the sick and the afflicted and to the development, over the opposition of a hostile Legislature, of a comprehensive, unified park system, having in mind not only present requirements but the needs and the welfare of the generations to come.

For ten years I battled against bitter Republican opposition to retain for the people of the State of New York the control of their water power, their greatest God-given resources, and have prevented their alienation and preserved them for our people and for our posterity.

I sponsored legislation which brought about reform of the ballot, on the passage of direct primary laws and provisions against corrupt practices in elections.

The first bill for a bonus by the State of New York to the World War veterans was signed during my administration.

Although a city man, I can say to you without fear of contradiction that I did more for agriculture and for its promotion in the State of New York than any Governor in recent history. Cooperative marketing was encouraged. New impetus was given to the construction of the State highways. State aid was furnished to towns and counties to bring the farm nearer to the city and, during my terms of office, there was appropriated in excess of $15,000,000 for the eradication of bovine tuberculosis.

The business of the State of New York was handled in a strictly business way. The number of public place holders was cut down. Appointments and promotions were made on a strictly merit basis. In consequence, there was effected a reduction in taxes to the farmer and the small home owner, from 1923 to 1928, of from two mills to one-half mill of the State's levy upon real property, together with a substantial reduction in the income tax.

Public improvements in the State, long neglected under Republican rule, are being carried out at a rate unprecedented in all its history.

Bear in mind that all this was accomplished without the cooperation of the Legislature, because during my entire career as Governor both branches of the Legislature have been Republican, except for a period of two years when one branch—the Senate—was Democratic. It was brought about because I took the issues to the people directly and brought the force of public opinion, regardless of party affiliation, to the support of these constructive measures.

During my governorship I have made appointment of scores of men to public office requiring the confirmation of the Senate, and while the Senate was in control of my party in only two out of the eight years I have been Governor, not a single appointment of mine was ever rejected.

The reason for this was that I made my appointments to public office in the State of New York without regard to politics, religion or any other consideration except the ability, the integrity and the fitness of the appointee and his capacity properly to serve the State.

Contrast this with the rejection of major appointments made by the President of the United States by a Senate of his own party.

I read in the press only recently that a Republican Congress passed four bills over the veto of the Republican President in one single day. During my entire eight years, the Legislature, hostile to me, never passed a single bill over my veto.

Has there been one flaw in my record, or one scandal of any kind connected with my administration that gives any meaning to this cry of Tammany rule, a cry which thousands of independent and Republican citizens of my own State treat with ridicule and contempt?

The Republican Party will leave no stone unturned to defeat me. I have reduced their organization in the State of New York to an empty shell. At the present time, $60,000,000 of public improvements are in progress in my State. If there was anything wrong or out of the way, does it not strike you, as men and women of common sense, that the Republican Party in New York would leave no stone unturned to bring it to light?

The fact is, they have searched, and searched in vain, for the slightest evidence of improper partisanship or conduct. They found no such thing; they could find no such thing; it did not exist. And in the face of this, Senator Owen and his kind have the nerve and the effrontery not to charge, but merely to insinuate, some evil which they are pleased to call Tammany rule.

One scandal connected with my administration would do more to help out the Republican National Committee in its campaign against me than all the millions of dollars now being spent by them in malicious propaganda. Unfortunately for them, they cannot find it, because the truth is it is not there. I challenge Senator Owen and all his kind to point to one single flaw upon which they can rest their case. But they won't find it. They won't try to find it, because I know what lies behind all this, and I will tell you before I sit down to-night.

I confess I take a just pride in this record. It represents years of earnest labor, conscientious effort and complete self-sacrifice to the public good in some endeavor to show my appreciation and gratitude to the people who have so signally honored me.

Don't you think that I am entitled to ask the people of this country to believe that I would carry into the service of the nation this same devotion and energy and sacrifice which I have given in service to the State? Don't you think that my party is entitled to make this argument to the American people, because it is not only the record itself that speaks in unmistakable language for me, it is the expressed approval of the leading fellow citizens of my State, who have never had the slighest affiliation with Tammany Hall, and many of whom have been its political opponents.

My election to the governorship four times has not been accomplished merely by Democratic votes, because New York is a normally Republican State. I have been elected by the votes of the Democrats, together with the votes of tens of thousands of patriotic, intelligent citizens of all forms of political belief who have placed the welfare of the State above party consideration.

Take the statement of a man who has not supported me for the governorship, Charles Evans Hughes; a statement not made for political purposes, but in presenting me to the Bar Association of New York City. He described me as "one who represents to us the expert in government and, I might say, a master in the science of politics."

He said of me, "the title that he holds is the proudest title that any American can hold, because it is a title to the esteem and affection of his fellow citizens."

Nicholas Murray Butler, President of Columbia University, in conferring upon me an honorary degree, stated that I was "alert, effective, public spirited and courageous, constantly speaking the true voice of the people."

The Very Rev. Howard Crobbins, Dean of the Episcopal Cathedral of St. John the Divine, stated that I had shown myself, "a singularly well-balanced, capable and forceful executive." He added: "He has been independent and fearless. He has had the interest of all the people of the State at heart and his sincerity and courage have won for him a nation-wide recognition."

Robert Lansing, Secretary of State under President Wilson, said of me: "His public career is convincing proof that he possesses the true spirit of public service, and is eminently fitted to fill with distinction and ability any office for which he might be chosen candidate."

Virginia G. Gildersleeve, Dean of Barnard College, stated that I had "made an excellent Governor and shown a knowledge of State affairs which very few of our Governors have ever possessed."

A group of distinguished educators, headed by Prof. John Dewey of Columbia University, said of my record of public education: "His whole attitude on education has been one of foresight and progress."

I could tax your patience for the rest of this evening with similar expressions from men and women who are the leaders of thought and affairs in the State of New York, independents in politics, most of them never affiliated with any political organization.

Do Senator Owen and the forces behind him know more about my record than these distinguished men and women who have watched it and studied it? But Senator Owen and his kind are not sincere. They know that this Tammany cry is an attempt to drag a red herring across the trail.

I know what lies behind all this and I shall tell you. I specifically refer to the question of my religion. Ordinarily, that word should never be used in a political campaign. The necessity for using it is forced on me by Senator Owen and his kind, and I feel that at least once in this campaign, I, as the candidate of the Democratic Party, owe it to the people of this country to discuss frankly and openly with them this attempt of Senator Owen and the forces behind him to inject bigotry, hatred, intolerance and un-American sectarian division into a campaign which should be an intelligent debate of the important issues which confront the American people.

In New York I would not have to discuss it. The people know me. But in view of the vast amount of literature anonymously circulated throughout this country, the cost of which must run into huge sums of money, I owe it to my country and my party to bring it out into the open. There is a well-founded belief that the major portion of this publication, at least, is being financed through political channels.

A recent newspaper account in the City of New York told the story of a woman who called at the Republican National headquarters in Washington, seeking some literature to distribute. She made the request that it be of a nature other than political. Those in charge of the Republican Publicity Bureau provided the lady with an automobile and she was driven to the office of a publication notorious throughout the country for its senseless, stupid, foolish attacks upon the Catholic Church and upon Catholics generally.

I can think of no greater disaster to this country than to have the voters of it divide upon religious lines. It is contrary to the spirit, not only of the Declaration of Independence, but of the Constitution itself. During all of our national life we have prided ourselves throughout the world on the declaration of the fundamental American truth that all men are created equal.

Our forefathers, in their wisdom, seeing the danger to the country of a division on religious issues, wrote into the Constitution of the United States in no uncertain words the declaration that no religious test shall ever be applied for public office, and it is a sad thing in 1928, in view of the countless billions of dollars that we have poured into the cause of public education, to see some American citizens proclaiming themselves 100 percent American, and in the document that makes that proclamation suggesting that I be defeated for the presidency because of my religious belief.

The Grand Dragon of the Realm of Arkansas, writing to a citizen of that State, urges my defeat because I am a Catholic, and in the letter suggests to the man, who happened to be a delegate to the Democratic convention, that by voting against me he was upholding American ideals and institutions as established by our forefathers.

The Grand Dragon that thus advised a delegate to the national convention to vote against me because of my religion is a member of an order known as Ku Klux Klan, who have the effrontery to refer to themselves as 100 percent Americans.

Yet totally ignorant of the history and tradition of this country and its institutions and, in the name of Americanism, they breathe into the hearts and souls of their members hatred of millions of their fellow countrymen because of their religious belief.

Nothing could be so out of line with the spirit of America. Nothing could be so foreign to the teachings of Jefferson. Nothing could be so contradictory of our whole history. Nothing could be so false to the teachings of our Divine Lord Himself. The world knows no greater mockery than the use of the blazing cross, the cross upon which Christ died, as a symbol to install into the hearts of men a hatred of their brethren, while Christ preached and died for the love and brotherhood of man.

I fully appreciate that here and there, in a great country like ours, there are to be found misguided people and, under ordinary circumstances, it might be well to be charitable and make full and due allowance for them. But this campaign, so far advanced, discloses such activity on their part as to constitute, in my opinion, a menace not alone to the party, but to the country itself.

I would have no objection to anybody finding fault with my public record circularizing the whole United States, provided he would tell the truth. But no decent, right-minded, upstanding American citizen can for a moment countenance the shower of lying statements, with no basis in fact, that have been reduced to printed matter and sent broadcast through the mails of this country.

One lie widely circulated, particularly through the southern part of the country, is that during my governorship I appointed practically nobody to office but members of my own church.

What are the facts? On investigation I find that in the cabinet of the Governor sit fourteen men. Three of the fourteen are Catholics, ten Protestants, and one of Jewish faith. In various bureaus and divisions of the Cabinet officers, the Governor appointed twenty-six people. Twelve of them are Catholics and fourteen of them are Protestants. Various other State officials, making up boards and commissions, and appointed by the Governor, make a total of 157 appointments, of which thirty-five were Catholics, 106 were Protestants, twelve were Jewish, and four I could not find out about.

I have appointed a large number of judges of all our courts, as well as a large number of county officers, for the purpose of filling vacancies. They total in number 177, of which sixty-four were Catholics, ninety were Protestants, eleven were Jewish, and twelve of the officials I was unable to find anything about so far as their religion was concerned.

This is a complete answer to the false, misleading and, if I may be permitted the use of the harsher word, lying statements that have found their way through a large part of this country in the form of printed matter.

If the American people are willing to sit silently by and see large amounts of money secretly pour into false and misleading propaganda for political purposes, I repeat that I see in this not only a danger to the party, but a danger to the country.

To such depths has this insidious manner of campaign sunk, that the little children in our public schools are being made the vehicles for the carrying of false and misleading propaganda. At Cedar Rapids, Iowa, the public prints tell us that a number of school girls asked their parents if it were true that there would be another war if Smith was elected. When questioned by their parents as to how they came to ask such questions, one of the girls said:

We were told at school that Wilson started the war in 1917, and if Governor Smith were elected he would start another war.

As contemptible as anything could possibly be is an article on the very front page of a publication devoted to the doings of a church wherein the gospel of Christ is preached. I refer to the Ashland Avenue Baptist, a publication coming from Lexington, Ky., in which a bitter and cruel attack is made upon me personally and is so ridiculous that ordinarily no attention should be paid to it. It speaks of my driving an automobile down Broadway at the rate of fifty miles an hour, and specially states I was driving the car myself while intoxicated.

Everybody who knows me knows full well I do not know how to drive an automobile, that I never tried it. As for the rest of the contemptible, lying statement, it is as false as this part.

On the inside of this paper, the morning worship on the following Sunday gives as the subject, "What think ye of Christ?" The man or set of men responsible for the publication of that wicked libel, in my opinion, do not believe in Christ. If they profess to, they at least do not follow His teachings. If I were in their place I would be deeply concerned about what Christ might think of me.

A similar personal slander against me was dragged out into the open about a week ago when a woman in the southern part of the country read what purported to be a letter from a woman in my own State. Fortunately, the names of both women were secured. One of my friends interviewed the woman in New York State, and she promptly denied having written such a letter. The woman in the southern part of the country refused to talk about it and refused to produce the letter.

I single out these few incidents as typical of hundreds. I well know that I am not the first public man who has been made the object of such baseless slander. It was poured forth on Grover Cleveland and upon Theodore Roosevelt, as well as upon myself. But as to me, the wicked motive of religious intolerance has driven bigots to attempt to inject these slanders into a political campaign. I here and now drag them into the open and I denounce them as a treasonable attack upon the very foundations of American liberty.

I have been told that politically it might be expedient for me to remain silent upon this subject, but so far as I am concerned no political expediency will keep me from speaking out in an endeavor to destroy these evil attacks.

There is abundant reason for believing that Republicans high in the councils of the party have countenanced a large part of this form of campaign, if they have not actually promoted it. A sin of omission is some times as grievous as a sin of commission. They may, through official spokes-men, disclaim as much as they please responsibility for dragging into a national campaign the question of religion, something that according to our Constitution, our history and our traditions has no part in any cam-paign for elective public office.

Giving them the benefit of all reasonable doubt, they at least remain silent on the exhibition that Mrs. Willebrandt made of herself before the Ohio Conference of the Methodist Episcopal Church when she said:

"There are two thousand pastors here. You have in your church more than 600,000 members of the Methodist Church in Ohio alone. That is enough to swing the election. The 600,000 have friends in other states. Write to them."

This is an extract from a speech made by her in favor of a resolution offered to the effect that the conference go on record as being unalter-ably opposed to the election of Governor Smith and to endorse the can-didacy of Herbert Hoover, the Republican candidate.

Mrs. Willebrandt holds a place of prominence in the Republican administration in Washington; she is an Assistant Attorney-General of the United States. By silence, after such a speech, the only inference one can draw is that the administration approves such political tactics. Mrs. Wille-brandt is not an irresponsible person. She was Chairman of the Commit-tee on Credentials in the Republican National Convention at Kansas City.

What would the effect be upon these same people if a prominent official of the government of the State of New York under me suggested to a gathering of the pastors of my church that they do for me what Mrs. Willebrandt suggests be done for Hoover?

It needs no words of mine to impress that upon your minds. It is dis-honest campaigning. It is un-American. It is out of line with the whole tradition and history of this government. And, to my way of thinking, is in itself sufficient to hold us up to the scorn of the thinking people of other nations.

One of the things, if not the meanest thing, in the campaign is a cir-cular pretending to place someone of my faith in the position of seeking votes for me because of my Catholicism. Like everything of its kind, of course it is unsigned, and it would be impossible to trace its authorship. It reached me through a member of the Masonic order who, in turn, received it in the mail. It is false in its every line. It was designed on its very face to injure me with members of churches other than my own.

I here emphatically declare that I do not wish any member of my faith in any part of the United States to vote for me on any religious grounds. I want them to vote for me only when in their hearts and con-sciences they become convinced that my election will promote the best interests of our country.

By the same token, I cannot refrain from saying that any person who votes against me simply because of my religion is not, to my way of thinking, a good citizen.

Let me remind the Democrats of this country that we belong to the party of that Thomas Jefferson whose proudest boast was that he was the author of the Virginia statute for religious freedom. Let me remind the citizens of every political faith that that statute of religious freedom has become a part of the sacred heritage of our land.

The constitutional guaranty that there should be no religious test for public office is not a mere form of words. It represents the most vital principle that ever was given any people.

I attack those who seek to undermine it, not only because I am a good Christian, but because I am a good American and a product of America and of American institutions. Everything I am, and everything I hope to be, I owe to those institutions.

The absolute separation of State and Church is part of the fundamental basis of our Constitution. I believe in that separation, and in all that it implies. That belief must be a part of the fundamental faith of every true American.

Let the people of this country decide this election upon the great and real issues of the campaign and upon nothing else.

For instance, you have all heard or read my Omaha speech on farm relief. Read the Democratic platform on farm relief, compare my speech and that platform plank with the platform plank of the Republican Party and the attitude of Mr. Hoover, so that you may decide for yourselves which of the two parties, or the two candidates, according to their spoken declarations, are best calculated to solve the problem that is pressing the people of this country for solution. By a study of that you will be conserving the interest of the cotton growers of this State and promoting its general prosperity.

Take my attitude on the development of our natural water power resources. Take the Democratic platform on that subject. Compare it with the Republican platform and with Mr. Hoover's attitude and record on the same subject, and find out from which of the two parties you can get and to which of the two candidates you can look forward with any degree of hope for the development of these resources under the control and ownership of the people themselves rather than their alienation for private gain.

Compare the Democratic platform with the Republican platform and Mr. Hoover's attitude with mine on the all-important question of flood control and the conservation of our land and property in valley of the Mississippi. And then take the record and find out from which party you got the greatest comfort and hope for a determination of that question.

Take the subject of the reorganization of the government in the interest of economy and a greater efficiency. Compare the platforms. Compare the speeches of acceptance, and be sure to look into the record of the Republican failure to carry out its promises along these lines during the last seven and a half years.

I declare it to be in the interest of the government, for its betterment, for the betterment and welfare of the people, the duty of every citizen to study the platforms of the two parties, to study the records of the candidates and to make his choice for the Presidency of the United States solely on the ground of what best promotes interest and welfare of our great republic and all its citizens.

If the contest is fought on these lines, as I shall insist it must be, I am confident of the outcome in November.

1932

— ☆ —

By this election year the Great Depression had reached its nadir. The *New York Times* average for twenty-five leading industrial stocks plummeted from a high of 452 in 1929 to a low of 58. Public construction was almost a billion dollars less than it had been in 1930. And, most telling of all, unemployment had reached the startling figure of nearly 13 million: nearly one out of every four Americans was unemployed; and in some large industrial cities—Chicago, for example—the figure reached one in three. Moreover, those able to find employment generally made only subsistence wages or worked so sporadically as hardly to justify their classification as "employed."

There was a gloom over the land when both political parties met in Chicago to nominate their candidates for the 1932 presidential election. The Republicans met first and renominated Herbert Hoover on the first ballot. In contrast to the listless Republican convention, the Democratic convention was marked by a spirited battle for the presidential nomination, with Governor Franklin D. Roosevelt of New York emerging as the winner on the fourth roll call.

Although Roosevelt had supported a comprehensive program of social legislation as governor of New York and had served as Assistant Secretary of the Navy in the Wilson administration, Walter Lippman called him "a pleasant man who, without any important qualifications for the office, would like to be President."

In an unprecedented step, Roosevelt flew to Chicago to deliver the first acceptance speech ever made before a national nominating convention. While the Democratic and Republican platforms were virtually identical on economic questions, Roosevelt casually pledged himself "to a new deal for the American people."

Roosevelt carried on an extensive campaign in 1932, traveling some 13,000 miles and making sixteen major speeches. (Partly this was due to the fact that Roosevelt was determined to demonstrate to the American electorate that the polio attack which permanently crippled him in 1921 would not be a handicap if elected.)

Most of Roosevelt's speeches dealt with very specific issues; a few were direct attacks on the Republican party in general and Hoover's economic philosophy in particular. In some of Roosevelt's speeches, such as his acceptance address in which he advocated a reforestation program, Roosevelt did allude to measures that would later become part of his New Deal. What was more obvious, however, were the glaring contradictions in his speeches. For example, he promised to increase aid to the unemployed and drastically to cut federal spending!

Curiously, Roosevelt's most important 1932 campaign address was one he never saw until he opened it up on the lectern. Written primarily by Adolf A. Berle, a member of Roosevelt's "brain trust," the Commonwealth Club speech reflected the ideas of his advisors rather than the candidate's own views at that juncture. Yet it was in this speech that the future president indicated the new departure his administration would take. Especially important was Roosevelt's assertion that the idea of "rugged individualism" was no longer applicable to a complex, industrial society. What was needed, Roosevelt argued, was a new relationship between government and society.

Clearly, Hoover worked harder and did more than any previous president to ameliorate the effects of a depression. But he remained intransigent, refusing to waver from his basic philosophy of self-help. Not until July, 1932, did the federal government begin allocating funds to the states, and then only in the form of loans. Fundamentally, this was due to Hoover's firm conviction that the American economic system was sound and that the Depression was a European import—a conviction that he repeated in his acceptance speech.

Hoover's busy schedule allowed him to make only nine important campaign speeches. In these addresses he tried to convince the American people that Roosevelt's policies were the entering wedge of a philosophy that would destroy the "American system," and that a temporary economic aberration did not warrant the destruction of a system that had provided so much to so many. On October 31st, at New York's Madison Square Garden, Hoover again emphasized that the 1932 election was "a contest between two philosophies of government."

FRANKLIN D. ROOSEVELT

Acceptance Speech

CHICAGO, ILLINOIS

July 2, 1932

Chairman Walsh, my friends of the Democratic National Convention of 1932:

I appreciate your willingness after these six arduous days to remain here, for I know well the sleepless hours which you and I have had. I regret that I am late, but I have no control over the winds of Heaven and could only be thankful for my Navy training.

The appearance before a National Convention of its nominee for President, to be formally notified of his selection, is unprecedented and unusual, but these are unprecedented and unusual times. I have started out on the tasks that lie ahead by breaking the absurd traditions that the candidate should remain in professed ignorance of what has happened for weeks until he is formally notified of that event many weeks later.

My friends, may this be the symbol of my intention to be honest and to avoid all hypocrisy or sham, to avoid all silly shutting of the eyes to the truth in this campaign. You have nominated me and I know it, and I am here to thank you for the honor.

Let it also be symbolic that in so doing I broke traditions. Let it be from now on the task of our Party to break foolish traditions. We will break foolish traditions and leave it to the Republican leadership, far more skilled in that art, to break promises.

Let us now and here highly resolve to resume the country's interrupted march along the path of real progress, of real justice, of real equality for all of our citizens, great and small. Our indomitable leader in that interrupted march is no longer with us, but there still survives today his spirit. Many of his captains, thank God, are still with us, to give us wise counsel. Let us feel that in everything we do there still lives with us, if not the body, the great indomitable, unquenchable, progressive soul of our Commander-in-Chief, Woodrow Wilson.

I have many things on which I want to make my position clear at the earliest possible moment in this campaign. That admirable document, the platform which you have adopted, is clear. I accept it 100 percent.

And you can accept my pledge that I will leave no doubt or ambiguity on where I stand on any question of moment in this campaign.

As we enter this new battle, let us keep always present with us some of the ideals of the Party: The fact that the Democratic Party by tradition and by the continuing logic of history, past and present, is the bearer of liberalism and of progress and at the same time of safety to our institutions. And if this appeal fails, remember well, my friends, that a resentment against the failure of Republican leadership—and note well that in this campaign I shall not use the words "Republican Party," but I shall use, day in and day out, the words, "Republican leadership"—the failure of Republican leaders to solve our troubles may degenerate into unreasoning radicalism.

The great social phenomenon of this depression, unlike others before it, is that it has produced but a few of the disorderly manifestations that too often attend upon such times.

Wild radicalism has made few converts, and the greatest tribute that I can pay to my countrymen is that in these days of crushing want there persists an orderly and hopeful spirit on the part of the millions of our people who have suffered so much. To fail to offer them a new chance is not only to betray their hopes but to misunderstand their patience.

To meet by reaction that danger of radicalism is to invite disaster. Reaction is no barrier to the radical. It is a challenge, a provocation. The way to meet that danger is to offer a workable program of reconstruction, and the party to offer it is the party with clean hands.

This, and this only, is a proper protection against blind reaction on the one hand and an improvised, hit-or-miss, irresponsible opportunism on the other.

There are two ways of viewing the Government's duty in matters affecting economic and social life. The first sees to it that a favored few are helped and hopes that some of their prosperity will leak through, sift through, to labor, to the farmer, to the small businessman. That theory belongs to the party of Toryism, and I had hoped that most of the Tories left this country in 1776.

But it is not and never will be the theory of the Democratic Party.

This is no time for fear, for reaction or for timidity. Here and now I invite those nominal Republicans who find that their conscience cannot be squared with the groping and the failure of their party leaders to join hands with us; here and now, in equal measure, I warn those nominal Democrats who squint at the future with their faces turned toward the past, and who feel no responsibility to the demands of the new time, that they are out of step with their Party.

Yes, the people of this country want a genuine choice this year, not a choice between two names for the same reactionary doctrine. Ours must be a party of liberal thought, of planned action, of enlightened international outlook, and of the greatest good to the greatest number of our citizens.

Now it is inevitable—and the choice is that of the times—it is inevitable that the main issue of this campaign should revolve about the clear fact of our economic condition, a depression so deep that it is without precedent in modern history. It will not do merely to state, as do Republican leaders to explain their broken promises of continued inaction, that the depression is worldwide. That was not their explanation of the apparent prosperity of 1928. The people will not forget the claim made by them then that prosperity was only a domestic product manufactured by a Republican President and a Republican Congress. If they claim paternity for the one they cannot deny paternity for the other.

I cannot take up all the problems today. I want to touch on a few that are vital. Let us look a little at the recent history and the simple economics, the kind of economics that you and I and the average man and woman talk.

In the years before 1929 we know that this country had completed a vast cycle of building and inflation; for ten years we expanded on the theory of repairing the wastes of the War, but actually expanding far beyond that, and also beyond our natural and normal growth. Now it is worth remembering, and the cold figures of finance prove it, that during that time there was little or no drop in the prices that the consumer had to pay, although those same figures proved that the cost of production fell very greatly; corporate profit resulting from this period was enormous; at the same time little of that profit was devoted to the reduction of prices. The consumer was forgotten. Very little of it went into increased wages; the worker was forgotten, and by no means an adequate proportion was even paid out in dividends—the stockholder was forgotten.

And, incidentally, very little of it was taken by taxation to the beneficent Government of those years.

What was the result? Enormous corporate surpluses piled up—the most stupendous in history. Where, under the spell of delirious speculation, did those surpluses go? Let us talk economics that the figures prove and that we can understand. Why, they went chiefly in two directions: first, into new and unnecessary plants which now stand stark and idle; and second, into the call-money market of Wall Street, either directly by the corporations, or indirectly through the banks. Those are the facts. Why blink at them?

Then came the crash. You know the story. Surpluses invested in unnecessary plants became idle. Men lost their jobs; purchasing power dried up; banks became frightened and started calling loans. Those who had money were afraid to part with it. Credit contracted. Industry stopped. Commerce declined, and unemployment mounted.

And there we are today.

Translate that into human terms. See how the events of the past three years have come home to specific groups of people: first, the group dependent on industry; second, the group dependent on agriculture; third, and made up in large part of members of the first two groups, the people who are called "small investors and depositors." In fact, the strongest possible tie between the first two groups, agriculture and industry, is the fact that the savings and to a degree the security of both are tied together in that third group—the credit structure of the Nation.

Never in history have the interests of all the people been so united in a single economic problem. Picture to yourself, for instance, the great groups of property owned by millions of our citizens, represented by credits issued in the form of bonds and mortgages—Government bonds of all kinds, Federal, State, county, municipal; bonds of industrial companies, of utility companies; mortgages on real estate in farms and cities, and finally the vast investments of the Nation in the railroads. What is the measure of the security of each of those groups? We know well that in our complicated, interrelated credit structure if any one of these credit groups collapses they may all collapse. Danger to one is danger to all.

How, I ask, has the present Administration in Washington treated the interrelationship of these credit groups? The answer is clear; It has not recognized that interrelationship existed at all. Why, the Nation asks, has Washington failed to understand that all of these groups, each and every one, the top of the pyramid and the bottom of the pyramid, must be considered together, that each and every one of them is dependent on every other; each and every one of them affecting the whole financial fabric?

Statesmanship and vision, my friends, require relief to all at the same time.

Just one word or two on taxes, the taxes that all of us pay toward the cost of Government of all kinds.

I know something of taxes. For three long years I have been going up and down this country preaching that Government—Federal and

State and local—costs too much. I shall not stop that preaching. As an immediate program of action we must abolish useless offices. We must eliminate unnecessary functions of Government—functions, in fact, that are not definitely essential to the continuance of Government. We must merge, we must consolidate subdivisions of Government, and, like the private citizen, give up luxuries which we can no longer afford.

By our example at Washington itself, we shall have the opportunity of pointing the way of economy to local government, for let us remember well that out of every tax dollar in the average State in this Nation, 40 cents enter the treasury in Washington, D. C., 10 or 12 cents only go to the State capitals, and 48 cents are consumed by the costs of local government in counties and cities and towns.

I propose to you, my friends, and through you, that Government of all kinds, big and little, be made solvent and that the example be set by the President of the United States and his Cabinet.

And talking about setting a definite example, I congratulate this convention for having had the courage fearlessly to write into its declaration of principles what an overwhelming majority here assembled really thinks about the 18th Amendment. This convention wants repeal. Your candidate wants repeal. And I am confident that the United States of America wants repeal.

Two years ago the platform on which I ran for Governor the second time contained substantially the same provision. The overwhelming sentiment of the people of my State, as shown by the vote of that year, extends, I know, to the people of many of the other States. I say to you now that from this date on the 18th Amendment is doomed. When that happens, we as Democrats must and will, rightly and morally, enable the States to protect themselves against the importation of intoxicating liquor where such importation may violate their State laws. We must rightly and morally prevent the return of the saloon.

To go back to this dry subject of finance, because it all ties in together —the 18th Amendment has something to do with finance, too—in a comprehensive planning for the reconstruction of the great credit groups, including Government credit, I list an important place for that prize statement of principle in the platform here adopted calling for the letting in of the light of day on issues of securities, foreign and domestic, which are offered for sale to the investing public.

My friends, you and I as common-sense citizens know that it would help to protect the savings of the country from the dishonesty of crooks and from the lack of honor of some men in high financial places. Publicity is the enemy of crookedness.

And now one word about unemployment, and incidentally about agriculture. I have favored the use of certain types of public works as a further emergency means of stimulating employment and the issuance of bonds to pay for such public works, but I have pointed out that no economic end is served if we merely build without building for a necessary purpose. Such works, of course, should insofar as possible be self-sustaining if they are to be financed by the issuing of bonds. So as to spread the points of all kinds as widely as possible, we must take definite steps to shorten the working day and the working week.

Let us use common sense and business sense. Just as one example, we know that a very hopeful and immediate means of relief, both for the unemployed and for agriculture, will come from a wide plan of the converting of many millions of acres of marginal and unused land into timberland through reforestation. There are tens of millions of acres east of the Mississippi River alone in abandoned farms, cut-over land, now growing up in worthless brush. Why, every European Nation has a definite land policy, and has had one for generations. We have none. Having none, we face a future of soil erosion and timber famine. It is clear that economic foresight and immediate employment march hand in hand in the call for the reforestation of these vast areas.

In so doing, employment can be given to a million men. That is the kind of public work that is self-sustaining, and therefore capable of being financed by the issuance of bonds which are made secure by the fact that the growth of tremendous crops will provide adequate security for the investment.

Yes, I have a very definite program for providing employment by that means. I have done it, and I am doing it today in the State of New York. I know that the Democratic Party can do it successfully in the Nation. That will put men to work, and that is an example of the action that we are going to have.

Now as a further aid to agriculture, we know perfectly well—but have we come out and said so clearly and distinctly?—we should repeal immediately those provisions of law that compel the Federal Government to go into the market to purchase, to sell, to speculate in farm products in a futile attempt to reduce farm surpluses. And they are the people who are talking of keeping Government out of business. The practical way to help the farmer is by an arrangement that will, in addition to lightening some of the impoverishing burdens from his back, do something toward the reduction of the surpluses of staple commodities that hang on the market. It should be our aim to add to the world prices of staple products the amount of a reasonable tariff protection, to give agriculture the same protection that industry has today.

And in exchange for this immediately increased return I am sure that the farmers of this Nation would agree ultimately to such planning of their production as would reduce the surpluses and make it unnecessary in later years to depend on dumping those surpluses abroad in order to support domestic prices. That result has been accomplished in other Nations; why not in America, too?

Farm leaders and farm economists, generally, agree that a plan based on that principle is a desirable first step in the reconstruction of agriculture. It does not in itself furnish a complete program, but it will serve in great measure in the long run to remove the pall of a surplus without the continued perpetual threat of world dumping. Final voluntary reduction of surplus is a part of our objective, but the long continuance and the present burden of existing surpluses make it necessary to repair great damage of the present by immediate emergency measures.

Such a plan as that, my friends, does not cost the Government any money, nor does it keep the Government in business or in speculation.

As to the actual wording of a bill, I believe that the Democratic Party stands ready to be guided by whatever the responsible farm groups themselves agree on. That is a principle that is sound; and again I ask for action.

One more word about the farmer, and I know that every delegate in this hall who lives in the city knows why I lay emphasis on the farmer. It is because one-half of our population, over 50,000,000 people, are dependent on agriculture; and, my friends, if those 50,000,000 people have no money, no cash, to buy what is produced in the city, the city suffers to an equal or greater extent.

That is why we are going to make the voters understand this year that this Nation is not merely a Nation of independence, but it is, if we are to survive, bound to be a Nation of interdependence—town and city, and North and South, East and West. That is our goal, and that goal will be understood by the people of this country no matter where they live.

Yes, the purchasing power of that half of our population dependent on agriculture is gone. Farm mortgages reach nearly ten billions of dollars today and interest charges on that alone are $560,000,000 a year. But that is not all. The tax burden caused by extravagant and inefficient local government is an additional factor. Our most immediate concern should be to reduce the interest burden on these mortgages.

Rediscounting of farm mortgages under salutary restrictions must be expanded and should, in the future, be conditioned on the reduction of interest rates. Amortization payments, maturities should likewise in this crisis be extended before rediscount is permitted where the mortgagor is sorely pressed. That, my friends, is another example of practical, immediate relief: Action.

I aim to do the same thing, and it can be done, for the small home-owner in our cities and villages. We can lighten his burden and develop his purchasing power. Take away, my friends, that spectre of too high an interest rate. Take away that spectre of the due date just a short time away. Save homes; save homes for thousands of self-respecting families, and drive out that spectre of insecurity from our midst.

Out of all the tons of printed paper, out of all the hours of oratory, the recriminations, the defenses, the happy-thought plans in Washington and in every State, there emerges one great, simple, crystal-pure fact that during the past ten years a Nation of 120,000,000 people has been led by the Republican leaders to erect an impregnable barbed wire entanglement around its borders through the instrumentality of tariffs which have isolated us from all the other human beings in all the rest of the round world. I accept that admirable tariff statement in the platform of this convention. It would protect American business and American labor. By our acts of the past we have invited and received the retaliation of other Nations. I propose an invitation to them to forget the past, to sit at the table with us, as friends, and to plan with us for the restoration of trade of the world.

Go into the home of the business man. He knows what the tariff has done for him. Go into the home of the factory worker. He knows why goods do not move. Go into the home of the farmer. He knows how the tariff has helped to ruin him.

At last our eyes are open. At last the American people are ready to acknowledge that Republican leadership was wrong and that the Democracy is right.

My program, of which I can only touch on these points, is based upon this simple moral principle: the welfare and the soundness of a Nation depend first upon what the great mass of the people wish and need; and second, whether or not they are getting it.

What do the people of America want more than anything else? To my mind, they want two things: work, with all the moral and spiritual values that go with it; and with work, a reasonable measure of security— security for themselves and for their wives and children. Work and security—these are more than words. They are more than facts. They are the spiritual values, the true goal toward which our efforts of reconstruction should lead. These are the values that this program is intended to gain; these are the values we have failed to achieve by the leadership we now have.

Our Republican leaders tell us economic laws—sacred, inviolable, unchangeable—cause panics which no one could prevent. But while they prate of economic laws, men and women are starving. We must lay hold of the fact that economic laws are not made by nature. They are made by human beings.

Yes, when—not if—when we get the chance, the Federal Government will assume bold leadership in distress relief. For years Washington has alternated between putting its head in the sand and saying there is no large number of destitute people in our midst who need food and clothing, and then saying the States should take care of them, if there are. Instead of planning two and a half years ago to do what they are now trying to do, they kept putting it off from day to day, week to week, and month to month, until the conscience of America demanded action.

I say that while primary responsibility for relief rests with localities now, as ever, yet the Federal Government has always had and still has a continuing responsibility for the broader public welfare. It will soon fulfill that responsibility.

And now, just a few words about our plans for the next four months. By coming here instead of waiting for a formal notification, I have made it clear that I believe we should eliminate expensive ceremonies and that we should set in motion at once, tonight, my friends, the necessary machinery for an adequate presentation of the issues to the electorate of the Nation.

I myself have important duties as Governor of a great State, duties which in these times are more arduous and more grave than at any previous period. Yet I feel confident that I shall be able to make a number of short visits to several parts of the Nation. My trips will have as their first objective the study at first hand, from the lips of men and women of all parties and all occupations, of the actual conditions and needs of every part of an interdependent country.

One word more: Out of every crisis, every tribulation, every disaster, mankind rises with some share of greater knowledge, of higher decency, of purer purpose. Today we shall have come through a period of loose thinking, descending morals, an era of selfishness, among individual men and women and among Nations. Blame not Governments alone for this. Blame ourselves in equal share. Let us be frank in acknowledgement of the truth that many amongst us have made obeisance to Mammon, that the profits of speculation, the easy road without toil, have lured us from the old barricades. To return to higher standards we must abandon the false prophets and seek new leaders of our own choosing.

Never before in modern history have the essential differences between the two major American parties stood out in such striking contrast as they do today. Republican leaders not only have failed in material things, they have failed in national vision, because in disaster they have held out no hope, they have pointed out no path for the people below to climb back to places of security and of safety in our American life.

Throughout the Nation, men and women, forgotten in the political philosophy of the Government of the last years look to us here for guidance and for more equitable opportunity to share in the distribution of national wealth.

On the farms, in the large metropolitan areas, in the smaller cities and in the villages, millions of our citizens cherish the hope that their old standards of living and of thought have not gone forever. Those millions cannot and shall not hope in vain.

I pledge you, I pledge myself, to a new deal for the American people. Let us all here assembled constitute ourselves prophets of a new order of competence and of courage. This is more than a political campaign; it is a call to arms. Give me your help, not to win votes alone, but to win in this crusade to restore America to its own people.

FRANKLIN D. ROOSEVELT

Campaign Speech

SAN FRANCISCO, CALIFORNIA

September 23, 1932

My friends:

I count it a privilege to be invited to address the Commonwealth Club. It has stood in the life of this city and State, and it is perhaps accurate to add, the Nation, as a group of citizen leaders interested in fundamental problems of Government, and chiefly concerned with achievement of progress in Government through non-partisan means. The privilege of addressing you, therefore, in the heat of a political campaign, is great. I want to respond to your courtesy in terms consistent with your policy.

I want to speak not of politics but of Government. I want to speak not of parties, but of universal principles. They are not political, except in that larger sense in which a great American once expressed a definition of politics, that nothing in all of human life is foreign to the science of politics.

I do want to give you, however, a recollection of a long life spent for a large part in public office. Some of my conclusions and observations have been deeply accentuated in these past few weeks. I have traveled far— from Albany to the Golden Gate. I have seen many people, and heard many things, and today, when in a sense my journey has reached the half-way mark, I am glad of the opportunity to discuss with you what it all means to me.

Sometimes, my friends, particularly in years such as these, the hand of discouragement falls upon us. It seems that things are in a rut, fixed, settled, that the world has grown old and tired and very much out of joint. This is the mood of depression, of dire and weary depression.

But then we look around us in America, and everything tells us that we are wrong. America is new. It is in the process of change and development. It has the great potentialities of youth, and particularly is this true of the great West, and of this coast, and of California.

I would not have you feel that I regard this as in any sense a new community. I have traveled in many parts of the world, but never have I felt the arresting thought of the change and development more than here, where the old, mystic East would seem to be near to us, where the currents of life and thought and commerce of the whole world meet us. This factor alone is sufficient to cause man to stop and think of the deeper meaning of things, when he stands in this community.

But more than that, I appreciate that the membership of this club consists of men who are thinking in terms beyond the immediate present, beyond their own immediate tasks, beyond their own individual interests. I want to invite you, therefore, to consider with me in the large, some of the relationships of Government and economic life that go deeply into our daily lives, our happiness, our future and our security.

The issue of Government has always been whether individual men and women will have to serve some system of Government or economics, or whether a system of Government and economics exists to serve individual men and women. This question has persistently dominated the discussion of Government for many generations. On questions relating to these things men have differed, and for time immemorial it is probable that honest men will continue to differ.

The final word belongs to no man; yet we can still believe in change and in progress. Democracy, as a dear old friend of mine in Indiana, Meredith Nicholson, has called it, is a quest, a never-ending seeking for better things, and in the seeking for these things and the striving for them, there are many roads to follow. But, if we map the course of these roads, we find that there are only two general directions.

When we look about us, we are likely to forget how hard people have worked to win the privilege of Government. The growth of the national Governments of Europe was a struggle for the development of a centralized force in the Nation, strong enough to impose peace upon ruling barons. In many instances the victory of the central Government, the creation of a strong central Government, was a haven of refuge to the individual. The people preferred the master far away to the exploitation and cruelty of the smaller master near at hand.

But the creators of national Government were perforce ruthless men.

They were often cruel in their methods, but they did strive steadily toward something that society needed and very much wanted, a strong central State able to keep the peace, to stamp out civil war, to put the unruly nobleman in his place, and to permit the bulk of individuals to live safely. The man of ruthless force had his place in developing a pioneer country, just as he did in fixing the power of the central Government in the development of Nations. Society paid him well for his services and its development. When the development among the Nations of Europe, however, had been completed, ambition and ruthlessness, having served their term, tended to overstep their mark.

There came a growing feeling that Government was conducted for the benefit of a few who thrived unduly at the expense of all. The people sought a balancing—a limiting force. There came gradually, through town councils, trade guilds, national parliaments, by constitution and by popular participation and control, limitations on arbitrary power.

Another factor that tended to limit the power of those who ruled, was the rise of the ethical conception that a ruler bore a responsibility for the welfare of his subjects.

The American colonies were born in this struggle. The American Revolution was a turning point in it. After the Revolution the struggle continued and shaped itself in the public life of the country. There were those who because they had seen the confusion which attended the years of war for American independence surrendered to the belief that popular Government was essentially dangerous and essentially unworkable. They were honest people, my friends, and we cannot deny that their experience had warranted some measure of fear. The most brilliant, honest and able exponent of this point of view was Hamilton. He was too impatient of slow-moving methods. Fundamentally he believed that the safety of the republic lay in the autocratic strength of its Government, that the destiny of individuals was to serve that Government, and that fundamentally a great and strong group of central institutions, guided by a small group of able and public spirited citizens, could best direct all Government.

But Mr. Jefferson, in the summer of 1776, after drafting the Declaration of Independence turned his mind to the same problem and took a different view. He did not deceive himself with outward forms. Government to him was a means to an end, not an end in itself; it might be either a refuge and a help or a threat and a danger, depending on the circumstances. We find him carefully analyzing the society for which he was to organize a Government. "We have no paupers. The great mass of our population is of laborers, our rich who cannot live without labor, either manual or professional, being few and of moderate wealth. Most of the laboring class possess property, cultivate their own lands, have families and from the demand for their labor, are enabled to exact from the rich and the competent such prices as enable them to feed abundantly, clothe above mere decency, to labor moderately and raise their families."

These people, he considered, had two sets of rights, those of "personal competency" and those involved in acquiring and possessing property. By "personal competency" he meant the right of free thinking, freedom of forming and expressing opinions, and freedom of personal living, each man according to his own lights. To insure the first set of rights, a Government must so order its functions as not to interfere with the individual. But even Jefferson realized that the exercise of the property rights might so interfere with the rights of the individual that the Government, without whose assistance the property rights could not exist, must intervene, not to destroy individualism, but to protect it.

You are familiar with the great political duel which followed; and how Hamilton, and his friends, building toward a dominant centralized power were at length defeated in the great election of 1800, by Mr. Jefferson's party. Out of that duel came the two parties, Republican and Democratic, as we know them today.

So began, in American political life, the new day, the day of the individual against the system, the day in which individualism was made the great watchword of American life. The happiest of economic conditions made that day long and splendid. On the Western frontier, land was substantially free. No one, who did not shirk the task of earning a living, was entirely without opportunity to do so. Depressions could, and did, come and go; but they could not alter the fundamental fact that most of the people lived partly by selling their labor and partly by extracting their livelihood from the soil, so that starvation and dislocation were practically impossible. At the very worst there was always the possibility of climbing into a covered wagon and moving west where the untilled prairies afforded a haven for men to whom the East did not provide a place. So great were our natural resources that we could offer this relief not only to our own people, but to the distressed of all the world; we could invite immigration from Europe, and welcome it with open arms. Traditionally, when a depression came a new section of land was opened in the West; and even our temporary misfortune served our manifest destiny.

It was in the middle of the nineteenth century that a new force was released and a new dream created. The force was what is called the industrial revolution, the advance of steam and machinery and the rise of the forerunners of the modern industrial plant. The dream was the dream of an economic machine, able to raise the standard of living for everyone; to bring luxury within the reach of the humblest; to annihilate distance by steam power and later by electricity, and to release everyone from the drudgery of the heaviest manual toil. It was to be expected that this would necessarily affect Government. Heretofore, Government had merely been called upon to produce conditions within which people could live happily, labor peacefully, and rest secure. Now it was called upon to aid in the consummation of this new dream. There was, however, a shadow over the dream. To be made real, it required use of the talents of men of tremendous will and tremendous ambition, since by no other force could the problems of financing and engineering and new developments be brought to a consummation.

So manifest were the advantages of the machine age, however, that the United States fearlessly, cheerfully, and, I think, rightly, accepted the bitter with the sweet. It was thought that no price was too high to pay for the advantages which we could draw from a finished industrial system. The history of the last half century is accordingly in large measure a history of a group of financial Titans, whose methods were not scrutinized with too much care, and who were honored in proportion as they produced the results, irrespective of the means they used. The financiers who pushed the railroads to the Pacific were always ruthless, often wasteful, and frequently corrupt; but they did build railroads, and we have them today. It has been estimated that the American investor paid for the American railway system more than three times over in the process; but despite this fact the net advantage was to the United States. As long as we had free land; as long as population was growing by leaps and bounds; as long as our industrial plants were insufficient to supply our own needs, society chose to give the ambitious man free play and unlimited reward provided only that he produced the economic plant so much desired.

During this period of expansion, there was equal opportunity for all and the business of Government was not to interfere but to assist in the development of industry. This was done at the request of business men themselves. The tariff was originally imposed for the purpose of "fostering our infant industry," a phrase I think the older among you will remember as a political issue not so long ago. The railroads were subsidized, sometimes by grants of money, oftener by grants of land; some of the most valuable oil lands in the United States were granted to assist the financing of the railroad which pushed through the Southwest. A nascent merchant marine was assisted by grants of money, or by mail subsidies, so that our steam shipping might ply the seven seas. Some of my friends tell me that they do not want the Government in business. With this I agree; but I wonder whether they realize the implications of the past. For while it has been American doctrine that the Government must not go into business in competition with private enterprises, still it has been traditional, particularly in Republican administrations, for business urgently to ask the Government to put at private disposal all kinds of Government assistance. The same man who tells you that he does not want to see the

Government interfere in business—and he means it, and has plenty of good reasons for saying so—is the first to go to Washington and ask the Government for a prohibitory tariff on his product. When things get just bad enough, as they did two years ago, he will go with equal speed to the United States Government and ask for a loan; and the Reconstruction Finance Corporation is the outcome of it. Each group has sought protection from the Government for its own special interests, without realizing that the function of Government must be to favor no small group at the expense of its duty to protect the right of personal freedom and of private property of all its citizens.

In retrospect we can now see that the turn of the tide came with the turn of the century. We were reaching our last frontier; there was no more free land and our industrial combinations had become great uncontrolled and irresponsible units of power within the State. Clear-sighted men saw with fear the danger that opportunity would no longer be equal; that the growing corporation, like the feudal baron of old, might threaten the economic freedom of individuals to earn a living. In that hour, our antitrust laws were born. The cry was raised against the great corporations. Theodore Roosevelt, the first great Republican Progressive, fought a Presidential campaign on the issue of "trust busting" and talked freely about malefactors of great wealth. If the Government had a policy it was rather to turn the clock back, to destroy the large combinations and to return to the time when every man owned his individual small business.

This was impossible; Theodore Roosevelt, abandoning the idea of "trust busting," was forced to work out a difference between "good" trusts and "bad" trusts. The Supreme Court set forth the famous "rule of reason" by which it seems to have meant that a concentration of industrial power was permissible if the method by which it got its power, and the use it made of that power, were reasonable.

Woodrow Wilson, elected in 1912, saw the situation more clearly. Where Jefferson had feared the encroachment of political power on the lives of individuals, Wilson knew that the new power was financial. He saw, in the highly centralized economic system, the despot of the twentieth century, on whom great masses of individuals relied for their safety and their livelihood, and whose irresponsibility and greed (if they were not controlled) would reduce them to starvation and penury. The concentration of financial power had not proceeded so far in 1912 as it has today; but it had grown far enough for Mr. Wilson to realize fully its implications. It is interesting, now, to read his speeches. What is called "radical" today (and I have reason to know whereof I speak) is mild compared to the campaign of Mr. Wilson. "No man can deny," he said, "that the lines of endeavor have more and more narrowed and stiffened; no man who knows anything about the development of industry in this country can have failed to observe that the larger kinds of credit are more and more difficult to obtain unless you obtain them upon terms of uniting your efforts with those who already control the industry of the country, and nobody can fail to observe that every man who tries to set himself up in competition with any process of manufacture which has taken place under the control of large combinations of capital will presently find himself either squeezed out or obliged to sell and allow himself to be absorbed." Had there been no World War—had Mr. Wilson been able to devote eight years to domestic instead of to international affairs—we might have had a wholly different situation at the present time. However, the then distant roar of European cannon, growing ever louder, forced him to abandon the study of this issue. The problem he saw so clearly is left with us as a legacy; and no one of us on either side of the political controversy can deny that it is a matter of grave concern to the Government.

A glance at the situation today only too clearly indicates that equality of opportunity as we have known it no longer exists. Our industrial plant is built; the problem just now is whether under existing conditions it is not overbuilt. Our last frontier has long since been reached, and there is practically no more free land. More than half of our people do not live on the farms or on lands and cannot derive a living by cultivating their own property. There is no safety valve in the form of a Western prairie to which those thrown out of work by the Eastern economic machines can go for a new start. We are not able to invite the immigration from Europe to share our endless plenty. We are now providing a drab living for our own people.

Our system of constantly rising tariffs has at last reacted against us to the point of closing our Canadian frontier on the north, our European markets on the east, many of our Latin-American markets to the south, and a goodly proportion of our Pacific markets on the west, through the retaliatory tariffs of those countries. It has forced many of our great industrial institutions which exported their surplus production to such countries, to establish plants in such countries, within the tariff walls. This has resulted in the reduction of the operation of their American plants, and opportunity for employment.

Just as freedom to farm has ceased, so also the opportunity in business has narrowed. It still is true that men can start small enterprises, trusting to native shrewdness and ability to keep abreast of competitors; but area after area has been preempted altogether by the great corporations, and even in the fields which still have no great concerns, the small man starts under a handicap. The unfeeling statistics of the past three decades show that the independent business man is running a losing race. Perhaps he is forced to the wall; perhaps he cannot command credit; perhaps he is "squeezed out," in Mr. Wilson's words, by highly organized corporate competitors, as your corner grocery man can tell you. Recently a careful study was made of the concentration of business in the United States. It showed that our economic life was dominated by some six hundred odd corporations who controlled two-thirds of American industry. Ten million small business men divided the other third. More striking still, it appeared that if the process of concentration goes on at the same rate, at the end of another century we shall have all American industry controlled by a dozen corporations, and run by perhaps a hundred men. Put plainly, we are steering a steady course toward economic oligarchy, if we are not there already.

Clearly, all this calls for a re-appraisal of values. A mere builder of more industrial plants, a creator of more railroad systems, an organizer of more corporations, is as likely to be a danger as a help. The day of the great promoter or the financial Titan, to whom we granted anything if only he would build, or develop, is over. Our task now is not discovery or exploitation of natural resources, or necessarily producing more goods. It is the soberer, less dramatic business of administering resources and plants already in hand, of seeking to reestablish foreign markets for our surplus production, of meeting the problem of underconsumption, of adjusting production to consumption, of distributing wealth and products more equitably, of adapting existing economic organizations to the service of the people. The day of enlightened administration has come.

Just as in older times the central Government was first a haven of refuge, and then a threat, so now in a closer economic system the central and ambitious financial unit is no longer a servant of national desire, but a danger. I would draw the parallel one step farther. We did not think because national Government had become a threat in the 18th century that therefore we should abandon the principle of national Government. Nor today should we abandon the principle of strong economic units called corporations, merely because their power is susceptible of easy abuse. In other times we dealt with the problem of an unduly ambitious central Government by modifying it gradually into a constitutional democratic Government. So today we are modifying and controlling our economic units.

As I see it, the task of Government in its relation to business is to assist the development of an economic declaration of rights, an economic constitutional order. This is the common task of statesman and business man. It is the minimum requirement of a more permanently safe order of things.

Happily, the times indicate that to create such an order not only is the proper policy of Government, but it is the only line of safety for our economic structures as well. We know, now, that these economic units cannot exist unless prosperity is uniform, that is, unless purchasing power is well distributed throughout every group in the Nation. That is why even the most selfish of corporations for its own interest would be glad to see wages restored and unemployment ended and to bring the Western farmer back to his accustomed level of prosperity and to assure a permanent safety to both groups. That is why some enlightened industries themselves endeavor to limit the freedom of action of each man and business group within the industry in the common interest of all; why business men everywhere are asking a form of organization which will bring the scheme of things into balance, even though it may in some measure qualify the freedom of action of individual units within the business.

The exposition need not further be elaborated. It is brief and incomplete, but you will be able to expand it in terms of your own business or occupation without difficulty. I think everyone who has actually entered the economic struggle—which means everyone who was not born to safe wealth—knows in his own experience and his own life that we have now to apply the earlier concepts of American Government to the conditions of today.

The Declaration of Independence discusses the problem of Government in terms of a contract. Government is a relation of give and take, a contract, perforce, if we would follow the thinking out of which it grew. Under such a contract rulers were accorded power, and the people consented to that power on consideration that they be accorded certain rights. The task of statesmanship has always been the re-definition of these rights in terms of a changing and growing social order. New conditions impose new requirements upon Government and those who conduct Government.

I held, for example, in proceedings before me as Governor, the purpose of which was the removal of the Sheriff of New York, that under modern conditions it was not enough for a public official merely to evade the legal terms of official wrong-doing. He owed a positive duty as well. I said in substance that if he had acquired large sums of money, he was when accused required to explain the sources of such wealth. To that extent this wealth was colored with a public interest. I said that in financial matters, public servants should, even beyond private citizens, be held to a stern and uncompromising rectitude.

I feel that we are coming to a view through the drift of our legislation and our public thinking in the past quarter century that private economic power is, to enlarge an old phrase, a public trust as well. I hold that continued enjoyment of that power by any individual or group must depend upon the fulfillment of that trust. The men who have reached the summit of American business life know this best; happily, many of these urge the binding quality of this greater social contract.

The terms of that contract are as old as the Republic, and as new as the new economic order.

Every man has a right to life; and this means that he has also a right to make a comfortable living. He may by sloth or crime decline to exercise that right; but it may not be denied him. We have no actual famine or dearth; our industrial and agricultural mechanism can produce enough and to spare. Our Government formal and informal, political and economic, owes to everyone an avenue to possess himself of a portion of that plenty sufficient for his needs, through his own work.

Every man has a right to his own property; which means a right to be assured, to the fullest extent attainable, in the safety of his savings. By no other means can men carry the burdens of those parts of life which, in the nature of things, afford no chance of labor; childhood, sickness, old age. In all thought of property, this right is paramount; all other property rights must yield to it. If, in accord with this principle, we must restrict the operations of the speculator, the manipulator, even the financier, I believe we must accept the restriction as needful, not to hamper individualism but to protect it.

These two requirements must be satisfied, in the main, by the individuals who claim and hold control of the great industrial and financial combinations which dominate so large a part of our industrial life. They have undertaken to be, not business men, but princes of property. I am not prepared to say that the system which produces them is wrong. I am very clear that they must fearlessly and competently assume the responsibility which goes with the power. So many enlightened business men know this that the statement would be little more than a platitude, were it not for an added implication.

This implication is, briefly that the responsible heads of finance and industry instead of acting each for himself, must work together to achieve the common end. They must, where necessary, sacrifice this or that private advantage; and in reciprocal self-denial must seek a general advantage. It is here that formal Government—political Government, if you choose—comes in. Whenever in the pursuit of this objective the lone wolf, the unethical competitor, the reckless promoter, the Ishmael or Insull whose hand is against every man's, declines to join in achieving an end recognized as being for the public welfare, and threatens to drag the industry back to a state of anarchy, the Government may properly be asked to apply restraint. Likewise, should the group ever use its collective power contrary to the public welfare, the Government must be swift to enter and protect the public interest.

The Government should assume the function of economic regulation only as a last resort, to be tried only when private initiative, inspired by high responsibility, with such assistance and balance as Government can give, has finally failed. As yet there has been no final failure, because there has been no attempt; and I decline to assume that this Nation is unable to meet the situation.

The final term of the high contract was for liberty and the pursuit of happiness. We have learned a great deal of both in the past century. We know that individual liberty and individual happiness mean nothing unless both are ordered in the sense that one man's meat is not another man's poison. We know that the old "rights of personal competency," the right to read, to think, to speak, to choose and live a mode of life, must be respected at all hazards. We know that liberty to do anything which deprives others of those elemental rights is outside the protection of any compact; and that Government in this regard is the maintenance of a balance, within which every individual may have a place if he will take it; in which every individual may find safety if he wishes it; in which every individual may attain such power as his ability permits, consistent with his assuming the accompanying responsibility.

All this is a long, slow talk. Nothing is more striking than the simple innocence of the men who insist, whenever an objective is present, on the prompt production of a patent scheme guaranteed to produce a result. Human endeavor is not so simple as that. Government includes the art of formulating a policy, and using the political technique to attain so much of that policy as will receive general support; persuading, leading, sacrificing, teaching always, because the greatest duty of a statesman is to educate. But in the matters of which I have spoken, we are learning rapidly, in a severe school. The lessons so learned must not be forgotten, even in the mental lethargy of a speculative upturn. We must build toward the time when a major depression cannot occur again; and if this means sacrificing the easy profits of inflationist booms, then let them go; and good riddance.

Faith in America, faith in our tradition of personal responsibility, faith in our institutions, faith in ourselves demand that we recognize the new terms of the old social contract. We shall fulfill them, as we fulfilled the obligation of the apparent Utopia which Jefferson imagined for us in 1776, and which Jefferson, Roosevelt and Wilson sought to bring to realization. We must do so, lest a rising tide of misery, engendered by our common failure, engulf us all. But failure is not an American habit; and in the strength of great hope we must all shoulder our common load.

☆

HERBERT C. HOOVER

Acceptance Speech

CONSTITUTION HALL, WASHINGTON, D. C.

August 11, 1932

Mr. Chairman and My Fellow Citizens:

In accepting the great honor you have brought me, I desire to speak so simply and so plainly that every man and woman in the United States who may hear or read my words cannot misunderstand.

The last three years have been a time of unparalleled economic calamity. They have been years of greater suffering and hardship than any which have come to the American people since the aftermath of the Civil War. As we look back over these troubled years we realize that we have passed through two stages of dislocation and stress.

Before the storm broke we were steadily gaining in prosperity. Our wounds from the war were rapidly healing. Advances in science and invention had opened vast vistas of new progress. Being prosperous, we became optimistic—all of us. From optimism some of us went to over-expansion in anticipation of the future, and from overexpansion to reckless speculation. In the soil poisoned by speculation grew those ugly weeds of waste, exploitation, and abuse of financial power. In this overproduction and speculative mania we marched with the rest of the world. Then three years ago came retribution by the inevitable world-wide slump in consumption of goods, in prices, and employment. At that juncture it was the normal penalty for a reckless boom such as we have witnessed a score of times in our history. Through such depressions we have always passed safely after a relatively short period of losses, of hardship and adjustment. We adopted policies in the Government which were fitting to the situation. Gradually the country began to right itself. Eighteen months ago there was a solid basis for hope that recovery was in sight.

Then there came to us a new calamity, a blow from abroad of such dangerous character as to strike at the very safety of the Republic. The countries of Europe proved unable to withstand the stress of the depression. The memories of the world had ignored the fact that the insidious diseases left by the Great War had not been cured. The skill and intelligence of millions in Europe had been blotted out by battle, disease, and starvation. Stupendous burdens of national debts had been built up. Poisoned springs of political instability lay in the treaties which closed the war.

Fears and hates held armaments to double those before the war. Governments were fallaciously seeking to build back by enlarged borrowing, by subsidizing industry and employment with taxes that slowly sapped the savings upon which industry must be rejuvenated and commerce solidly built. Under these strains the financial systems of many foreign countries crashed one by one.

New blows from decreasing world consumption of goods and from failing financial systems rained upon us. We are part of a world the disturbance of whose remotest populations affects our financial system, our employment, our markets, and prices of our farm products. Thus beginning eighteen months ago, the world-wide storm rapidly grew to hurricane force and the greatest economic emergency in all history. Unexpected, unforeseen, and violent shocks with every month brought new dangers and new emergencies. Fear and apprehension gripped the heart of our people in every village and city.

If we look back over the disasters of these three years, we find that three quarters of the population of the globe has suffered from the flames of revolution. Many nations have been subject to constant change and vacillation of government. Others have resorted to dictatorship or tyranny in desperate attempts to preserve some sort of social order.

I may pause for one short illustration of the character of one single destructive force arising from these causes which we have been compelled to meet. That was its effect upon our financial structure. Foreign countries, in the face of their own failures not believing that we had the courage or ability to meet this crisis, withdrew from the United States over $2,400,000,000, including a billion in gold. Our own alarmed citizens withdrew over $1,600,000,000 of currency from our banks into hoarding. These actions, combined with the fears they generated, caused a shrinkage of credit available for conduct of industry and commerce by several times even these vast sums. Its visible expression was bank and business failures, demoralization of security and real property values, commodity prices, and employment. This was but one of the invading forces of destruction.

Two courses were open. We might have done nothing. That would have been utter ruin. Instead, we met the situation with proposals to private business and the Congress of the most gigantic program of economic defense and counter attack ever evolved in the history of the Republic. We put it into action.

Our measures have repelled these attacks of fear and panic. We have maintained the financial integrity of our Government. We have coöperated to restore and stabilize the situation abroad. As a nation we have paid every dollar demanded of us. We have used the credit of the Government to aid and protect our institutions, public and private. We have provided methods and assurances that there shall be none to suffer from hunger and cold. We have instituted measures to assist farmers and home owners. We have created vast agencies for employment. Above all, we have maintained the sanctity of the principles upon which this Republic has grown great.

In a large sense the test of success of our program is simple. Our people, while suffering great hardships, have been and will be cared for. In the long view our institutions have been sustained intact and are now functioning with increasing confidence of the future. As a nation we are undefeated and unafraid. Government by the people has not been defiled.

With the humility of one who by necessity has stood in the midst of this storm I can say with pride that the distinction for these accomplishments belongs not to the Government or to any individual. It is due to the intrepid soul of our people. It is to their character, their fortitude, their initiative, and their courage that we owe these results. We of this generation did not build the great Ship of State. But the policies I have inaugurated have protected and aided its navigation in this storm. These policies and programs have not been partisan. I gladly give tribute to those members of the Democratic Party in Congress whose patriotic coöperation against factional and demagogic opposition has assisted in a score of great undertakings. I likewise give credit to Democratic as well as Republican leaders among our citizens for their coöperation and help.

A record of these dangers and these policies in the last three years will be set down in books. Much of it is of interest only to history. Our interest now is the future. I dwell upon these policies and problems only where they illustrate the questions of the day and our course in the future. As a government and as a people we still have much to do. We must continue the building of our measures of restoration. We must profit by the lessons of this experience.

Before I enter upon a discussion of these policies I wish to say something of my conception of the relation of our Government to the people and of the responsibilities of both, particularly as applied to these times. The spirit and devising of this Government by the people was to sustain a dual purpose—on the one hand to protect our people among nations and in domestic emergencies by great national power, and on the other to preserve individual liberty and freedom through local government.

The function of the Federal Government in these times is to use its reserve powers and its strength for the protection of citizens and local governments by supporting our institutions against forces beyond their control. It is not the function of the Government to relieve individuals of their responsibilities to their neighbors, or to relieve private institutions of their responsibilities to the public, or of local government to the States, or of State governments to the Federal Government. In giving that protection and that aid the Federal Government must insist that all of them exert their responsibilities in full. It is vital that the programs of the Government shall not compete with or replace any of them but shall add to their initiative and their strength. It is vital that by the use of public revenues and public credit in emergency the Nation shall be strengthened and not weakened.

And in all these emergencies and crises, and in all our future policies, we must also preserve the fundamental principles of our social and economic system. That system is founded upon a conception of ordered freedom. The test of that freedom is that there should be maintained equality of opportunity to every individual so that he may achieve for himself the best to which his character, ability, and ambition entitle him. It is only by this release of initiative, this insistence upon individual responsibility, that we accrue the great sums of individual accomplishment which carry this Nation forward. This is not an individualism which permits men to run riot in selfishness or to override equality of opportunity for others. It permits no violation of ordered liberty. In the race after the false gods of materialism men and groups have forgotten their country. Equality of opportunity contains no conception of exploitation by any selfish, ruthless, classs-minded men or groups. They have no place in the American system. As against these stand the guiding ideals and concepts of our Nation. I propose to maintain them.

The solution of our many problems which arise from the shifting scene of national life is not to be found in haphazard experimentation or by revolution. It must be through organic development of our national life under these ideals. It must secure that coöperative action which builds initiative and strength outside of government. It does not follow, because our difficulties are stupendous, because there are some souls timorous enough to doubt the validity and effectiveness of our ideals and our system, that we must turn to a State-controlled or State-directed social or economic system in order to cure our troubles. That is not liberalism; it is tyranny. It is the regimentation of men under autocratic bureaucracy with all its extinction of liberty, of hope, and of opportunity. Of course, no man of understanding says that our system works perfectly. It does not. The human race is not perfect. Nevertheless, the movement of a true civilization is toward freedom rather than regimentation. This is our ideal.

Ofttimes the tendency of democracy in presence of national danger is to strike blindly, to listen to demagogues and slogans, all of which would destroy and would not save. We have refused to be stampeded into such courses. Ofttimes democracy elsewhere in the world has been unable to move fast enough to save itself in emergency. There have been disheartening delays and failures in legislation and private action which have added to the losses of our people, yet this democracy of ours has proved its ability to act.

Our emergency measures of the last three years form a definite strategy dominated in the background by these American principles and ideals, forming a continuous campaign waged against the forces of destruction on an ever widening or constantly shifting front.

Thus we have held that the Federal Government should in the presence of great national danger use its powers to give leadership to the initiative, the courage, and the fortitude of the people themselves; but it must insist upon individual, community, and state responsibility. That it should furnish leadership to assure the coördination and unity of all existing agencies, governmental and private, for economic and humanitarian action. That where it becomes necessary to meet emergencies beyond the power of these agencies by the creation of new government instrumentalities, they should be of such character as not to supplant or weaken, but rather to supplement and strengthen, the initiative and enterprise of the people. That they must, directly, or indirectly, serve all the people. Above all, that they should be set up in such form that once the emergency is passed they can and must be demobilized and withdrawn, leaving our governmental, economic, and social structure strong and whole.

We have not feared boldly to adopt unprecedented measures to meet the unprecedented violence of the storm. But, because we have kept ever before us these eternal principles of our nation, the American Government in its ideals is the same as it was when the people gave the Presidency into my trust. We shall keep it so. We have resolutely rejected the temptation, under pressure of immediate events, to resort to those panaceas and short cuts which, even if temporarily successful, would ultimately undermine and weaken what has slowly been built and molded by experience and effort throughout these hundred and fifty years.

It was in accordance with these principles that in the first stage of the depression I called the leaders of business and of labor and agriculture to meet with me and induced them, by their own initiative, to organize against panic with all its devastating destruction; to uphold wages until the cost of living was adjusted; to spread existing employment through shortened hours; and to advance construction work, public and private, against future need.

In pursuance of that same policy, I each winter thereafter assumed the leadership in mobilizing all the voluntary and official organizations throughout the country to prevent suffering from hunger and cold, and to protect the million families stricken by drought. When it became advisable to strengthen the States that could not longer carry the full burden of relief to distress, I held that the Federal Government should do so through loans to the States and thus maintain the fundamental responsibility of the States. We stopped the attempt to turn this effort to the politics of selfish sectional demands. We kept it based upon human need.

It is in accordance with these principles that, in aid to unemployment, we are expending some six hundred millions in Federal construction of such public works as can be justified as bringing early and definite returns. We have opposed the distortion of these needed works into pork-barrel nonproductive works which impoverish the Nation.

It is in accord with these principles and purposes that we have made provision for one billion five hundred millions of loans to self-supporting works so that we may increase employment in productive labor. We rejected projects of wasteful nonproductive works allocated for the purpose of attracting votes instead of affording relief. Thereby, instead of wasteful drain upon the taxpayer, we secure the return of their cost to Government agencies and at the same time we increase the wealth of the Nation.

It was in accordance with these principles that we have strengthened the capital of the Federal land banks—that, on the one hand, confidence in their securities should not be impaired, and on the other, that farmers indebted to them should not be unduly deprived of their homes. The Farm Board by emergency loans to the farmers' coöperatives served to stem panics in agricultural prices and saved hundreds of thousands of farmers and their creditors from bankruptcy. We have created agencies to prevent bankruptcy and failure of their coöperative organizations, and we are erecting new instrumentalities to give credit facilities for live-stock growers and the orderly marketing of farm products.

It was in accordance with these principles that in the face of the looming European crises we sought to change the trend of European economic degeneration by my proposal of the German moratorium and the standstill agreements as to German private debts. We stemmed the tide of collapse in Germany and the consequent ruin of its people, with its repercussion on all other nations of the world. In furtherance of world stability we have made proposals to reduce the cost of world armaments by a billion dollars a year.

It was in accordance with these principles that I first secured the creation by private initiative of the National Credit Association, whose efforts prevented the failure of hundreds of banks, and loss to countless thousands of depositors who had loaned all their savings to them.

As the storm grew in intensity we created the Reconstruction Finance Corporation with a capital of two billions to uphold the credit structure of the Nation, and by thus raising the shield of Government credit we prevented the wholesale failure of banks, of insurance companies, of building and loan associations, of farm-mortgage associations, of livestock-loan associations, and of railroads in all of which the public interest is paramount. This disaster has been averted through the saving of more than 5,000 institutions and the knowledge that adequate assistance was available to tide others over the stress. This was done not to save a few stockholders, but to save twenty-five millions of American families, every one of whose very savings and employment might have been wiped out and whose whole future would have been blighted had those institutions gone down.

It was in accordance with these principles that we expanded the functions and powers of the Federal Reserve banks that they might counteract the stupendous shrinkage of credit due to fear, to hoarding, and to foreign withdrawals.

It is in accordance with these principles that we are now in process of establishing a new system of home loan banks so that through added strength by coöperation in the building and loan associations, the savings banks, and the insurance companies we may relax the pressure of forfeiture upon home owners and procure the release of new resources for the construction of more homes and the employment of more men.

It was in accordance with these principles that we have insisted upon a reduction of governmental expenses, for no country can squander itself to prosperity on the ruins of its taxpayers, and it was in accordance with these purposes that we have sought new revenues to equalize the diminishing income of the Government in order that the power of the Federal Government to meet the emergency should be impregnable.

It is in accordance with these principles that we have joined in the development of a world economic conference to bulwark the whole international fabric of finance, monetary values, and the expansion of world commerce.

It is in accordance with these principles that I am today organizing the private industrial and financial resources of the country to coöperate effectively with the vast governmental instrumentalities which we have in motion, so that through their united and coördinated efforts we may move from defense to powerful attack upon the depression along the whole national front.

These programs, unparalleled in the history of depressions in any country and in any time, to care for distress, to provide employment, to aid agriculture, to maintain the financial stability of the country, to safeguard the savings of the people, to protect their homes, are not in the past tense—they are in action. I shall propose such other measures, public and private, as may be necessary from time to time to meet the changing situations and to further speed economic recovery. That recovery may be slow, but we will succeed.

And come what may, I shall maintain through all these measures the sanctity of the great principles under which the Republic over a period of one hundred and fifty years has grown to be the greatest nation on earth.

I should like to digress for one instant for an observation on the last three years which should exhilarate the faith of all Americans—that is the profound growth of the sense of social responsibility which this depression has demonstrated.

No government in Washington has hitherto considered that it held so broad a responsibility for leadership in such times. Despite hardships, the devotion of our men and women to those in distress is demonstrated by the national averages of infant mortality, general mortality, and sickness, which are less today than in times of prosperity. For the first time in the history of depressions, dividends, profits, and cost of living have been reduced before wages have suffered. We have been more free from industrial conflict through strikes and lockouts and all forms of social disorder than even in normal times. The Nation is building the initiative of men toward new fields of social coöperation and endeavor.

So much for the great national emergency and the principles of government for which we stand and their application to the measures we have taken.

There are national policies wider than the emergency, wider than the economic horizon. They are set forth in our platform. Having the responsibility of this office, my views upon them are clearly and often set out in the public record. I may, however, summarize some of them.

1. I am squarely for a protective tariff. I am against the proposal of "a competitive tariff for revenue" as advocated by our opponents. That would place our farmers and our workers in competition with peasant and sweated labor products.

2. I am against their proposals to destroy the usefulness of the bipartisan Tariff Commission, the establishment of whose effective powers we secured during this administration twenty-five years after it was first advocated by President Theodore Roosevelt. That instrumentality enables us to correct any injustice and to readjust the rates of duty to shifting economic change, without constant tinkering and orgies of logrolling in Congress. If our opponents will descend from vague generalizations to any particular schedule, if it be higher than necessary to protect our people or insufficient for their protection, it can be remedied by this bipartisan commission.

3. My views in opposition to cancellation of war debts are a matter of detailed record in many public statements and a recent message to the Congress. They mark a continuity of that policy maintained by my predecessors. I am hopeful of such drastic reduction of world armament as will save the taxpayers in debtor countries a large part of the cost of their payments to us. If for any particular annual payment we were offered

some other tangible form of compensation, such as the expansion of markets for American agriculture and labor, and the restoration and maintenance of our prosperity, then I am sure our citizens would consider such a proposal. But it is a certainty that these debts must not be canceled or the burdens transferred to our people.

4. I insist upon an army and navy of a strength which guarantees that no foreign soldier will land on American soil. That strength is relative to other nations. I favor every arms reduction which preserves that relationship.

5. I favor rigidly restricted immigration. I have by executive direction, in order to relieve us of added unemployment, already reduced the inward movement to less than the outward movement. I shall adhere to that policy.

6. I have repeatedly recommended to the Congress a revision of the railway transportation laws, in order that we may create greater stability and greater assurance of vital service in all our transportation. I shall persist in it.

7. I have repeatedly recommended the Federal regulation of interstate power. I shall persist in that. I have opposed the Federal Government undertaking the operation of the power business. I shall continue that opposition.

8. I have for years supported the conservation of national resources. I have made frequent recommendations to the Congress in respect thereto, including legislation to correct the waste and destruction of these resources through the present interpretations of the antitrust laws. I shall continue to urge such action.

9. This depression has exposed many weaknesses in our economic system. There have been exploitation and abuse of financial power. We will fearlessly and unremittingly reform such abuses. I have recommended to the Congress the reform of our banking laws. Unfortunately this legislation has not yet been enacted. The American people must have protection from insecure banking through a stronger system. They must be relieved from conditions which permit the credit machinery of the country to be made available without adequate check for wholesale speculation in securities with ruinous consequences to millions of our citizens and to national economy. I recommended to the Congress emergency relief for depositors in closed banks. For seven years I have repeatedly warned against private loans abroad for nonproductive purposes. I shall persist in those matters.

10. I have insisted upon a balanced Budget as the foundation of all public and private financial stability and of all public cónfidence. I shall insist on the maintenance of that policy. Recent increases in revenues,

while temporary, should be again examined, and if they tend to sap the vitality of industry, and thus retard employment, they must be revised.

11. The first necessity of the Nation, the wealth and income of whose citizens has been reduced, is to reduce expenditures in government, national, state, and local. It is the relief of taxes from the backs of men which liberates their powers. It is through lower expenditures that we get lower taxes. This must be done. Considerable reduction in Federal expenditures has been attained. If we except those extraordinary expenditures imposed upon us by the depression, it will be found that the Federal Government is operating for $200,000,000 less annually today than four years ago. The Congress rejected recommendations from the administration which would have saved an additional $150,000,000 this fiscal year. The opposition leadership insisted, as the price of vital reconstruction legislation and over my protest, upon adding $300,000,000 of costs to the taxpayer through public works inadvisable at this time. I shall repeat my proposals for economy. The opposition leadership in the House of Representatives in the last four months secured passage by the House of $3,000,000,000 in such raids. They have been stopped. I shall continue to oppose raids upon the Federal Treasury.

12. I have repeatedly for seven years urged the Congress either themselves to abolish obsolete bureaus and commissions and to reorganize the whole Government structure in the interest of economy, or to give someone the authority to do so. I have succeeded partially in securing authority, but I regret that no substantial act under it is to be effective until approved by the next Congress.

13. With the collapse in world prices and depreciated currencies the farmer was never so dependent upon his tariff protection for recovery as he is at the present time. We shall hold to that. We have enacted many measures of emergency relief to agriculture. They are having effect. I shall keep them functioning until the strain is past. The original purpose of the Farm Board was to strengthen the efforts of the farmer to establish his own farmer-owned, farmer-controlled marketing agencies. It has greatly succeeded in this purpose, even in these times of adversity. The departure of the Farm Board from its original purpose by making loans to farmers' coöperatives to preserve prices from panic served the emergency, but such action in normal times is absolutely destructive to the farmers' interests.

We still have vast problems to solve in agriculture. No power on earth can restore prices except by restoration of general recovery and markets. Every measure we have taken looking to general recovery is of benefit to the farmer. There is no relief to the farmer by extending government bureaucracy to control his production and thus curtail his liberties, nor by subsidies that bring only more bureaucracy and ultimate collapse. I shall oppose them.

The most practicable relief to the farmer today aside from the general economic recovery is a definite program of readjustment and coördination of national, state, and local taxation which will relieve real property, especially the farms, from unfair burdens of taxation which the current readjustment in values has brought about. To that purpose I propose to devote myself.

14. I have always favored the development of rivers and harbors and highways. These improvements have been greatly expedited. We shall continue that work to completion. After twenty years of discussion between the United States and the great nation to the north, I have signed a treaty for the construction of the Great Lakes–St. Lawrence seaway. That treaty does not injure the Chicago to the Gulf waterway, the work upon which, together with the whole Mississippi system, I have expedited, and in which I am equally interested. We shall undertake this great seaway, the greatest public improvement upon our continent, with its consequent employment of many men as quickly as the treaty is ratified.

15. Our views upon sound currency require no elucidation. They are indelibly a part of Republican history and policies. We have affirmed them by preventing the Democratic majority in the House from effecting wild schemes of uncontrolled inflation.

16. I have furnished to the Congress and to the States authoritative information upon the urgent need of reorganization of law enforcement agencies, the courts and their procedure, that we may reduce the lawlessness and crime in the country. I have recommended specific reforms to the Congress. I shall again press this necessity.

17. Upon my recommendations the Congress has enacted the most extensive measures of prison reform of two generations. As a result, and despite the doubling of the number of persons under Federal restraint in three years, we are today returning them to society far better fitted for citizenship.

18. There are many other important subjects fully set forth in the platform and in my public statements in the past.

19. The leadership of the Federal Government is not to be confined to economic and international questions. There are problems of the home, of education of children, of citizenship, the most vital of all to the future of the Nation. Except in the case of aid to States which I have recommended for stimulation of the protection and health of children, they are not matters of legislation. We have given leadership to the initiative of our people for social advancement through organization against illiteracy, through the White House conferences on protection and health of children, through the National Conference on Home Ownership, through stimulation to social and recreational agencies. There are the visible evi-

dences of spiritual leadership by government. They will be continued and constantly invigorated.

20. My foreign policies have been devoted to strengthening the foundations of world peace. We inaugurated the London naval treaty which reduced arms and limited the ratios between the fleets of the three powers. We have made concrete proposals at Geneva to reduce armaments of the world by one third. It would save the taxpayers of the world a billion a year. It would save us over $200,000,000 a year. It would reduce fear and danger of war. We have expanded the arbitration of disputes. I have recommended joining the World Court under proper reservations preserving our freedom of action. We have given leadership in transforming the Kellogg–Briand pact from an inspiring outlawry of war to an organized instrument for peaceful settlements backed by definite mobilization of world public opinion against aggression. We shall, under the spirit of that pact, consult with other nations in times of emergency to promote world peace. We shall enter no agreements committing us to any future course of action or which call for use of force to preserve peace.

Above all, I have projected a new doctrine into international affairs, the doctrine that we do not and never will recognize title to possession of territory gained in violation of the peace pacts. That doctrine has been accepted by all the nations of the world on a recent critical occasion, and within the last few days has been accepted again by all the nations of the Western Hemisphere. That is public opinion made tangible and effective.

This world needs peace. It must have peace with justice. I shall continue to strive unceasingly, with every power of mind and spirit, to explore every possible path that leads toward a world in which right triumphs over force, in which reason rules over passion, in which men and women may rear their children not to be devoured by war but to pursue in safety the nobler arts of peace.

I shall continue to build on that design.

Across the path of the Nation's consideration of these vast problems of economic and social order there has arisen a bitter controversy over the control of the liquor traffic. I have always sympathized with the high purpose of the Eighteenth Amendment, and I have used every power at my command to make it effective over the entire country. I have hoped it was the final solution of the evils of the liquor traffic against which our people have striven for generations. It has succeeded in great measure in those many communities where the majority sentiment is favorable to it. But in other and increasing number of communities there is a majority sentiment unfavorable to it. Laws opposed by majority sentiment create resentment which undermines enforcement and in the end produces degeneration and crime.

Our opponents pledge the members of their party to destroy every vestige of constitutional and effective Federal control of the traffic. That means over large areas the return of the saloon system with its corruption, its moral and social abuse which debauched the home, its deliberate interference with those States endeavoring to find honest solution, its permeation of political parties, and its pervasion of legislatures, which even touched at the capital of the Nation. The Eighteenth Amendment smashed that régime as by a stroke of lightning. I cannot consent to the return of that system.

At the same time we must recognize the difficulties which have developed in making the Eighteenth Amendment effective and that grave abuses have grown up. In order to secure the enforcement of the amendment under our dual form of government, the constitutional provision called for concurrent action on one hand by the State and local authorities and on the other by the Federal Government. Its enforcement requires independent but coincident action of both agencies. An increasing number of States and municipalities are proving themselves unwilling to engage in such enforcement. Owing to these forces there is in large sections an increasing illegal traffic in liquor. But worse than this there has been in those areas a spread of disrespect not only for this law but for all laws, grave dangers of practical nullification of the Constitution, a degeneration in municipal government, and an increase in subsidized crime and violence. I cannot consent to the continuation of this régime.

I refuse to accept either of these destinies, on the one hand to return to the old saloon with its political and social corruption, or on the other to endure the bootlegger and the speakeasy with their abuses and crime. Either is intolerable. These are not the ways out.

Our objective must be a sane solution, not a blind leap back to old evils. Moreover, such a step backward would result in a chaos of new evils never yet experienced, because the local systems of prohibitions and controls which were developed over generations have been in large degree abandoned under the amendment.

The Republican platform recommends submission of the question to the States, that the people themselves may determine whether they desire a change, but insists that this submission shall propose a constructive and not a destructive change. It does not dictate to the conscience of any member of the party.

The first duty of the President of the United States is to enforce the laws as they exist. That I shall continue to do to the utmost of my ability. Any other course would be the abrogation of the very guaranties of liberty itself.

The Constitution gives the President no power or authority with respect to changes in the Constitution itself; nevertheless, my countrymen have a right to know my conclusions upon this matter. They are clear and need not be misunderstood. They are based upon the broad facts I have stated, upon my experience in this high office, and upon the deep conviction that our purpose must be the elimination of the evils of this traffic from this civilization by practical measures.

It is my belief that in order to remedy present evils a change is necessary by which we resummon a proper share of initiative and responsibility which the very essence of our Government demands shall rest upon the States and local authorities. That change must avoid the return of the saloon.

It is my conviction that the nature of this change, and one upon which all reasonable people can find common ground, is that each State shall be given the right to deal with the problem as it may determine, but subject to absolute guarantees in the Constitution of the United States to protect each State from interference and invasion by its neighbors, and that in no part of the United States shall there be a return of the saloon system with its inevitable political and social corruption and its organized interference with other States.

American statesmanship is capable of working out such a solution and making it effective.

My fellow citizens, the discussion of great problems of economic life and of government often seems abstract and cold. But within their right solution lie the happiness and hope of a great people. Without such solution all else is mere verbal sympathy.

Today millions of our fellow countrymen are out of work. Prices of the farmers' products are below a living standard. Many millions more who are in business or hold employment are haunted by fears for the future. No man with a spark of humanity can sit in my place without suffering from the picture of their anxieties and hardships before him day and night. They would be more than human if they were not led to blame their condition upon the government in power. I have understood their sufferings and have worked to the limits of my strength to produce action that would really help them.

Much remains to be done to attain recovery. The emergency measures now in action represent an unparalleled use of national power to relieve distress, to provide employment, to serve agriculture, to preserve the stability of the Government, to maintain the integrity of our institutions. Our policies prevent unemployment caused by floods of imported goods and laborers. Our policies preserve peace. They embrace coöperation with other nations in those fields in which we can serve. With patience and perseverance these measures will succeed.

Despite the dislocation of economic life our great tools of production and distribution are more efficient than ever before; our fabulous natural resources, our farms, our homes, our skill are unimpaired. From the hard-won experience of this depression we shall build stronger methods of prevention and stronger methods of protection to our people from the abuses which have become evident. We shall march to far greater accomplishment.

With united effort we can and will turn the tide toward the restoration of business, employment, and agriculture. It will call for the utmost devotion and wisdom. Every reserve of American courage and vision must be called upon to sustain us and to plan wisely for the future.

Through it all our first duty is to preserve unfettered that dominant American spirit which has produced our enterprise and individual character. That is the bedrock of the past, and that is the guaranty of the future. Not regimented mechanisms but free men is our goal. Herein is the fundamental issue. A representative democracy, progressive and unafraid to meet its problems, but meeting them upon the foundations of experience and not upon the wave of emotion or the insensate demands of a radicalism which grasps at every opportunity to exploit the sufferings of a people.

With these courses we shall emerge from this great national strain with our American system of life and government strengthened. Our people will be free to reassert their energy and enterprise in a society eager to reward in full measure those whose industry serves its well-being. Our youth will find the doors of equal opportunity still open.

The problems of the next few years are not only economic. They are also moral and spiritual. The present check to our material success must deeply stir our national conscience upon the purposes of life itself. It must cause us to revalue and reshape our drift from materialism to a higher note of individual and national ideals.

Underlying every purpose is the spiritual application of moral ideals which are the fundamental basis of happiness in a people. This is a land of homes, churches, schoolhouses dedicated to the sober and enduring satisfactions of family life and the rearing of children in an atmosphere of ideals and religious faith. Only with these high standards can we hold society together, and only from them can government survive or business prosper. They are the sole insurance to the safety of our children and the continuity of the Nation.

If it shall appear that while I have had the honor of the Presidency I have contributed the part required from this high office to bringing the Republic through this dark night, and if in my administration we shall see the break of dawn to a better day, I shall have done my part in the world. No man can have a greater honor than that.

I have but one desire: that is, to see my country again on the road to prosperity which shall be more sane and lasting through the lesson of experience, to see the principles and ideals of the American people perpetuated.

I rest the case of the Republican Party on the intelligence and the just discernment of the American people. Should my countrymen again place upon me the responsibilities of this high office, I shall carry forward the work of reconstruction. I shall hope long before another four years have passed to see the world prosperous and at peace and every American home again in the sunshine of genuine progress and genuine prosperity. I shall seek to maintain untarnished and unweakened those fundamental traditions and principles upon which our Nation was founded and upon which it has grown. I shall invite and welcome the help of every man and woman in the preservation of the United States for the happiness of its people. This is my pledge to the Nation and to Almighty God.

HERBERT C. HOOVER

Campaign Speech

MADISON SQUARE GARDEN, NEW YORK CITY

October 31, 1932

This campaign is more than a contest between two men. It is more than a contest between two parties. It is a contest between two philosophies of government.

We are told by the opposition that we must have a change, that we must have a new deal. It is not the change that comes from normal development of national life to which I object, but the proposal to alter the whole foundations of our national life which have been builded through generations of testing and struggle, and of the principles upon which we have builded the Nation. The expressions our opponents use must refer to important changes in our economic and social system and our system of Government, otherwise they are nothing but vacuous words. And I realize that in this time of distress many of our people are asking whether our social and economic system is incapable of that great primary function of providing security and comfort of life to all of the firesides of our 25,000,000 homes in America, whether our social system provides for the fundamental development and progress of our people, whether our form of government is capable of originating and sustaining that security and progress.

This question is the basis upon which our opponents are appealing to the people in their fears and distress. They are proposing changes and so-called new deals which would destroy the very foundations of our American system.

Our people should consider the primary facts before they come to the judgment—not merely through political agitation, the glitter of promise, and the discouragement of temporary hardships—whether they will support changes which radically affect the whole system which has been builded up by 150 years of the toil of our fathers. They should not approach the question in the despair with which our opponents would clothe it.

Our economic system has received abnormal shocks during the past three years, which temporarily dislocated its normal functioning. These shocks have in a large sense come from without our borders, but I say to you that our system of government has enabled us to take such strong action as to prevent the disaster which would otherwise have come to our Nation. It has enabled us further to develop measures and programs which are now demonstrating their ability to bring about restoration and progress.

We must go deeper than platitudes and emotional appeals of the public platform in the campaign, if we will penetrate to the full significance of the changes which our opponents are attempting to float upon the wave of distress and discontent from the difficulties we are passing through. We can find what our opponents would do after searching the record of their appeals to discontent, group and sectional interest. We must search for them in the legislative acts which they sponsored and passed in the Democratic-controlled House of Representatives in the last session of Congress. We must look into measures for which they voted and which were defeated. We must inquire whether or not the presidential and vice presidential candidates have disavowed these acts. If they have not, we must conclude that they form a portion and are a substantial indication of the profound changes proposed.

And we must look still further than this as to what revolutionary changes have been proposed by the candidates themselves.

We must look into the type of leaders who are campaigning for the Democratic ticket, whose philosophies have been well known all their lives, whose demands for a change in the American system are frank and forceful. I can respect the sincerity of these men in their desire to change our form of government and our social and economic system, though I shall do my best tonight to prove they are wrong. I refer particularly to Senator Norris, Senator LaFollette, Senator Cutting, Senator Huey Long,

Senator Wheeler, William R. Hearst, and other exponents of a social philosophy different from the traditional American one. Unless these men feel assurance of support to their ideas they certainly would not be supporting these candidates and the Democratic Party. The seal of these men indicates that they have sure confidence that they will have voice in the administration of our government.

I may say at once that the changes proposed from all these Democratic principals and allies are of the most profound and penetrating character. If they are brought about this will not be the America which we have known in the past.

Let us pause for a moment and examine the American system of government, of social and economic life, which it is now proposed that we should alter. Our system is the product of our race and of our experience in building a nation to heights unparalleled in the whole history of the world. It is a system peculiar to the American people. It differs essentially from all others in the world. It is an American system.

It is founded on the conception that only through ordered liberty, through freedom to the individual, and equal opportunity to the individual will his initiative and enterprise be summoned to spur the march of progress.

It is by the maintenance of equality of opportunity and therefore of a society absolutely fluid in freedom of the movement of its human particles that our individualism departs from the individualism of Europe. We resent class distinction because there can be no rise for the individual through the frozen strata of classes, and no stratification of classes can take place in a mass livened by the free rise of its particles. Thus in our ideals the able and ambitious are able to rise constantly from the bottom to leadership in the community.

This freedom of the individual creates of itself the necessity and the cheerful willingness of men to act coöperatively in a thousand ways and for every purpose as occasion arises; and it permits such voluntary coöperations to be dissolved as soon as they have served their purpose, to be replaced by new voluntary associations for new purposes.

There has thus grown within us, to gigantic importance, a new conception. That is, this voluntary coöperation within the community. Coöperation to perfect the social organization; coöperation for the care of those in distress; coöperation for the advancement of knowledge, of scientific research, of education; for coöperative action in the advancement of many phases of economic life. This is self-government by the people outside of Government; it is the most powerful development of individual freedom and equal opportunity that has taken place in the century and a half since our fundamental institutions were founded.

It is in the further development of this coöperation and a sense of its responsibility that we should find solution for many of our complex problems, and not by the extension of government into our economic and social life. The greatest function of government is to build up that coöperation, and its most resolute action should be to deny the extension of bureaucracy. We have developed great agencies of coöperation by the assistance of the Government which promote and protect the interests of individuals and the smaller units of business. The Federal Reserve System, in its strengthening and support of the smaller banks; the Farm Board, in its strengthening and support of the farm coöperatives; the Home Loan Banks, in the mobilizing of building and loan associations and savings banks; the Federal Land Banks, in giving independence and strength to land mortgage associations; the great mobilization of relief to distress, the mobilization of business and industry in measures of recovery, and a score of other activities are not socialism—they are the essence of protection to the development of free men.

The primary conception of this whole American system is not the regimentation of men but the coöperation of free men. It is founded upon the conception of responsibility of the individual to the community, of the responsibility of local government to the state, of the state to the National Government.

It is founded on a peculiar conception of self-government designed to maintain this equal opportunity to the individual, and through decentralization it brings about and maintains these responsibilities. The centralization of government will undermine responsibilities and will destroy the system.

Our government differs from all previous conceptions, not only in this decentralization but also in the separation of functions between the legislative, executive and judicial arms of government, in which the independence of the judicial arm is the keystone of the whole structure.

It is founded on a conception that in times of emergency, when forces are running beyond control of individuals or other coöperative action, beyond the control of local communities and of states, then the great reserve powers of the Federal Government shall be brought into action to protect the community. But when these forces have ceased there must be a return of state, local, and individual responsibility.

The implacable march of scientific discovery with its train of new inventions presents every year new problems to government and new problems to the social order. Questions often arise whether, in the face of the growth of these new and gigantic tools, democracy can remain master in its own house, can preserve the fundamentals of our American system. I contend that it can; and I contend that this American system of ours has demonstrated its validity and superiority over any other system yet invented by human mind.

It has demonstrated it in the face of the greatest test of our history—that is the emergency which we have faced in the past three years.

When the political and economic weakness of many nations of Europe, the result of the World War and its aftermath, finally culminated in collapse of their institutions, the delicate adjustment of our economic and social life received a shock unparalleled in our history. No one knows that better than you of New York. No one knows its causes better than you. That the crisis was so great that many of the leading banks sought directly or indirectly to convert their assets into gold or its equivalent with the result that they practically ceased to function as credit institutions; that many of our citizens sought flight for their capital to other countries; that many of them attempted to hoard gold in large amounts. These were but indications of the flight of confidence and of the belief that our government could not overcome these forces.

Yet these forces were overcome—perhaps by narrow margins—and this action demonstrates what the courage of a nation can accomplish under the resolute leadership in the Republican Party. And I say the Republican Party, because our opponents, before and during the crisis, proposed no constructive program; though some of their members patriotically supported ours. Later on the Democratic House of Representatives did develop the real thought and ideas of the Democratic Party, but it was so destructive that it had to be defeated, for it would have destroyed, not healed.

In spite of all these obstructions we did succeed. Our form of government did prove itself equal to the task. We saved this Nation from a quarter of a century of chaos and degeneration, and we preserved the savings, the insurance policies, gave a fighting chance to men to hold their homes. We saved the integrity of our government and the honesty of the American dollar. And we installed measures which today are bringing back recovery. Employment, agriculture, business—all of these show the steady, if slow, healing of our enormous wound.

I therefore contend that the problem of today is to continue these measures and policies to restore this American system to its normal functioning, to repair the wounds it has received, to correct the weaknesses and evils which would defeat that system. To enter upon a series of deep changes to embark upon this inchoate new deal which has been propounded in this campaign would be to undermine and destroy our American system.

Before we enter upon such courses, I would like for you to consider what the results of this American system have been during the last thirty years—that is, one single generation. For if it can be demonstrated that by means of this, our unequaled political, social, and economic system, we have secured a lift in the standards of living and a diffusion of comfort and hope to men and women, the growth of equal opportunity, the widening of all opportunity, such as had never been seen in the history of the world, then we should not tamper with it or destroy it; but on the contrary we should restore it and, by its gradual improvement and perfection, foster it into new performance for our country and for our children.

Now, if we look back over the last generation we find that the number of our families and, therefore, our homes, have increased from sixteen to twenty-five million, or 62 percent. In that time we have builded for them 15,000,000 new and better homes. We have equipped 20,000,000 homes with electricity; thereby we have lifted infinite drudgery from women and men. The barriers of time and space have been swept away. Life has been made freer, the intellectual vision of every individual has been expanded by the installation of 20,000,000 telephones, 12,000,000 radios, and the service of 20,000,000 automobiles. Our cities have been made magnificent with beautiful buildings, parks and playgrounds. Our countryside has been knit together with splendid roads. We have increased by twelve times the use of electrical power and thereby taken sweat from the backs of men. In this broad sweep real wages and purchasing power of men and women have steadily increased. New comforts have steadily come to them. The hours of labor have decreased, the 12-hour day has disappeared, even the 9-hour day has almost gone. We are now advancing the 5-day week. The portals of opportunity to our children have ever widened. While our population grew by but 62 percent, we have increased the number of children in high schools by 700 percent, those in institutions of higher learning by 300 percent. With all our spending we multiplied by six times the savings in our banks and in our building and loan associations. We multiplied by 1,200 percent the amount of our life insurance. With the enlargement of our leisure we have come to a fuller life; we gained new visions of hope, we more nearly realize our national aspirations and give increasing scope to the creative power of every individual and expansion of every man's mind.

Our people in those 30 years grew in the sense of social responsibility. There is profound progress in the relation of the employer and employed. We have more nearly met with a full hand the most sacred obligation of man, that is, the responsibility of a man to his neighbor. Support to our schools, hospitals, and institutions for the care of the afflicted surpassed in totals of billions the proportionate service in any period of history in any nation in the world.

Three years ago there came a break in this progress. A break of the same type we have met fifteen times in a century and yet we have overcome them. But 18 months later came a further blow by shocks transmitted to us by the earthquakes of the collapse in nations throughout the world as the aftermath of the World War. The workings of our system were dislocated. Millions of men and women are out of jobs. Business men and farmers suffer. Their distress is bitter. I do not seek to minimize the depth of it. We may thank God that in view of this storm 30,000,000 still have their jobs; yet this must not distract our thought from the suffering of the other 10,000,000.

But I ask you what has happened. This 30 years of incomparable improvement in the scale of living, the advance of comfort and intellectual life, inspiration, and ideals did not arise without right principles animating the American system which produced them. Shall that system be discarded because vote-seeking men appeal to distress and say that the machinery is all wrong and that it must be abandoned or tampered with? Is it not more sensible to realize the simple fact that some extraordinary force has been thrown into the mechanism, temporarily deranging its operation? Is it not wiser to believe that the difficulty is not with the principles upon which our American system is founded and designed through all these generations of inheritance? Should not our purpose be to restore the normal working of that system which has brought to us such immeasurable benefits, and not destroy it?

And in order to indicate to you that the proposals of our opponents will endanger or destroy our system, I propose to analyze a few of the proposals of our opponents in their relation to these fundamentals.

First. A proposal of our opponents which would break down the American system is the expansion of Government expenditure by yielding to sectional and group raids on the Public Treasury. The extension of Government expenditures beyond the minimum limit necessary to conduct the proper functions of the Government enslaves men to work for the Government. If we combine the whole governmental expenditures— National, state, and municipal—we will find that before the World War each citizen worked, theoretically, 25 days out of each year for the Government. In 1924 he worked 46 days a year for the Government. Today he works for the support of all forms of government 61 days· out of the year.

No nation can conscript its citizens for this proportion of men's time without national impoverishment and destruction of their liberties. Our Nation cannot do it without destruction to our whole conception of the American system. The Federal Government has been forced in this emergency to unusual expenditures but in partial alleviation of these extraordinary and unusual expenditures, the Republican Administration has made a successful effort to reduce the ordinary running expenses of the Government. Our opponents have persistently interfered with such policies. I only need recall to you that the Democratic House of Representatives passed bills in the last session that would have increased our expenditures by $3,500,000,000, or 87 percent. Expressed in day's labor, this would have meant the conscription of 16 days' additional work from every citizen for the Government. This I stopped. Furthermore, they refused to accept recommendations from the Administration in respect to $150,000,000 to $200,000,000 of reductions in ordinary expenditures, and finally they forced upon us increasing expenditure of $322,000,000. In spite of this, the ordinary expenses of the Government have been reduced upwards of $200,000,000 during this present administration. They will be decidedly further reduced. But the major point I wish to make—the disheartening part of these proposals of our opponents—is that they represent successful pressures of minorities. They would appeal to sectional and group political support, and thereby impose terrific burdens upon every home in the country. These things can and must be resisted. But they can only be resisted if there shall be live and virile public support to the Administration, in opposition to political log-rolling and the sectional and group raids on the Treasury for distribution of public money, which is cardinal in the congeries of elements which make up the Democratic party.

These expenditures proposed by the Democratic House of Representatives for the benefit of special groups and special sections of our country directly undermine the American system. Those who pay are, in the last analysis, the man who works at the bench, the desk, and on the farm. They take away his comfort, stifle his leisure, and destroy his equal opportunity.

Second. Another proposal of our opponents which would destroy the American system is that of inflation of the currency. The bill which passed the last session of the Democratic House called upon the Treasury of the United States to issue $2,300,000,000 in paper currency that would be unconvertible into solid values. Call it what you will, greenbacks or fiat money. It was that nightmare which overhung our own country for years after the Civil War.

In our special situation today the issuance of greenbacks means the immediate departure of this country from the gold standard, as there could be no provision for the redemption of such currency in gold. The new currency must obviously go to immediate and constantly fluctuating discount when associated with currency convertible in gold.

The oldest law of currency is that bad money drives out the good, for a population—every individual—will hoard good currency and endeavor to get rid of the bad. The invariable effect is the withdrawal of a vast sum of good currency from circulation, and at once the Government is forced to print more and more bad paper currency. No candidate and no speaker in this campaign has disavowed this action of the Democratic House. In spite of this visible experience within recollection of this generation, with all its pitiable results, fiat money is proposed by the Democratic Party as a potent measure for relief from this depression.

The use of this expedient by nations in difficulty since the war in Europe has been one of the most tragic disasters to equality of opportunity, the independence of man.

I quote from a revealing speech by Mr. Owen D. Young upon the return of the Dawes Commission:

He stated, "the currency of Germany was depreciating so rapidly that the industries paid their wages daily, and sometimes indeed twice a day. Standing with the lines of employees was another line of wives and mothers waiting for the marks. The wife grabbed the paper from her husband's hand and rushed to the nearest provision store to spend it quickly before the rapid depreciation had cut its purchasing power in two.

"When the chairman of the syndicate of the German Trade Unions, Herr Grasseman, appeared before the Dawes Committee, I put to him this question: 'What can this committee do for German labor?'

"I expected the answer to be some one of the slogans of labor: An 8-hour day, old age or disability pensions, insurance against unemployment—something of that kind. Much to my surprise the answer came promptly.

" 'What your committee must do for German labor is to give us a stable currency. Do you know' Herr Grasseman said 'that for many months it has been impossible for a wage earner in Germany to perform any of his moral obligations?

" 'Knowing that a child was coming to the family at a certain time, there was no way by which the husband, through effort or sacrifice or savings, could guarantee his wife a doctor and a nurse when that event arrived. One knowing that his mother was stricken with a fatal disease could not by any extra effort or sacrifice or saving be in a position to insure her a decent burial on her death.

" 'Your committee must,' Herr Grasseman added 'just as a basic human thing, give us a stable currency and thereby insure to the worker that his wages will have the same purchasing power when he wants to spend them as they had when he earned them.' "

And I ask: Is that the preservation of opportunity and the protection of men by government?

Third. In the last session the Congress, under the personal leadership of the Democratic Vice Presidential candidate, and their allies in the Senate, enacted a law to extend the Government into personal banking business. This I was compelled to veto, out of fidelity to the whole American system of life and government. I may repeat a part of that veto message—and it remains unchallenged by any Democratic leader. I said:

"It would mean loans against security for any conceivable purpose on any conceivable security to anybody who wants money. It would place the Government in private business in such fashion as to violate the very principle of public relations upon which we have builded our Nation, and renders insecure its very foundations. Such action would make the Reconstruction Corporation the greatest banking and money-lending institution of all history. It would constitute a gigantic centralization of banking and finance to which the American people have been properly opposed over a hundred years. The purpose of the expansion is no longer in the spirit of solving a great major emergency but to establish a privilege whether it serves a great national end or not."

I further stated:

"It would require the setting up of a huge bureaucracy, to establish branches in every county and town in the United States. Every political pressure would be assembled for particular persons. It would be within the power of these agencies to dictate the welfare of millions of people, to discriminate between competitive business at will, and to deal favor and disaster amongst them. The organization would be constantly subjected to conspiracies and raids of predatory interests, individuals, and private corporations. Huge losses and great scandals must inevitably result. It would mean the squandering of public credit to be ultimately borne by the taxpayer."

I stated further that—

'This proposal violates every sound principle of public finance and of our government. Never before has so dangerous a suggestion been made to our country. Never before has so much power for evil been placed at the unlimited discretion of seven individuals."

They failed to pass this bill over my veto. But you must not be deceived. This is still in their purposes as a part of the new deal.

Fourth. Another proposal of our opponents which would wholly alter our American system of life is to reduce the protective tariff to a competitive tariff for revenue. The protective tariff and its results upon our economic structure has become gradually embedded into our economic life since the first protective tariff act passed by the American Congress under the administration of George Washington. There have been gaps at times of Democratic control when this protection has been taken away. But it has been so embedded that its removal has never failed to bring disaster. Whole towns, communities, and forms of agriculture with their homes, schools, and churches have been built up under this system of protection. The grass will grow in streets of a hundred cities, a thousand towns; the weeds will overrun the fields of millions of farms if that protection be taken away. Their churches and school houses will decay.

Incidentally another one of the proposals of our opponents which is to destroy equal opportunity both between individuals and communities is their promise to repeal the independent action of the bipartisan Tariff

Commission and thereby return the determination of import duties to the old logrolling greed of group or sectional interests of congressional action in review of the tariff.

Fifth. Another proposal is that the Government go into the power business. Three years ago, in view of the extension of the use of transmission of power over state borders and the difficulties of state regulatory bodies in the face of this interstate action, I recommended to the Congress that such interstate power should be placed under regulation by the Federal Government in coöperation with the state authorities.

That recommendation was in accord with the principles of the Republican Party over the past 50 years, to provide regulation where public interest had developed in tools of industry which was beyond control and regulation of the states.

I succeeded in creating an independent Power Commission to handle such matters, but the Democratic House declined to approve the further powers to this commission necessary for such regulation.

I have stated unceasingly that I am opposed to the Federal Government going into the power business. I have insisted upon rigid regulation. The Democratic candidate has declared that under the same conditions which may make local action of this character desirable, he is prepared to put the Federal Government into the power business. He is being actively supported by a score of Senators in this campaign, many of whose expenses are being paid by the Democratic National Committee, who are pledged to Federal Government development and operation of electrical power.

I find in the instructions to campaign speakers issued by the Democratic National Committee that they are instructed to criticize my action in the veto of the bill which would have put the Government permanently into the operation of power at Muscle Shoals with a capital from the Federal Treasury of over $100,000,000. In fact 31 Democratic Senators, being all except 3, voted to override that veto. In that bill was the flat issue of the Federal Government permanently in competitive business. I vetoed it because of principle and not because it was especially the power business. In that veto I stated that I was firmly opposed to the Federal Government entering into any business, the major purpose of which is competition with our citizens. I said:

"There are national emergencies which require that the Government should temporarily enter the field of business but that they must be emergency actions and in matters where the cost of the project is secondary to much higher consideration. There are many localities where the Federal Government is justified in the construction of great dams and reservoirs, where navigation, flood control, reclamation or stream regulation are of dominant importance, and where they are beyond the capacity or purpose of private or local government capital to construct. In these cases, power is often a by-product and should be disposed of by contract or lease. But for the Federal Government to deliberately go out to build up and expand such an occasion to the major purpose of a power and manufacturing business is to break down the initiative and enterprise of the American people; it is destruction of equality of opportunity amongst our people; it is the negation of the ideals upon which our civilization has been based.

"This bill raises one of the important issues confronting our people. That is squarely the issue of Federal Government ownership and operation of power and manufacturing business not as a minor by-product but as a major purpose. Involved in this question is the agitation against the conduct of the power industry. The power problem is not to be solved by the Federal Government going into the power business, nor it is to be solved by the project in this bill. The remedy for abuses in the conduct of that industry lies in regulation and not by the Federal Government entering upon the business itself. I have recommended to the Congress on various occasions that action should be taken to establish Federal regulation of interstate power in coöperation with state authorities. This bill would launch the Federal Government upon a policy of ownership of power utilities upon a basis of competition instead of by the proper Government function of regulation for the protection of all the people. I hesitate to contemplate the future of our institutions, of our government, and of our country if the preoccupation of its officials is to be no longer the promotion of justice and equal opportunity but is to be devoted to barter in the markets. That is not liberalism; it is degeneration."

From their utterances in this campaign and elsewhere we are justified in the conclusion that our opponents propose to put the Federal Government in the power business with all its additions to Federal bureaucracy, its tyranny over state and local governments, its undermining of state and local responsibilities and initiative.

Sixth. I may cite another instance of absolutely destructive proposals to our American system by our opponents.

Recently there was circulated through the unemployed in this country a letter from the Democratic candidate in which he stated that he

"would support measures for the inauguration of self-liquidating public works such as the utilization of water resources, flood control, land reclamation, to provide employment for all surplus labor at all times."

I especially emphasize that promise to promote "employment for all surplus labor at all times." At first I could not believe that anyone would be so cruel as to hold out a hope so absolutely impossible of realization to these 10,000,000 who are unemployed. But the authenticity of this promise has been verified. And I protest against such frivolous promises being held out to a suffering people. It is easily demonstrable that no such employment can be found. But the point I wish to make here and now is the mental attitude and spirit of the Democratic Party to attempt it. It is another mark of the character of the new deal and the destructive changes which mean the total abandonment of every principle upon which this government and the American system is founded. If it were possible to give this employment to 10,000,000 people by the Government, it would cost upwards of $9,000,000,000 a year.

The stages of this destruction would be first the destruction of Government credit, the value of Government securities, the destruction of every fiduciary trust in our country, insurance policies and all. It would pull down the employment of those who are still at work by the high taxes and the demoralization of credit upon which their employment is dependent. It would mean the pulling and hauling of politics for projects and measures, the favoring of localities, sections, and groups. It would mean the growth of a fearful bureaucracy which, once established, could never be dislodged. If it were possible, it would mean one-third of the electorate with Government jobs earnest to maintain this bureaucracy and to control the political destinies of the country.

Incidentally, the Democratic candidate has said on several occasions that we must reduce surplus production of agricultural products and yet he proposes to extend this production on a gigantic scale through expansion of reclamation and new agricultural areas to the ruin of the farmer.

I have said before, and I want to repeat on this occasion that the only method by which we can stop the suffering and unemployment is by returning our people to their normal jobs in their normal homes, carrying on their normal functions of living. This can be done only by sound processes of protecting and stimulating recovery of the existing economic system upon which we have builded our progress thus far—preventing distress and giving such sound employment as we can find in the meantime.

Seventh. Recently, at Indianapolis, I called attention to the statement made by Governor Roosevelt in his address on October 25 with respect to the Supreme Court of the United States. He said:

"After March 4, 1929, the Republican Party was in complete control of all branches of the Government—Executive, Senate and House, and, I may add for good measure, in order to make it complete, the Supreme Court as well."

I am not called upon to defend the Supreme Court of the United States from this slurring reflection. Fortunately that court has jealously maintained over the years its high standard of integrity, impartiality, and freedom from influence of either the Executive or Congress, so that the confidence of the people is sound and unshaken.

But is the Democratic candidate really proposing his conception of the relation of the Executive and the Supreme Court? If that is his idea, he is proposing the most revolutionary new deal, the most stupendous breaking of precedent, the most destructive undermining of the very safeguard of our form of government yet proposed by a presidential candidate.

Eighth. In order that we may get at the philosophical background of the mind which pronounces the necessity for profound change in our American system and a new deal, I would call your attention to an address delivered by the Democratic candidate in San Francisco, early in October:

He said:

"Our industrial plant is built. The problem just now is whether under existing conditions it is not overbuilt. Our last frontier has long since been reached. There is practically no more free land. There is no safety valve in the western prairies where we can go for a new start. . . . The mere building of more industrial plants, the organization of more corporations is as likely to be as much a danger as a help. . . . Our task now is not the discovery of natural resources or necessarily the production of more goods, it is the sober, less dramatic business of administering the resources and plants already in hand . . . establishing markets for surplus production, of meeting the problem of under-consumption, distributing the wealth and products more equitably and adopting the economic organization to the service of the people. . . ."

There are many of these expressions with which no one would quarrel. But I do challenge the whole idea that we have ended the advance of America, that this country has reached the zenith of its power, the height of its development. That is the counsel of despair for the future of America. That is not the spirit by which we shall emerge from this depression. That is not the spirit that made this country. If it is true, every American must abandon the road of countless progress and unlimited opportunity. I deny that the promise of American life has been fulfilled, for that means we have begun the decline and fall. No nation can cease to move forward without degeneration of spirit.

I could quote from gentlemen who have emitted this same note of pessimism in economic depressions going back for 100 years. What Governor Roosevelt has overlooked is the fact that we are yet but on the frontiers of development of science, and of invention. I have only to remind you that discoveries in electricity, the internal-combustion engine, the radio—all of which have sprung into being since our land was settled—have in themselves represented the greatest advances in America. This philosophy upon which the Governor of New York proposes to conduct the Presidency of the United States is the philosophy of stagnation, of despair. It is the end of hope. The destinies of this country should not be dominated by that spirit in action. It would be the end of the American system.

I have recited to you the progress of this last generation. Progress in that generation was not due to the opening up of new agricultural land; it was due to the scientific research, the opening of new invention, new flashes of light from the intelligence of our people. These brought the improvements in agriculture and in industry. There are a thousand inventions for comfort in the lockers of science and invention which have not yet come to light; all are but on their frontiers. As for myself I am confident that if we do not destroy this American system, if we continue to stimulate scientific research, if we continue to give it the impulse of initiative and enterprise, if we continue to build voluntary coöperative action instead of financial concentration, if we continue to build it into a system of free men, my children will enjoy the same opportunity that have come to me and the whole 120,000,000 of my countrymen. I wish to see American Government conducted in this faith and in this hope.

If these measures, these promises, which I have discussed; or these failures to disavow these projects; this attitude of mind, mean anything, they mean the enormous expansion of the Federal Government; they mean the growth of bureaucracy such as we have never seen in our history. No man who has not occupied my position in Washington can fully realize the constant battle which must be carried on against incompetence, corruption, tyranny of government expanded into business activities. If we first examine the effect on our form of government of such a program, we come at once to the effect of the most gigantic increase in expenditure ever known in history. That alone would break down the savings, the wages, the equality of opportunity among our people. These measures would transfer vast responsibilities to the Federal Government from the states, the local governments, and the individuals. But that is not all; they would break down our form of government. Our legislative bodies can not delegate their authority to any dictator, but without such delegation every member of these bodies is impelled in representation of the interest of his constituents constantly to seek privilege and demand service in the use of such agencies. Every time the Federal Government extends its arm, 531 Senators and Congressmen become actual boards of directors of that business.

Capable men can not be chosen by politics for all the various talents required. Even if they were supermen, if there were no politics in the selection of the Congress, if there were no constant pressure for this and for that, so large a number would be incapable as a board of directors of any institution. At once when these extensions take place by the Federal Government, the authority and responsibility of state governments and institutions are undermined. Every enterprise of private business is at once halted to know what Federal action is going to be. It destroys initiative and courage. We can do no better than quote that great statesman of labor, the late Samuel Gompers, in speaking of a similar situation:

"It is a question of whether it shall be government ownership or private ownership under control. If I were a minority of one in this convention, I would want to cast my vote so that the men of labor shall not willingly enslave themselves to government in their industrial effort."

We have heard a great deal in this campaign about reactionaries, conservatives, progressives, liberals, and radicals. I have not yet heard an attempt by any one of the orators who mouth these phrases to define the principles upon which they base these classifications. There is one thing I can say without any question of doubt—that is, that the spirit of liberalism is to create free men; it is not the regimentation of men. It is not the extension of bureaucracy. I have said in this city before now that you can not extend the mastery of government over the daily life of a people without somewhere making it master of people's souls and thoughts. Expansion of government in business means that the Government in order to protect itself from the political consequences of its errors is driven irresistibly without peace to greater and greater control of the Nation's press and platform. Free speech does not live many hours after free industry and free commerce die. It is a false liberalism that interprets itself into Government operation of business. Every step in that direction poisons the very roots of liberalism. It poisons political equality, free speech, free press, and equality of opportunity. It is the road not to liberty but to less liberty. True liberalism is found not in striving to spread bureaucracy, but in striving to set bounds to it. True liberalism seeks all legitimate freedom first in the confident belief that without such freedom the pursuit of other blessings is in vain. Liberalism is a force truly of the spirit proceeding from the deep realization that economic freedom can not be sacrificed if political freedom is to be preserved.

Even if the Government conduct of business could give us the maximum of efficiency instead of least efficiency, it would be purchased at the cost of freedom. It would increase rather than decrease abuse and corruption, stifle initiative and invention, undermine development of leadership, cripple mental and spiritual energies of our people, extinguish equality of opportunity, and dry up the spirit of liberty and progress. Men who are going about this country announcing that they are liberals because of their promises to extend the Government in business are not liberals, they are reactionaries of the United States.

And I do not wish to be misquoted or misunderstood. I do not mean that our government is to part with one iota of its national resources without complete protection to the public interest. I have already stated that democracy must remain master in its own house. I have stated that abuse and wrongdoing must be punished and controlled. Nor do I wish to be misinterpreted as stating that the United States is a free-for-all and devil-take-the-hindermost society.

The very essence of equality of opportunity of our American system is that there shall be no monopoly or domination by any group or section in this country, whether it be business, sectional or a group interest. On the contrary, our American system demands economic justice as well as political and social justice; it is not a system of laissez faire.

I am not setting up the contention that our American system is perfect. No human ideal has ever been perfectly attained, since humanity itself is not perfect. But the wisdom of our forefathers and the wisdom of the 30 men who have preceded me in this office hold to the conception that progress can only be attained as the sum of accomplishments of free individuals, and they have held unalterably to these principles.

In the ebb and flow of economic life our people in times of prosperity and ease naturally tend to neglect the vigilance over their rights. Moreover, wrongdoing is obscured by apparent success in enterprise. Then insidious diseases and wrongdoings grow apace. But we have in the past seen in times of distress and difficulty that wrongdoing and weakness come to the surface and our people, in their endeavors to correct these wrongs, are tempted to extremes which may destroy rather than build.

It is men who do wrong, not our institutions. It is men who violate the laws and public rights. It is men, not institutions, which must be punished.

In my acceptance speech four years ago at Palo Alto I stated that—

"One of the oldest aspirations of the human race was the abolition of poverty: By poverty I mean the grinding by under-nourishment, cold, ignorance, fear of old age to those who have the will to work."

I stated that—

"In America today we are nearer a final triumph over poverty than in any land. The poorhouse has vanished from amongst us; we have not reached that goal, but given a chance to go forward, we shall, with the help of God, be in sight of the day when poverty will be banished from this Nation."

Our Democratic friends have quoted this passage many times in this campaign. I do not withdraw a word of it. When I look about the world even in these times of trouble and distress I find it more true in this land than anywhere else under the traveling sun. I am not ashamed of it, because I am not ashamed of holding ideals and purposes for the progress of the American people. Are my Democratic opponents prepared to state that they do not stand for this ideal or this hope? For my part, I propose to continue to strive for it, and I hope to live to see it accomplished.

One of the most encouraging and inspiring phases of this whole campaign has been the unprecedented interest of our younger men and women. It is in this group that we find our new homes being founded, our new families in which the children are being taught those basic principles of love and faith and patriotism. It is in this group that we find the starting of business and professional careers with courageous and hopeful faces turned to the future and its promise. It is this group who must undertake the guardianship of our American system and carry it forward to its greater achievements.

Inevitably in the progress of time, our country and its institutions will be entirely in their hands. The burdens of the depression have fallen on the younger generation with equal and perhaps greater severity than upon the elders. It has affected not only their economic well-being, but has tended also to shatter many illusions. But their faith in our country and its institutions has not been shaken. I am confident that they will resist any destruction to our American system of political, economic and social life.

It is a tribute to America and its past and present leaders and even more a tribute to this younger generation that, contrary to the experience of other countries, we can say tonight that the youth of America is more staunch than many of their elders. I can ask no higher tribute from my party for the maintenance of the American system and the program of my administration than the support being given by the younger men and women of our country. It has just been communicated to me that tonight at this time, in every county and almost every precinct of our country, 3,000,000 members of the Young Republican League are meeting for the support of a Republican victory November 8th—a victory for the American system.

My countrymen, the proposals of our opponents represent a profound change in American life—less in concrete proposal, bad as that may be, than by implication and by evasion. Dominantly in their spirit they represent a radical departure from the foundations of 150 years which have made this the greatest nation in the world. This election is not a mere shift from the ins to the outs. It means deciding the direction our Nation will take over a century to come.

My conception of America is a land where men and women may walk in ordered liberty, where they may enjoy the advantages of wealth not concentrated in the hands of a few but diffused through the lives of all, where they build and safeguard their homes, give to their children full opportunities of American life, where every man shall be respected in the faith that his conscience and his heart direct him to follow, where people secure in their liberty shall have leisure and impulse to seek a fuller life. That leads to the release of the energies of men and women, to the wider vision and higher hope; it leads to opportunity for greater and greater service not alone of man to man in our country but from our country to the world. It leads to health in body and a spirit unfettered, youthful, eager with a vision stretching beyond the farthest horizons with an open mind, sympathetic and generous. But that must be builded upon our experience with the past, upon the foundations which have made our country great. It must be the product of our truly American system.

☆

1936

—— ☆ ——

Few contemporary political observers would have taken seriously the November 2, 1936 election prognostication of the Democratic party's national chairman, James J. Farley, that Roosevelt would win every state save two: Maine and Vermont. Earlier, Arthur Krock of the *New York Times* wrote that "the Republican party will poll a far larger popular vote than in 1932. . . . Roosevelt's big majorities are over." And the *Literary Digest*, which had predicted correctly every presidential election since 1920, went even further, asserting that the Republican party would win the election of 1936.

On Election Day, November 3rd, the American electorate followed Farley's script faithfully. But Roosevelt's overwhelming victory was more than just a personal triumph. It was an unequivocal declaration on the part of the American people that big government was to remain a permanent feature of American society.

In 1936 the Republican party held its presidential nominating convention in Cleveland. There they designated Alfred Moosman Landon, the progressive governor of Kansas, as their candidate. Landon was one of only seven GOP governors in the land, and was the only chief executive that the Republican party elected in 1932. Although the Republicans accepted the need for certain reform measures, their platform was fundamentally a condemnation of the New Deal.

123

After renominating Roosevelt and chronicling the achievements of the New Deal in their platform, the Democratic party was again addressed by their candidate. In his acceptance speech at Philadelphia Roosevelt sounded the clarion call of his campaign. The election, he stated, would be a struggle against the "economic royalists." The time had come, he continued, to return to the people the fruits of their labor.

Roosevelt's campaign strategy was to make himself the candidate of a liberal, progressive movement that cut across party lines. His opponents were not the Republican people or Alf Landon (whom he never mentioned by name), but the "economic royalists," such as the American Liberty League, an organization of arch-conservative business leaders who courted anti-New Dealers of both parties.

In his campaign speeches Roosevelt rarely addressed himself to the future. Instead, he stressed the accomplishments of the New Deal, punctuating his remarks with comparisons between 1932 and 1936—comparisons that led people in Bridgeport, Connecticut to welcome the President with "Thank God for Roosevelt" signs. In one of the President's more arresting speeches, he associated his administration with the preservation of the capitalistic system.

Beginning with his acceptance speech at Topeka, Kansas, Landon recited the Republic platform and was very specific in his attacks on Roosevelt's New Deal measures, including social security, which was probably the most popular piece of New Deal legislation. In addition, Landon tried to show that not only had the New Deal failed to solve some of the nation's most salient problems—problems for which it was granted extraordinary power—but that it had, in fact, created additional problems. By aggrandizing power, Landon claimed, Roosevelt had upset the constitutional balance of power. These charges, coupled with Landon's challenge that Roosevelt categorically announce his position on all of the major issues of the day, were the basic themes of Landon's speeches. His October 29th campaign address in New York is indicative of this style.

FRANKLIN D. ROOSEVELT

Acceptance Speech

PHILADELPHIA, PENNSYLVANIA

June 27, 1936

Senator Robinson, members of the Democratic convention, my friends.

We meet at a time of great moment to the future of the nation. It is an occasion to be dedicated to the simple and sincere expression of an attitude toward problems, the determination of which will profoundly affect America.

I come not only as the leader of a party—not only as a candidate for high office, but as one upon whom many critical hours have imposed and still impose a grave responsibility.

For the sympathy, help and confidence with which Americans have sustained me in my task I am grateful. For their loyalty I salute the members of our great party, in and out of official life in every part of the Union. I salute those of other parties, especially those in Congress who on so many occasions put partisanship aside. I thank the Governors of the several States, their Legislatures, their State and local officials who participated unselfishly and regardless of party in our efforts to achieve recovery and destroy abuses. Above all, I thank the millions of Americans who have borne disaster bravely and have dared to smile through the storm.

America will not forget these recent years—will not forget that the rescue was not a mere party task—it was the concern of all of us. In our strength we rose together, rallied our energies together, applied the old rules of common sense, and together survived.

In those days we feared fear. That was why we fought fear. And today, my friends, we have won against the most dangerous of our foes— we have conquered fear.

But I cannot, with candor, tell you that all is well with the world. Clouds of suspicion, tides of ill-will and intolerance gather darkly in many places. In our own land we enjoy, indeed, a fullness of life greater than that of most nations. But the rush of modern civilization itself has raised for us new difficulties, new problems which must be solved if we are to preserve to the United States the political and economic freedom for which Washington and Jefferson planned and fought.

Philadelphia is a good city in which to write American history. This is fitting ground on which to reaffirm the faith of our fathers; to pledge ourselves to restore to the people a wider freedom—to give to 1936 as the founders gave to 1776—an American way of life.

The very word freedom, in itself and of necessity, suggests freedom from some restraining power. In 1776, we sought freedom from the tyranny of a political autocracy—from the eighteenth century royalists who held special privileges from the crown. It was to perpetuate their privilege that they governed without the consent of the governed; that they denied the right of free assembly and free speech; that they restricted the worship of God; that they put the average man's property and the average man's life in pawn to the mercenaries of dynastic power—that they regimented the people.

And so it was to win freedom from the tyranny of political autocracy that the American Revolution was fought. That victory gave the business of governing into the hands of the average man, who won the right with his neighbors to make and order his own destiny through his own government. Political tyranny was wiped out at Philadelphia on July 4, 1776.

Since that struggle, however, man's inventive genius released new forces in our land which reordered the lives of our people. The age of machinery, of railroads, of steam and electricity; the radio and telegraph; mass production, mass distribution—all of these combined to bring forward a new civilization and with it a new problem for those who would remain free.

For out of this modern civilization economic royalists carved new dynasties. New kingdoms were built upon concentration of control over material things. Through new uses of corporations, banks and securities, new machinery of industry and agriculture, of labor and capital—all undreamed of by the fathers—the whole structure of modern life was impressed into this royal service.

There was no place among this royalty for our many thousands of small business men and merchants who sought to make a worthy use of the American system of initiative and profit. They were no more free than the worker or the farmer. Even honest and progressive-minded men of wealth, aware of their obligation to their generation, could never know just where they fitted into this dynastic scheme of things.

It was natural and perhaps human that the privileged princes of these new economic dynasties, thirsting for power, reached out for control over government itself. They created a new despotism and wrapped it in the robes of legal sanction. In its service, new mercenaries sought to regiment the people, their labor and their properties. And as a result the average man once more confronts the problem that faced the Minute Man.

The hours men and women worked, the wages they received, the conditions of their labor—these had passed beyond the control of the people, and were imposed by this new industrial dictatorship. The savings of the average family, the capital of the small business man, the investments set aside for old age—other people's money—these were tools which the new economic royalty used to dig itself in.

Those who tilled the soil no longer reaped the rewards which were their right. The small measure of their gains was decreed by men in distant cities.

Throughout the nation, opportunity was limited by monopoly. Individual initiative was crushed in the cogs of a great machine. The field open for free business was more and more restricted. Private enterprise became too private. It became privileged enterprise, not free enterprise.

An old English judge once said: "Necessitous men are not free men." Liberty requires opportunity to make a living—a living decent according to the standard of the time, a living which gives man not only enough to live by, but something to live for.

For too many of us the political equality we once had won was meaningless in the face of economic inequality. A small group had concentrated into their own hands an almost complete control over other people's property, other people's money, other people's labor—other people's lives. For too many of us life was no longer free; liberty no longer real; men could no longer follow the pursuit of happiness.

Against economic tyranny such as this the citizen could only appeal to the organized power of government. The collapse of 1929 showed up the despotism for what it was. The election of 1932 was the people's mandate to end it. Under that mandate it is being ended.

The royalists of the economic order have conceded that political freedom was the business of the government, but they have maintained that economic slavery was nobody's business. They granted that the government could protect the citizen in his right to vote but they denied that the government could do anything to protect the citizen in his right to work and live.

Today we stand committed to the proposition that freedom is no half-

and-half affair. If the average citizen is guaranteed equal opportunity in the polling place, he must have equal opportunity in the market place.

The economic royalists complain that we seek to overthrow the institutions of America. What they really complain of is that we seek to take away their power. Our Allegiance to American institutions requires the overthrow of this kind of power. In vain they seek to hide behind the flag and the Constitution. In their blindness they forget what the flag and the Constitution stand for. Now, as always, the flag and the Constitution stand for democracy, not tyranny; for freedom, not subjection, and against a dictatorship by mob rule and the overprivileged alike.

The brave and clear platform adopted by this convention, to which I heartily subscribe, sets forth that government in a modern civilization has certain inescapable obligations to its citizens, among which are protection of the family and the home, the establishment of a democracy of opportunity and aid to those overtaken by disaster.

But the resolute enemy within our gates is ever ready to beat down our words unless in greater courage we will fight for them.

For more than three years we have fought for them. This convention in every word and deed has pledged that that fight will go on.

The defeats and victories of these years have given to us as a people a new understanding of our government and of ourselves. Never since the early days of the New England town meeting have the affairs of government been so widely discussed and so clearly appreciated. It has been brought home to us that the only effective guide for the safety of the most worldly of worlds is moral principle.

We do not see faith, hope and charity as unattainable ideals, but we use them as stout supports of a nation fighting the fight for freedom in a modern civilization.

Faith—in the soundness of democracy in the midst of dictatorships.

Hope—renewed because we know so well the progress we have made.

Charity—in the true spirit of that grand old word. For charity literally translated from the original means love, the love that understands, that does not merely share the wealth of the giver, but in true sympathy and wisdom helps men to help themselves.

We seek not merely to make government a mechanical implement, but to give it the vibrant personal character that is the embodiment of human charity.

We are poor indeed if this nation cannot afford to lift from every recess of American life the dread fear of the unemployed that they are not needed in the world. We cannot afford to accumulate a deficit in the books of human fortitude.

In the place of the palace of privilege we seek to build a temple out of faith and hope and charity.

It is a sobering thing to be a servant of this great cause. We try in our daily work to remember that the cause belongs not to us but to the people. The standard is not in the hands of you and me alone. It is carried by America. We seek daily to profit from experience, to learn to do better as our task proceeds.

Governments can err—Presidents do make mistakes, but the immortal Dante tells us that divine justice weighs the sins of the cold-blooded and the sins of the warm-hearted in different scales.

Better the occasional faults of a government that lives in a spirit of charity than the consistent omissions of a government frozen in the ice of its own indifference.

There is a mysterious cycle in human events. To some generations much is given. Of others much is expected. This generation of Americans has a rendezvous with destiny.

In this world of ours, in other lands, there are some people who, in times past, have lived and fought for freedom, and seem to have grown too weary to carry on the fight. They have sold their heritage of freedom for the illusion of a living. They have yielded their democracy.

I believe in my heart that only our success can stir their ancient hope. They begin to know that here in America we are waging a great war. It is not alone a war against want and destitution and economic demoralization. It is a war for the survival of democracy. We are fighting to save a great and precious form of government for ourselves and for the world.

I accept the commission you have tendered me. I join with you. I am enlisted for the duration of the war.

FRANKLIN D. ROOSEVELT

Campaign Speech

CHICAGO, ILLINOIS

October 14, 1936

Mr. Chairman, Governor Horner, Mayor Kelly, my friends of the great State of Illinois:

I seem to have been here before. Four years ago I dropped into this city from the airways—an old friend come in a new way—to accept in this hall the nomination for the Presidency of the United States. I came to a

Chicago fighting with its back to the wall—factories closed, markets silent, banks shaky, ships and trains empty. Today those factories sing the song of industry; markets hum with bustling movement; banks are secure; ships and trains are running full. Once again it is Chicago as Carl Sandburg saw it—"The City of the big shoulders"—the city that smiles. And with Chicago a whole Nation that had not been cheerful for years is full of cheer once more.

On this trip through the Nation I have talked to farmers, I have talked to miners, I have talked to industrial workers; and in all that I have seen and heard one fact has been clear as crystal—that they are part and parcel of a rounded whole, and that none of them can succeed in his chosen occupation if those in the other occupations fail in their prosperity. I have driven home that point.

Tonight, in this center of business, I give the same message to the business men of America—to those who make and sell the processed goods the Nation uses and to the men and women who work for them.

To them I say:

Do you have a deposit in the bank? It is safer today than it has ever been in our history. It is guaranteed. Last October 1st marked the end of the first full year in fifty-five years without a single failure of a national bank in the United States. Is that not on the credit side of the Government's account with you?

Are you an investor? Your stocks and bonds are up to five- and six-year high levels.

Are you a merchant? Your markets have the precious life-blood of purchasing power. Your customers on the farms have better incomes and smaller debts. Your customers in the cities have more jobs, surer jobs, better jobs. Did not your Government have something to do with that?

Are you in industry? Industrial earnings, industrial profits are the highest in four, six, or even seven years! Bankruptcies are at a new low. Your Government takes some credit for that.

Are you in railroads? Freight loadings are steadily going up. Passenger receipts are steadily going up—have in some cases doubled—because your Government made the railroads cut rates and make money.

Are you a middleman in the great stream of farm products? The meat and grain that move through your yards and elevators have a steadier supply, a steadier demand and steadier prices than you have known for years. And your Government is trying to keep it that way.

Some people say that all this recovery has just happened. But in a complicated modern world recoveries from depressions do not just happen. The years from 1929 to 1933, when we waited for recovery just to happen, prove the point.

But in 1933 we did not wait. We acted. Behind the growing recovery of today is a story of deliberate Government acceptance of responsibility to save business, to save the American system of private enterprise and economic democracy—a record unequaled by any modern Government in history.

What had the previous Administration in Washington done for four years? Nothing. Why? For a very fundamental reason. That Administration was not industrially-minded or agriculturally-minded or business-minded. It was high-finance-minded—manned and controlled by a handful of men who in turn controlled and by one financial device or another took their toll from the greater part of all other business and industry.

Let me make one simple statement. When I refer to high finance I am not talking about all great bankers, or all great corporation executives, or all multimillionaires—any more than Theodore Roosevelt, in using the term "malefactors of great wealth," implied that all men of great wealth were "malefactors." I do not even imply that the majority of them are bad citizens. The opposite is true.

Just in the same way, the overwhelming majority of business men in this country are good citizens and the proportion of those who are not is probably about the same proportion as in the other occupations and professions of life.

When I speak of high finance as a harmful factor in recent years, I am speaking about a minority which includes the type of individual who speculates with other people's money—and you in Chicago know the kind I refer to—and also the type of individual who says that popular government cannot be trusted and, therefore, that the control of business of all kinds and, indeed, of Government itself should be vested in the hands of one hundred or two hundred all-wise individuals controlling the purse-strings of the Nation.

High finance of this type refused to permit Government credit to go directly to the industrialist, to the business man, to the homeowner, to the farmer. They wanted it to trickle down from the top, through the intricate arrangements which they controlled and by which they were able to levy tribute on every business in the land.

They did not want interest rates to be reduced by the use of Government funds, for that would affect the rate of interest which they themselves wanted to charge. They did not want Government supervision over financial markets through which they manipulated their monopolies with other people's money.

And in the face of their demands that Government do nothing that they called "unsound," the Government, hypnotized by its indebtedness to them, stood by and let the depression drive industry and business toward bankruptcy.

America is an economic unit. New means and methods of transportation and communications have made us economically as well as politically a single Nation.

Because kidnappers and bank robbers could in high-powered cars speed across state lines it became necessary, in order to protect our people, to invoke the power of the Federal Government. In the same way, speculators and manipulators from across State lines, and regardless of State laws, have lured the unsuspecting and the unwary to financial destruction. In the same way across State lines, there have been built up intricate corporate structures, piling bond upon stock and stock upon bond—huge monopolies which were stifling independent business and private enterprise.

There was no power under Heaven that could protect the people against that sort of thing except a people's Government at Washington. All that this Administration has done, all that it proposes to do—and this it does propose to do—is to use every power and authority of the Federal Government to protect the commerce of America from the selfish forces which ruined it.

Always, month in and month out, during these three and a half years, your Government has had but one sign on its desk—"Seek only the greater good of the greater number of Americans." And in appraising the record, remember two things. First, this Administration was called upon to act after a previous Administration and all the combined forces of private enterprise had failed. Secondly, in spite of all the demand for speed, the complexity of the problem and all the vast sums of money involved, we have had no Teapot Dome.

We found when we came to Washington in 1933, that the business and industry of the Nation were like a train which had gone off the rails into a ditch. Our first job was to get it out of the ditch and start it up the track again as far as the repair shops. Our next job was to make repairs—on the broken axles which had gotten it off the road, on the engine which had been worn down by gross misuse.

What was it that the average business man wanted Government to do for him—to do immediately in 1933?

1. Stop deflation and falling prices—and we did it.

2. Increase the purchasing power of his customers who were industrial workers in the cities—and we did it.

3. Increase the purchasing power of his customers on the farms—and we did it.

4. Decrease interest rates, power rates and transportation rates—and we did it.

5. Protect him from the losses due to crime, bank robbers, kidnappers, blackmailers—and we did it.

How did we do it? By a sound monetary policy which raised prices.

By reorganizing the banks of the Nation and insuring their deposits. By bringing the business men of the Nation together and encouraging them to pay higher wages, to shorten working hours, and to discourage that minority among their own members who were engaging in unfair competition and unethical business practices.

Through the A.A.A., through our cattle-buying program, through our program of drought relief and flood relief, through the Farm Credit Administration, we raised the income of the customers of business who lived on the farms. By our program to provide work for the unemployed, by our C.C.C. camps, and other measures, greater purchasing power was given to those who lived in our cities.

Money began going round again. The dollars paid out by Government were spent in the stores and shops of the Nation; and spent again to the wholesaler; and spent again to the factory; and spent again to the wage earner; and then spent again in another store and shop. The wheels of business began to turn again; the train was back on the rails.

Mind you, it did not get out of the ditch itself, it was hauled out by your Government.

And we hauled it along the road. P.W.A., W.P.A., both provided normal and useful employment for hundreds of thousands of workers. Hundreds of millions of dollars got into circulation when we liquidated the assets of closed banks through the Reconstruction Finance Corporation; millions more when we loaned money for home building and home financing through the Federal Housing program, hundreds of millions more in loans and grants to enable municipalities to build needed improvements; hundreds of millions more through the C.C.C. camps.

I am not going to talk tonight about how much our program to provide work for the unemployed meant to the Nation as a whole. That cannot be measured in dollars and cents. It can be measured only in terms of the preservation of the families of America.

But so far as business goes, it can be measured in terms of sales made and goods moving.

The train of American business is moving ahead.

But you people know what I mean when I say it is clear that if the train is to run smoothly again the cars will have to be loaded more evenly. We have made a definite start in getting the train loaded more evenly, in order that axles may not break again.

For example, we have provided a sounder and cheaper money market and a sound banking and securities system. You business men know how much legitimate business you lost in the old days because your customers were robbed by fake securities or impoverished by shaky banks.

By our monetary policy we have kept prices up and lightened the burden of debt. It is easier to get credit. It is easier to repay.

We have encouraged cheaper power for the small factory owner to lower his cost of production.

We have given the business man cheaper transportation rates.

But above all, we have fought to break the deadly grip which monopoly has in the past been able to fasten on the business of the Nation.

Because we cherished our system of private property and free enterprise and were determined to preserve it as the foundation of our traditional American system, we recalled the warning of Thomas Jefferson that "widespread poverty and concentrated wealth cannot long endure side by side in a democracy."

Our job was to preserve the American ideal of economic as well as political democracy, against the abuse of concentration of economic power that had been insidiously growing up among us in the past fifty years, particularly during the twelve years of preceding Administrations. Free economic enterprise was being weeded out at an alarming pace.

During those years of false prosperity and during the more recent years of exhausting repression, one business after another, one small corporation after another, their resources depleted, had failed or had fallen into the lap of a bigger competitor.

A dangerous thing was happening. Half of the industrial corporate wealth of the country had come under the control of less than two hundred huge corporations. That is not all. These huge corporations in some cases did not even try to compete with each other. They themselves were tied together by interlocking directors, interlocking bankers, interlocking lawyers.

This concentration of wealth and power has been built upon other people's money, other people's business, other people's labor. Under this concentration independent business was allowed to exist only by sufferance. It has been a menace to the social system as well as to the economic system which we call American democracy.

There is no excuse for it in the cold terms of industrial efficiency.

There is no excuse for it from the point of view of the average investor.

There is no excuse for it from the point of view of the independent business man.

I believe, I have always believed, and I will always believe in private enterprise as the backbone of economic well-being in the United States.

But I know, and you know, and every independent business man who has had to struggle against the competition of monopolies knows, that this concentration of economic power in all-embracing corporations does not represent private enterprise as we Americans cherish it and propose to foster it. On the contrary, it represents private enterprise which has become a kind of private government, a power unto itself—a regimentation of other people's money and other people's lives.

Back in Kansas I spoke about bogey-men and fairy tales which the real Republican leaders, many of whom are part of this concentrated power, are using to spread fear among the American people.

You good people have heard about these fairy tales and bogey-men too. You have heard about how antagonistic to business this Administration is supposed to be. You have heard all about the dangers which the business of America is supposed to be facing if this Administration continues.

The answer to that is the record of what we have done. It was this Administration which saved the system of private profit and free enterprise after it had been dragged to the brink of ruin by these same leaders who now try to scare you.

Look at the advance in private business in the last three and a half years; and read there what we think about private business.

Today for the first time in seven years the banker, the storekeeper, the small factory owner, the industrialist, can all sit back and enjoy the company of their own ledgers. They are in the black. That is where we want them to be; that is where our policies aim them to be; that is where we intend them to be in the future.

Some of these people really forget how sick they were. But I know how sick they were. I have their fever charts. I know how the knees of all of our rugged individualists were trembling four years ago and how their hearts fluttered. They came to Washington in great numbers. Washington did not look like a dangerous bureaucracy to them then. Oh, no! It looked like an emergency hospital. All of the distinguished patients wanted two things—a quick hypodermic to end the pain and a course of treatment to cure the disease. They wanted them in a hurry; we gave them both. And now most of the patients seem to be doing very nicely. Some of them are even well enough to throw their crutches at the doctor.

The struggle against private monopoly is a struggle for, and not against, American business. It is a struggle to preserve individual enterprise and economic freedom.

I believe in individualism. I believe in it in the arts, the sciences and professions. I believe in it in business. I believe in individualism in all of these things—up to the point where the individualist starts to operate at the expense of society. The overwhelming majority of American business men do not believe in it beyond that point. We have all suffered in the past from individualism run wild. Society has suffered and business has suffered.

Believing in the solvency of business, the solvency of farmers and the solvency of workers, I believe also in the solvency of Government. Your Government is solvent.

The net Federal debt today is lower in proportion to the income of the Nation and in proportion to the wealth of the Nation than it was on March 4, 1933.

In the future it will become lower still because with the rising tide of national income and national wealth, the very causes of our emergency spending are starting to disappear. Government expenditures are coming down and Government income is going up. The opportunities for private enterprise will continue to expand.

The people of America have no quarrel with business. They insist only that the power of concentrated wealth shall not be abused.

We have come through a hard struggle to preserve democracy in America. Where other Nations in other parts of the world have lost that fight, we have won.

The business men of America and all other citizens have joined in a firm resolve to hold the fruits of that victory, to cling to the old ideals and old fundamentals upon which America has grown great.

ALFRED M. LANDON

Acceptance Speech

TOPEKA, KANSAS

July 23, 1936

Mr. Chairman, Members of the Notification Committee, Ladies and Gentlemen:

I accept the nomination of the Republican party for the Presidency of the United States. In accepting this leadership I pray for divine guidance to make me worthy of the faith and the confidence which you have shown in me.

This call, coming to one whose life has been that of the every-day American, is proof of that freedom of opportunity which belongs to the people under our government. It carries with it both an honor and a responsibility. In a republic these cannot be separated.

Tonight, facing this honor and responsibility, I hope for the gift of simple and straightforward speech. I want every man and woman in this nation to understand my every word, for I speak of issues deeply concerning us all.

The citizen who assumes the direction of the executive branch of our government takes an oath that he will "faithfully execute the office of President of the United States, and will," to the best of his ability, "preserve, protect and defend the Constitution of the United States." This oath carries the obligation so to use executive power that it will fulfill the purposes for which it was delegated.

No man, in common good faith to his fellow-citizens, may rightfully assume the duties of the high office of Chief Executive and take the oath that goes with the office unless he shall intend to keep and shall keep his oath inviolate.

It is with a full understanding of the meaning of this oath that I accept this nomination.

The 1936 platform of the Republican party has my complete adherence. It sets out the principles by which we can achieve the full national life that our resources entitle us to enjoy.

There is not time to lay our whole program before you tonight; I can touch only upon a few phases of it. The others I hope to discuss with you in detail as the campaign progresses.

First, I shall take up the question of recovery and relief. I shall follow this by discussing a matter closely allied to both debt and taxes. Our farm policy and the problems of labor will bring me to a brief discussion of international relations. And last, I shall take up our constitutional government and the forces that threaten it.

I intend to approach the issues fairly, as I see them, without rancor or passion. If we are to go forward permanently, it must be with a united nation—not with a people torn by appeals to prejudice and divided by class feeling.

The time has come to pull together.

No people can make headway where great numbers are supported in idleness. There is no future on the relief roles. The law of this world is that man shall eat bread by the sweat of his brow. The whole American people want to work at full time and at full pay. They want homes and a chance for their children, reasonable security, and the right to live according to American standards. They want to share in a steady progress. We bind ourselves with a pledge we shall not ignore, thrust aside, or forget, to devote our whole energy to bringing these things about.

The world has tried to conquer this depression by different methods. None of them has been fully successful. Too frequently recovery has been hindered, if not defeated, by political considerations.

Our own country has tried one economic theory after another. The present administration asked for, and received, extraordinary powers upon the assurance that these were to be temporary. Most of its proposals did not follow familiar paths to recovery. We knew they were being undertaken hastily and with little deliberation.

But because the measures were supposed to be temporary, because everybody hoped they would prove successful, and because the people wanted the administration to have a fair trial, Congress and the country united in support of its efforts at the outset.

Now it becomes our duty to examine the record as it stands. The record shows that these measures did not fit together into any definite program of recovery. Many of them worked at cross-purposes and defeated themselves. Some developed into definite hindrances to recovery. They had the effect generally of extending control by Washington into the remotest corners of the country. The frequent and sudden changes in the administration's policy caused a continual uneasiness.

As a result, recovery has been set back again and again. This was not all of the failure. Practical progressives have suffered the disheartening experience of seeing many liberal objectives discredited during the past three years by careless thinking, unworkable laws and incompetent administration.

The nation has not made the durable progress, either in reform or recovery, that we had the right to expect.

For it must be remembered that the welfare of our people is not recorded on the financial pages of the newspapers. It cannot be measured in stock market prices. The real test is to be found in the ability of the average American to engage in business, to obtain a job, to be a self-supporting and a self-respecting member of his community.

Judged by the things that make us a nation of happy families, the New Deal has fallen far short of success. The proof of this is in the record. The record shows that in 1933 the primary need was jobs for the unemployed. The record shows that in 1936 the primary need still is jobs for the unemployed.

The time has come to stop this fumbling with recovery. American initiative is not a commodity to be delivered in pound packages through a governmental bureau. It is a vital force in the life of our nation and it must be freed!

The country is ripe for recovery. We are far behind in expenditures for upkeep and improvements and for expansion.

The total of this demand—in industry, in new enterprises, in our homes and on our farms—amounts to billions of dollars. Once all this consumer demand is released the problem will be not where to find work for the workers but where to find workers for the work.

One of the signs of the ending of past depressions was the launching of new business ventures. It is true that most of them were small. Altogether, however, they provided work for many millions of people. In the present depression this demand for work has not yet appeared. Few new ventures have been started. Why? Because the small business man, the working-man who would like to become his own boss—the average American—has hesitated to start out for himself. He lacks confidence in the soundness of Federal policy; he is afraid of what may come next.

We must dispel his fear, restore his confidence and place our reliance once more in the initiative, intelligence and courage of these makers of jobs and opportunities. That is why I say, in all earnestness, that the time has come to unshackle initiative and free the spirit of American enterprise.

We must be freed from incessant governmental intimidation and hostility. We must be freed from excessive expenditures and crippling taxation. We must be freed from the effects of an arbitrary and uncertain monetary policy. And through a vigorous enforcement of the anti-trust laws we must be freed from private monopolistic control.

Once these things are done, the energies of the American economic system will remedy the ravages of depression and restore full activity and full employment.

Out of this depression has come not only the problem of recovery but also the equally grave problem of caring for the unemployed until recovery is attained. Their relief at all times is a matter of plain duty.

We of our party pledge that this obligation will never be neglected. In extending help, however, we will handle the public funds as a public trust. We will recognize that all citizens, irrespective of color, race, creed or party affiliation, have an equal right to this protection. We would consider it base beyond words to make loyalty or service to party a condition upon which the needy unemployed might obtain help. Those who use public funds to build their political machines forfeit all right to political consideration from true Americans.

Let me emphasize that while we propose to follow a policy of economy in government expenditures those who need relief will get it. We will not take our economies out of the allotments to the unemployed. We will take them out of the hides of the political exploiters. The question is not—as stated by the administration—how much money the American people are willing to spend for relief. The question is how much waste the American people are willing to stand for in the administration of relief.

The destruction of human values by this depression has been far greater than the American people suffered during the World War. When the depression began millions of dependable men and women had employment. They were the solid citizenry of America; they had lived honestly and had worked hard. They had dealt fairly with the Government, which, in turn, had depended upon their support.

Then they found themselves deprived of employment by economic forces over which they had no control. Little by little they spent their life savings while vainly seeking new jobs.

We shall undertake to aid these innocent victims of the depression.

In addition, we shall amend the Social Security Act to make it workable. We recognize that society, acting through government, must afford as large a measure of protection as it can against involuntary unemployment and dependency in old age. We pledge that the Federal Government will do its proper share in that task.

But it must be kept in mind that the security of all of us depends on the good management of our common affairs. We must be able to produce and accumulate enough to finance our normal progress, as well as to take care of ourselves and of those entitled to protection.

Mounting debts and increasing taxes constitute a threat to all of these aims. They absorb the funds that might be used to create new things or to reduce the cost of present goods. Taxes, both visible and invisible, add to the price of everything. By taking more and more out of the family purse they leave less for the family security. Let us not be misled by those who tell us that others will be made to carry the burden for us. A simple inquiry into the facts and figures will show that our growing debts and taxes are so enormous that, even if we tax to the utmost limits those who are best able to pay, the average taxpayer will still have to bear the major part. While spending billions of dollars of borrowed money may create a temporary appearance of prosperity, we and our children, as taxpayers, have yet to pay the bill. For every single dollar spent we will pay back two dollars!

Crushing debts and taxes are usually incurred, as they are being incurred today, under the guise of helping people—the same people who must finally pay them. They invariably retard prosperity and they sometimes lead to situations in which the rights of the people are destroyed. This is the lesson of history and we have seen it occur in the modern world.

Our party holds nothing to be of more urgent importance than putting our financial house in order. For the good of all of us, we must re-establish responsibility in the handling of government finances. We must recognize that a government does not have an unlimited supply of money to spend. It must husband its resources just as truly as does the head of a family. Unless it follows such a course it cannot afford the services which the people themselves expect.

No sound national policy looking to the national welfare will neglect the farmer. This is not because the farmer needs or wishes to be coddled, or that he asks for undue help. It is necessary because the needs of a great nation require that its food producers shall always stand upon a social and economic plane in keeping with the national importance of their service.

The present administration's efforts to produce this result have not been successful. Payments under the triple-A did help to tide farmers over a difficult period. But, even before it was ruled out by the Supreme Court, the triple-A was rapidly disorganizing American agriculture. Some of its worst effects continue. By its policies the administration has taken the American farmer out of foreign markets and put the foreign farmer into the American market. The loss of markets, both at home and abroad, far outweighs the value of all the benefits paid to farmers.

Worst than this, from the standpoint of the public, is the fact that the administration, through its program of scarcity, has gambled with the needed food and feed supplies of the country. It overlooked the fact that mother nature cannot be regimented.

The time has now come when we must replace this futile program with one that is economically and socially right.

The wealth of our soil must be preserved. We shall establish effective soil conservation and erosion control policies in connection with a national land use and flood-prevention program—and keep it all out of politics.

Our farmers are entitled to all of the home market they can supply without injustice to the consumer. We propose a policy that protects them in this right.

Some of our farmers, dependent in part upon foreign markets, suffer from disadvantages arising from world disorder. Until these disadvantages are eliminated we propose to pay cash benefits in order to cushion our farm families against the disastrous effects of price fluctuations and to protect their standard of living.

The American people, now as always, are responsive to distress caused by disasters, such as the present drought. Our platform reflects that spirit. We shall fulfill its pledge to give every reasonable assistance to producers in areas suffering from such temporary afflictions, so that they may again get on a self-supporting basis.

Our farm program as a whole will be made to serve a vital national purpose.

The family type of farm has long constituted one of the cherished foundations of our social strength. It represents human values that we must not lose. Widespread ownership of moderate-sized tracts of land was the aim of the Republican Homestead Act. This conception of agriculture is one phase of the general principle that we stand for—preserving freedom of opportunity in all walks of life.

The benefits which will be paid under our program will go no higher than the production level of the family type of farm.

Another matter of deep concern is the welfare of American labor. The general well-being of our country requires that labor shall have the position and rewards of prosperity to which it is entitled. I firmly believe that labor has the right to protect this position and to achieve those rewards by organizing in labor unions. Surely the history of labor in the United States has demonstrated that working conditions, wages and hours have been improved through self-organization.

The right of labor to organize means to me the right of employees to join any type of union they prefer, whether it covers their plant, their craft or their industry. It means that, in the absence of a union contract, an employee has an equal right to join a union or to refuse to join a union.

Under all circumstances, so states the Republican platform, employees are to be free from interference from any source, which means, as I read it, entire freedom from coercion or intimidation by the employer, any fellow-employee or any other person.

The government must maintain itself in the position of an umpire: First, to protect the public interest, and, second, to act as a mediator between conflicting groups. One of the greatest problems of this country is to develop effective methods of conciliation.

Taking a dispute after it gets into a tangle and rushing it to the doorstep of the President is a bad way to handle a labor situation or any other situation.

In international affairs also the Republican party has always worked for the advancement of justice and peace. Following the early tradition of our country, it has consistently urged the adjustment of international disputes in accordance with law, equity and justice. We have now again declared our continued loyalty to this principle.

Republican Presidents sent delegates to the Hague conferences and one of them took the leading part in the termination of the Russo-Japanese War. Another Republican President called a conference which for the first time produced a reduction and limitation of arms on a wide scale. Still another led in securing the treaty outlawing wars.

In purpose and achievement our party has a record which points the way to further helpful service in creating international understanding, in removing the causes of war and in reducing and limiting arms.

We shall take every opportunity to promote among the nations a peace based upon justice and human rights. We shall join in no plan that would take from us that independence of judgment which has made the United States a power for good in the world. We shall join in no plan that might involve us in a war in the beginning of which we had no part, or that would build a false peace on the foundation of armed camps.

I turn now to the basic principles upon which our nation is founded. America has always stood, and now stands, first of all for human rights, for "the life, liberty and pursuit of happiness" of the great Declaration. The prime needs of men have not changed since that Declaration, though new means from time to time may be necessary to meet those needs. But the great safeguards against tyranny and oppression must not be cast away and lost. They must be saved that men may live free to pursue their happiness, safe from any kind of exploitation.

One cannot face this occasion and the prospect flowing from it without a sobering reflection upon the beginnings, growth, and destiny of our nation. Our government was founded to give life to certain vital principles. The people embodied these basic principles of human rights in the Federal and State Constitutions. Thus, the people themselves, of their own free will, set up this government. And it is still the government of the people. Any change which the people want they can have by following the procedure they themselves laid down.

But for any official or branch of government to attempt such a change, without authority from the people, is to do an unwarranted and illegal act. It is a substitution of personal for constitutional government. If added power is needed, the people have set out how that authority may be had from them if they wish to give it.

This, in its broad essentials, is the basic structure of our government.

As our economic life has become more complex and specialized some need, real or apparent, has often been urged as an excuse for a further grant of power from the people. They have sometimes given, sometimes withheld, the desired power.

There has now appeared in high places, however, a new and dangerous impulse. This is the impulse to take away and lodge in the Chief Executive, without the people's consent, the powers which they have kept in their State governments or which they have reserved in themselves.

In its ultimate effect upon the welfare of the whole people, this, then, is the most important question now before us: Shall we continue to delegate more and more power to the Chief Executive or do we desire to preserve the American form of government? Shall we continue to recognize that certain rights reside with the people, that certain powers are reserved for the States, and that certain functions are delegated to the Federal Government?

Now I know that many of us, at one time or another, have become dissatisfied and impatient with the efforts of our local and State administrations to solve our difficulties.

At such times it has seemed to us that only a larger, more powerful unit of government could meet the need.

For those who have followed such a line of reasoning I have the understanding that comes from experience. As a young man I was attracted to the idea of centralizing in the Federal Government full power to correct the abuses growing out of a more complex social order. When the people rejected this alternative, I was as disappointed as any one. But in spite of this rejection, I have lived to see many of those abuses substantially corrected by the forty-eight State Legislatures in their fields and by the Federal Government in its field of interstate commerce.

More recently, as a small independent oil producer, I saw my industry ask for Federal regulation because of a selfish exploitation of a natural resource, which, once wasted, cannot be replaced. When Federal regulation failed the industry made progress in the solution of the problem by turning to State action, supplemented with interstate compacts as provided by the amazing foresight of the makers of the Constitution.

It is not my belief that the Constitution is above change. The people have the right, by the means they have prescribed, to change their form of government to fit their wishes. If they could not do this, they would not be free. But change must come by and through the people and not by usurpation. Changes should come openly, after full and free discussion, and after full opportunity for the people to express their will.

The Republican party, however, does not believe that the people wish to abandon the American form of government.

We propose to maintain the constitutional balance of power between the States and the Federal Government.

We propose to use the full power of the Federal Government to break up private monopolies and to eliminate private monopolistic practices.

In other words, the Republican party proposes to restore and to maintain a free competitive system—a system under which, and only under which, can there be independence, equality of opportunity, and work for all.

A free competitive system is necessary to a free government. Neither political nor civil liberty long survive the loss of economic liberty. Each and all of these liberties, with the precious human rights which they involve, must be preserved intact and inviolate.

If I am elected Chief Executive of this nation I propose to restore our government to an efficient as well as constitutional basis.

I shall call to my aid those men best qualified to conduct the public business—and I mean just that.

I shall stand back of them.

I shall hold them responsible for doing their jobs.

I shall cooperate whole-heartedly with Congress in an effective reorganization of the numerous government agencies, to get rid of those that are not necessary, to eliminate duplication, to insure better administration, and to save the taxpayers' money.

I hold that it is the right of our people to have their greatest public service enterprise—their government—well administered.

These are some of the aims and proposals of a Republican administration that would enter office under a pledge to conduct the public business with honesty, frugality, courage and common sense.

In common with all my countrymen, I look forward to the America that is to be.

It should be a nation in which the old, wrong things are going out and the new, right things are coming in.

It should be a country which produces more and more until there is plenty for all, and with a fair chance for all to earn their share.

It should be a land in which equal opportunity shall prevail and special privilege shall have no place.

It should be an America that shall bring to bear the whole of her great spiritual force in a common effort to drive the curse of war from the earth; an America that, for the sake of all mankind as well as ourselves, shall never lose the faith that human freedom is a practical ideal.

It is in these aims and in these works that I vision the manifest destiny of America. Everything we need for their realization we can find, I firmly believe, within the principles under which this nation has grown to greatness. God grant us, one and all, the strength and the wisdom to do our part in bringing these things to pass.

☆

ALFRED M. LANDON

Campaign Speech

NEW YORK CITY

October 29, 1936

We are drawing to the end of a great campaign—a campaign that trancends all party lines. Tonight I am here, not alone as the representative of a great party; I am here as the representative of a great cause—a cause in which millions of my fellow-citizens are joined—a cause in which Democrats, independents and Republicans are fighting shoulder to shoulder.

Let me begin by restating the basic principles of my political creed.

I believe in our constitutional form of government—a government established by the people, responsible to the people and alterable only in accordance with the will of the people.

I believe in our indivisible union of indestructible States.

I believe in the American system of free enterprise, regulated by law.

I believe in the liberty of the individual as guaranteed by the Constitution.

I believe in the rights of minorities as protected by the Constitution.

I believe in the liberties secured by the Bill of Rights and in their maintenance as the best protection against bigotry and all intolerance, whether of race, color or creed.

I believe in an independent Supreme Court and judiciary, secure from executive or legislative invasion.

I believe that in the future, as in the past, the hopes of our people can best be realized by following the American way of life under the American Constitution.

I believe in the principles of civic righteousness exemplified by Theodore Roosevelt and I pledge myself to go forward along the trail he blazed.

In the light of this creed I have already outlined my stand on the chief issues of the campaign. Tonight I am going to review my position and contrast it with that of my opponent.

It is fitting that I should start with the problem of agriculture. Your City of New York is the greatest market for farm products in the country. As consumers you want an ample supply of food at fair prices. As wage-earners you need the buying power of a prosperous farm population.

The welfare of agriculture is also the welfare of industry. A fair adjustment between the two is not a matter of politics, it is a matter of national necessity.

Now let us look at the record.

In direct defiance of the 1932 Democratic platform, which condemned the unsound policy of crop restriction, the Triple A was enacted. The Triple A restricted agricultural production by 36,000,000 acres.

This administration has rewarded scarcity and penalized plenty. Not only has it failed to correct the basic ills of agriculture, it has added to them. I am from a great agricultural State and I know.

I know how this program dislocated our agricultural system. I know, for instance, that almost overnight it forced the Southern farmer out of cotton into crops competing with the North and West. It led him into dairy farming and the raising of livestock. This affected not only the farmer of the North and West. It also affected the farmer of the South, who lost a large part of his cotton export market.

Luckily for this administration, the full damage of its program has been hidden by the droughts.

Government has a moral obligation to help repair the damage caused to the farmer by this administration's destructive experiments. Farming, by its very nature, cannot readjust itself as rapidly as industry to the after-effects of economic planning. During the period of readjustment, and until foreign markets are reopened, the government must help the farmer.

We can do this without violating the Constitution. We can do this without imposing such burdens as the processing tax upon the consumer. We can do this within the limits of a balanced budget. And don't forget I am going to balance the budget.

The Republican party also proposes a sound long-term program of conservation and land use. This is the only permanent solution of the farm problem and is essential to the preservation of the nation's land resources. We propose to stop muddling and meddling and to begin mending.

And what does the President mean to do for agriculture? Is he going to continue the policy of scarcity?

The answer is: No one can be sure.

Now let us turn to industry. What was the basic declaration of the Democratic platform of 1932? It was that the anti-trust laws—the laws protecting the little fellow from monopoly—should be strengthened and enforced.

And what did the administration do? It created the NRA. This law gave the sanction of government to private monopoly. It endorsed the vicious policy of price-fixing. It disregarded the interest of 130,000,000 Americans as consumers. It attempted to tell every business man, large and small, how to run his business.

The NRA was the direct opposite of the American system of free competition. It was an attempt to supplant American initiative with Washington dictation. And what happened? Monopolies prospered and a little New Jersey pants-presser went to jail.

I am against private monopoly. I am against monopolistic practices. I am against the monopoly of an all-powerful central government. And while I am President I intend to see that the anti-trust laws are strengthened and enforced without fear or favor.

I intend to see that government bureaucracy never again starts choking business. I intend to see that American initiative has a chance to give jobs to American workers. And I intend to broaden the market for American products by encouraging freer interchange of goods in world trade.

And what does the President propose for industry? He pays tribute to free initiative at Chicago on a Wednesday and to planned economy at Detroit on a Thursday. One day the President's son says the NRA will be revived. The next day the President's son says it will not. When the President was asked about NRA last Tuesday in a press conference, he said: "You pay your money and you take your choice." What does he mean?

The answer is: No one can be sure.

Growing out of the troubles of agriculture and industry is the intensely human problem of unemployment. What is the record on this?

In 1932 the President said that 11,000,000 Americans were looking for work. Today, according to the American Federation of Labor, there are still 11,000,000 Americans looking for work. Yet the President boasts of recovery—in one city in terms of a baseball game and in another city in terms of a patient he has cured.

These fellow-citizens of ours can and will be re-employed. There is no need for one-fifth of our working population to be condemned to live in an economic world apart. There is work to be done in this country—more than enough to give jobs to all the unemployed. This work will start just as soon as uncertainty in government policies is replaced by confidence.

There can be no confidence when the government is proud of spending more than it takes in.

There can be no confidence when the government creates uncertainty about the value of money.

There can be no confidence when the government threatens to control every detail of our economic life.

There can be no confidence when the government proclaims that the way to have more is to produce less.

In short, there can be no confidence while this administration remains in power.

As Chief Executive I intend to follow a course that will restore confidence.

I intend to be open and aboveboard on the policies of my administration.

I intend in the task of reconstruction to make use of the best talent available irrespective of party.

I intend to throw out all plans based on scarcity.

I intend to put an end to this administration's policy of 'try anything once.' The time has come for a steady hand at the wheel.

And what does the President propose to restore confidence? Another 'breathing-spell'?

The answer is: No one can be sure.

Of course re-employment cannot come overnight. In the meantime those in need must have relief. Consider the administration's record here.

The Democratic platform in 1932 condemned the 'improper and excessive use of money in political activities.'

In defiance of this pledge we have had an outrageous use of public money for political purposes. Public funds appropriated for relief have been used in an attempt to buy the votes of our less fortunate citizens. But it will not do them any good. The votes of the American people are not for sale.

As Chief Executive I intend to see that relief is purged of politics. There is ample money in this country to take care of those in need. When

I am President they will be taken care of. This is the plain will of the American people.

And what does the President propose to do about relief? How does he propose to free the victims of the depression from political exploitation?

The answer is: No one can be sure.

In a highly industrialized society we must provide for the protection of the aged.

The present administration claims it has done this through its Social Security Act. But the act does not give security. It is based upon a conception that is fundamentally wrong. It assumes that the American people are so improvident that they must be compelled to save by a paternal government.

Beginning next Jan. 1, workers, no matter how small their wages, will have their pay docked—they will have their pay docked for the purpose of building up a phantom reserve fund—a fund that any future Congress can spend any time it sees fit and for any purpose it sees fit.

I cannot understand how any administration would dare to perpetrate such a fraud upon our workers.

The Republican party proposes to replace this unworkable hodge-podge by a plan that is honest, fair and financially sound. We propose that the funds for security payments shall be provided as we go along. We propose that they shall be obtained from a direct and specific tax widely distributed. We propose that all American citizens over 65 shall receive whatever additional income is necessary to keep them from need.

I repeat: The workers will start to pay for the present plan next Jan. 1. They will pay as wage-earners through a direct deduction from their pay. They will pay both as wage-earners and consumers through the tax levied on their employers' payrolls. And don't let any one tell you otherwise. Even the Democratic Attorney General of New York admits this. Last March, before the New York Court of Appeals, he said that a tax on employers' payrolls, although levied on the employer, will be—and I quote —"shifted either to wage-earners or consumers or both."

And what does the President propose to do about these taxes? Is he going to continue a plan that takes money from workers without any assurance that they will get back what they put in?

The answer is: No one can be sure.

Since the NRA was declared unconstitutional—and largely because it was declared unconstitutional—there has been some improvement in business.

But there has been no reduction in the total of government spending. In the year ended last June the Federal Government spent nearly $9,000,000,000. This is an all-time peace-time high.

We will spend this year over $900,000,000 more for the ordinary routine expenditures of government than in 1934. And we will spend $1,500,000,000 more for relief than in 1934.

Under this administration seventy-five new agencies have been created. Two hundred and fifty thousand additional employees have been foisted on the taxpayers. The Federal payroll has reached the staggering sum of $1,500,000,000 a year.

As I said at Chicago, any one at all familiar with what has been going on could almost count on the fingers of one hand foolish experiments the government could cut out and save at least $1,000,000,000 any time it wanted to.

I pledge myself to put an end to extravagance and waste. I pledge myself to stop the policy that glorifies spending. I pledge myself to balance the budget.

And what is the President going to do? Is he going to stop his policy of spending for spending's sake?

The answer is: No one can be sure.

I come finally to the underlying and fundamental issue of this campaign. This is the question of whether our American form of government is to be preserved.

Let us turn once more to the record.

The President has been responsible for nine acts declared unconstitutional by the Supreme Court.

He has publicly urged Congress to pass a law, even though it had reasonable doubts as to its constitutionality.

He has publicly belittled the Supreme Court of the United States.

He has publicly suggested that the Constitution is an outworn document.

He has retained in high office men outspoken in their contempt for the American form of government.

He has sponsored laws which have deprived States of their Constitutional rights.

Every one of these actions—and the list is by no means complete—strikes at the heart of the American form of government.

Our Constitution is not a lifeless piece of paper. It is the underlying law of the land and the charter of the liberties of our people. The people, and they alone, have the right to amend or destroy it. Until the people in their combined wisdom decide to make the change, it is the plain duty of the people's servants to keep within the Constitution. It is the plain meaning of the oath of office that they shall keep within the Constitution.

Our Federal system allows great leeway. But if changes in our civilization make amendment to the Constitution desirable it should be amended. It has been amended in the past. It can be in the future.

I have already made my position clear on this question. I am on record that, if proper working conditions cannot be regulated by the States, I shall favor a constitutional amendment giving the States the necessary powers.

And what are the intentions of the President with respect to the Constitution? Does he believe changes are required? If so, will an amendment be submitted to the people, or will he attempt to get around the Constitution by tampering with the Supreme Court?

The answer is: No one can be sure.

We want more than a material recovery in this country. We want a moral and spiritual recovery as well. We have been allowing material things to obscure the great religious and spiritual values. But life is more than bread. Character is the supreme thing. We have been weakening those very qualities upon which character is built. It would be tragedy if in our attempt to win prosperity we should lose our own souls. It would be an overwhelming disaster if we should forget that it is righteousness that exalteth a nation.

Forty-eight hours from tonight, standing where I am standing, there will be a President of the United States. He will be seeking re-election.

A little more than forty-eight hours after he has spoken, the American people will be streaming to the polls.

Here once again I ask him to speak what is in his mind. It is his duty, not only as President, but also as an American, to tell what his purposes and intentions really are. It is his duty, as it is my duty, to trust the "combined wisdom of the people." For the Constitution, which he swore to uphold, stands squarely on the "combined wisdom of the people." When the ballot speaks, it speaks the "combined wisdom of the people."

The people of this country will not trust a man who does not trust them. If he trusts them he will answer the questions being asked from one end of the country to the other.

Does he favor reviving the principles of the National Recovery Act? Or does he favor the American system of free initiative?

Does he favor reviving the principles of the Agricultural Adjustment Act? Or does he favor allowing the farmer to be a lord on his own farm?

Does he favor concentrating more and more power in the hands of the Chief Executive? Or does he favor a return to the American form of government?

These three things are inseparable. If he wants the AAA, he must have the NRA. If he wants the NRA, he must have the AAA. And both are impossible without increased powers for the Chief Executive.

And so, in closing this meeting, I leave a challenge with the President. I say to him: Mr. President, I am willing to trust the people. I am willing to stand up and say openly that I am against economic planning by the government. I am against the concentration of power in the hands of the Chief Executive.

Tell us where you stand, Mr. President. Tell us not in generalities, but clearly, so that no one can mistake your meaning. And tell us why you have evaded the issue until the eve of the election.

I leave my gage at your feet.

My gage is the gauge of your confidence, Mr. President, your confidence in the American people.

My gage is the gauge of your duty, Mr. President, your duty to the American people.

My gage is the gauge of your faith, Mr. President, your faith in the American people.

By the words that you speak in forty-eight hours the American people will know the measure of your confidence and your duty and your faith in their wisdom.

☆

1940

———— ☆ ————

Roosevelt's second administration was conspicuous for its interminable difficulties. First came the unsuccessful attempt to "pack" the Supreme Court in early 1937—an effort which perceptibly damaged Roosevelt's reputation; then came the "Roosevelt recession," which further hurt his stature; next came the President's disastrous attempt to "purge" conservative members of his own party in the mid-term elections of 1938; finally, there was Hitler's invasion of Poland on September 1, 1939. What Americans were witnessing was the beginning of the end of the New Deal.

Against this background the Republican convention opened at Philadelphia on June 24th. It took the party six ballots to nominate their candidate, Wendell Willkie, a forty-eight year old Wall Street attorney who had never held a political post. Born in Elwood, Indiana, Willkie moved to New York in 1929; by 1933 he was president of Commonwealth and Southern, a utility holding corporation.

Because Willkie's corporation controlled several electric power companies in the Tennessee Valley, he came into conflict with the Tennessee Valley Authority, the New Deal agency which competed with private industry for the distribution of electric power in that area. Willkie's protracted struggle with the TVA brought him national recognition and established him as a leading advocate of private enterprise.

The 1940 Republican party's platform supported state action over federal intervention on the home front and espoused an equivocal position on foreign policy, calling for aid to "all people fighting for liberty," provided that aid was not in contravention of international law or incompatible with the nation's own defense requirements.

After his nomination Willkie briefly appeared before the convention, where the one-time Democrat who had voted for Roosevelt in 1932 said: "And so, you Republicans, I call upon you to join me." His formal acceptance speech—the only address in which he did not deviate from the text—was delivered in his home town.

Interestingly, Willkie was sympathetic toward the New Deal's social legislation and in basic agreement with Roosevelt's foreign policy. Essentially, Willkie opposed the general outlines of the New Deal rather than its individual features. His principal criticism of the New Deal was that it assumed a defeatist posture. Rather than trying to usher in new industry, he charged, it was committed to regulating old enterprise. In short, the New Deal was supplying static solutions to a revolutionary situation. It was retarding the American economy at a time when it required expansion. What was required, Willkie affirmed, was new leadership.

Willkie's attacks on the New Deal and its "third-term candidate" did little to galvanize public opinion. By the fall, Willkie was a candidate in search of an issue. It was during this phase of his campaign that he began criticizing Roosevelt's foreign policy. In an October 17th campaign address at St. Louis, Willkie combined all his criticisms of the New Deal and leveled a three-pronged attack against the third-term candidate who had failed to restore production and who was unwittingly leading us into war.

The Democrats assembled in Chicago on July 15th. At the convention Roosevelt's Secretary of Commerce, Harry Hopkins, worked assiduously to make it appear as though Roosevelt was being drafted for a third-term. In addition, Hopkins sought to secure the nomination of Roosevelt's choice for his running-mate, Secretary of Agriculture Henry A. Wallace. Both men were nominated on the first ballot.

For the first time in three conventions Roosevelt was unable to deliver his acceptance speech in person. In a radio broadcast from Washington the President announced that he was running again not as a Democrat, but as a man who felt a "call to service." The preservation of global freedom, he went on, could not be entrusted to "untrained hands, inexperienced hands."

In his campaign speeches Roosevelt traced the accomplishments of the New Deal and attacked the Republican party's position on foreign policy. It was during this campaign that Roosevelt uttered one of his most frequently quoted remarks. Speaking in Boston on October 30th, he made the following pledge to the parents of America: "I have said this before, but I shall say it again and again and again: Your boys are not going to be sent into any foreign wars."

But it was in Cleveland, on November 2nd, that Roosevelt delivered what is believed to be the most eloquent and moving speech of his career. There he presented his vision of America, an America without poverty and with equal opportunity for all, an America that would be a beacon of liberty to the world.

FRANKLIN D. ROOSEVELT

Acceptance Speech

VIA RADIO TO CONVENTION, WASHINGTON, D. C.

July 19, 1940

Members of the Convention—my friends:

It is very late; but I have felt that you would rather that I speak to you now than wait until tomorrow.

It is with a very full heart that I speak tonight. I must confess that I do so with mixed feelings—because I find myself, as almost everyone does sooner or later in his lifetime, in a conflict between deep personal desire for retirement on the one hand, and that quiet, invisible thing called "conscience" on the other.

Because there are self-appointed commentators and interpreters who will seek to misinterpret or question motives, I speak in a somewhat personal vein; and I must trust to the good faith and common sense of the American people to accept my own good faith—and to do their own interpreting.

When, in 1936, I was chosen by the voters for a second time as President, it was my firm intention to turn over the responsibilities of Government to other hands at the end of my term. That conviction remained with me. Eight years in the Presidency, following a period of bleak depression, and covering one world crisis after another, would normally entitle any man to the relaxation that comes from honorable retirement.

During the spring of 1939, world events made it clear to all but the blind or the partisan that a great war in Europe had become not merely a possibility but a probability, and that such a war would of necessity deeply affect the future of this nation.

When the conflict first broke out last September, it was still my intention to announce clearly and simply, at an early date, that under no conditions would I accept reelection. This fact was well known to my friends, and I think was understood by many citizens.

It soon became evident, however, that such a public statement on my part would be unwise from the point of view of sheer public duty. As President of the United States, it was my clear duty, with the aid of the Congress, to preserve our neutrality, to shape our program of defense, to meet rapid changes, to keep our domestic affairs adjusted to shifting world conditions, and to sustain the policy of the Good Neighbor.

It was also my obvious duty to maintain to the utmost the influence of this mighty nation in our effort to prevent the spread of war, and to sustain by all legal means those governments threatened by other governments which had rejected the principles of democracy.

Swiftly moving foreign events made necessary swift action at home and beyond the seas. Plans for national defense had to be expanded and adjusted to meet new forms of warfare. American citizens and their welfare had to be safeguarded in many foreign zones of danger. National unity in the United States became a crying essential in the face of the development of unbelievable types of espionage and international treachery.

Every day that passed called for the postponement of personal plans and partisan debate until the latest possible moment. The normal conditions under which I would have made public declaration of my personal desires were wholly gone.

And so, thinking solely of the national good and of the international scene, I came to the reluctant conclusion that such declaration should not be made before the national Convention. It was accordingly made to you within an hour after the permanent organization of this Convention.

Like any other man, I am complimented by the honor you have done me. But I know you will understand the spirit in which I say that no call of Party alone would prevail upon me to accept reelection to the Presidency.

The real decision to be made in these circumstances is not the acceptance of a nomination, but rather an ultimate willingness to serve if chosen by the electorate of the United States. Many considerations enter into this decision.

During the past few months, with due Congressional approval, we in the United States have been taking steps to implement the total defense of America. I cannot forget that in carrying out this program I have drafted into the service of the nation many men and women, taking them away from important private affairs, calling them suddenly from their homes and their businesses. I have asked them to leave their own work, and to contribute their skill and experience to the cause of their nation.

I, as the head of their Government, have asked them to do this. Regardless of party, regardless of personal convenience, they came—they answered the call. Every single one of them, with one exception, has come to the nation's Capital to serve the nation.

These people, who have placed patriotism above all else, represent those who have made their way to what might be called the top of their professions or industries through their proven skill and experience.

But they alone could not be enough to meet the needs of the times.

Just as a system of national defense based on man power alone, without the mechanized equipment of modern warfare, is totally insufficient for adequate national defense, so also planes and guns and tanks are wholly insufficient unless they are implemented by the power of men trained to use them.

Such man power consists not only of pilots and gunners and infantry and those who operate tanks. For every individual in actual combat service, it is necessary for adequate defense that we have ready at hand at least four or five other trained individuals organized for non-combat services.

Because of the millions of citizens involved in the conduct of defense, most right thinking persons are agreed that some form of selection by draft is as necessary and fair today as it was in 1917 and 1918.

Nearly every American is willing to do his share or her share to defend the United States. It is neither just nor efficient to permit that task to fall upon any one section or any one group. For every section and every group depend for their existence upon the survival of the nation as a whole.

Lying awake, as I have on many nights, I have asked myself whether I have the right, as Commander-in-Chief of the Army and Navy, to call on men and women to serve their country or to train themselves to serve and, at the same time, decline to serve my country in my own personal capacity, if I am called upon to do so by the people of my country.

In times like these—in times of great tension, of great crisis—the compass of the world narrows to a single fact. The fact which dominates our world is the fact of armed aggression, the fact of successful armed aggression, aimed at the form of Government, the kind of society that we in the United States have chosen and established for ourselves. It is a fact which no one longer doubts—which no one is longer able to ignore.

It is not an ordinary war. It is a revolution imposed by force of arms, which threatens all men everywhere. It is a revolution which proposes not to set men free but to reduce them to slavery—to reduce them to slavery in the interest of a dictatorship which has already shown the nature and the extent of the advantage which it hopes to obtain.

That is the fact which dominates our world and which dominates the lives of all of us, each and every one of us. In the face of the danger which confronts our time, no individual retains or can hope to retain, the right of personal choice which free men enjoy in times of peace. He has a first obligation to serve in the defense of our institutions of freedom—a first obligation to serve his country in whatever capacity his country finds him useful.

Like most men of my age, I had made plans for myself, plans for a private life of my own choice and for my own satisfaction, a life of that kind to begin in January, 1941. These plans, like so many other plans, had been made in a world which now seems as distant as another planet. Today all private plans, all private lives, have been in a sense repealed by an overriding public danger. In the face of that public danger all those who can be of service to the Republic have no choice but to offer themselves for service in those capacities for which they may be fitted.

Those, my friends, are the reasons why I have had to admit to myself, and now to state to you, that my conscience will not let me turn my back upon a call to service.

The right to make that call rests with the people through the American method of a free election. Only the people themselves can draft a President. If such a draft should be made upon me, I say to you, in the utmost simplicity, I will, with God's help, continue to serve with the best of my ability and with the fullness of my strength.

To you, the delegates of this Convention, I express my gratitude for the selection of Henry Wallace for the high office of Vice President of the United States. His first-hand knowledge of the problems of Government in every sphere of life and in every single part of the nation—and indeed of the whole world—qualifies him without reservation. His practical idealism will be of great service to me individually and to the nation as a whole.

And to the Chairman of the National Committee, the Postmaster General of the United States—my old friend Jim Farley—I send, as I have often before and shall many times again, my most affectionate greetings. All of us are sure that he will continue to give all the leadership and support that he possibly can to the cause of American democracy.

In some respects, as I think my good wife suggested an hour or so ago—the next few months will be different from the usual national campaigns of recent years.

Most of you know how important it is that the President of the United States in these days remain close to the seat of Government. Since last Summer I have been compelled to abandon proposed journeys to inspect many of our great national projects from the Alleghenies to the Pacific Coast.

Events move so fast in other parts of the world that it has become my duty to remain either in the White House itself or at some near-by point where I can reach Washington and even Europe and Asia by direct telephone—where, if need be, I can be back at my desk in the space of a very few hours. And in addition, the splendid work of the new defense machinery will require me to spend vastly more time in conference with the responsible administration heads under me. Finally, the added task which the present crisis has imposed also upon the Congress, compelling them to forego their usual adjournment, calls for constant cooperation between the Executive and Legislative branches, to the efficiency of which I am glad indeed now to pay tribute.

I do expect, of course, during the coming months to make my usual periodic reports to the country through the medium of press conferences and radio talks. I shall not have the time or the inclination to engage in purely political debate. But I shall never be loath to call the attention of the nation to deliberate or unwitting falsifications of fact, which are sometimes made by political candidates.

I have spoken to you in a very informal and personal way. The exigencies of the day require, however, that I also talk with you about things which transcend any personality and go very deeply to the roots of American civilization.

Our lives have been based on those fundamental freedoms and liberties which we Americans have cherished for a century and a half. The establishment of them and the preservation of them in each succeeding generation have been accomplished through the processes of free elective Government—the democratic-republican form, based on the representative system and the coordination of the executive, the legislative and the judicial branches.

The task of safeguarding our institutions seems to me to be twofold. One must be accomplished, if it becomes necessary, by the armed defense forces of the nation. The other, by the united effort of the men and women of the country to make our Federal and State and local Governments responsive to the growing requirements of modern democracy.

There have been occasions, as we remember, when reactions in the march of democracy have set in, and forward-looking progress has seemed to stop.

But such periods have been followed by liberal and progressive times which have enabled the nation to catch up with new developments in fulfilling new human needs. Such a time has been the past seven years. Because we had seemed to lag in previous years, we have had to develop, speedily and efficiently, the answers to aspirations which had come from every State and every family in the land.

We have sometimes called it social legislation; we have sometimes called it legislation to end the abuses of the past; we have sometimes called it legislation for human security; and we have sometimes called it legislation to better the condition of life of the many millions of our fellow citizens, who could not have the essentials of life or hope for an American standard of living.

Some of us have labeled it a wider and more equitable distribution of wealth in our land. It has included among its aims, to liberalize and broaden the control of vast industries—lodged today in the hands of a relatively small group of individuals of very great financial power.

But all of these definitions and labels are essentially the expression of one consistent thought. They represent a constantly growing sense of human decency, human decency throughout our nation.

This sense of human decency is happily confined to no group or class. You find it in the humblest home. You find it among those who toil, and among the shopkeepers and the farmers of the nation. You find it, to a growing degree, even among those who are listed in that top group which has so much control over the industrial and financial structure of the nation. Therefore, this urge of humanity can by no means be labeled a war of class against class. It is rather a war against poverty and suffering and ill-health and insecurity, a war in which all classes are joining in the interest of a sound and enduring democracy.

I do not believe for a moment, and I know that you do not believe either, that we have fully answered all the needs of human security. But we have covered much of the road. I need not catalogue the milestones of seven years. For every individual and every family in the whole land know that the average of their personal lives has been made safer and sounder and happier than it has ever been before. I do not think they want the gains in these directions to be repealed or even to be placed in the charge of those who would give them mere lip-service with no heart service.

Yes, very much more remains to be done, and I think the voters want the task entrusted to those who believe that the words "human betterment" apply to poor and rich alike.

And I have a sneaking suspicion too, that voters will smile at charges of inefficiency against a Government which has boldly met the enormous problems of banking, and finance and industry which the great efficient bankers and industrialists of the Republican Party left in such hopeless chaos in the famous year 1933.

But we all know that our progress at home and in the other American nations toward this realization of a better human decency—progress along free lines—is gravely endangered by what is happening on other continents. In Europe, many nations, through dictatorships or invasions, have been compelled to abandon normal democratic processes. They have been compelled to adopt forms of government which some call "new and efficient."

They are not new, my friends, they are only a relapse—a relapse into ancient history. The omnipotent rulers of the greater part of modern Europe have guaranteed efficiency, and work, and a type of security.

But the slaves who built the pyramids for the glory of the dictator Pharoahs of Egypt had that kind of security, that kind of efficiency, that kind of corporative state.

So did the inhabitants of that world which extended from Britain to Persia under the undisputed rule of the proconsuls sent out from Rome.

So did the henchmen, the tradesmen, the mercenaries and the slaves of the feudal system which dominated Europe a thousand years ago.

So did the people of those nations of Europe who received their kings and their government at the whim of the conquering Napoleon.

Whatever its new trappings and new slogans, tyranny is the oldest and most discredited rule known to history. And whenever tyranny has replaced a more human form of Government it has been due more to internal causes than external. Democracy can thrive only when it enlists the devotion of those whom Lincoln called the common people. Democracy can hold that devotion only when it adequately respects their dignity by so ordering society as to assure to the masses of men and women reasonable security and hope for themselves and for their children.

We in our democracy, and those who live in still unconquered democracies, will never willingly descend to any form of this so-called security of efficiency which calls for the abandonment of other securities more vital to the dignity of man. It is our credo—unshakable to the end—that we must live under the liberties that were first heralded by Magna Carta and placed into glorious operation through the Declaration of Independence, the Constitution of the United States and the Bill of Rights.

The Government of the United States for the past seven years has had the courage openly to oppose by every peaceful means the spread of the dictator form of Government. If our Government should pass to other hands next January—untried hands, inexperienced hands—we can merely hope and pray that they will not substitute appeasement and compromise with those who seek to destroy all democracies everywhere, including here.

I would not undo, if I could, the efforts I made to prevent war from the moment it was threatened and to restrict the area of carnage, down to the last minute. I do not now soften the condemnation expressed by Secretary Hull and myself from time to time for the acts of aggression that have wiped out ancient liberty-loving, peace-pursuing countries which had scrupulously maintained neutrality. I do not recant the sentiments of sympathy with all free peoples resisting such aggression, or begrudge the material aid that we have given to them. I do not regret my consistent endeavor to awaken this country to the menace for us and for all we hold dear.

I have pursued these efforts in the face of appeaser fifth columnists who charged me with hysteria and war-mongering. But I felt it my duty, my simple, plain, inescapable duty, to arouse my countrymen to the danger of the new forces let loose in the world.

So long as I am President, I will do all I can to insure that that foreign policy remain our foreign policy.

All that I have done to maintain the peace of this country and to prepare it morally, as well as physically, for whatever contingencies may be in store, I submit to the judgment of my countrymen.

We face one of the great choices of history.

It is not alone a choice of Government by the people versus dictatorship.

It is not alone a choice of freedom versus slavery.

It is not alone a choice between moving forward or falling back.

It is all of these rolled into one.

It is the continuance of Civilization as we know it versus the ultimate destruction of all that we have held dear—religion against godlessness; the ideal of justice against the practice of force; moral decency versus the firing squad; courage to speak out, and to act, versus the false lullaby of appeasement.

But it has been well said that a selfish and greedy people cannot be free.

The American people must decide whether these things are worth making sacrifices of money, of energy, and of self. They will not decide by listening to mere words or by reading mere pledges, interpretations and claims. They will decide on the record—the record as it has been made—the record of things as they are.

The American people will sustain the progress of a representative democracy, asking the Divine Blessing as they face the future with courage and with faith.

☆

FRANKLIN D. ROOSEVELT

Campaign Speech

CLEVELAND, OHIO

November 2, 1940

Mr. Chairman, ladies and gentlemen:

In making this, my final national address of the campaign, I express once more my deep regret that I could not carry out my wish to go to other States in the great Middle West, in the South and across the Mississippi River. It has been solely in the interest of peace and the maintenance of peace that your great Secretary of State and I have felt that we should both remain within easy distance of the National Capital in these trying days.

Tonight in Cleveland, I am happy, through this great audience of my old friends, to give this message to America.

For the past seven years I have had the high honor and the grave responsibility of leadership of the American people. In those seven years, the American people have marched forward, out of a wilderness of depression and despair.

They have marched forward right up to the very threshold of the future—a future which holds the fulfillment of our hopes for real freedom, real prosperity, real peace.

I want that march to continue for four more years. And for that purpose, I am asking your vote of confidence.

There are certain forces within our own national community, composed of men who call themselves American but who would destroy America. They are the forces of dictatorship in our land—on one hand, the Communists, and on the other, the Girdlers.

It is their constant purpose in this as in other lands to weaken democracy, to destroy the free man's faith in his own cause.

In this election all the representatives of those forces, without exception, are voting against the New Deal.

You and I are proud of that opposition. It is positive proof that what we have built and strengthened in the past seven years *is* democracy!

This generation of Americans is living in a tremendous moment of history.

The surge of events abroad has made some few doubters among us ask: Is this the end of a story that has been told? Is the book of democracy now to be closed and placed away upon the dusty shelves of time?

My answer is this: All we have known of the glories of democracy— its freedom, its efficiency as a mode of living, its ability to meet the aspirations of the common man—all these are merely an introduction to the greater story of a more glorious future.

We Americans of today—all of us—we are characters in this living book of democracy.

But we are also its author. It falls upon us now to say whether the chapters that are to come will tell a story of retreat or a story of continued advance.

I believe that the American people will say: "Forward!"

We look at the old world of Europe today. It is an ugly world, poisoned by hatred and greed and fear. We can see what has been the inevitable consequence of that poison—war.

We look at the country in which we live. It is a great country, built by generations of peaceable, friendly men and women who had in their hearts faith that the good life can be attained by those who will work for it.

We know that we are determined to defend our country—and with our neighbors to defend this Hemisphere. We are strong in our defense. Every hour and every day we grow stronger.

Our foreign policy is shaped to express the determination of our Government and the will of our people in our dealings with other nations. Those dealings, in the past few years, have been more difficult, more complex than ever before.

There is nothing secret about our foreign policy. It is not a secret from the American people—and it is not a secret from any Government anywhere in the world. I have stated it many times before, not only in words but in action. Let me restate it like this:

The first purpose of our foreign policy is to keep our country out of war. At the same time, we seek to keep foreign conceptions of Government out of the United States.

That is why we make ourselves strong; that is why we muster all the reserves of our national strength.

The second purpose of this policy is to keep war as far away as possible from the shores of the entire Western Hemisphere. Our policy is to promote such friendly relations with the Latin-American Republics and with Canada, that the great powers of Europe and Asia will know that they cannot divide the people of this hemisphere one from another. And if you go from the North Pole to the South Pole, you will know that it is a policy of practical success.

Finally, our policy is to give all possible material aid to the nations which still resist aggression, across the Atlantic and Pacific Oceans.

And let me make it perfectly clear that we intend to commit none of the fatal errors of appeasement.

We in this Nation of many States have found the way by which men of many racial origins may live together in peace.

If the human race as a whole is to survive, the world must find the way by which men and nations can live together in peace. We cannot accept the doctrine that war must be forever a part of man's destiny.

We do know what would be the foreign policy of those who are doubters about our democracy.

We do not know what would be the foreign policy of those who are obviously trying to sit on both sides of the fence at the same time. Ours is the foreign policy of an Administration which has undying faith in the strength of our democracy today, full confidence in the vitality of our democracy in the future, and a consistent record in the cause of peace

Our strength is measured not only in terms of the might of our armaments. It is measured not only in terms of the horsepower of our machines.

The true measure of our strength lies deeply imbedded in the social and economic justice of the system in which we live.

For you can build ships and tanks and planes and guns galore; but they will not be enough. You must place behind them an invincible faith in the institutions which they have been built to defend.

The dictators have devised a new system—or, rather, a modern, streamlined version of a very ancient system.

But Americans will have none of that. They will never submit to domination or influence by Naziism or Communism. They will hesitate to support those of whom they are not absolutely sure.

For Americans are determined to retain for themselves the right of free speech, free religion, free assembly and the right which lies at the basis of all of them—the right to choose the officers of their own Government in free elections.

We intend to keep our freedom—to defend it from attacks from without and against corruption from within. We shall defend it against the forces of dictatorship, whatever disguises and false faces they may wear.

But we have learned that freedom in itself is not enough.

Freedom of speech is of no use to a man who has nothing to say.

Freedom of worship is of no use to a man who has lost his God.

Democracy, to be dynamic, must provide for its citizens opportunity as well as freedom.

We of this generation have seen a rebirth of dynamic democracy in America in these past few years.

The American people have faced with courage the most severe problems of all of our modern history.

The start toward a solution of these problems had to be made seven years ago by providing the bare necessities of life—food and shelter and clothing. The American people insisted that those obligations were a concern of Government; they denied that the only solution was the poorhouse.

Your Government assumed its proper function as the working representative of the average men and women of America. And the reforms in our social structure that we have achieved—these permanent reforms are your achievement.

The New Deal has been the creation of you, the American people.

You provided work for free men and women in America who could find no work.

Idle men were given the opportunity on roads to be built, homes to be erected, rivers to be harnessed, power to be made for farm and home and industry.

You used the powers of Government to stop the depletion of the top soil of America, to stop decline in farm prices, to stop foreclosures of homes and farms.

You wrote into the law the right of working men and women to bargain collectively, and you set up the machinery to enforce that right.

You turned to the problems of youth and age. You took your children out of the factory and shop and outlawed the right of anyone to exploit the labor of those children; and you gave to those children the chance to prepare in body and spirit the molding of an even fuller and brighter day for themselves. For the youth of the land you provided chances for jobs and for education. And for old age itself you provided security and rest.

You made safe the banks which held your savings. You stopped, once and for all, gambling with other people's money—money changing in the temple.

You advanced to other objectives. You gained them, you consolidated them and advanced again.

The task which this generation had to do has been begun. The forward march of democracy is under way. Its advance must not and will not stop.

During those years while our democracy moved forward, your Government has worked with you and for you. Your Government has at times been checked. But always, with the aid and the counsel of all the people, we have resumed our march.

Now we are asked to stop in our tracks. We are asked to turn about, to march back into the wilderness from which we came.

Of course we will not turn backward. We will not turn back because we are the inheritors of a tradition of pioneering, exploring, experimenting and adventuring. We will not be scared into retreating by threats from the doubters of democracy.

Neither will we be bribed by extravagant promises of fabulous wealth.

Those who offer such promises try to delude us with a mirage on the far horizon—a mirage of an island of dreams, with palaces and palms and plums.

And it is a curious fact of nature that a mirage is always upside down, above the horizon.

But then, the mirage—upside down or right-side up—isn't there at all. Now you see it—and now you don't.

Of course we shall continue to strengthen all these dynamic reforms in our social and economic life; to keep the processes of democracy side by side with the necessities and possibilities of modern industrial production.

Of course we shall continue to make available the good things of life created by the genius of science and technology—to use them, however, not for the enjoyment of the few but for the welfare of all.

For there lies the road to democracy that is strong.

Of course we intend to preserve and build up the land of this country —its soil, its forests and its rivers—all the resources with which God has endowed the people of the United States.

Of course we intend to continue to build up the bodies and the minds of the men, women and children of the Nation—through democratic education and a democratic program for health.

For there lies the road to democracy that is strong.

Of course we intend to continue our efforts to protect our system of private enterprise and private property, but to protect it from monopoly of financial control on the one hand and from Communistic wrecking on the other.

Of course we shall continue our efforts to prevent economic dictatorship as well as political dictatorship.

Of course we intend to continue to build up the morale of this country, not as blind obedience to some leader, but as the expression of confidence in the deeply ethical principles upon which this Nation and its democracy were founded.

For there lies the road to democracy that is strong.

The progress of our country, as well as the defense of our country, requires national unity. We need the cooperation of every single American—our workers, the great organizers and technicians in our factories, our farmers, our professional men and women, our workers in industry, our mothers, our fathers, our youth—all the men and women who love America just a little bit more than they love themselves.

And if we can have the assistance of all these, we can promise that such a program can make this country prosperous and free and strong—to be a light of the world and a comfort to all people.

And all the forces of evil shall not prevail against it.

For so it is written in the Book, and so it is written in the moral law, and so it is written in the promise of a great era of world peace.

This Nation which is arming itself for defense has also the intelligence to save its human resources by giving them that confidence which comes from useful work.

This Nation which is creating a great navy has also found the strength to build houses and begin to clear the slums of its cities and its countryside.

This Nation which has become the industrial leader of the world has the humanity to know that the people of a free land need not suffer the disease of poverty and the dread of not being wanted.

It is the destiny of this American generation to point the road to the future for all the world to see. It is our prayer that all lovers of freedom may join us—the anguished common people of this earth for whom we seek to light the path.

I see an America where factory workers are not discarded after they reach their prime, where there is no endless chain of poverty from generation to generation, where impoverished farmers and farm hands do not become homeless wanderers, where monopoly does not make youth a beggar for a job.

I see an America whose rivers and valleys and lakes—hills and streams and plains—the mountains over our land and nature's wealth deep under the earth—are protected as the rightful heritage of all the people.

I see an America where small business really has a chance to flourish and grow.

I see an America of great cultural and educational opportunity for all its people.

I see an America where the income from the land shall be implemented and protected by a Government determined to guarantee to those who hoe it a fair share in the national income.

An America where the wheels of trade and private industry continue to turn to make the goods for America. Where no businessman can be stifled by the harsh hand of monopoly, and where the legitimate profits of legitimate business are the fair reward of every businessman—big and little—in all the Nation.

I see an America with peace in the ranks of labor.

An America where the workers are really free and—through their great unions undominated by any outside force, or by any dictator within—can take their proper place at the council table with the owners and managers of business. Where the dignity and security of the working man and woman are guaranteed by their own strength and fortified by the safeguards of law.

An America where those who have reached the evening of life shall live out their years in peace and security. Where pensions and insurance for these aged shall be given as a matter of right to those who through a long life of labor have served their families and their nation as well.

I see an America devoted to our freedom—unified by tolerance and by religious faith—a people consecrated to peace, a people confident in strength because their body and their spirit are secure and unafraid.

During these years while our democracy advanced on many fields of battle, I have had the great privilege of being your President. No personal ambition of any man could desire more than that.

It is a hard task. It is a task from which there is no escape day or night.

And through it all there have been two thoughts uppermost in my mind—to preserve peace in our land; and to make the forces of democracy work for the benefit of the common people of America.

Seven years ago I started with loyal helpers and with the trust and faith and support of millions of ordinary Americans.

The way was difficult—the path was dark, but we have moved steadily forward to the open fields and the glowing light that shines ahead.

The way of our lives seems clearer now, if we but follow the charts and the guides of our democratic faith.

There is a great storm raging now, a storm that makes things harder for the world. And that storm, which did not start in this land of ours, is the true reason that I would like to stick by these people of ours until we reach the clear, sure footing ahead.

We will make it—we will make it before the next term is over.

We will make it; and the world, we hope, will make it, too.

When that term is over there will be another President, and many more Presidents in the years to come, and I think that, in the years to come, that word "President" will be a word to cheer the hearts of common men and women everywhere.

Our future belongs to us Americans.

It is for us to design it; for us to build it.

In that building of it we shall prove that our faith is strong enough to survive the most fearsome storms that have ever swept over the earth.

In the days and months and years to come, we shall be making history—hewing out a new shape for the future. And we shall make very sure that that future of our bears the likeness of liberty.

Always the heart and the soul of our country will be the heart and the soul of the common man—the men and the women who never have ceased to believe in democracy, who never have ceased to love their families, their homes and their country.

The spirit of the common man is the spirit of peace and good will. It is the spirit of God. And in His faith is the strength of all America.

☆

WENDELL L. WILLKIE

Acceptance Speech

ELWOOD, INDIANA

August 17, 1940

The ceremony of an acceptance speech is a tradition of our pioneer past— before the days of rapid communication. You all know that I accepted at Philadelphia the nomination of the Republican party for President of the United States. But I take pride in the traditions and not in change for the mere sake of overthrowing precedents.

An acceptance speech is a candidate's keynote, a declaration of his broad principles. It cannot possibly review the issues in detail. I shall, however, cover each of them frankly during this campaign. Here I give you an outline of the political philosophy that is in my heart. We are here today to represent a sacred cause—the preservation of American democracy.

Obviously, I cannot lead this cause alone. I need the help of every American—Republican, Democrat or Independent—Jew, Catholic, or Protestant—people of every color, creed and race. Party lines are down. Nothing could make that clearer than the nomination by the Republicans of a liberal Democrat who changed his party affiliation because he found democracy in the Republican party and not in the New Deal party.

And as the leader of the Republican party let me say this. We go into our campaign as into a crusade. Revitalized and reunited, and joined by millions who share in our cause, we dedicate ourselves to the principles of American liberty, and we shall fight this campaign on the basis of those principles, not on the basis of hate, jealousy, or personalities. The leaders of the Republican party, in Congress and in the party organization, have made me that pledge. I have given that pledge to them. And I extend it to all who will join in this cause. What we need in this country is a new leadership that believes in the destiny of America. I represent here today the forces that will bring that leadership to you.

There is a special reason why I have come back to Elwood, Indiana, to make this acceptance speech. I have an engagement to keep in this town. It was made a long time ago with a young man I knew well.

This young man was born and raised in Elwood. He attended the Elwood public schools. He worked in your factories and stores. He started the practice of law in your courts. As I look back upon him, I realize that he had plenty of faults. But he had also three steadfast convictions. He was devoted to the ideal of individual liberty. He hated all special privileges and forms of oppression. And he knew without any doubt that the greatest country on earth was the United States of America.

That boy was myself thirty or thirty-five years ago. I still adhere to those convictions. To him, to his generation, to his elders, and to the youth of today I pledge my word that I shall never let them down.

In former days America was described as a country in which any young man might become President. It is still that kind of country. The thousands of my fellow townsmen standing hereabout know how distant seemed that opportunity to me thirty years ago. We must fight to preserve America as a country in which every girl and boy has every opportunity for any achievement.

To the millions of our young men and women who have been deliberately disillusioned by the political influences I now oppose; to the millions who no longer believe in the future of their land—to them I want to say in all humility—this boy I knew started like you, without money or position; but America gave him the opportunity for a career. I want to assure a similar opportunity to every boy and girl of today who is willing to stand on his own feet, and work and fight.

I have more reason than most of you to feel strongly about this because the United States gave to my family their first chance for a free life. The ancestors of both my father and my mother, like the ancestors of millions of Americans, lived in Central Europe. They were humble people—not members of the ruling or wealthy classes. Their opportunities were restricted by discriminatory laws and class distinctions. One was exiled because of his religion; another was persecuted because he believed in the principles of the French Revolution; and still another was jailed for insisting on the right of free speech.

As their descendant, I have fought from boyhood against all those restrictions, discriminations and tyrannies. And I am still fighting.

My grandparents lived in Germany. They were supporters of the democratic revolutions in that country, and when the revolutions failed they fled to the United States. How familiar that sounds! Today, also, people are being oppressed in Europe. The story of the barbarous and worse than medieval persecution of the Jews—a race that has done so much to improve the culture of these countries and our own—is the most tragic in human history. Today there are millions of refugees who desire sanctuary and opportunity in America, just as in my grandparents' time. The protection of our own labor and agriculture prevents us from admitting more than a few of them. But their misery and suffering make us resolve to preserve our country as a land free of hate and bitterness, of racial and class distinction. I pledge you that kind of America.

My mother was born in this country. My father was three or four years old when his parents settled in northern Indiana. It was then a trackless forest. As a young man he helped to clear that forest. He worked his way through the Fort Wayne Methodist College, taught school, and became Superintendent of Schools here in Elwood. My mother was also a school teacher. Whenever they had time, they both studied law and eventually both took up the practice of law. I doubt if any two people ever appreciated or loved this country more than they.

As you who lived here with them well know, they were fiercely democratic. They hated oppression, autocracy, or arbitrary control of any kind. They believed in the qualities that have made America great—an independent spirit, an inquiring mind, a courageous heart. At school they taught those virtues to many of you who are here today. At home they taught them to their children. It is a tribute to their teaching that when the United States entered the World War in 1917, three of their four boys were volunteers, in the uniform of the American forces, within one month after war was declared. They withheld no sacrifices for the preservation of the America of 1917. In an even more dangerous world, we must not withhold any sacrifice necessary for the preservation of the America of 1940.

Today we meet in a typical American town. The quiet streets, the pleasant fields that lie outside, the people going casually about their business, seem far removed from the shattered cities, the gutted buildings, and the stricken people of Europe. It is hard for us to realize that the war in Europe can affect our daily lives. Instinctively we turn aside from the recurring conflicts over there, the diplomatic intrigue, the shifts of power that the last war failed to end.

Yet—instinctively also—we know that we are not isolated from those suffering people. We live in the same world as they, and we are created in the same image. In all the democracies that have recently fallen, the people were living the same peaceful lives that we live. They had similar ideals of human freedom. Their methods of trade and exchange were similar to ours. Try as we will, we cannot brush the pitiless picture of their destruction from our vision, or escape the profound effects of it upon the world in which we live.

No man is so wise as to foresee what the future holds or to lay out a plan for it. No man can guarantee to maintain peace. Peace is not something that a nation can achieve by itself. It also depends on what some other country does. It is neither practical, nor desirable, to adopt a foreign program committing the United States to future action under unknown circumstances.

The best that we can do is to decide what principle shall guide us.

For me, that principle can be simply defined:

In the foreign policy of the United States, as in its domestic policy, I would do everything to defend American democracy and I would refrain from doing anything that would injure it.

We must not permit our emotions—our sympathies or hatreds—to move us from that fixed principle.

For instance, we must not shirk the necessity of preparing our sons to take care of themselves in case the defense of America leads to war. I shall not undertake to analyze the legislation on this subject that is now before Congress, or to examine the intentions of the Administration with regard to it. I concur with many members of my party, that these intentions must be closely watched. Nevertheless, in spite of these considerations, I cannot ask the American people to put their faith in me, without recording my conviction that some form of selective service is the only democratic way in which to secure the trained and competent manpower we need for national defense.

Also, in the light of my principle, we must honestly face our relationship with Great Britain. We must admit that the loss of the British Fleet would greatly weaken our defense. This is because the British Fleet has for years controlled the Atlantic, leaving us free to concentrate in the Pacific. If the British Fleet were lost or captured, the Atlantic might be dominated by Germany, a power hostile to our way of life, controlling in that event most of the ships and shipbuilding facilities of Europe.

This would be a calamity for us. We might be exposed to attack on the Atlantic. Our defense would be weakened until we could build a navy and air force strong enough to defend both coasts. Also, our foreign trade would be profoundly affected. That trade is vital to our prosperity. But if we had to trade with a Europe dominated by the present German trade policies, we might have to change our methods to some totalitarian form. This is a prospect that any lover of democracy must view with consternation.

The objective of America is in the opposite direction. We must, in the long run, rebuild a world in which we can live and move and do business in the democratic way.

The President of the United States recently said: "We will extend to the opponents of force the material resources of this nation, and at the same time we will harness the use of those resources in order that we ourselves, in the Americas, may have equipment and training equal to the task of any emergency and every defense."

I should like to state that I am in agreement with these two principles, as I understand them—and I don't understand them as implying military involvement in the present hostilities. As an American citizen I am glad to pledge my wholehearted support to the President in whatever action he may take in accordance with these principles.

But I cannot follow the President in his conduct of foreign affairs in this critical time. There have been occasions when many of us have wondered if he is deliberately inciting us to war. I trust that I have made it plain that in the defense of America, and of our liberties, I should not hesitate to stand for war. But like a great many other Americans I saw what war was like at first hand in 1917. I know what war can do to demoralize civil liberties at home. And I believe it to be the first duty of a President to try to maintain peace.

But Mr. Roosevelt has not done this. He has dabbled in inflammatory statements and manufactured panics. Of course, we in America like to speak our minds freely, but this does not mean that at a critical period in history our President should cause bitterness and confusion for the sake of a little political oratory. The President's attacks on foreign powers have been useless and dangerous. He has courted a war for which the country is hopelessly unprepared—and which it emphatically does not want. He has secretly meddled in the affairs of Europe, and he has even unscrupulously encouraged other countries to hope for more help than we are able to give.

"Walk softly and carry a big stick" was the motto of Theodore Roosevelt. It is still good American doctrine for 1940. Under the present administration the country has been placed in the false position of shouting insults and not even beginning to prepare to take the consequences.

But while he has thus been quick to tell other nations what they ought to do, Mr. Roosevelt has been slow to take the American people into his confidence. He has hesitated to report facts, to explain situations, or to define realistic objectives. The confusion in the nation's mind has been largely due to this lack of information from the White House.

If I am elected President, I plan to reverse both of these policies. I should threaten foreign governments only when our country was threatened by them and when I was ready to act; and I should consider our diplomacy as part of the people's business concerning which they were entitled to prompt and frank reports to the limit of practicability.

Candor in these times is the hope of democracy. We must not kid ourselves any longer. We must begin to tell ourselves the truth—right here —and right now.

We have been sitting as spectators of a great tragedy. The action on the stage of history has been relentless.

For instance, the French people were just as brave and intelligent as the Germans. Their armies were considered the best in the world. France and her allies won the last war. They possessed all the material resources they needed. They had wealth and reserves of credit all over the earth. Yet the Germans crushed France like an eggshell.

The reason is now clear: The fault lay with France herself.

France believed in the forms of democracy and in the idea of freedom. But she failed to put them to use. She forgot that freedom must be dynamic, that it is forever in the process of creating a new world. This was the lesson that we of America had taught to all countries.

When the European democracies lost that vision, they opened the way to Hitler. While Germany was building a great new productive plant, France became absorbed in unfruitful political adventures and flimsy economy theories. Her government was trying desperately to cover the people's nakedness with a garment that was not big enough.

The free men of France should have been weaving themselves a bigger garment. For in trying to pull the small one around themselves they tore it to pieces.

And in this tragedy let us find our lesson. The foreign policy of the United States begins right here in our own land. The first task of our country in its international affairs is to become strong at home. We must regain prosperity, restore the independence of our people, and protect our defensive forces. If that is not done promptly we are in constant danger. If that is done no enemy on earth dare attack us. I propose to do it.

We must face a brutal, perhaps, a terrible fact. Our way of life is in competition with Hitler's way of life.

This competition is not merely one of armaments. It is a competition of energy against energy, production against production, brains against brains, salesmanship against salesmanship.

In facing it we should have no fear. History shows that our way of life is the stronger way. From it has come more wealth, more industry, more happiness, more human enlightment than from any other way. Free men are the strongest men.

But we cannot just take this historical fact for granted. We must make it live. If we are to outdistance the totalitarian powers, we must arise to a new life of adventure and discovery. We must make a wider horizon for the human race. It is to that new life that I pledge myself.

I promise, by returning to those same American principles that overcame German autocracy once before, both in business and in war, to outdistance Hitler in any contests he choses in 1940 or after. And I promise that when we beat him, we shall beat him on our own terms, in our own American way.

The promises of the present administration cannot lead you to victory against Hitler, or against anyone else. This administration stands for principles exactly opposite to mine. It does not preach the doctrine of growth. It preaches the doctrine of division. We are not asked to make more for ourselves. We are asked to divide among ourselves that which we already have. The New Deal doctrine does not seek risk, it seeks safety. Let us call it the "I pass" doctrine. The New Deal dealt it, and refused to make any more bets on the American future.

Why, that is exactly the course France followed to her destruction! Like the Blum government in France, so has our government become entangled in unfruitful adventures. As in France, so here, we have heard talk of class distinctions and of economic groups preying upon other groups. We are told that capital hates labor and labor capital. We are told that the different kinds of men, whose task it is to build America, are enemies of one another. And I am ashamed to say that some Americans have made political capital of that supposed enmity.

As for me, I want to say here and now that there is no hate in my heart, and that there will be none in my campaign. It is my belief that there is no hate in the hearts of any group of Americans for any other American group—except as the New Dealers seek to put it there for political purposes. I stand for a new companionship in an industrial society.

Of course, if you start like the New Deal with the idea that we shall never have many more automobiles or radios, that we cannot develop many new inventions of importance, that our standard of living must remain what it is, the rest of the argument is easy. Since a few people have more than they need and millions have less than they need, it is necessary to redivide the wealth and turn it back from the few to the many.

But this can only make the poor poorer and the rich less rich. It does not really distribute wealth. It distributes poverty.

Because I am a businessman, formerly connected with a large company, the doctrinaires of the opposition have attacked me as an opponent of liberalism. But I was a liberal before many of these men had heard the word, and I fought for many of the reforms of the elder LaFollette, Theodore Roosevelt, and Woodrow Wilson before another Roosevelt adopted— and distorted—liberalism.

I learned my liberalism right here at home. From the factories that came into this town many years ago, large fortunes were made by a few individuals, who thereby acquired too much power over our community. Those same forces were at work throughout the rest of the nation. By

1929 the concentration of private power had gone further than it should ever go in a democracy.

We all know that such concentration of power must be checked. Thomas Jefferson disliked regulation, yet he said that the prime purpose of government in a democracy is to keep men from injuring each other. We know from our own experience that the less fortunate or less skillful among us must be protected from encroachment. That is why we support what is known as the liberal point of view. That is why we believe in reform.

I believe that the forces of free enterprise must be regulated. I am opposed to business monopolies. I believe in collective bargaining, by representatives of labor's own free choice, without any interference and in full protection of those obvious rights. I believe in the maintenance of minimum standards for wages and of maximum standards for hours. I believe that such standards should constantly improve. I believe in the federal regulation of interstate utilities, of securities markets, and of banking. I believe in federal pensions, in adequate old age benefits, and in unemployment allowances.

I believe that the Federal government has a responsibility to equalize the lot of the farmer, with that of the manufacturer. If this cannot be done by parity of prices, other means must be found—with the least possible regimentation of the farmer's affairs. I believe in the encouragement of cooperative buying and selling, and in the full extension of rural electrification.

The purpose of all such measures is indeed to obtain a better distribution of the wealth and earning power of this country. But I do not base my claim to liberalism solely on my faith in such reforms. American liberalism does not consist merely in reforming things. It consists also in making things.

The ability to grow, the ability to make things, is the measure of man's welfare on this earth. To be free, man must be creative.

I am a liberal because I believe that in our industrial age there is no limit to the productive capacity of any man. And so I believe that there is no limit to the horizon of the United States.

I say that we must substitute for the philosophy of distributed scarcity the philosophy of unlimited productivity. I stand for the restoration of full production and reemployment by private enterprise in America.

And I say that we must henceforth ask certain questions of every reform, and of every law to regulate business or industry. We must ask: Has it encouraged our industries to produce? Has it created new opportunities for our youth? Will it increase our standard of living? Will it encourage us to open up a new and bigger world?

A reform that cannot meet these tests is not a truly liberal reform.

It is an "I pass" reform. It does not tend to strengthen our system, but to weaken it. It exposes us to aggressors, whether economic or military. It encourages class distinctions and hatreds. And it will lead us inevitably, as I believe we are now headed, toward a form of government alien to ours, and a way of life contrary to the way that our parents taught us here in Elwood.

It is from weakness that people reach for dictators and concentrated government power. Only the strong can be free.

And only the productive can be strong.

When the present administration came to power in 1933, we heard a lot about the forgotten man. The Government, we were told, must care for those who had no other means of support. With this proposition all of us agreed. And we still hold firmly to the principle that those whom private industry cannot support must be supported by government agency, whether federal or state.

But I want to ask anyone in this audience who is, or has been, on relief whether the support that the Government gives him is enough. Is it enough for the free and able-bodied American to be given a few scraps of cash or credit with which to keep himself and his children just this side of starvation and nakedness? Is that what the forgotten man wanted us to remember?

What that man wanted us to remember was his chance—his right—to take part in our great American adventure.

But this administration never remembered that. It launched a vitriolic and well-planned attack against those very industries in which the forgotten man wanted a chance.

It carried on a propaganda campaign to convince the people that businessmen are iniquitous.

It seized upon its taxing power for political purposes. It has levied taxes to punish one man, to force another to do what he did not want to do, to take a crack at a third whom some government agency disliked, or to promote the experiments of a brain-trust. The direct effect of the New Deal taxes has been to inhibit opportunity. It has diverted the money of the rich from productive enterprises to government bonds, so that the United States treasury—and no one else—may have plenty to spend. Thus, much of the money of the rich is invested in tax-exempt securities.

In this connection let me say that, in its plan for tax revision, the Republican party will follow two simple principles. Taxes shall be levied in accordance with each one's ability to pay. And the primary purpose of levying them will be to raise money. We must—and can—raise more money at less relative cost to the people. We must do it without inflicting on the poor the present disproportionate load of *hidden* taxes.

The New Deal's attack on business has had inevitable results. The investor has been afraid to invest his capital, and therefore billions of dollars now lie idle in the banks. The businessman has been afraid to expand his operations, and therefore millions of men have been turned away from the employment offices. Low incomes in the cities, and irresponsible experiments in the country, have deprived the farmer of his markets.

For the first time in our history, American industry has remained stationary for a decade. It offers no more jobs today than it did ten years ago—and there are 6,000,000 more persons seeking jobs. As a nation of producers we have become stagnant. Much of our industrial machinery is obsolete. And the national standard of living has declined.

It is a statement of fact, and no longer a political accusation, that the New Deal has failed in its program of economic rehabilitation. And the victims of its failures are the very persons whose cause it professes to champion.

The little business men are victims because their chances are more restricted than ever before.

The farmers are victims because many of them are forced to subsist on what is virtually a dole, under centralized direction from Washington.

The nine or ten million unemployed are victims because their chances for jobs are fewer.

Approximately 6,000,000 families are victims because they are on relief.

And unless we do something about it soon, 130,000,000 people—an entire nation—will become victims, because they stand in need of a defense system which this administration has so far proved itself powerless to create anywhere except on paper.

To accomplish these results, the present administration has spent sixty billion dollars.

And I say there must be something wrong with a theory of government or a theory of economics, by which, after the expenditure of such a fantastic sum, we have less opportunity than we had before.

The New Deal believes, as frequently declared, that the spending of vast sums by the government is a virtue in itself. They tell us that government spending insures recovery. Where is the recovery?

The New Deal stands for doing what has to be done by spending as much money as possible. I propose to do it by spending as little money as possible. This is one great issue in domestic policy and I propose in this campaign to make it clear.

And I make this grave charge against this administration:

I charge that the course this administration is following will lead us, like France, to the end of the road. I say that this course will lead us to economic disintegration and dictatorship.

I say that we must substitute for the philosophy of spending, the philosophy of production. You cannot buy freedom. You must make freedom.

This is a serious charge. It is not made lightly. And it cannot be lightly avoided by the opposition.

I, therefore, have a proposal to make.

The President stated in his acceptance speech that he does not have either "the time or the inclination to engage in purely political debate." I do not want to engage in purely political debate, either. But I believe that the tradition of face to face debate is justly honored among our American political traditions. I believe that we should set an example, at this time, of the workings of American democracy. And I do not think that the issues at stake are "purely political." In my opinion they concern the life and death of democracy.

I propose that during the next two and a half months, the President and I appear together on public platforms in various parts of the country, to debate the fundamental issues of this campaign. These are the problems of our great domestic economy, as well as of our national defense: The problems of agriculture, of labor, of industry, of finance, of the government's relationship to the people, and of our preparations to guard against assault. And also I should like to debate the question of the assumption by this President, in seeking a third term, of a greater public confidence than was accorded to our presidential giants, Washington, Jefferson, Jackson, Lincoln, Cleveland, Theodore Roosevelt, and Woodrow Wilson.

I make this proposal respectfully to a man upon whose shoulders rest the cares of the state. But I make it in dead earnest.

I accept the nomination of the Republican party for President of the United States.

I accept it in the spirit in which I know it was given at our convention in Philadelphia—the spirit of dedication. I herewith dedicate myself with all my heart, with all my mind, and with all my soul to making this nation strong.

But I say this, too. In the pursuit of that goal I shall not lead you down the easy road. If I am chosen the leader of this democracy as I am now of the Republican party, I shall lead you down the road of sacrifice and of service to your country.

What I am saying is a far harsher thing than I should like to say in this speech of acceptance—a far harsher thing than I would have said had the old world not been swept by war during the past year. I am saying to you that we cannot rebuild our American democracy without hardship, without sacrifice, even—without suffering. I am proposing that course to you as a candidate for election by you.

When Winston Churchill became Prime Minister of England a few months ago, he made no sugar-coated promises. "I have nothing to offer you," he said, "but blood, tears, toil, and sweat." Those are harsh words, brave words; yet if England lives, it will be because her people were told the truth and accepted it. Fortunately, in America, we are not reduced to "blood and tears." But we shall not be able to avoid the "toil and sweat."

In these months ahead of us, every man who works in this country—whether he works with his hands or with his mind—will have to work a little harder. Every man and woman will feel the burden of taxes. Every housewife will have to plan a little more carefully. I speak plainly because you must not be deceived about the difficulties of the future. You will have to be hard of muscle, clear of head, brave of heart.

Today great institutions of freedom, for which humanity has spilled so much blood, lie in ruins. In Europe those rights of person and property —the civil liberties—which your ancestors fought for, and which you still enjoy, are virtually extinct. And it is my profound conviction that even here in this country, the Democratic party, under its present leadership, will prove incapable of protecting those liberties of yours.

The Democratic party today stands for division among our people; for the struggle of class against class and faction against faction; for the power of political machines and the exploitation of pressure groups. Liberty does not thrive in such soil.

The only soil in which liberty can grow is that of a united people. We must have faith that the welfare of one is the welfare of all. We must know that the truth can only be reached by the expression of our free opinions, without fear and without rancor. We must acknowledge that all are equal before God and before the law. And we must learn to abhor those disruptive pressures, whether religious, political, or economic, that the enemies of liberty employ.

The Republican party and those associated with it, constitute a great political body that stands preeminently for liberty—without commitments, without fear, and without contradictions. This party believes that your happiness must be achieved through liberty rather than in spite of liberty. We ask you to turn your eyes upon the future, where your hope lies. We see written there the same promise that has always been written there: the promise that strong men will perform strong deeds.

With the help of Almighty Providence, with unyielding determination and ceaseless effort, we must and we shall make that American promise come true.

☆

WENDELL L. WILLKIE

Campaign Speech

ST. LOUIS, MISSOURI

October 17, 1940

I am delighted to be here in St. Louis. I have a very pleasant recollection of my visit here prior to the Republican National Convention. Tonight I want to talk to you upon a subject about which my convictions are very deep and very strong. It is of course true that the people who live on the sea coasts of these United States, on the Atlantic and the Pacific, are closer to the problem of foreign affairs than are the people who live in the interior.

But I am sure the people who live on the sea coasts will agree that policy for the United States cannot be a true policy, it cannot be a realistic policy, unless it gives full expression to the ideals and the hopes of this great American interior.

Here in the valley of the Mississippi we can look outward in our mind's eye, across the Alleghenies to the Atlantic, and across the Rockies to the Pacific. We can see in giant perspective the position of America on this earth. We can see in Europe the advance of bloody armies across nations that were once numbered in the democratic world. We have seen those armies advance across fields where some of our boys lie buried.

And when we turn to the other direction and look out across the Pacific we find that the same insatiate and aggressive dictator that has made a shambles of Europe, has now joined in alliance with Japan, an alliance that seems to be aimed at these United States.

We may perhaps take comfort in the fact that Japan is very far away. And likewise, we may perhaps also take comfort in the recent intimation by the Japanese Foreign Office that the new alliance is not really aimed at these United States. We deeply hope that that is right.

Nevertheless, in the light of the record, we must view that alliance with profound misgivings.

Now, my fellow Americans, this situation has been brewing for a number of years, since the World War as a matter of fact, and perhaps before. But tonight I want to confine my discussion to the last four or five years.

In those four or five years the Administration in Washington has been very active in foreign affairs. It has been active, so it tells us, in promoting the cause of peace. And it has tried to persuade the American people of the wisdom of its foreign policy.

There are some people in America today who admit frankly that this Administration has failed in its most elementary duties at home. They admit frankly that the New Deal has demoralized American industry, created widespread unemployment and brought America to the verge of bankruptcy.

And yet these same persons tell us that this Administration has been so wise and so effective in its foreign policy that it ought to be re-elected for a third term.

Now I am in agreement with some of the basic international objectives of the Administration at the present time. I shall return to those objectives presently, to define them for you.

But I wish to make it plain tonight that I do not think the New Deal has been either wise or effective in foreign affairs. I do not think it has contributed to peace. As a matter of fact, I believe it has contributed to war. And I believe so because of a fundamental misunderstanding, a fundamental failure to understand, the role that America must play among the nations of the earth.

In order to define what I believe to be the proper role of America, the proper function of America, I am now going to quote some passages at considerable length. There were written about America by a European statesman, in my judgment the most courageous and most far-sighted statesman in the world today. I am referring to Winston Churchill, the Prime Minister of England.

Now I want you to listen very carefully to these passages. The first one was written in December of 1937. Now listen very carefully. These are the words of Winston Churchill, not the words of Wendell Willkie, although, when you hear them you will suspect that they were taken from my writing.

"There is one way above all others," said Mr. Churchill "in which the United States can aid the European democracies." Now this was in 1937 he said this. "Let her regain and maintain her prosperity."

"A prosperous United States," he says "exerts an immense beneficent force upon world affairs. A United States, on the other hand, thrown into financial and economic collapse spreads evil far and wide, and weakens France and England just at the time when they have most need to be strong."

Now let me proceed with Winston Churchill.

"The Washington Administration," I'm still quoting Mr. Churchill, "has waged so ruthless a war on private enterprise that the United States . . . is actually . . . leading the world back into the trough of depression. . . .

The effect has been to range the Executive of the United States agencies of the capitalistic system. . . ."

Now mark you, that passage was written in 1937. That is what Winston Churchill thought about what the New Deal had done to its own recovery and to the effect it had had upon the world.

Now let me proceed with Mr. Churchill.

"Even in time of peace," he said, "even in time of peace the economic and financial policy of the United States may exercise an appreciable check upon the war preparations of potential dictators."

That was Winston Churchill in 1937, who said that if the Washington Administration had permitted economic recovery in the United States Hitler would have been checked.

But what did the Washington Administration do? Now please don't take it in the language of Wendell Willkie, take it in the language of Winston Churchill, one year later, namely, in 1938, and again I quote him.

"Economic and financial disorder in the United States," said Mr. Churchill in 1938, "not only depresses all sister countries, but weakens them in those very forces which either mitigate the hatreds of race or provide the means to resist tyranny. The first service which the United States can render the world cause is to become prosperous and also to become well armed."

I'm still quoting Mr. Churchill. Let's see what else he has to say.

"The warfare between big business and the Administration continues at a grievous pace. These great forces do not seem to realize how much they are dependent, one upon another. The President," this is still Winston Churchill, "continues blithely now to disturb, now to console, business and finance. He blows hot, he blows cold, and confidence does not return.

"Immense use is made of the national borrowing power for relieving unemployment which would largely cure itself, if even for a single year the normal conditions of confidence were restored."

Does that sound much different from what Wendell Willkie has been preaching to the American people?

Well, let's see what else this forthright far-sighted statesman said about these United States in 1938.

"Party politics," he goes on, "invade every aspect of our economic life. The authority and prestige which spring from the great armament of a free people may be undermined by financial and political disorder."

Then he utters this hope, which I certainly reutter here tonight:

"But we must hope that other counsels will prevail."

That was what America looked like in 1938 to the stateman beyond the seas. It is not, of course, the carefully decorated picture of American foreign policy that the New Deal has drawn for the American people. But it is a forthright picture drawn by a man on whom has fallen the terrible task of defending the democratic world.

Now I know there are many who believe that the Atlantic and the Pacific Oceans are so broad that Americans need not worry concerning what happens on the other side of them.

Those oceans are indeed broad. We can say with the utmost confidence, standing here in the center of America: We do not want to send our boys over there again. And we do not intend to send them over there again. And if you elect me President we won't.

But by the same token I believe if you re-elect the third-term candidate they will be sent. We cannot and we must not undertake to maintain by arms the peace of Europe.

But, my fellow-Americans, those broad oceans were not intended by their Creator to be barriers. They ought to be broad blue highways of commerce and of trade.

When trade travels across the oceans and the frontiers, a new demand is set up, directly and indirectly, for the products you manufacture here in St. Louis and the crops you grow here in Missouri. That demand, in turn, is created by the purchases of American industry, by the buying of tin and rubber and nickel and other commodities that our industries need.

The role of the United States among the nations is not the settlement of boundary disputes or of racial disputes. It is not the maintenance of a balance of power in Europe. The role of the United States, at least the role it should occupy, the peacetime role, is something far more congenial to our people. It is to create purchasing power and to raise the standard of living, first for ourselves, and as a result of raising it for ourselves, thereby raising the standard of living for others.

That is the aim. When we fail in that aim we weaken the democratic world. During the past several years, since Winston Churchill penned those penetrating lines, we have failed utterly to achieve that aim, and we have seen a great part of the democratic world collapse.

But some say all that is water over the dam. We may perhaps look forward to some future time, under some future Administration, when America may have a chance to play that peacetime role. They say today the world is at war. The New Deal, so these people say, is necessary to the fulfillment of the wartime, not the peacetime, role of the United States.

But I ask, what role is this? What is this role to which the New Deal is indispensable?

Again we are speaking here in the middle of the American continent and as we look across those oceans what do we find standing between us and the decline of our trade and commerce?

What do we find standing between our free enterprise and the totalitarian method of production by slavery?

What do we find standing between our free institutions which we cherish and the barbaric philosophy of slavery to the State?

We find, we find Great Britain. We find the heroic British people standing.

We find those people across the Atlantic. We find them north of us in Canada. We find them remotely, and in smaller numbers, across the Pacific in Australia and in Asia.

As we stand here looking out to the east and to the west we find the British people living on the very rim of our freedom.

So I ask again: What is the role under these circumstances that the United States should play in this war-torn world?

What is this role to which the New Deal says it is so indispensable?

Is it that we should send an expeditionary force over there? Is it that we should join again in a foreign war? Is that the role to which the New Deal thinks itself indispensable? Is that the reason for the provocative statements, the gratuitous insults, the whispers, the rumors that keep coming out of Washington?

I ask the question frankly. I ask it in deadly earnest. Because you and I know that that is not our role.

We cannot send an expeditionary force out to that rim. We have no such force. And even if we had that force it would do no good. It isn't what those people need. It isn't even what they've asked us for.

The reinforcement of that rim of freedom can be accomplished in one way. And only in one way. It can be accomplished only by a thing that the New Deal does not understand, namely, production.

We must produce more, and more, and more. We must produce airplanes. We must produce hundreds of other things. That is our role. That is the role that we must employ to reinforce that rim of freedom.

But, but people of Missouri, when we have reached that resolution, we uncover a terrible fact, a perfectly terrible fact. We have not got those things to send to Great Britain. We haven't even got them for ourselves.

And here is another terrible fact. Here is the worst fact of all: We are not even making those things in any substantial quantity. We are not helping the way we ought to help, the way we must help if we are not to be left utterly alone in this bloody and this barbarous world.

And why is this? Why are we so incapable of doing the very thing that we know we ought to do and for which America has heretofore always been famed for doing?

It is because for the past five years this Administration which knew, which could not help from knowing what was happening in the world, failed utterly and failed completely to grasp the real function of America in a war-torn world.

This Administration failed to see—failed most tragically to see—that the key to war, as well as the key to peace, is America, American production, production.

I have shown on many occasions that this Administration has been aware of the need for adequate defense for nearly five years. It itself said so in January, 1936.

But what was done about it at that time? Our agencies of production were abused, attacked, smothered under a wave of political propaganda.

Our Navy was not built up. Our Army was not modernized. Our arsenals were allowed to sink into decrepitude. Our aircraft industry was not encouraged—we have today only a few hundred modern military planes.

As a result we don't even have the capacity in America to make those things today.

And, as a further result, everything we send to Britain is a sacrifice to our own defense. We must make the awful choice as to whether to supply Britain or ourselves first. We cannot supply either one adequately, much less both.

I have said before that I am in favor of aiding Britain at some sacrifice to our own defense program. But I want to point out here, that it is a sacrifice, and that sacrifice is entirely due to the New Deal's fault.

And worse, much worse, our entire industrial system is demoralized. The expansion of our capacity will be even slower than it would have been had we been producing even on a normal basis.

We do not start this huge task from a normal level. We start it from a depression level and a depression level that the policies of the New Deal have caused.

Therefore, my fellow Americans, I put the proposition to you very, very seriously.

Here is an Administration which has maintained itself in power chiefly by attacking American industry.

Here is an Administration which does not understand industry— which does not understand, which has never studied the most elementary principles of production.

Here is an Administration which, from 1933 through 1937, failed to understand the relationship of America to a world at peace, and from 1937 onward has failed to grasp the relationship of America in a world at war.

Here is an Administration which now—even now—refuses to give adequate power to men who understand production; which insists, which insists upon clearing the entire defense program over the desk of a single man who is seeking to violate one of the most cherished traditions of this Republic, in running for a third term.

Do you seriously believe that this Administration is capable of meeting this crisis, which it has so entirely brought about itself?

Do you seriously believe that it is capable of reinforcing the rim of freedom quickly and effectively?

Do you seriously believe that it can supply America with the indispensable weapons of defense and at the same time send appropriate aid to Great Britain?

Are you confident that it will never send our boys over there, in a desperate and futile effort to cover up its own errors in failing to bring about production?

In the history of the world there has never been such a huge production job. It's the greatest job of production that has ever challenged the imagination of man. It surpasses by far what we attempted at the time of the last World War.

And I can also truthfully say that no Administration in the history of America has ever understood less about the problems and the necessity of production than this one.

Let us not be fooled by scenery. Let us not be fooled by poses and attitudes and clever words. The production of words never saved any man's life in battle.

America has contributed to make this crisis in the world today. And the men responsible for that fact are the men of the third-term party, who are seeking re-election, strange as it may seem, on the international issue.

I am speaking not only to you people of Missouri. I am speaking tonight to millions, from the Pacific to the Atlantic, from Canada to Mexico. I plead with all of you. Let us see America as it really is.

In peacetime America must conduct herself with a consciousness that she is a great economic force in the world. If her actions are irresponsible they are capable of disrupting the economics of the world.

Our role, therefore, in peacetime is to produce, to raise the purchasing power, to lift the standard of living, not alone of ourselves but of others, to lift the standard of living of others who aspire to the democratic way of life.

And our position in wartime is exactly the same. It is still production —production to reinforce the rim of freedom far beyond our borders.

The failure of America to produce, whether in peace or in war, makes havoc of the democratic world.

Let us be very clear about that. The fact that the New Deal stopped the recovery that was coming about in 1937 helped wreck France and England and helped to promote Hitler.

Let us see ourselves as we really are. What happens when we fail in this twofold responsibility of production in peacetime and production in wartime?

What happens when America fails to produce? Why, war happens. Yes, when our instruments and agencies of production fail, war threatens even us.

Alliances are made against us. Threats are flung against us. Our interests are violated. Our neighbors to the south are invaded by the emissaries of dictators to wean them away from us.

War is never the road to peace. Appeasement is not the road to peace. Production is the road to peace and the only road to peace.

Today the emergency is increased by our own dire need for a defense system. Until we can show power with our air force, our Navy, our Army and until we have mobilized industry to supply them, no foreign power that we may devise can be effective.

The primary object of a defense system should be to defend ourselves and to support our neighbor, Canada, to the north and other neighbors to the south. When we make that defense system strong—and only when we make it strong—we can realistically hope for peace in this hemisphere.

More than ever before in history, the American people now hold the fate of other nations in their hands. More than ever before in history, it is for them to mold the shape of things to come.

This shape, this unknown shape, will be born on a single day: on that day next month when the people choose their government for the next four years.

On that day let them not choose a government for which peace is just a word; a government of attitudes and poses, a government whose promises still are, and will remain on order.

Let them choose rather a government that will make peace a reality; a government that will get things done to make them strong. A government that can turn to any dictator and say:

"This is America, and America is on hand."

☆

1944

— ☆ —

On July 11, 1944, one week before the Democratic national convention met in Chicago, President Roosevelt released a letter stating that, as a "good soldier," he would again accept renomination. For just as Roosevelt believed that he had to be elected in 1940 in order to destroy the forces of fascism and preserve freedom, so he was now convinced that he had to be reelected in order to prosecute the war to a victorious conclusion, and, equally important, to help establish a world organization that would maintain peace and democracy.

But the election of 1944 did not promise to produce the landslide victories of years past. Americans had been demonstrating their displeasure with Roosevelt for several years. Farmers were disturbed by agricultural price controls, consumers were dissatisfied with rationing, workers disapproved of wage restrictions. These feelings were manifested in the mid-term elections of 1942, when the Republicans won 47 new seats in the House and 9 in the Senate.

At their convention in Chicago, the Republicans nominated Governor Thomas E. Dewey of New York on their first ballot. After winning a national reputation as an energetic prosecutor, Dewey was elected District Attorney of Manhattan in 1937. Following his defeat by Herbert Lehman in the 1938 gubernatorial election, Dewey sought his party's 1940 presidential nomination. Although he won most of the primaries, the nomination went to Wendell Willkie.

Upon his election as governor of New York in 1942, Dewey promised that he would serve out his full four-year term. As a result of this pledge, he never declared his candidacy; nor did he personally canvas the nation looking for support.

In his acceptance speech Dewey declared that the present administration had already demonstrated its failure to solve the major problems of the Depression, such as employment, and that it had "grown old in office." Conscious of the fact that Roosevelt's position as Commander-in-Chief gave the President a decided advantage in 1944, Dewey focused his attention on domestic issues, although he assured the American people that a change of administration would not affect the conduct of the war. In addition, the Republican platform committed itself to the cause of victory and to America's participation in a postwar organization to maintain world peace.

Dewey faced a difficult challenge in 1944. His campaign strategy called on him to extend himself to independent voters by means of a prudent criticism of the New Deal while, at the same time, accepting most of Roosevelt's social legislation. In one speech, in fact, he called on the government to expand social security and old-age unemployment coverage. This led the *New York Times* to write: "Mr. Dewey just about completed the process of running for the Presidency on the domestic platform of the New Deal."

The Republican candidate lodged his most trenchant criticism against the New Deal in his opening campaign address at Philadelphia. There he held the Democrats responsible for the continuation of the Depression, indicted them for what he labeled their "defeatism," and urged an end to the "most wasteful, extravagant and incompetent Administration in the history of the nation."

While the Democrats were willing to accept F.D.R. for a fourth term and to uphold his policies in their platform, they refused to renominate Vice President Henry Wallace, whose liberalism had estranged many Southerners and big-city bosses. On the second ballot the convention chose Senator Harry S. Truman of Missouri as Roosevelt's running mate.

From San Diego, Roosevelt thanked the convention for the nomination and told them that once again events would compel him to wage a limited campaign. His party's primary responsibility, he stated, would be to win the war, establish the peace, and to reconvert the economy for the returning veterans.

Roosevelt's greatest asset in 1944 was that he was the wartime leader of the Allies and that few Americans were willing to change horses in midstream. These facts, however, did not prevent him from delivering some major campaign speeches. Of the few speeches he did make, his first, delivered on September 23rd before the International Brotherhood of Teamsters in Washington, was unquestionably one of Roosevelt's most politically astute statements. Roosevelt spent several weeks preparing the text, popularly referred to as the "Fala" speech.

In an informal, conversational style, Roosevelt told his audience that the Republican party became conscious of the common man periodically, once every four years. He then called on the American people to allow the Democrats to conclude the war so that peace and comity would become permanent features in international relations.

The speech had a threefold effect: first, it explained Roosevelt's political position; second, it dispelled rumors that he was too ill to serve again; finally, it aroused interest in the election.

FRANKLIN D. ROOSEVELT

Acceptance Speech

RADIO BROADCAST, SAN DIEGO, CALIFORNIA

July 20, 1944

Mr. Chairman, ladies and gentlemen of the convention, my friends:

I have already indicated to you why I accept the nomination that you have offered me in spite of my desire to retire to the quiet of private life.

You in this convention are aware of what I have sought to gain for the nation and you have asked me to continue.

It seems wholly likely that within the next four years our armed forces and those of our allies will have gained a complete victory over Germany and Japan sooner or later, and that the world once more will be at peace under a system, we hope, that will prevent a new World War.

In any event, whenever that times comes, new hands will then have full opportunity to realize the ideals which we seek.

In the last three elections, the people of the United States have transcended party affiliation, not only Democrats but also forward-looking Republicans, and millions of independent voters have turned to progressive leadership, a leadership which has sought consistently and with fair success to advance the average American citizen who had been so forgotten during the period after the last war.

I am confident that they will continue to look to that same kind of liberalism to built our safer economy for the future. I am sure that you will understand me when I say that my decision expressed to you formally tonight is based solely on a sense of obligation to serve if called upon to do so by the people of the United States.

I shall not campaign, in the usual sense, for the office. In these days of tragic sorrow, I do not consider it fitting and, besides, in these days of global warfare, I shall not be able to find the time. I shall, however, feel free to report to the people the facts about matters of concern to them and, especially, to correct any misrepresentation.

During the past few days, I have been going across the whole width of the continent to a naval base, where I am speaking to you now from the train. As I was crossing the fertile lands and the wide plains and the Great Divide, I could not fail to think of the new relationship between the people of our farms and cities and villages and the people of the rest of the world overseas, on the islands of the Pacific, in the Far East, in the outer Americas, in Britain and Normandy and Germany and Poland and Russia itself.

For Oklahoma, Louisiana and California farmers are becoming a part of all these distant spots, as greatly as Massachusetts and Virginia were a part of the European picture in 1778. Today, Oklahoma and California are being defended in Normandy and Saipan, and that vitally affects the security and the well-being of every human being in Oklahoma and California.

Mankind changes the scope and the breadth of its thought and vision slowly indeed. In the days of the Roman Empire, eyes were focused on Europe, on the Mediterranean area. The civilization in the Far East was barely known of. The American continents were unheard of, and even after the people of Europe began to spill over to these continents, the people of North America in colonial days knew only their Atlantic seaboard and a tiny portion of the other Americas, and they turned mostly for trade and international relationships to Europe.

Africa at that time was considered only as the provider of human chattels. Asia was essentially unknown to our ancestors.

During the ninetenth century, during that era of development and expansion on this continent, we felt a national isolation, geographic, economic and political, an isolation from the vast world which lay overseas. Not until this generation, roughly this century, people here and elsewhere were compelled more and more to widen the orbit of their vision to include every part of the world.

Yes, it has been a wrench, perhaps, but a very necessary one. It is good that we are all getting that broader vision, for we shall need it after the war. The isolationists and the ostriches who plagued our thinking before Pearl Harbor are becoming slowly extinct.

The people of America now know that all nations of the world, large and small, will have to play their appropriate part in keeping the peace by force, and in deciding peacefully the disputes which might lead to war.

We all know how truly the world has become one, that if Germany and Japan, for example, were to come through this war with their philosophies established and their armies intact, our own grandchildren would again have to be fighting in their day for their liberties and their lives.

Some day soon, we shall all be able to fly to any other part of the world within twenty-four hours. Oceans will no longer figure as greatly in our physical defense as they have in the past for our own safety and for our own economic good. Therefore, if for no other reason, we must take a leading part in the maintenance of peace and in the increase of trade among all nations of the world.

And that is why your Government for many, many months has been laying plans and studying the problems of the near future, preparing itself to act so that the people of the United States may not suffer hardships after the war, may continue constantly to improve its standards and may join with other nations in doing the same.

There are even now working toward that end the best staff in all our history, men and women of all parties and from every part of the nation. I realize that "planning" is a word which in some places brings forth sneers, but, frankly, before our entry into the war, it was planning which made possible the magnificent organization and the equipment of the Army and Navy of the United States which are fighting for us and for our salvation today.

Improvement through planning is of necessity the order of the day. Even in military affairs things do not stand still. An army or a navy trained and equipped and fighting according to a 1932 model would not have been a safe reliance in 1944. And, if we are to progress in our civilization, improvement is necessary in other fields, in the physical things that are a part of our daily lives, and in the concepts of social justice at home and abroad.

I am now at this naval base in the performance of my duty under the Constitution. The war waits for no elections. Decisions must be made, plans must be laid, strategy must be carried out. They do not concern merely a party or a group. They will affect the daily lives of Americans for generations to come.

What is the job before us in 1944? First, to win the war, to win the war fast, and to win it overpoweringly.

Second, to form world-wide international organizations and to arrange to use the armed force of the sovereign nations of the world to make another war impossible within the foreseeable future.

Third, to build an economy for our returning veterans and for all

Americans which will provide employment and provide decent standards of living.

The people of the United States will decide this fall whether they wish to turn over this 1944 job, this world-wide job, to inexperienced or immature hands, to those who opposed Lend-Lease and international cooperation against the forces of aggression and tryanny until they could read the polls of popular sentiment, or whether they wish to leave it to those who saw the danger from abroad, who met it head-on, and who now have seized the offensive and carried the war to its present stages of success, to those who by international conferences and united actions have begun to build that kind of common understanding and cooperative experience which will be so necessary in the world to come.

They will also decide, these people of ours, whether they will entrust the task of postwar reconversion to those who offered the veterans of the last war bread lines and apple selling, and who finally led the American people down to the abyss of 1932, or whether they will leave it to those who rescued American business and agriculture and industry and finance and labor in 1933, and who have already planned and put through much legislation to help our veterans resume their normal occupation in a well-ordered, reconversioned process.

They will not decide these questions by reading glowing words or platform pledges. The mouthings of those who are willing to promise anything and everything, contradictions, inconsistencies, impossibilities, anything which might snare a few votes here and a few votes there.

They will decide on the record, the record written on the seas, on the land, in the skies. They will decide on the record of our domestic accomplishments in recovery and reform since March 4, 1933, and they will decide on the record of our war production and food production, unparalleled in all history, in spite of the sneers of those in high places who said, "It can't be done."

They will decide on the record of the International Food Conferences of UNRRA, the relief organization of the International Labor Conference, of the International Education Conference, of the International Monetary Conference, and they will decide on the record written in the Atlantic Charter, at Casablanca, at Cairo, at Moscow, at Teheran.

We have made mistakes—who has not? Things have not always been perfect. Are they ever perfect in human affairs?

But the objective, the objective at home and abroad, has always been clear before us. Constantly we have made steady, sure progress toward that objective. The record is plain and unmistakable as to that, a record for everyone to read.

☆

FRANKLIN D. ROOSEVELT

Campaign Speech

WASHINGTON, D. C.

September 23, 1944

Mr. Tobin—I should say Dan, I always have—Ladies and Gentlemen:

I am very much touched and I am very happy in your applause, and very happy at the informality of this dinner with old friends of mine.

You know, though, this is not the first time that we have met together on this basis and I am particularly happy that this national campaign opens in your presence as it did four years ago. And I don't mind mentioning the fact that Dan Tobin and I are just a little bit superstitious.

Well, here we are, here we are again after four years—and what years they have been!

You know I am actually four years older—which is a fact that seems to annoy some people. In fact, in the mathematical field there are millions of Americans who are more than eleven years older than when we started in to clear up the mess that was dumped into our laps in 1933.

We all know that certain people will make it a practice to depreciate the accomplishments of labor—who even attack labor as unpatriotic.

They keep this business up usually for three years and six months in a row. But then, for some strange reason, they change their tune—every four years—just before election day.

When votes are at stake they suddenly discover that they really love labor, and that they are anxious to protect labor from its old friends.

I got quite a laugh, for example—and I am sure that you did—when I read this plank in the Republican platform adopted at their National Convention last July:

"The Republican party accepts the purposes of the National Labor Relations Act, the Wage and Hour Act, the Social Security Act, and all other Federal statutes designed to promote and protect the welfare of American working men and women, and we promise a fair and just administration of those laws."

You know many of the Republican leaders and Congressmen and candidates who shouted enthusiastic approval of that plank in that convention hall would not even recognize these progressive laws if they met them in broad daylight. Indeed, they have personally spent years of effort and energy—and much money—in fighting every one of those laws in Congress, and in the press, and in the courts, ever since this Administration began to advocate them and enact them into legislation.

This is a fair example of their insincerity and of their inconsistency.

The whole purpose of Republican oratory these days seems to be to switch labels. The object is to persuade the American people that the Democratic party was responsible for the 1929 crash and the depression and that the Republican party was responsible for all social progress under the New Deal.

Now, imitation may be the sincerest form of flattery—but I am afraid, I am afraid, that in this case it is the most obvious common or garden variety of fraud. .

For it is perfectly true that there are enlightened, liberal elements in the Republican party, and they have fought hard and honorably to bring the party up to date and to get it in step with the forward march of the American progress. But these liberal elements were not able to drive the Old Guard Republicans from their entrenched positions.

Can the Old Guard pass itself off as the New Deal?

I think not.

We have seen many marvelous stunts in the circus, but no performing elephant could turn a hand-spring without falling flat on its back.

I need not recount to you the centuries of history that have been crowded into these four years since I saw you last.

There were some—in the Congress and out—who raised their voices against our preparations for defense—before and after 1939—objected to them, raised their voices against them as hysterical warmongering, who cried out against our help to the Allies as provocative and dangerous.

We remember those voices.

They would like to have us forget them now. But in 1940 and 1939 (my it seems a long time ago) they were loud voices. Happily they were in the minority and—fortunately for ourselves, and for the world—they could not stop America.

There are some politicians who kept their heads buried in the sand while the storms of Europe and Asia were headed our way, who said that the Lend-Lease Bill "would bring an end" (and I am quoting) "to free government in the United States," and who said (and I am quoting) "only hysteria entertains the idea that Germany, Italy or Japan contemplate war on us."

These men, these very men are now asking the American people to entrust to them the conduct of our foreign policy and our military policy.

What the Republican leaders are now saying in effect is this: "Oh, just forget what we used to say, we've changed our minds now—we have been reading the public opinion polls about these things, and now we know what the American people want."

And they say, "Don't leave the task of making the peace to those old men who first urged it, and who have laid already the foundations for it, and who have had to fight all of us, inch by inch, during the last five years to do it. Why, just turn it all over to us. We'll do it so skillfully that we won't lose a single isolationist vote or a single isolationist campaign contribution."

I think there is one thing that you know. I am too old for that. I cannot talk out of both sides of my mouth at the same time.

The Government of the United States welcomes all sincere supporters of the cause of effective world collaboration in the making of a lasting peace. Millions of Republicans all over the nation are with us—and have been with us in our unshakable determination to build the solid structure of peace. And they, too, will resent this campaign talk by those who first woke up to the facts of international life a few short months ago—when they began to study the polls of public opinion.

Those who today have the military responsibility for waging this war in all parts of the globe are not helped by the statements of men who, without responsibility and without the knowledge of the facts, lecture the chiefs of staff of the United States as to the best means of dividing our armed forces and our military resources between the Atlantic and the Pacific, between the Army and the Navy and among the commanding generals of the different theatres of war. And I may say that the commanding generals are making good in a big way.

When I addressed you four years ago I said this, I said: "I know that America will never be disappointed in its expectations that labor will always continue to do its share of the job, the job we now face, and do it patriotically and effectively and unselfishly."

Today we know that America has not been disappointed. In his order of the day when the Allied armies first landed in Normandy, two months ago, General Eisenhower said, "Our home fronts have given us overwhelming superiority in weapons and munitions of war."

The country knows that there is a breed, luckily enough innumerous, called labor baiters. I know that those labor baiters among the opposition who are there, but who, instead of calling attention to the achievements of labor in this war, prefer to pick on the occasional strikes that have occurred—strikes that have been condemned by every responsible national labor leader. I ought to say, parenthetically, all but one. And that, and that one labor leader, incidentally, is not conspicuous among my supporters.

Labor baiters forget that, at our peak, American labor and management have turned out airplanes at the rate of 109,000 a year; tanks—57,000 a year; combat vessels—573 a year; landing vessels to get the troops ashore —51,000 a year; cargo ships—19,000,000 tons a year. (Henry Kaiser is here tonight, I am glad to say.) And small arms ammunition—oh, I can't understand it, don't believe you can either—23 billion rounds a year.

But a strike is news, and generally appears in shrieking headlines— and, of course, they say labor is always to blame.

The fact is that, since Pearl Harbor, only one-tenth of one percent of manhours have been lost by strikes. Can you beat that! But you know even those candidates who burst out in election-year, election-year affection for social legislation and for labor in general, still think that you ought to be good boys and stay out of politics. And above all, they hate to see any working man or woman contribute a dollar bill to any wicked political party.

Of course, it's all right for the large financiers and industrialists and monopolists to contribute tens of thousands of dollars—but their solicitude for that dollar which the men and women in the ranks of labor contribute is always very touching.

They are, of course, perfectly willing to let you vote—unless you happen to be a soldier, or a sailor overseas, or a merchant seaman carrying the munitions of war. In that case, they have made it pretty hard for you to vote at all—for there are some political candidates who think that they may have a chance of election if only the total vote is small enough.

And while I am on the subject of voting let me urge every American citizen—man or woman—to use your sacred privilege of voting, no matter which candidate you expect to support. Our millions of soldiers and sailors and merchant seamen have been handicapped or prevented from voting by those politicians—prevented from voting by those politicians and those candidates who think that they stand to lose by such votes. You here at home have the freedom of the ballot. Irrespective of party you should register and vote this November. I think that is a matter of plain good citizenship.

Words come easily, but they do not change the record. You are, most of you, old enough to remember what things were like for labor in 1932.

You remember the closed banks and the breadlines and the starvation wages; the foreclosures of homes and farms, and the bankruptcies of business; the "Hoovervilles," and the young men and women of the nation facing a hopeless, jobless future; the closed factories and mines and mills; the ruined and abandoned farms; the stalled railroads; the empty docks; the blank despair of a whole nation—and the utter impotence of the Federal Government.

You remember the long hard road, with its gains and its setbacks, which we have traveled together ever since those days.

Now there are some politicians, of course, who do not remember that far back, and there are some who remember but find it convenient to forget. No, the record is not to be washed away that easily.

The opposition in this year has already imported into this campaign a very interesting thing because it's foreign—they have imported the propaganda technique invented by the dictators abroad. Remember a number of years ago there was a book, *Mein Kampf*. Written by Hitler himself. The technique was all set out in Hitler's book—and it was copied by the aggressors of Italy and Japan. According to that technique, you should never use a small falsehood; always a big one, for its very fantastic nature would make it more credible—if only you keep repeating it over and over and over again.

Well, let's take some simple illustrations that come to mind. For example, although I rubbed my eyes when I read it, we have been told that it was not a Republican depression, but a Democratic depression from which this nation was saved in 1933. That this Administration—this one today—is responsible for all the suffering and misery that the history books and the American people have always thought had been brought about during the twelve ill-fated years when the Republican party was in power.

Now, there is an old and somewhat lugubrious adage which says: "Never speak of a rope in the house of a man who's been hanged." In the same way, if I were a Republican leader speaking to a mixed audience, the last word in the whole dictionary that I would think of using is that word "depression." You know they pop up all the time.

For another example, I learned much to my amazement—that the policy of this Administration was to keep men in the Army when the war is over because there might be no jobs for them in civil life.

Well, the very day that this fantastic charge was first made a formal plan for the method of speedy discharge from the Army had already been announced by the War Department—a plan based on the wishes of the soldiers themselves.

This callous and brazen falsehood about demobilization was—of course, a very simple thing it was—an effort to stimulate fear among American mothers and wives and sweethearts. And, incidentally, it was hardly calculated to bolster the morale of our soldiers and sailors and airmen who are fighting our battles all over the world.

But perhaps the most ridiculous of these campaign falsifications is the one that this Administration failed to prepare for the war that was coming. I doubt whether even Goebbels would have tried that one.

For even he would never have dared hope that the voters of America had already forgotten that many of the Republican leaders in the Congress and outside the Congress tried to thwart and block nearly every attempt that this Administration made to warn our people and arm our nation.

Some of them called our 50,000-airplane program fantastic. Many of those very same leaders who fought every defense measure that we proposed are still in control of the Republican party—look at the names— were in control of its national convention in Chicago and would be in control of the machinery of the Congress and of the Republican party in the event of a Republican victory this fall.

These Republican leaders have not been content with attacks on me, or on my wife, or on my sons—no, not content with that, they now include my little dog, Fala. Well, of course, I don't resent attacks and my family don't resent attacks, but Fala does resent them. You know, you know Fala's Scotch and, being a Scottie, as soon as he learned that the Republican fiction writers in Congress and out had concocted a story that I had left him behind on an Aleutian island and had sent a destroyer back to find him—at a cost to the taxpayers of two or three or eight or twenty million dollars—his Scotch soul was furious. He has not been the same dog since.

I am accustomed to hearing malicious falsehoods about myself—such as that old, worm-eaten chestnut that I have represented myself as indispensable. But I think I have a right to resent, to object to libelous statements about my dog.

Well, I think we all recognize the old technique. The people of this country know the past too well to be deceived into forgetting. Too much is at stake to forget. There are tasks ahead of us which we must now complete with the same will, the same skill and intelligence and devotion that have already led us so far along the road to victory.

There is the task of finishing victoriously this most terrible of all wars as speedily as possible and with the least cost on lives.

There is the task of setting up international machinery to assure that peace, once established, will not again be broken.

And there is the task that we face here at home—the task of reconverting our economy for the purposes of war from the purposes of war to the purposes of peace.

These peace-building tasks were faced once before, nearly a generation ago. They were botched—b-o-t-c-h-ed—they were botched by a Republican Administration. That must not happen this time. We will not let it happen this time.

And, fortunately, we do not begin from scratch. Much has been done. Much more is under way. The fruits of victory this time will not be apples sold on street corners.

Many months ago, many months ago the Administration set up necessary machinery for an orderly peacetime mobilization, demobilization. The Congress has passed much more legislation continuing the agencies needed for demobilization—with additional powers to carry out their functions.

I know that the American people—business and labor and agriculture —have the same will, basic will, to do for peace what they have done for war. And I know that they can sustain a national income that will assure full production and full employment under our democratic system of private enterprise, with Government encouragement and aid whenever and wherever that is necessary.

The keynote back of all this literature that we read, the keynote of all that we propose to do in reconversion can be found in the one word— "jobs."

We shall lease or dispose of our Government-owned plants and facilities and our surplus war property and land on the basis of how they can be best operated by private enterprise to give jobs to the greatest number.

We shall follow a wage policy that will sustain the purchasing power of labor—for that means more production and more jobs. You and I know that the present policies on wages and prices were conceived to serve the need of the great masses of the people. They stopped inflation. They kept prices on a relatively stable level. Through the demobilization period policies will be carried out with the same objective in mind—to serve the needs of the great masses of the people.

This is not the time in which men can be forgotten as they were in the Republican catastrophe that we inherited. The returning soldiers, the workers by their machines, the farmers in the field, the miners, the men and women in offices and shops, do not intend to be forgotten.

No, they know that they are not surplus. Because they know that they are America.

We must set targets and objectives for the future which will seem impossible, like the airplane, to those who live in and are weighted down by the dead past.

And for months, and today and in the future we are organizing and will continue to put forth the logistics of the peace just as Marshall and King and Arnold, MacArthur, Eisenhower and Nimitz are organizing these logistics of this war.

I think that the victory of the American people and their Allies in this war will be far more than a victory against Fascism and reaction and the dead hand of despotism of the past. The victory of the American people and their Allies in this war will be a victory for democracy. It will constitute such an affirmation of the strength and power and vitality of government by the people as history has never before witnessed.

And so, my friends, with that affirmation of the vitality of democratic government behind us, that demonstration of its resilience and its capacity for decision and for action—with that knowledge of our own strength and power—we move forward with God's help to the greatest epoch of free achievement by free men that the world has ever known.

☆

THOMAS E. DEWEY

Acceptance Speech

CHICAGO, ILLINOIS

June 28, 1944

Mr. Chairman and fellow Americans:

I am profoundly moved by the trust you have placed in me. I deeply feel the responsibility which goes with your nomination for President of the United States at this grave hour of our nation's history.

That I have not sought this responsibility, all of you know. I told the people of my State, two years ago, that it was my intention to devote my full term as governor exclusively to their service. You have decided otherwise. In accordance with the principles of our republican form of government you have laid upon me the highest duty to which an American can be called. No one has a right to refuse such a call. With the help of God, I will try to be worthy of the trust. I accept the nomination.

I am happy and proud to be associated with my good friend from the State of Ohio, John W. Bricker. For many months, John Bricker has gone from state to state telling the people of the issues, of the great need for better government, for the sound principles of government, and the leadership which will come to it with a Republican victory this year. Never before have I seen such good sportsmenship as that displayed by John Bricker here this morning and I am proud to be associated with him.

I come to this great task a free man. I have made no pledges, promises or commitments, expressed or implied, to any man or woman. I shall make none, except to the American people.

These pledges I do make:

To men and women of the Republican Party everywhere I pledge my utmost efforts in the months ahead. In return, I ask for your support. Without it, I cannot discharge the heavy obligation you lay upon me.

To Americans of every party I pledge that on Jan. 20 next year our government will again have a cabinet of the ablest men and women to be found in America. The members of that Cabinet will expect and will receive full delegation of the powers of their office. They will be capable of administering those powers. They will each be experienced in the task to be done and young enough to do it. This election will bring an end to one-man government in America.

To Americans of every party I pledge a campaign dedicated to one and above all others—that this nation under God may continue in the years ahead a free nation of free men.

At this moment on battlegrounds around the world Americans are dying for the freedom of our country. Their comrades are pressing on in the face of hardship and suffering. They are pressing on for total victory and for the liberties of all of us.

Everything we say or do today and in the future must be devoted to the single purpose of that victory. Then, when victory is won, we must devote ourselves with equal unity of purpose to re-winning at home the freedom they have won at such desperate cost abroad.

To our allies let us send from this convention one message from our hearts: The American people are united with you to the limit of our resources and manpower, devoted to the single task of victory and the establishment of a firm and lasting peace.

To every member of the axis powers, let us send this message from this Convention: By this political campaign, which you are unable to understand, our will to victory will be strengthened, and with every day you further delay surrender the consequences to you will be more severe.

That we shall win this war none of us and few of our enemies can now have any doubt. But how we win this war is of major importance for the years ahead. We won the last war but it didn't stay won. This time we must also win the purposes for which we are fighting. Germany must never again nourish the delusion that she could have won. We must carry to Japan a defeat so crushing and complete that every last man among them knows that he has been beaten. We must not merely defeat the armies and the navies of our enemies. We must defeat, once and for all, their will to make war. In their hearts as well as with their lips, let them be taught to say: "Never again."

The military conduct of the war is outside this campaign. It is and must remain completely out of politics. General Marshall and Admiral King are doing a superb job. Thank God for both of them. Let me make it crystal clear that a change of administration next January cannot and will not involve any change in the military conduct of the war. If there is not now any civilian interference with the military and naval commands, a change in administration will not alter this status. If there is civilian interference, the new administration will put a stop to it forthwith.

But the war is being fought on the home front as well as abroad, while all of us are deeply proud of the military conduct of the war, can we honestly say that the home front could not bear improvement? The present administration in Washington has been in office for more than 11 years. Today, it is at war with Congress, and at war with itself. Squabbles between Cabinet members, feuds between rival bureaucrats and bitterness between the President and his own party members, in and out of Congress, have become the order of the day. In the vital matters of taxation, price control, rationing, labor relations, manpower, we have become familiar with the spectacle of wrangling, bungling and confusion.

Does anyone suggest that the present national administration is giving either efficient or competent government? We have not heard that claim made, even by its most fanatical supporters. No, all they tell us is that in its young days it did some good things. That we freely grant. But now it has grown old in office. It has become tired and quarrelsome. It seems that the great men who founded this nation really did know what they were talking about when they said that three terms were too many.

When we have won the war, we shall still have to win the peace. We are agreed, all of us, that America will participate with other sovereign nations in a cooperative effort to prevent future wars. Let us face up boldly to the magnitude of that task. We shall not make secure the peace of the world by mere words. We can't do it simply by drawing up a fine-sounding treaty. It can not be the work of any one man or of a little group of rulers who meet together in private conferences. The structure of peace must be built. It must be the work of many men. We must have as our representatives in this task the ablest men and women America can produce, and the structure they join in building must rest upon the solid rock of a united American public opinion.

I am not one of those who despair of achieving that end. I am utterly confident we can do it. For years, we have had men in Washington who were notoriously weak in certain branches of arithmetic but they specialized in division. They've been playing up minor differences of opinion among our people until the people of other countries might have thought that America was cleft in two.

But all the while there was a larger, growing area of agreement. Recently the overwhelming majesty of that broad area of agreement has become obvious. The Republican Party can take pride in helping to define it and broaden it. There are only a few, a very few, who really believe that America should try to remain aloof from the world. There are only a relatively few who believe it would be practical for America or her allies to renounce all sovereignty and join a Super-state. I certainly would not deny these two extremes the right to their opinions; but I stand firmly with the overwhelming majority of my fellow citizens in that great wide area of agreement. That agreement was clearly expressed by the Republican Mackinac Declaration and was adopted in the foreign policy plank of this Convention.

No organization for peace will last if it is slipped through by stealth or trickery or the momentary hypnotism of high-sounding phrases. We shall have to work and pray and be patient and make sacrifices to achieve a really lasting peace. That is not too much to ask in the name of those who have died for the future of our country. This is no task for men who specialize in dividing our people. It is no task to be entrusted to stubborn men, grown old and tired and quarrelsome in office. We learned that in 1919.

The building of the peace is more than a matter of international co-operation. God has endowed America with such blessings as to fit her for a great role in the world. We can only play that role if we are strong and healthy and vigorous as nature has equipped us to be. It would be a tragedy if after this war Americans returned from our armed forces and failed to find the freedom and opportunity for which they fought. This must be a land where every man and woman has a fair chance to work and get ahead. Never again must free Americans face the spectre of long-continued, mass unemployment. We Republicans are agreed that full employment shall be a first objective of national policy. And by full employment I mean a real chance for every man and woman to earn a decent living.

What hope does the present administration offer here? In 1940, the year before this country entered the war, there were still 10,000,000 unemployed. After seven years of unequalled power and unparalleled spending, the New Deal had failed utterly to solve that problem. It never solved that problem. It was left to be solved by war. Do we have to have a war to get jobs?

What are we now offered? Only the dreary prospect of a continued war economy after the war, with interference piled on interference and petty tyrannies rivaling the very regimentation against which we are now at war.

The present administration has never solved this fundamental problem of jobs and opportunity. It can never solve this problem. It has never even understood what makes a job. It has never been for full production. It has lived in chattering fear of abundance. It has specialized in curtailment and restriction. It has been consistently hostile to and abusive of American business and American industry, although it is in business and industry that most of us make our living.

In all the record of the past 11 years is there anything that suggests the present administration can bring about high-level employment after this war? Is there any reason to believe that those who have so signally failed in the past can succeed in the future? The problem of jobs will not be easily solved; but it will never be solved at all unless we get a new, progressive administration in Washington—and that means a Republican administration.

For one hundred and fifty years America was the hope of the world. Here on this great broad continent we had brought into being something for which men had longed throughout all history. Here, all men were held to be free and equal. Here, government derived its just powers from the consent of the governed. Here men believd passionately in freedom, independence—the God-given right of the individual to be his own master. Yet, with all of this freedom—I insist—because of this freedom—ours was a land of plenty. In a fashion unequalled anywhere else in the world, America grew and strengthened; our standard of living became the envy of the world. In all lands, men and women looked toward America as the pattern of what they, themselves, desired. And because we were what we were, good will flowed toward us from all corners of the earth. An American was welcomed everywhere and looked upon with admiration and regard.

At times, we had our troubles; made our share of mistakes; but we faltered only to go forward with renewed vigor. It remained for the past eleven years, under the present national administration, for continuing unemployment to be accepted with resignation as the inevitable condition of a nation past its prime.

It is the New Deal which tells us that America has lost its capacity to grow. We shall never build a better world by listening to those counsels of defeat. Is America old and worn out as the New Dealers tell us? Look to the beaches of Normandy for the answer. Look to the reaches of the wide Pacific—to the corners of the world where American men are fighting. Look to the marvels of production in the war plants in our own cities and towns. I say to you: our country is just fighting its way through to new horizons. The future of America has no limit.

True, we now pass through dark and troubled times, scarcely a home escapes the touch of dread anxiety and grief; yet in this hour the American spirit rises, faith returns—faith in our God, faith in our fellowman, faith in the land our fathers died to win, faith in the future, limitless and bright, of this, our country.

In the name of that faith we shall carry our cause in the coming months to the American people.

☆

THOMAS E. DEWEY

Campaign Speech

PHILADELPHIA, PENNSYLVANIA

September 7, 1944

Governor Martin, Governor Edge, fellow Americans:

Tonight we open a campaign to decide the course of our country for many years to come. The next national Administration will take office Jan. 20, 1945, and will serve until 1949. Those years, 1945 to 1949, will be largely—and we pray wholly—peacetime years.

For nearly three years our nation has been engaged in a world war. Today our armed forces are winning victory after victory. Total, smashing victory is in sight. Germany and Japan shall be given the lessons of their lives—right in Berlin and Tokyo.

America—our America which loves peace so dearly—is proving once again that it can wage war mightily. That it can crush any aggressor who threatens the freedom which we love even more than peace. The American people have risen to the challenge. The war is being won on the battlefronts. It is also being won in the factory, the office, the farm, the mine and the home.

Yes, we are proving that we can wage war. But what are the prospects of success as a nation at peace? The answer depends entirely on the outcome of this election.

At the very outset I want to make one thing clear. This is not merely a campaign against an individual or a political party. It is not merely a campaign to displace a tired, exhausted, quarreling and bickering Administration with a fresh and vigorous Administration.

This is a campaign against an Administration which was conceived in defeatism, which failed for eight straight years to restore our domestic economy, which has been the most wasteful, extravagant and incompetent Administration in the history of the nation and, worst of all, one which has lost faith in itself and in the American people.

This basic issue was clearly revealed in the recent announcement by the Director of Selective Service in Washington. He said that when Germany and Japan have been defeated it will still be necessary to demobilize the armed forces very gradually. And why? Because, he said, "We can keep people in the Army about as cheaply as we could create an agency for them when they are out."

Let me repeat that. He said we can keep people in the Army about as cheaply as we could create an agency for them when they are out.

For six months we have been hearing statements from the New Deal underlings in Washington that this was the plan. Now it is out in the open. They have been working up to it. Because they are afraid of peace. They are afraid of a continuance of their own failures to get this country going again. They are afraid of America.

I do not share that fear. I believe that our members of the armed forces should be transported home and released at the earliest moment practicable after victory. I believe that the occupation of Germany and Japan should very soon be confined to those who voluntarily choose to remain in the Army when peace comes. I am not afraid of the future of America—either immediate or distant. I am sure of our future, if we get a National Administration which believes in the United States of America.

The New Deal was founded on the philosophy that our frontiers are behind us and that all we have left to do is to quarrel among ourselves over the division of what we have. Mr. Roosevelt himself said in 1932:

"Our industrial plant is built . . . our task is not . . . necessarily producing more goods. It is the soberer, less dramatic business of administering resources and plants already in hand."

The New Deal operated on that philosophy for seven straight peacetime years with unlimited power and unlimited money. At the end of that time, in 1939, the New Deal gave its own official verdict on its failure by this cold admission: "The American economic machine is stalled on dead center."

The Administration knows that the war, with all its tragic toll of death, debt and destruction, is the only thing that saved it. They are deadly afraid that they will go back to resumption of their own failures. That is why they are afraid to let men out of the Army. That is why they say it is cheaper to keep men in the Army than to let them come home when peace has been won.

Now let us get another point straight for the records right here at the beginning. In the last hundred years we have had eleven periods during which business and employment were well below normal. During that period the average depression lasted two years. In the entire hundred years the longest depression of all was five years and the next longest was four years—up to the last one.

When this Administration took office the depression was already over three years old. Then what happened? In 1934, when the depression was then five years old—that's longer than any other depression in a whole century, we still had 12,000,000 unemployed in America. By 1940 the depression was almost eleven years old. This Administration had been in power for more than seven straight years and there were still 10,000,000 Americans unemployed.

It took a world war to get jobs for the American people.

Let's get one thing clear and settled. Who was President of the United States during the depression that lasted from 1933 until some time in 1940, when war orders from all over the world began to bring us full employment again? It was the New Deal that kept this country in a continuous state of depression for seven straight years. They lived on a depression. It was the New Deal that made, that managed to make a three-year depression last eleven straight years—over twice as long as any other depression in a whole century.

And now Washington is getting all set for another depression. They intend to keep the young men in the Army. The New Deal spokesmen are daily announcing that reconversion will be difficult, if not impossible. They say that relief rolls will be enormous. They drearily promise us that we shall need to prepare for an army of unemployed bigger than the armies we have put in the field against the Germans and the Japanese. That's what's wrong with the New Deal. That's why it's time for a change.

The reason for this long continued failure is twofold. First, because there never was a worse job of running the Government of this country in all its history. When one agency fails, the New Deal just piles another one on and we pay for both. When both fail they invent a third and we pay for all three. When men quarrel, there isn't anybody to put a stop to it in our Government. When agencies get snarled up there is no one in authority to unsnarl them. Meanwhile, the people's business goes to pot and the people are the victims.

Right in the final crisis of this war, the most critical of all war agencies —the War Production Board—fell apart right before our eyes. This is also the board, and don't forget it, this is also the board in charge of reconversion and jobs. Yet we have seen quarreling, disunity and public recriminations day after day, as one competent man after another resigned and the head of the board was sent to China. This isn't a new experience; others have been sent to China. And we have seen this very thing happen to agency after agency. The cost of the war effort, to the country, can never be calculated. And it's time the people put an end to it, because no one else will.

When the WPB fell apart, so did your chance under this Administration for jobs after this war is over. For now the New Dealers have moved in, and their handiwork, their promise for America has never been jobs—but the dole.

The other reason for this long continued failure—the reason why they are now dismally preparing for another depression—is because this Administration has so little faith in the United States. They believe in the defeatist philosophy that our industrial plant is built, that our task is not to produce more goods but to fight among ourselves over what we have.

I believe that we have not even begun to build our industrial plant. We have not exhausted our inventive genius. We have not exhausted our capacity to produce more goods for our people. No living man has yet dreamed of the limit to which we can go if we have a Government which believes in the American economic system and in the American people.

This Administration is convinced that only, only by surrendering a little bit of freedom for every little bit of security can we achieve social security. That is exactly what our enemies thought. So their people first lost their freedom and then they lost their security. I cannot accept that course for America. I believe—I know—that if we achieve real social security, we can achieve it only if we do keep our freedom.

There can be—there must be—jobs and opportunity for all, without discrimination on account of race, creed, color or national origin. There must be jobs in industry, in agriculture, in mines, in stores, in offices, at a high level of wages and salaries. There must be opportunity and incentive for men and women to go into business for themselves.

The war has proved that despite the New Deal, America can mightily increase its frontiers of production. With competent government America can produce mightily for peace. And the standard of living of our people is limited only by the amount of goods and services we are able to produce.

The New Deal prepares to keep men in the Army because it is afraid of a resumption of its own depression. They can't think of anything for us to do once we stop building guns and tanks. But to those who believe in America there's lots to do.

Why, just take housing, for example. If we simply build the homes the American people need in order to be decently housed, it will keep millions of men employed for years. After twelve years of the New Deal the housing of the American people has fallen down so badly that just to come up to the standards of 1930 we shall need to build a million homes a year for many years to come. And this does not include the enormous need for farm housing repairs and alterations.

Why by the end of this year we shall have an immediate need for 6,000,000 automobiles just to put the same number of cars back on the road that were there in 1941. We shall need after the war 3,500,000 vacuum cleaners, 7,000,000 clocks, 23,000,000 radio sets, 5,000,000 refrigerators, 3,000,000 washing machines, and millions of other household appliances.

There are 600 different articles made of steel and iron which have not been manufactured since 1942. All of this means production and production means jobs. But that kind of production, that kind of jobs are beyond the experience and beyond the vision of the New Deal.

Why the transportation industry—the railroads, the whole moving, growing aircraft industry and the motor—is just waiting to get going, and to burst into production such as we've never seen in the history of our country.

The mighty energy we found lying dormant and unused in this country at the beginning of the war must be turned from destruction to creation. There can and must be jobs for all who want them and a free, open door for every man who wants to start out in business for himself.

We know from long experience that we shall not provide jobs and restore small business by the methods of the New Deal. We cannot keep our freedom and at the same time continue experimentation with a new policy every day by the national Government. We cannot succeed with a controlled and regulated society under a Government which destroys incentive, chokes production, fosters disunity and discourages men with vision and imagination from creating employment and opportunity.

The New Deal really believes that unemployment is bound to be with us permanently and it says so. They will change this 12-year-old tune between now and election. They do it every time. But they always come back to it after election. The New Deal really believes that we cannot have good social legislation and also have good jobs for all. I believe with all my heart and soul that we can have both.

Of course we need security regulation. Of course we need bank deposit insurance. Of course we need price support for agriculture. Of course the farmers of this country cannot be left to the hazards of a world price while they buy their goods at an American price. Of course we need unemployment insurance and old-age pensions and also relief whenever there are not enough jobs. Of course the rights of labor to organize and bargain collectively are fundamental. My party blazed the trail in that field by passage of the Railway Labor Act in 1926.

But we must also have a Government which believes in enterprise and Government policies which encourage enterprise. We must see to it that a man who wants to start a business is encouraged to start it, that the man who wants to expand a growing business is encouraged to expand it. We must see to it that the job-producing enterprises of America are stimulated to produce more jobs. We must see to it that the man who wants to produce more jobs is not throttled by the Government—but knows that he has a Government as eager for him to succeed as he is himself.

We cannot have jobs and opportunity if we surrender our freedom to Government control. I say we do not need to surrender our freedom to Government control in order to have the economic security to which we are entitled as free men. I say we can have both opportunity and security within the framework of a free society. That is what the American people will say at the election next November.

With the winning of the war in sight, there are two overshadowing problems. First, the making and keeping of the peace of the world so that your children and my children shall not face this tragedy all over again. This great objective, to which we are all so deeply devoted, I shall talk about at Louisville tomorrow night on the radio.

The other problem is whether we shall replace the tired and quarrelsome defeatism of the present Administration with a fresh and vigorous Government which believes in the future of the United States, and knows how to act on that belief.

Such action involves many things: tax policies, regulatory policies, labor policies, opportunity for small business, the bureaucracies which are attempting to regulate every detail of the lives of our people and these are all of major importance. I will discuss each of them in detail before this campaign is over. I will discuss them in plain English and say what we propose to do about them, so that there shall be no misunderstanding.

I am interested—desperately interested in bringing to our country a rebirth of faith in our future. I am deeply interested in bringing a final end to the defeatism and failure of this Administration in its domestic policies. I am deeply devoted to the principle that victory in this war shall mean victory for freedom and for the permanent peace of the world. Our place in a peaceful world can and shall be made secure. But nothing on earth will make us secure unless we are strong, unless we are productive and unless we have faith in ourselves. We can and we will recover our future and go forward in the path of freedom and security. I have unlimited faith that the American people will choose that path next November.

☆

1948

—— ☆ ——

When Roosevelt died of a massive cerebral hemorrhage on April 12, 1945, Vice President Harry S. Truman was totally unprepared to assume leadership. "Boys, if you ever pray," Truman told reporters, "pray for me now. I don't know whether you fellows ever had a load of hay fall on you," he continued, "but when they told me yesterday what had happened, I felt like the moon, the stars and all the planets had fallen on me."

In November, 1948, few Americans believed that Harry Truman would have to sustain his burden much longer, for there were several candidates who were willing to relieve this Atlas of his charge. Yet what occurred on Election Day, 1948, was unquestionably the greatest political upset in American history.

Once in power, Truman believed himself to be the guardian of of the New Deal—the guardian of its legislation as well as its spirit. Beginning in September, 1945, Truman began outlining what would come to be known as the Fair Deal: full-employment legislation, farm-price supports, public housing, health insurance, the nationalization of the atom, the creation of a permanent Fair Employment Practices Commission, and a modernization of New Deal legislation affecting such areas as social security, minimum wages, and conservation.

Yet at the same time that he wanted to consolidate and expand the New Deal, Truman also had the challenging task of reconverting

America's wartime economy for peaceful purposes. Truman came under heavy attack during these days. After years of sacrifice, Americans wanted a conclusion of wage and price controls. Labor demanded higher wages but insisted that price controls be retained; businessmen insisted that they be allowed to raise their prices but that the government maintain control over wages; the agricultural sector opposed price controls but pressed for a retention of price supports.

Perhaps only a Solomon could have held such diverse and contradictory interests in equilibrium. Small wonder, then, that in the mid-term elections of 1946 the Republicans recaptured both houses of Congress for the first time since 1928.

The new 80th Congress immediately established itself as a bastion of conservatism, passing such controversial legislation as the Taft-Hartley Act over Truman's veto. The President retaliated by flooding Congress with a host of liberal measures, including civil rights legislation—an area in which the Truman administration broke new ground.

The Republican party opened its convention in Philadelphia on June 21st. Before a national television audience (this was the first time that a presidential nominating convention had been televised) the Republicans returned to their 1940 candidate, Thomas E. Dewey, on the third ballot. In their platform the Republicans supported the containment of communism and the United Nations.

Dewey's acceptance speech was a harbinger of his campaign addresses, a call for Americans to band together to achieve "spiritual unity." Primarily because he felt that victory was assured, (public opinion polls predicted that he would "win in a walk") Dewey's campaign speeches were very general so as not to alienate any wing of his party. Like his speech at Des Moines, Iowa, on September 20th, his addresses sounded more like Fourth of July orations than campaign addresses.

Although Truman had little difficulty in staving off a "dump Truman" movement at his party's convention in Philadelphia, the convention was not a successful affair for the President. When the party accepted a civil rights plank in its platform, thirty-five delegates from Mississippi and Alabama withdrew.

Shortly thereafter the Southern States' Rights party met at Birmingham, Alabama, to nominate J. Strom Thurmond, the governor of South Carolina, as the presidential candidate of the Dixiecrats. For some time now Southerners believed that their power in Congress was being emasculated at the expense of the large industrial areas in the North. Equally important, they felt that the federal government was encroaching on the management of their daily lives, particularly in the area of race relations. Therefore, the Dixiecrats specifically inserted in their platform a plank that sanctioned "the segregation of the races."

Essentially, the States' Rights party's strategy was to sweep the South's 127 electoral votes and to throw the election into the House of Representatives, where they could influence the selection of the president.

Not only were the Democrats being attacked from the right, but there was also thunder on the left. On July 22nd the Progressive party met in Philadelphia to nominate Henry A. Wallace, Truman's deposed Secretary of Commerce, as their standard bearer. Wallace was a staunch supporter of the New Deal, but also a firm critic of Truman's foreign policy, arguing that containment would lead to war. Since domestic and foreign policy were inextricably interwoven in Wallace's mind, his campaign centered its criticisms on the administration's containment policy. But Wallace's campaign was seriously handicapped by communist elements within his party and by events abroad, such as the communist coup against the liberal regime in Czechoslovakia and the Soviet blockade of West Berlin.

Truman began his campaign with his acceptance speech at Philadelphia, in which he dramatically announced that he would call the 80th Congress into special session and challenge them to pass progressive legislation. Truman's strategy was to shift the battleground, to make the election a struggle between President and Congress, rather than Truman vs. Dewey.

In his campaign Truman covered over 20,000 miles and made some 250 speeches, most of which were "whistle stop" addresses delivered from the platform of his train. Such speeches accommodated his informal style, which came across better in person than via the radio. Each one of his speeches was very specific, and concentrated on an issue that was important to the people he was addressing. Truman's October 24th address at Harlem (the first speech given there by an American president) is an example of his style.

HARRY S. TRUMAN

Acceptance Speech

PHILADELPHIA, PENNSYLVANIA

July 15, 1948

I am sorry that the microphones are in your way, but they have to be where they are because I've got to be able to see what I'm doing, as I always am able to see what I am doing.

I can't tell you how very much I appreciate the honor which you've just conferred upon me. I shall continue to try to deserve it. I accept the nomination, and I want to thank this convention for its unanimous nomination of my good friend and colleague, Senator Barkley, of Kentucky.

He's a great man and a great public servant. Senator Barkley and I will win this election and make these Republicans like it, don't you forget that. We'll do that because they're wrong and we're right, and I'll prove it to you in just a few minutes.

This convention met to express the will and reaffirm the beliefs of the Democratic party. There have been differences of opinion. These differences have been settled by a majority vote, as they should be, and now it's time for us to get together and beat the common enemy and it's up to you.

We'll be working together for victory and a great cause. Victory has become a habit of our party. It's been elected four times in succession and I'm convinced it will be elected a fifth time next November.

The reason is that the people know the Democratic party is the people's party and the Republican party is the party of special interests and it always has been and always will be.

The record of the Democratic party is written in the accomplishments of the last sixteen years. I don't need to repeat them. They have been very ably placed before this convention by the keynote speaker, the candidate for Vice-President, and by the permanent chairman.

Confidence and security have been brought to the American people by the Democratic party. Farm income has increased from less than $2,500,000,000 in 1933 to more than $18,000,000,000 in 1947. Never in the world were the farmers of any republic or any kingdom or any other country, as prosperous as the farmers of the United States, and if they don't do their duty by the Democratic party they're the most ungrateful people in the world.

The wages and salaries in this country have increased from $29,000,000,000 in 1933 to more than $128,000,000,000 in 1947. That's labor, and labor never had but one friend in politics, and that was the Democratic party and Franklin D. Roosevelt.

And I'll say to labor just what I've said to the farmers. They are the most ungrateful people in the world if they pass the Democratic party by this year.

The total national income has increased from less than $40,000,000,000 in 1933 to $203,000,000,000 in 1947, the greatest in all the history of the world. These benefits have been spread to all the people because it's the business of the Democratic party to see that the people get a fair share of these things.

This last Eightieth Congress proved just the opposite for the Republicans. The record on foreign policy of the Democratic party is that the United States has been turned away permanently from isolationism, and we've converted the greatest and best of the Republicans to our viewpoint on that subject.

The United States has to accept its full responsibility for leadership in international affairs. We have been the backers and the people who organized and started the United Nations, first started under that great Democratic President Woodrow Wilson in the League of Nations. The League was sabotaged by the Republicans in 1920, and we must see that the United Nations continues a strong and going body, so we can have everlasting peace in the world.

We've removed the trade barriers in the world, which is the best asset we can have for peace. Those trade barriers must not be put back into operation again. We have started a foreign-aid program which means the recovery of Europe and China and the Far East. We instituted the program for Greece and Turkey, and I'll say to you that all these things were done in a co-operative bi-partisan manner.

The foreign-relations committees of the Senate and the House were taken into the full confidence of the President in every one of these moves.

As I've said time and time again, foreign policy should be the policy of the whole nation, and not a policy of one party or the other. Partisanship should stop at the water's edge, and I shall continue to preach that through this whole campaign.

I'd like to say a word or two now about what I think the Republican philosophy is, and I'll speak from actions and from history and from experience. The situation in 1932 was due to the policy of the Republican party control of the government of the United States.

The Republican party favors the privileged few and not the common, every-day man. Ever since its inception, that party has been under the control of special privilege, and they concretely proved it in the Eightieth Congress. They proved it by the things they did to the people and not for them. They proved it by the things they failed to do.

Now let's look at some of them, just a few. Time and time again I recommended the extension of price control before it expired on June 30, 1946. I asked for that extension in September, 1945. In November, 1945, in a message on the State of the Union in 1946. That price control legislation didn't come to my desk until June 30, 1946, on the day on which it was supposed to expire, and it was such a rotten bill that I couldn't sign it.

Then thirty days after that they sent me one that was just as bad and I had to sign it, because they quit and went home.

It was said when O. P. A. died that prices would adjust themselves, for the benefit of the country. They've adjusted themselves all right. They've gone all the way off the chart in adjusting themselves at the expense of the consumer and for the benefit of the people who hold the goods.

I called a special session of Congress in November, 1947—Nov. 17, 1947—and I set out a ten-point program for the welfare and benefit of this country; among other things, stand-by price controls. I got nothing. The Congress has still done nothing.

Way back, four and a half years ago while I was in the Senate we passed the housing bill in the Senate known as the Wagner-Ellender-Taft bill. It was a bill to clear the slums in the big cities, and to help erect low-rent housing. That bill, as I said, passed the Senate four years ago, but it died in the House. That bill was reintroduced in the Eightieth Congress as the Taft-Ellender-Wagner bill—the name was slightly changed.

But it was practically the same bill and it passed the Senate, but was allowed to die in the House of Representatives. The Banking and Currency Committee sat on that bill, and it was finally forced out of the committee when the Rules Committee took charge, and it's still in the Rules Committee.

But desperate pleas from Philadelphia, in that convention that met here three weeks ago, didn't get that housing bill passed. They passed a bill that's called a housing bill, which isn't worth the paper it's written on.

In the field of labor, we needed moderate legislation to promote labor-management relations. But Congress instead passed the so-called Taft-Hartley act, which has disrupted labor-management relations and will cause strife and bitterness for years to come if it's not repealed, and the Democratic platform says it's got to be repealed.

I tried to strengthen the Labor Deparment. The Republican platform in 1944 said if they were in power they'd build up a strong Labor Department. Do you know what they've done to the Labor Department? They've simply torn it up. There's only one bureau left that's functioning and they've cut the appropriation on that so it can hardly function.

I recommended an increase in the minimum wage. What did they do? Nothing, absolutely nothing. I suggested that the schools in this country are crowded, teachers underpaid, and that there is a shortage of teachers. One of the greatest national needs is more and better schools.

I urged the Congress to provide $300,000,000 to aid the states in meeting the present educational crisis. The Congress did nothing about it. Time and again I have recommended improvements in the social security law, including extending protection to those not now covered, to increase the amount of the benefits, reduce the eligibility age of women from sixty-five to sixty years. Congress studied the matter for two years but couldn't find time to extend increased benefits, but it did find time to take social security benefits away from 750,000 people.

And they passed that over my veto.

I repeatedly asked the Congress to pass a health program. The nation suffers from lack of medical care. That situation can be remedied any time the Congress wants to act upon it. Everybody knows that I recommended to the Congress a civil-rights program. I did so because I believe it to be my duty under the Constitution. Some of the members of my own party disagreed with me violently on this matter, but they stand up and do it openly. People can tell where they stand. But the Republicans all profess to be for these measures, but the Eightieth Congress didn't act and they had enough men there to do it, and they could have had cloture, and they didn't have to have a filibuster. There were enough people in that Congress to vote for cloture.

Now everybody likes to have a little surplus. But we must reduce the national debt in times of prosperity, and when tax relief can be given without regard to those who need it most, and not go to those who need it least, as this Republican rich-man's tax bill did when they passed it over my veto, on the third try.

The first one of these tax bills they sent me was so rotten that they couldn't even stomach it themselves. They finally did send one that was somewhat improved, but it still helps the rich and sticks the knife into the back of the poor.

Now the Republicans came here a few weeks ago and they wrote up a platform. I hope you've all read that platform. They adopted a platform, and that platform had a lot of promises and statements of what the Republican party is for and what they would do if they were in power.

They promised to do in that platform a lot of things I've been asking them to do, and that they've refused to do when they had the power. The Republican platform cries about cruelly high prices. I have been trying to get them to do something about high prices ever since they met the first time.

Now listen to this one. This one is equally as bad and as cynical. The Republican platform comes out for slum clearance and low rental housing. I've been trying to get them to pass that housing bill ever since they met the first time, and it's still resting in the Rules Committee today.

The Republican platform pledges equality of educational opportunity. I've been trying to get them to do something about that ever since they came there, and that bill is at rest in the House of Representatives.

The Republican platform urges extending and increasing social security benefits. Think of that—increasing social security benefits, and yet when they had the opportunity they took 750,000 people off the social security roles.

I wonder if they think they can fool the people of the United States with such poppycock as that?

There's a long list of these promises in that Republican platform and if it weren't so late I'd tell you about all of them.

I discussed a number of these failures of the Republican Eightieth Congress, and everyone of them is important. Two of them are of major concern to every American family; the failure to do anything about high prices, and the failure to do anything about housing.

My duty as President requires that I use every means within my power to get the laws the people need on matters of such importance and urgency. I am therefore calling this Congress back into session on the 26th of July.

On the twenty-sixth day of July, which out in Missouri they call Turnip Day, I'm going to call that Congress back and I'm going to ask them to pass laws halting rising prices and to meet the housing crisis which they say they're for in their platform. At the same time I shall ask them to act on other vitally needed measures such as aid to education, which they say they're for; a national health program, civil-rights legislation, which they say they're for; an increase in the minimum wage—which I doubt very much they're for; an extension of social security coverage and increased benefits, which they say they're for; funds for projects needed in our program to provide public power and cheap electricity.

By indirection, this Eightieth Congress has tried to sabotage the power policy which the United States has pursued for fourteen years. That power lobby is just as bad as the real estate lobby, which is sitting on the housing bill. I shall ask for adequate and decent law for displaced persons in place of the anti-Semitic, anti-Catholic law which this Eightieth Congress passed.

Now my friends, if there is any reality behind that Republican platform, we ought to get some action out of the short session of the Eightieth Congress. They could do this job in fifteen days if they wanted to do it. They'll still have time to go out and run for office. They're going to try and dodge their responsibility, they're going to drag all the red herrings they can across this campaign. But I'm here to say to you that Senator Barkley and I are not going to let them get away with it.

Now what that worst Eightieth Congress does in its special session will be the test. The American people will not decide by listening to mere words or by reading a mere platform. They will decide on the record. The record as it has been written. And in the record is the stark truth that the battle lines for 1948 are the same as they were back in 1932 when the nation lay prostrate and helpless as the result of Republican misrule and inaction.

In 1932 we were attacking the citadel of special privilege and greed; we were fighting to drive the money changers from the temple. Today in 1948 we are the defenders of the stronghold of democracy and of equal opportunity. The haven of the ordinary people of this land and not of the favored classes or of the powerful few.

The battle cry is just the same now as it was in 1932 and I paraphrase the words of Franklin D. Roosevelt as he issued the challenge in accepting his nomination at Chicago: This is more than a political call to arms. Give me your help. Not to win votes alone, but to win in this new crusade and keep America secure and safe for its own people.

Now my friends, with the help of God, and the wholehearted push which you can put behind this campaign, we can save this country from a continuation of the Eightieth Congress and from misrule from now on. I must have your help! You must get in and push and win this election. The country can't afford another Republican Congress.

☆

HARRY S. TRUMAN

Campaign Speech

HARLEM, NEW YORK

October 29, 1948

Dr. Johnson, and members of the Ministerial Alliance which has given me this award:

I am exceedingly grateful for it. I hope I shall always deserve it. This, in my mind, is a most solemn occasion. It's made a tremendous impression upon me.

Franklin Roosevelt was a great champion of human rights. When he led us out of the depression to the victory over the Axis, he enabled us to build a country in which prosperity and freedom must exist side by side. This is the only atmosphere in which human rights can thrive.

Eventually, we are going to have an America in which freedom and opportunity are the same for everyone. There is only one way to accomplish that great purpose, and that is to keep working for it and never take a backward step.

I am especially glad to receive the Franklin Roosevelt award on this day—October 29. This date means a great deal to me personally, and it is a significant date in the history of human freedom in this country.

One year ago today, on October 29, 1947, the President's Committee on Civil Rights submitted to me, and to the American people, its momentous report.

That report was drawn up by men and women who had the honesty to face the whole problem of civil rights squarely, and the courage to state their conclusions frankly.

I created the Civil Rights Committee because racial and religious intolerance began to appear after World War II. They threatened the very freedoms we had fought to save.

We Americans have a democratic way of acting when our freedoms are threatened.

We get the most thoughtful and representative men and women we can find, and we ask them to put down on paper the principles that represent freedom and a method of action that will preserve and extend that freedom. In that manner, we get a declaration of purpose and a guide for action that the whole country can consider.

That is the way in which the Declaration of Independence was drawn up.

That is the way in which the Constitution of the United States was written.

The report that the Civil Rights Committee prepared is in the tradition of these great documents.

It was the authors of the Declaration of Independence who stated the principle that all men are created equal in their rights, and that it is to secure these rights that governments are instituted among men.

It was the authors of the Constitution who made it clear that, under our form of government, all citizens are equal before the law, and that the Federal Government has a duty to guarantee to every citizen equal protection of the laws.

The Civil Rights Committee did more than repeat these great principles. It described a method to put these principles into action, and to make them a living reality for every American, regardless of his race, his religion, or his national origin.

When every American knows that his rights and his opportunities are fully protected and respected by the Federal, State, and local governments, then we will have the kind of unity that really means something.

It is easy to talk of unity. But it is the work that is done for unity that really counts.

The job that the Civil Rights Committee did was to tell the American people how to create the kind of freedom that we need in this country.

The Civil Rights Committee described the kind of freedom that comes when every man has an equal chance for a job—not just the hot and heavy job—but the best job he is qualified for.

The Committee described the kind of freedom that comes when every American boy and girl has an equal chance for an education.

The Committee described the kind of freedom that comes when every citizen has an equal opportunity to go to the ballot box and cast his vote and have it counted.

The Committee described the kind of freedom that comes when every man, woman, and child is free from the fear of mob violence and intimidation.

When we have that kind of freedom, we will face the evil forces that are abroad in the world—whatever or wherever they may be—with the strength that comes from complete confidence in one another and from complete faith in the working of our own democracy.

One of the great things that the Civil Rights Committee did for the country was to get every American to think seriously about the principles that make our country great.

More than 1 million copies of the full text of the civil rights report have been printed in books and newspapers.

More than 30 different pamphlets based on the report have been printed and distributed by private organizations.

Millions of Americans have heard the report discussed on the radio.

In making its recommendations, the Civil Rights Committee did not limit itself to action by the President or by the executive branch. The Committee's recommendations included action by every branch of the Federal Government, by State and local governments, and by private organizations, and by individuals.

That is why it is so important that the Civil Rights Committee's report be studied widely. For in the last analysis, freedom resides in the actions of each individual. That is the reason I like to hear that scriptural reading from the Gospel according to St. Luke. That's just exactly what it means. It means you and I must act out what we say in our Constitution and our Bill of Rights. It is in his mind and heart—and to his mind and heart—that we must eventually speak to the individual.

After the Civil Rights Committee submitted its report, I asked Congress to do ten of the things recommended by the Committee.

You know what they did about that.

So I went ahead and did what the President can do, unaided by the Congress.

I issued two Executive orders.

One of them established the President's Committee on Equality of Treatment and Opportunity in the Armed Services.

The other one covered regulations governing fair employment practices within the Federal establishment.

In addition to that, the Department of Justice went into the Supreme Court and aided in getting a decision outlawing restrictive covenants.

Several States and municipalities have taken action on the recommendations of the Civil Rights Committee, and I hope more will follow after them.

Today the democratic way of life is being challenged all over the world. Democracy's answer to the challenge of totalitarianism is its promise of equal rights and equal opportunity for all mankind.

The fulfillment of this promise is among the highest purposes of government.

Our determination to attain the goal of equal rights and equal opportunity must be resolute and unwavering.

For my part, I intend to keep moving toward this goal with every ounce of strength and determination that I have.

☆

THOMAS E. DEWEY

Acceptance Speech

PHILADELPHIA, PENNSYLVANIA

June 24, 1948

Speaker Martin and fellow Republicans:

You, the elected representatives of our Republican Party, have again given to me the highest honor you can bestow—your nomination for President of the United States.

I thank you with all my heart for your friendship and your confidence. I am profoundly sensible of the responsibility that goes with this nomination. I pray God that I may deserve this opportunity to serve our country. In all humility, I accept the nomination.

I am happy to be able to say to you that I come to you unfettered by a single obligation or promise to any living person. I come free to join with you in selecting to serve our nation the finest men and women in the country, free to unite our party and our country in meeting the grave challenge of our time.

United we can match this challenge with depth of understanding and largeness of spirit; with a unity which is above recrimination, above partisanship, and above self-interest. These are articles of faith from which the greatness of America has been fashioned. Our people are eager to know again the upsurging power of that faith. They are turning to us to put such a faith at the heart of our national life. That is what we are called upon to do, and that is what we will do.

In this historic Convention, you have had placed before you six other candidates, all high-minded men of character and ability and deeply devoted to their country—Senator Raymond E. Baldwin, General Douglas MacArthur, Governor Harold E. Stassen, Senator Robert A. Taft, Senator Arthur Vandenberg, and Governor Earl Warren. Never has any party produced so many fine, able, distinguished, and patriotic men.

I am deeply moved and grateful for the generous and gracious statements they have made in this hall tonight. I hope that I may be worthy of the trust. This has been a difficult choice in an honorable contest. It has been a stirring demonstration of the life and vitality and ideals of our Republican Party.

There has been honest contention, spirited disagreement, and I believe considerable hot argument. But do not let anybody be misled by that. You have given here in this hall a moving and dramatic proof of how Americans, who honestly differ, close ranks and move forward, for the Nation's well-being, shoulder to shoulder. Let me assure you that beginning next January 20, there will be teamwork in the Government of the United States of America.

The responsibility and the opportunity that have come to our party are the greatest in the history of free government. For tonight our future —our peace, our prosperity, the very fate of freedom—hangs in a precarious balance.

Mere victory in an election is not our purpose, it is not our task. Our task is to fill our victory with such meaning for mankind everywhere, yearning for freedom, that they will take heart and move forward out of this desperate darkness of today into the light of freedom's promise.

Our platform proclaims the guideposts that will mark our steadfast and certain endeavor in a fearful world. This magnificent statement of principles is concise and to the point.

You unanimously adopted it, and I am very proud to support it. That platform will be the heart of the message I will take to the country. After January 20th, it will be the cornerstone of our Republican Administration.

Fortunately, we are a united party. Our nation stands tragically in need of that same unity.

Our people are turning away from the meaner things that divide us, and they have a yearning to move to higher ground, to find a common purpose in the finer things which unite us. We, the Republican Party, must be the instrument of achieving that aspiration. We must be the means by which America's full powers are released and this uncertain future filled again with opportunity. That is our pledge. That will be, for the American people, the fruit of our victory.

If this unity is to be won and kept, it must have great dimensions. Its boundaries must be far above and beyond politics. Freedom can be saved —it can only be saved—if free men everywhere make this unity their common cause.

Unity in such a cause must be the chief cornerstone of peace. A peace won at the expense of liberty is a peace too dearly bought. Such a peace would not endure. Above all other purposes, we must labor by every peaceful means to build a world order founded upon justice and righteousness. That kind of world will have peace. That kind of peace will be worth having. That is the crowning responsibility that our people have laid upon us in this solemn hour. That is the crowning task to which we here dedicate ourselves.

The unity we seek is more than material. It is more than a matter of things and measures. It is most of all spiritual. Our problem is not outside ourselves. Our problem is within ourselves. We have found the means to blow this world of ours apart, physically. We have not yet found the spiritual means to put together the world's broken pieces, to bind up its wounds, to make a good society, a community of men of good will that fits our dreams. We have devised noble plans for a new world. Without a new spirit, our noblest plans will come to nought. We pray that, in the days ahead, a full measure of that spirit may be ours.

The next Presidential term will see the completion of the first half of the twentieth century. So far it has been a century of amazing progress and of terrible tragedy. We have seen the world transformed. We have seen mankind's age-long struggle against nature crowned by extraordinary success.

Yet our triumphs have been darkened by bitter defeats in the equally ancient struggle of men to live together in peace, security and understanding. For this age of progress, this twentieth century, has been dominated by two terrible world wars and, between the wars, the worst economic depression in the history of mankind.

We must learn to do better. The period that is drawing to a close has been one of scientific achievement. The era that is opening before us must be a period of human and spiritual achievement.

We propose, in this Convention, and as a party, and as a government, to continue to carry forward the great technological gains of our age. We shall harness the unimaginable possibilities of atomic energy, to bring men and women a larger, fuller life. But there is something more important than all this. With all the energy, intelligence and determination which mortal heart and mind can summon to the task, we must solve the problem of establishing a just and lasting peace in the world, and of securing to our own and other like-minded people the blessings of freedom and of individual opportunity.

To me, to be a Republican in this hour is to dedicate one's life to the freedom of men. As long as the world is half free and half slave, we must peacefully labor to help men everywhere to achieve liberty.

We have declared our goal to be a strong and free America in a free world of free men—free to speak their own minds, free to develop new ideas, free to publish whatever they believe, free to move from place to place, free to choose their occupations, free to enjoy and to save and to use the fruits of their labor, and free to worship God, each according to his own concept of His grace and His mercy.

When these rights are secure in this world of ours, the permanent ideals of the Republican Party shall have been realized.

The ideals of the American people are the ideals of the Republican Party. We have tonight, and in these days which preceded, here in Philadelphia lighted a beacon, in this cradle of our own independence. We have lighted a beacon to give eternal hope that men may live in liberty with human dignity and before God, and loving Him, stand erect and free.

☆

THOMAS E. DEWEY

Campaign Speech

DES MOINES, IOWA

September 20, 1948

Mr. Chairman, Senator Wilson, Senator Hickenlooper and fellow Americans:

I appreciate more deeply than I can tell you your wonderful welcome. Tonight we enter upon a campaign to unite all America.

On Jan. 20, we will enter on a new era. We propose to install in Washington an Administration which has faith in the American people, a warm understanding of their needs and the competence to meet those needs.

We will rediscover the essential unit of our people and the spiritual strength that makes our country great.

We'll begin to move forward again shoulder to shoulder toward an even greater America and a better life for every American, in a nation working effectively for the peace of the world.

This is my pledge to my fellow-citizens, the declaration of the principles and purposes of your next Administration.

I pledge to you that, as President, every act of mine will be determined by one principle above all others: Is this good for our country?

I pledge to you that my administration will be made up of men and women devoted to that same principle—of men and women whose love of their country comes ahead of every other consideration. They will know how to translate their devotion to our country into constructive action.

I pledge to you a foreign policy based upon the firm belief that we can have peace. That policy will be made effective by men and women who really understand the nature of the threat to peace and who have the vigor, the knowledge and the experience required to wage that peace.

I pledge to you a Government of team-work. The executive heads of your Government will be really qualified for their positions after Jan. 20 and they will be given full responsibility to do their job without loose talk, factional quarreling or appeals to group prejudice. They will know how to work together as a team and one of the most important members of that team will be the distinguished Governor of California, the next Vice President of the United States, Earl Warren.

I pledge to you an Administration which will know how to work with the elected representatives of the people in the Congress, an Administration that wants to work with them and will do so. The unity we need for the nation will be practiced in the nation's Capitol.

I pledge to you that on next Jan. 20 there will begin in Washington the biggest unraveling, unsnarling operation in our nation's history.

I pledge to you an Administration which knows in its mind and believes in its heart that every American is dependent on every other American; that no segment of our people can prosper without the prosperity of all; that in truth we must all go forward together.

This is what you may expect from your next, your Republican administration. It will be a government in which every member is enlisted to advance the well-being of all our people and is dedicated to the release of the enthusiasm, the energy and the enterprise of our people: a government that has faith in America and is resolved to prove its faith by its works.

This is the road on which I propose that we set out all together. As we advance we shall carry America's destiny with us. We shall also carry the hope of freedom and the living promise to a stricken world that men can be free and that free men can live in peace.

We're living in sorely troubled times. The unhappy difficulties of today are familiar to every one of us. Three years after the end of the war the world has still not found peace. As we wage the peace, we face problems as momentous as a any nation has ever confronted in history, either in peace or in war.

Our sons and daughters—the young people in all our grade schools, our high schools and our colleges have lived—it seems impossible but it's true—they have lived their whole lives in a troubled world. Their plans for education, for getting married—for getting ahead, are delayed and disrupted. Against the dangers of a sorely troubled world they are being called upon to keep America strong.

The wife and mother who's been out shopping today to buy meat for her family and clothes for her children has been up against the hard fact of high prices. Every married veteran living in a Quonset hut, or doubled up with his family, is up against the cruel fact that we do not have enough good homes for our people. Every family living in a crowded, unsanitary, cold-water tenement has the same urgent needs. Hard-working, frugal Americans find they don't make enough to lay anything by for a rainy day or for sickness, or unemployment, or old age.

Millions of Americans, too, face the intolerable fact that because of their race or their color or the way they choose to worship God, they are denied rights which are their birthrights and which, by American principle and law, are their just due.

These are some of the difficulties that confront us. It won't be easy to meet them, and I want no one to think that I believe it will be easy. These times require the cooperation of everyone of us and the highest order of devotion and intense labor by your Government. But it's part of my faith in America to believe that with restoration of faith in ourselves, of competence in our Government, of unity of purpose among our people there is nothing, as a people, we cannot do.

I deeply believe that with an administration which can unite our people will have taken the greatest single step toward solving these problems. This is our most urgent need.

Every four years, under our Constitution, it's our right as Americans to hear a full and thoughtful discussion of the issues before us. As this campaign progresses I shall place before you my views concerning every aspect of the grave problems at home and abroad and the steps, the concrete steps, which I propose that we meet them.

I will not contend that all our difficulties today have been brought about by the present National Administration. They haven't. Some of these unhappy conditions are the result of circumstances beyond the control of any government. Any fair-minded person would agree that others are merely the result of the Administration's lack of judgment, or of faith in our people. Only part are deliberately caused for political purposes. But it's not too important how these conditions came about. The important thing is that, as Americans, we turn our faces forward and set about curing them with a stout purpose and a full heart. We can enlarge the opportunities of all our people and move toward peace with all the world.

And to all those in this country or abroad who hate freedom, as well as to all our friends everywhere who love freedom and look to us for aid and leadership, let me make this one thing very clear: So far as I am concerned—so far as the Republican party is concerned, this campaign will not create division among our people. Instead this campaign will unite us as we have never been united before. It will unite us so strongly that no force will again attack us and we will labor unceasingly and with unity to find common grounds of firm and peaceful agreement with all the nations of this earth.

As we chart our course for the years ahead, we must find the stars by which to sail. We must look to the fundamentals of our country. They're easy to find. Our America is not the lucky product of a rich continent discovered by seafaring adventurer looking for a pot of gold. The roots of our country are not material. They are moral and spiritual. Of course we are deeply concerned about things to live with. But we are also concerned about the values by which we live. You and I know that we can surmount our unhappy times by a restoration of our ideas and faith in our country.

We know that, we know it because we are Americans. It's no accident that our country stands like a beacon of hope to all the world today. Our magnificent America is the end result of the deep convictions of a great people devoted above everything else to faith in their God and the liberty and precious importance of every single human being.

We believe in freedom for our neighbors across the street or across the seas—the same freedom we expect for ourselves. We believe in honesty, loyalty, fair play, concern for our neighbors, the innate ability of men to achieve; these convictions, arched over by our faith in God, are the inner meaning of the American way of life. That is why the eyes of freedom-loving people everywhere in this troubled world are turning with hope to us. That is our America for which we cannot and will not fail.

But we are in a world and in a time when these convictions are doubted and sneered at and denied. The priceless rights of freedom of speech, of assembly, of religion, of the press, academic freedom, the fundamental freedom of choice of occupation, even of the right to own a car or a home or a farm—all these are denied to many millions of regimented people throughout the world. The ideals and the rights we hold to be good are held to be evil in those countries. No other fact about our world is of such ominous importance.

We live in a world in which tyranny is on the march. The evil idea is on the march that man is not destined to be free but to be enslaved. That idea is backed by a mobilization of enormous force. Millions of families who have known freedom are in fear of evil, unfamiliar footsteps and at every moment they expect the knock on the door. Millions who still enjoy freedom live in fear that today or tomorrow some crisis or excuse will be seized upon to blot out their freedom too.

Millions of human beings, it may be tens of millions—nobody knows —are being starved and worked to death in concentration camps and at slave labor. And yet, at this very moment in the history of the world the promise of America and the truth of what America believes are being vindicated. The oppressed peoples of these lands know there is a better life. They know there is a better way. The truth about America seeps through every obstacle of iron and steel. In millions of hearts the hope that is America is flaming. That's why we in America have such a solemn obligation to love and cherish all the freedoms we enjoy; that's why we have such a solemn obligation, every single one of us, not to divide our country but to unite it for all purposes and for all time.

We are the last, best hope of earth. Neither barbed wire nor bayonet have been able to suppress the will of men and women to cross from tyranny to freedom.

Let's call up some of them as witnesses. Let them testify to this thing we believe in. Call up Jan Masaryk of Czechoslovakia, the heroic son of a heroic father. We may never know whether he took his life or was murdered. But we do know this, that however it came, he preferred death to a life cut off from freedom. Jan Masaryk is our witness.

Call up Archbishop Stepinac who lies today in a Communist prison, a living martyr to the cause of freedom of religion. Call up Nicola Petkov, the executed leader of the free forces of Bulgaria. Call up General Bor Komorowski and Stanislaw Mikolajczyk, the great exiled leaders of Poland who gladly brushed elbows with death to escape from tyranny. All these are our witnesses.

Call up the athletes who came out from behind the iron curtain to compete in the Olympics only last month and refused to go home. Call up Oksana Kasenkina, the Russian school teacher. She was picked by the secret police to come to our country to teach the children of Soviet diplomats. She could not even understand the language of our country, but in her heart she came to understand America. And when she jumped to death or freedom from the window of her diplomatic prison, she gave her testimony. That was the day—the very same tragic day—that the American people were told that the exposure of communism in our own Government is a "red herring."

With mankind as our witness this is no time for doubting the rightness of free governments. This is a time—above all times—for a great American affirmation. Our faith reaffirmed holds our destiny and the hope of all the world.

As we look around us we can count our blessings and be humbly proud and grateful we are Americans.

Our fathers came from an old world in which few men knew the meaning of liberty. Yet they dared to found a nation and stake its future on their belief in what men could do if only they were free. The America of today is the living, towering symbol of the eternal rightness of that faith.

We've sometimes fallen short, we've sometimes failed, but in our hearts we believe and know that every man and woman and child has something of the Divine in him, that every single individual is of priceless importance and that free men against whatever odds have an unbeatable quality. That faith is my faith. It's the faith of our people. It's the faith in which we will go forward.

Never let anyone tell you that America's unfinished job is too big. Never let anyone tell you that we can meet our problems in this country only by surrendering to the devices borrowed from the police states. The free system is the only one where we can make a mistake and have a heaven-sent opportunity to cure it. It's the only one where opportunity always exists to improve. The free system is the only one where men can freely change their governments by peaceful means. This land of ours, almost alone in all the world, is still the place where youth—where every young man and every young woman—is free to plan for the future and to make their dreams come true.

As a nation we're troubled today by many problems and we must remove many fears. We're troubled by high prices and we must end the maladjustments which cause them. We need more homes for our people. We must widen the opportunities for our youth. We must increase the security for our older people. We must protect our enterprise system from monopoly, while encouraging free and fuller production for the benefit of all our citizens. We must, and we will, maintain support prices so our farmers can go ahead confidently with full production of the food our growing nation needs. We must, and we will, preserve the gains of labor so that its confidence and production will grow and flourish. We must work against intolerance and bigotry, against racial and religious discrimination. Above all we must confidently face the immense labor of making peace in this world and act wisely and with courage to achieve it.

As I make specific proposals dealing with these problems of ours in the course of this campaign, they will not be the product of any wishful thinking. I have no trick answers and no easy solutions. I will not offer one solution to one group and another solution to another group.

The American people have a right to expect honest answers and I propose to give them. The specific proposals I will make as this campaign goes along will not be born of fear—and I may add there will be no threats in any of them. They will come from my own deep faith in America. They will not set faction against faction or group against group. They will aim to join us together as a whole people in a more perfect union.

As we go on from here together, we shall know that our advance is carrying us into unexplored territory—on into the atomic age. Man has, at last, begun to tap the powers of the universe. We can do much, we Americans, to see that this new age is not one of catastrophe, but one of unimagined promise and achievements. That is our purpose. That is the measure of our opportunity. For such a future let us summon new wisdom, new courage and a new vision. Let us say, as one people: We welcome the challenge of tomorrow.

Let us go forward into this future as courageous, united Americans, bound together by an invincible faith that liberty and justice under God, is the most precious thing on earth.

☆

1952

—— ☆ ——

Before the Republican national convention opened in Chicago on July 7, 1952, most delegates thought that they were going to the "windy city" to nominate Senator Robert A. Taft of Ohio, "Mr. Republican," as their presidential candidate. Although the son of former President William Howard Taft supported civil rights legislation and other liberal measures such as public housing, Taft was an ardent conservative, especially on matters of foreign policy. Taft had criticized Roosevelt's measures before Pearl Harbor and opposed NATO after the war.

It was because of Taft's stand on foreign affairs that the internationalist wing of the Republican party attempted to draft a candidate who would maintain the bipartisan coalition on foreign policy. While General Dwight D. Eisenhower had been beckoned before, by Democrats as well as Republicans, it was not until June, 1952, that Eisenhower confirmed he was a Republican. And it was not until a few weeks before the convention that he began to campaign actively for the nomination.

While Taft's forces controlled the national committee and the convention machinery, Eisenhower's forces were able to outmaneuver the Taft delegates on the convention floor and to capture the nomination for the general on the first ballot.

The Republican party's condemnation of the Truman administra-

239

tion's handling of "Korea, communism, and corruption" within its administration was almost inconsequential, for with Ike on their side they sensed victory. In his brief acceptance speech the general placed himself above mundane party battles and politics and pledged himself to lead the American people in yet another crusade, "a great crusade—for Freedom in America and Freedom in the world."

As the Republican forces left Chicago, the Democrats moved in. With Truman already out of the running (he announced his decision on March 29, 1952), the Democrats drafted Governor Adlai E. Stevenson of Illinois on the third ballot, although the former New Dealer did not become a candidate until the convention was a few days old. In his acceptance speech Stevenson called on the Democratic party to "talk sense to the American people" and to use the campaign as an "opportunity to educate and elevate" the nation.

Clearly, one of Eisenhower's first tasks was to make peace with Taft. This was accomplished at a September 12th conference at Eisenhower's home in New York City. At this meeting Eisenhower agreed to accept Taft's domestic programs, especially the senator's request that federal spending be drastically reduced.

But on September 18th Ike's campaign came to an abrupt halt. On that day the *New York Post* released a story which charged that Eisenhower's running mate, Senator Richard M. Nixon of California, had been a recipient of a "slush fund." This was particularly troubling to Eisenhower because the Republican party had been attacking corruption in the Truman administration. Many of Eisenhower's leading supporters, such as the *Washington Post* and the *New York Herald Tribune*, called for Nixon's resignation.

On September 23rd Nixon presented his case to the American people via television. His autobiographical "Checkers" speech was a triumph. Following his appearance the Republican national committee was flooded with over 200,000 telegrams supporting Nixon.

Ike's 1952 campaign was one of the best-orchestrated campaigns in American history. In fact, one could argue that it was the first modern "Madison Avenue" campaign. His appearance at Philadelphia, for instance, called for Eisenhower to be photographed with his right hand on the Liberty Bell. In addition, this was the first campaign to use television as a major vehicle for shaping public opinion.

Eisenhower himself travelled 33,000 miles, visiting 44 states and delivering some 228 speeches. As the campaign progressed he shifted his emphasis to an area that most people associated him with: foreign policy. Ike began attacking the administration's handling of the Korean War, particularly its inability to resume meaningful negotiations which, he charged, were allowing the North Koreans to regroup. These messages reached their crescendo at Detroit on October 24th, when the general announced: "I shall go to Korea."

Stevenson too waged an extensive campaign, covering some 32,500 miles and 32 states. Stevenson agreed with Truman's policy of containment, but went a little further than the President on the issue of civil rights. While he called the war against the communists in Korea a battle against "the anti-Christ," he could not challenge the general on foreign policy. All he could do in this campaign was to summarize the basic issues and to try to point out the contradictions in Eisenhower's speeches. This was Stevenson's aim in his witty and eloquent address at Brooklyn, New York on October 31st.

DWIGHT D. EISENHOWER

Acceptance Speech

CHICAGO, ILLINOIS

July 11, 1952

Mr. Chairman, my Fellow Republicans:

May I first thank you on behalf of Mrs. Eisenhower and myself for the warmth of your welcome. For us both this is our first entry into a political convention and it is a heartwarming one. Thank you very much.

And before I proceed with the thoughts that I should like to address briefly to you, may I have the temerity to congratulate this convention on the selection of their nominee for Vice-President. A man who has shown statesmanlike qualities in many ways, but as a special talent an ability to ferret out any kind of subversive influence wherever it may be found and the strength and persistence to get rid of it.

Ladies and Gentlemen, you have summoned me on behalf of millions of your fellow Americans to lead a great crusade—for Freedom in America and Freedom in the world. I know something of the solemn responsibility of leading a crusade. I have led one. I take up this task, therefore, in a spirit of deep obligation. Mindful of its burdens and of its decisive importance. I accept your summons. I will lead this crusade.

Our aims—the aims of this Republican crusade—are clear: to sweep from office an administration which has fastened on every one of us the wastefulness, the arrogance and corruption in high places, the heavy burdens and anxieties which are the bitter fruit of a party too long in power.

Much more than this, it is our aim to give to our country a program of progressive policies drawn from our finest Republican traditions; to unite us wherever we have been divided; to strengthen freedom wherever among any group is has been weakened; to build a sure foundation for sound prosperity for all here at home and for a just and sure peace throughout our world.

To achieve these aims we must have total victory; we must have more Republicans in our state and local offices; more Republican governments in our states; a Republican majority in the United States House of Representatives and in the United States Senate; and, of course, a Republican in the White House.

Today is the first day of this great battle. The road that leads to Nov. 4 is a fighting road. In that fight I will keep nothing in reserve.

Before this I stood on the eve of battle. Before every attack it has always been my practice to seek out our men in their camps and on the roads and talk with them face to face about their concerns and discuss with them the great mission to which we were all committed.

In this battle to which all of us are now committed it will be my practice to meet and talk with Americans face to face in every section, every corner, every nook and cranny of this land.

I know that such a momentous campaign cannot be won by a few or by divided or by uncertain forces. So to all those from the precinct level up who have worked long hours at difficult tasks in support of our party— and for our party's candidates—I extend an earnest call to join up; join up for longer hours and harder work and even greater devotion to this cause. I call on you to bring into this effort your neighbors next door and across the street. This is not a job for any one of us or for just a few of us.

Since this morning I have had helpful and heartwarming talks with Senator Taft, Governor Warren and Governor Stassen. I wanted them to know, as I want you to know, that in the hard fight ahead we will work intimately together to promote the principles and aims of our party. I was strengthened and heartened by their instant agreement to support this cause to the utmost. Their cooperation means that the Republican party will unitedly move forward in a sweeping victory.

We are now at a moment in history when, under God, this nation of ours has become the mightiest temporal power and the mightiest spiritual force on earth. The destiny of mankind—the making of a world that will be fit for our children to live in—hangs in the balance on what we say and what we accomplish in these months ahead.

We must use our power wisely for the good of all our people. If we do this, we will open a road into the future on which today's Americans, young and old, and the generations that come after them, can go forward—go forward to a life in which there will be far greater abundance of material, cultural, and spiritual rewards than our forefathers or we ever dreamed of.

We will so undergird our freedom that today's aggressors and those who tomorrow may rise up to threaten us, will not merely be deterred but stopped in their tracks. Then we will at last be on the road to real peace.

The American people look to us to direct our nation's might to these purposes.

As we launch this crusade we call to go forward with us the youth of America. This cause needs their enthusiasm, their devotion, and the lift their vision of the future will provide. We call to go forward with us the women of America; our workers, farmers, businessmen. As we go to the country, Americans in every walk of life can have confidence that our single-minded purpose is to serve their interest, guard and extend their rights and strengthen the America that we so love.

The noble service to which we Republicans summon all Americans is not only for one campaign or for one election. Our summons is to a lifetime enrollment. And our party shall always remain committed to a more secure, a brighter and an even better future for all our people.

We go out from here with unbounded trust in the American people. We go out from here to merit their unbounded trust in us.

Wherever I am, I will end each day of this coming campaign thinking of millions of American homes, large and small; of fathers and mothers working and sacrificing to make sure that their children are well cared for, free from fear; full of good hope for the future, proud citizens of a country that will stand among the nations as the leader of a peaceful and prosperous world.

Ladies and gentlemen, my dear friends that have heaped upon me such honors, it is more than a nomination I accept today. It is a dedication —a dedication to the shining promise of tomorrow. As together we face that tomorrow, I beseech the prayers of all our people and the blessing and guidance of Almighty God.

☆

DWIGHT D. EISENHOWER

Campaign Speech

DETROIT, MICHIGAN

October 24, 1952

In this anxious autumn for America, one fact looms above all others in our people's mind. One tragedy challenges all men dedicated to the work of peace. One word shouts denial to those who foolishly pretend that ours is not a nation at war.

This fact, this tragedy, this word is: Korea.

A small country, Korea has been, for more than two years, the battleground for the costliest foreign war our nation has fought, excepting the two world wars. It has been the burial ground for 20,000 American dead. It has been another historic field of honor for the valor and skill and tenacity of American soldiers.

All these things it has been—and yet one thing more. It has been a symbol—a telling symbol—of the foreign policy of our nation.

It has been a sign—a warning sign—of the way the Administration has conducted our world affairs.

It has been a measure—a damning measure—of the quality of leadership we have been given.

Tonight I am going to talk about our foreign policy and of its supreme symbol—the Korean war. I am not going to give you elaborate generalizations—but hard, tough facts. I am going to state the unvarnished truth.

What, then, are the plain facts?

The biggest fact about the Korean war is this: It was never inevitable, it was never inescapable, no fantastic fiat of history decreed that little South Korea—in the summer of 1950—would fatally tempt Communist aggressors as their easiest victim. No demonic destiny decreed that America had to be bled this way in order to keep South Korea free and to keep freedom itself self-respecting.

We are not mute prisoners of history. That is a doctrine for totalitarians, it is no creed for free men.

There is a Korean war—and we are fighting it—for the simplest of reasons: Because free leadership failed to check and to turn back Communist ambition before it savagely attacked us. The Korean war—more perhaps than any other war in history—simply and swiftly followed the collapse of our political defenses. There is no other reason than this: We failed to read and to outwit the totalitarian mind.

I know something of this totalitarian mind. Through the years of World War II, I carried a heavy burden of decision in the free world's crusade against the tyranny then threatening us all. Month after month, year after year, I had to search out and to weigh the strengths and weaknesses of an enemy driven by the lust to rule the great globe itself.

World War II should have taught us all one lesson. The lesson is this: To vacillate, to hesitate—to appease even by merely betraying unsteady purpose—is to feed a dictator's appetite for conquest and to invite war itself.

That lesson—which should have firmly guided every great decision of our leadership through these later years—was ignored in the development of the Administration's policies for Asia since the end of World War II. Because it was ignored, the record of these policies is a record of appalling failure.

The record of failure dates back—with red-letter folly—at least to September of 1947. It was then that Gen. Albert Wedemeyer—returned from a Presidential mission to the Far East—submitted to the President this warning: "The withdrawal of American military forces from Korea would result in the occupation of South Korea by either Soviet troops or, as seems more likely, by the Korean military units trained under Soviet auspices in North Korea."

That warning and his entire report were disregarded and suppressed by the Administration.

The terrible record of these years reaches its dramatic climax in a series of unforgettable scenes on Capitol Hill in June of 1949. By then the decision to complete withdrawal of American forces from Korea—despite menacing signs from the North—had been drawn up by the Department of State. The decision included the intention to ask Congress for aid to Korea to compensate for the withdrawal of American forces.

This brought questions from Congress. The Administration parade of civilian and military witnesses before the House Foreign Affairs Committee was headed by the Secretary of State. He and his aides faced a group of Republican Congressmen both skeptical and fearful.

What followed was historic and decisive.

I beg you to listen carefully to the words that followed, for they shaped this nation's course from that date to this.

Listen, then:

First: Republican Congressman John Lodge of Connecticut asked "(do) you feel that the Korean Government is able to fill the vacuum caused by the withdrawal of the occupation forces?"

The Administration answered: "Definitely."

Second: A very different estimate of the risk involved came from Republican Congressman Walter Judd of Minnesota. He warned: "I think the thing necessary to give security to Korea at this stage of the game is the presence of a small American force and the knowledge (on the Soviet side) that attack upon it would bring trouble with us."

"I am convinced," Representative Judd continued, "that if we keep even a battalion there, they are not going to move. And if the battalion is not there"—listen now to his warning—"the chances are they will move within a year."

What a tragedy that the Administration shrugged off that accurate warning!

Third: The Secretary of State was asked if he agreed that the South Koreans alone—and I quote—"will be able to defend themselves against any attack from the northern half of the country." To this the Secretary answered briskly: "We share the same view. Yes, sir."

Rarely in Congressional testimony has so much misinformation been compressed so efficiently into so few words.

Fourth: Republican Congressman Lodge had an incisive comment on all this. "That," he said, "is wishful thinking. . . . I am afraid it confesses a kind of fundamental isolationism that exists in certain branches of the Government, which I think is a very dangerous pattern. I think the presence of our troops there is a tremendous deterrent to the Russians."

Finally: This remarkable scene of the summer of 1949 ends with a memorable document. The minority report of five Republican members of the House Foreign Affairs Committee on July 26, 1949, submitted this solemn warning.

Listen to it:

"It is reliably reported that Soviet troops, attached to the North Korean puppet armies, are in position of command as well as acting as advisors. . . . This development may well presage the launching of a full-scale military drive across the Thirty-eighth Parallel.

"Our forces . . . have been withdrawn from South Korea at the very instant when logic and common sense both demanded no retreat from the realities of the situation."

The report continues: "Already along the Thirty-eighth Parallel aggression is speaking with the too-familiar voices of howitzers and cannons. Our position is untenable and indefensible.

"The House should be aware of these facts."

These words of eloquent, reasoned warning were spoken eleven months before the Korean war broke.

Behind these words was a fervent, desperate appeal. That appeal was addressed to the Administration. It begged at least some firm statement of American intention that might deter the foreseen attack.

What was the Administration answer to that appeal?

The first answer was silence—stubborn, sullen silence for six months.

Then, suddenly, came speech—a high Government official at long last speaking out on Asia. It was now January of 1950. What did he say? He said, "The United States Government will not provide military aid or advice to Chinese forces on Formosa."

Then, one week later, the Secretary of State announced his famous "defense perimeter"—publicly advising our enemies that, so far as nations outside this perimeter were concerned, "no person can guarantee these areas against military attack." Under these circumstances, it was cold comfort to the nations outside this perimeter to be reminded that they could appeal to the United Nations.

These nations, of course, included Korea. The armies of communism, thus informed, began their big build-up. Six months later they were ready to strike across the Thirty-eighth Parallel. They struck on June 25, 1950.

On that day, the record of political and diplomatic failure of this Administration was completed and sealed.

The responsibility for this record cannot be dodged or evaded. Even if not a single Republican leader had warned so clearly against the coming disaster, the responsibility for the fateful political decisions would still rest wholly with the men charged with making those decisions—in the Department of State and in the White House. They cannot escape that responsibility now or ever.

When the enemy struck, on that June day of 1950, what did America do? It did what it always has done in all its times of peril. It appealed to the heroism of its youth.

This appeal was utterly right and utterly inescapable. It was inescapable not only because this was the only way to defend the idea of collective freedom against savage aggression. That appeal was inescapable because there was now in the plight into which we had stumbled no other way to save honor and self-respect.

The answer to that appeal has been what any American knew it would be. It has been sheer valor—valor on all the Korean mountainsides that, each day, bear fresh scars of new graves.

Now—in this anxious autumn—from these heroic men there comes back an answering appeal. It is no whine, no whimpering plea. It is a question that addresses itself to simple reason. It asks: Where do we go from here? When comes the end? Is there an end?

These questions touch all of us. They demand truthful answers. Neither glib promises nor glib excuses will serve. They would be no better than the glib prophecies that brought us to this pass.

To these questions there are two false answers—both equally false. The first would be any answer that dishonestly pledged an end to war in

Korea by any imminent, exact date. Such a pledge would brand its speaker as a deceiver.

The second and equally false answer declares that nothing can be done to speed a secure peace. It dares to tell us that we, the strongest nation in the history of freedom, can only wait—and wait—and wait. Such a statement brands its speaker as a defeatist.

My answer—candid and complete—is this:

The first task of a new Administration will be to review and re-examine every course of action open to us with one goal in view: To bring the Korean war to an early and honorable end. This is my pledge to the American people.

For this task a wholly new Administration is necessary. The reason for this is simple. The old Administration cannot be expected to repair what it failed to prevent.

Where will a new Administration begin?

It will begin with its President taking a simple, firm resolution. That resolution will be: To forego the diversions of politics and to concentrate on the job of ending the Korean war—until that job is honorably done.

That job requires a personal trip to Korea.

I shall make that trip. Only in that way could I learn how best to serve the American people in the cause of peace.

I shall go to Korea.

That is my second pledge to the American people.

Carefully, then, this new Administration, unfettered by past decisions and inherited mistakes, can review every factor—military, political and psychological—to be mobilized in speeding a just peace.

Progress along at least two lines can instantly begin. We can—first— step up the program of training and arming the South Korean forces. Manifestly, under the circumstances of today, United Nations forces can- not abandon that unhappy land. But just as troops of the Republic of Korea covet and deserve the honor of defending their frontiers, so should we give them maximum assistance to insure their ability to do so.

Then, United Nations forces in reserve positions and supporting roles would be assurance that disaster would not again strike.

We can—secondly—shape our psychological warfare program into a weapon capable of cracking the Communist front.

Beyond all this we must carefully weigh all interrelated courses of action. We will, of course, constantly confer with associated free nations of Asia and with the cooperating members of the United Nations. Thus we could bring into being a practical plan for world peace.

That is my third pledge to you.

As the next Administration goes to work for peace, we must be guided at every instant by that lesson I spoke of earlier. The vital lesson is this:

To vacillate, to appease, to placate is only to invite war—vaster war—bloodier war. In the words of the late Senator [Arthur H.] Vandenberg, appeasement is not the road to peace; it is only surrender on the installment plan.

I will always reject appeasement.

And that is my fourth pledge to you.

A nation's foreign policy is a much graver matter than rustling papers and bustling conferences. It is much more than diplomatic decisions and trade treaties and military arrangements.

A foreign policy is the face and voice of a whole people. It is all that the world sees and hears and understands about a single nation. It expresses the character and the faith and the will of that nation. In this, a nation is like any individual of our personal acquaintance; the simplest gesture can betray hesitation or weakness, the merest inflection of voice can reveal doubt or fear.

It is in this deep sense that our foreign policy has faltered and failed.

For a democracy, a great election, such as this, signifies a most solemn trial. It is the time when—to the bewilderment of all tyrants—the people sit in judgment upon the leaders. It is the time when these leaders are summoned before the bar of public decision. There they must give evidence both to justify their actions and explain their intentions.

In the great trial of this election, the judges—the people—must not be deceived into believing that the choice is between isolationism and internationalism. That is a debate of the dead past. The vast majority of Americans of both parties know that to keep their own nation free, they bear a majestic responsibility for freedom through all the world. As practical people, Americans also know the critical necessity of unimpaired access to raw materials on other continents for our own economic and military strength.

Today the choice—the real choice—lies between policies that assume that responsibility awkwardly and fearfully—and policies that accept that responsibility with sure purpose and firm will. The choice is between foresight and blindness, between doing and apologizing, between planning and improvising.

In rendering their verdict, the people must judge with courage and with wisdom. For—at this date—any faltering in America's leadership is a capital offense against freedom.

In this trial, my testimony, of a personal kind, is quite simple. A soldier all my life, I have enlisted in the greatest cause of my life—the cause of peace.

I do not believe it a presumption for me to call the effort of all who have enlisted with me—a crusade.

I use that word only to signify two facts. First: We are united and devoted to a just cause of the purest meaning to all humankind. Second: We know that—for all the might of our effort—victory can come only with the gift of God's help.

In this spirit—humble servants of a proud ideal—we do soberly say: This is a crusade.

☆

ADLAI E. STEVENSON

Acceptance Speech

CHICAGO, ILLINOIS

July 26, 1952

I accept your nomination—and your program.

I should have preferred to hear those words uttered by a stronger, a wiser, a better man than myself. But, after listening to the President's speech, I feel better about myself!

None of you, my friends, can wholly appreciate what is in my heart. I can only hope that you may understand my words. They will be few.

I have not sought the honor you have done me. I *could* not seek it because I aspired to another office, which was the full measure of my ambition. One does not treat the highest office within the gift of the people of Illinois as an alternative or as a consolation prize.

I *would* not seek your nomination for the Presidency because the burdens of that office stagger the imagination. Its potential for good or evil now and in the years of our lives smothers exultation and converts vanity to prayer.

I have asked the Merciful Father—the Father of us all—to let this cup pass from me. But from such dread responsibility one does not shrink in fear, in self-interest, or in false humility.

So, "If this cup may not pass from me, except I drink it, Thy will be done."

That my heart has been troubled, that I have not sought this nomination, that I could not seek it in good conscience, that I would not seek it in honest self-appraisal, is not to say that I value it the less. Rather it is that I revere the office of the Presidency of the United States.

And now, my friends, that you have made your decision, I will fight to win that office with all my heart and soul. And, with your help, I have no doubt that we will win.

You have summoned me to the highest mission within the gift of any people. I could not be more proud. Better men than I were at hand for this mighty task, and I owe to you and to them every resource of mind and of strength that I possess to make your deed today a good one for our country and for our party. I am confident too, that your selection of a candidate for Vice President will strengthen me and our party immeasurably in the hard, the implacable work that lies ahead for all of us.

I know you join me in gratitude and respect for the great Democrats and the leaders of our generation whose names you have considered here in this Convention, whose vigor, whose character, whose devotion to the Republic we love so well have won the respect of countless Americans and have enriched our party. I shall need them, we shall need them, because I have not changed in any respect since yesterday. Your nomination, awesome as I find it, has not enlarged my capacities. So I am profoundly grateful and emboldened by their comradeship and their fealty, and I have been deeply moved by their expressions of good will and support. And I cannot, my friends, resist the urge to take the one opportunity that has been afforded me to pay my humble respects to a very great and good American, whom I am proud to call my kinsman, Alben Barkley of Kentucky.

Let me say, too, that I have been heartened by the conduct of this Convention. You have argued and disagreed, because as Democrats you care and you care deeply. But you have disagreed and argued without calling each other liars and thieves, without despoiling our best traditions in any naked struggles for power.

And you have written a platform that neither equivocates, contradicts nor evades. You have restated our party's record, its principles and its purposes, in language that none can mistake, and with a firm confidence in justice, freedom and peace on earth that will raise the hearts and the hopes of mankind for that distant day when no one rattles a saber and no one drags a chain.

For all these things I am grateful to you. But I feel no exultation, no sense of triumph. Our troubles are all ahead of us. Some will call us appeasers; other will say we are the war party. Some will say we are reactionary. Others will say that we stand for socialism. There will be the inevitable cries of "throw the rascals out"; "it's time for a change"; and so on and so on.

We'll hear all those things and many more besides. But we will hear nothing that we have not heard before. I am not too much concerned with partisan denunciation, with epithets and abuse, because the workingman, the farmer, the thoughtful businessmen, all know that they are better off than ever before and they all know that the greatest danger to free enterprise in this country died with the great depression under the hammer blows of the Democratic Party.

Nor am I afraid that the precious two-party system is in danger. Certainly the Republican Party looked brutally alive a couple of weeks ago, and I mean both Republican parties! Nor am I afraid that the Democratic Party is old and fat and indolent. After 150 years it has been old for a long time; and it will never be indolent as long as it looks forward and not back, as long as it commands the allegiance of the young and the hopeful who dream the dreams and see the visions of a better America and a better world.

You will hear many sincere and thoughtful people express concern about the continuation of one party in power for twenty years. I don't belittle this attitude. But change for the sake of change has no absolute merit in itself. If our greatest hazard is preservation of the values of Western civilization, in our self-interest alone, if you please, is it the part of wisdom to change for the sake of change to a party with a split personality; to a leader, whom we all respect, but who has been called upon to minister to a hopeless case of political schizophrenia?

If the fear is corruption in official position, do you believe with Charles Evans Hughes that guilt is personal and knows no party? Do you doubt the power of any political leader, if he has the will to do so, to set his own house in order without his neighbors having to burn it down?

What does concern me, in common with thinking partisans of both parties, is not just winning the election, but how it is won, how well we can take advantage of this great quadrennial opportunity to debate issues sensibly and soberly. I hope and pray that we Democrats, win or lose, can campaign not as a crusade to exterminate the opposing party, as our opponents seem to prefer, but as a great opportunity to educate and elevate a people whose destiny is leadership, not alone of a rich and prosperous, contented country as in the past, but of a world in ferment.

And, my friends, more important than winning the election is governing the nation. That is the test of a political party—the acid, final test. When the tumult and the shouting die, when the bands are gone and the lights are dimmed, there is the stark reality of responsibility in an hour of history haunted with those gaunt, grim specters of strife, dissension and materialism at home, and ruthless, inscrutable and hostile power abroad.

The ordeal of the twentieth century—the bloodiest, most turbulent era of the Christian age—is far from over. Sacrifice, patience, understanding and implacable purpose may be our lot for years to come. Let's face it. Let's talk sense to the American people. Let's tell them the truth, that there are no gains without pains, that we are now on the eve of great decisions, not easy decisions, like resistance when you're attacked, but a long, patient, costly struggle which alone can assure triumph over the great enemies of man—war, poverty and tyranny—and the assaults upon human dignity which are the most grievous consequences of each.

Let's tell them that the victory to be won in the twentieth century, this portal to the Golden Age, mocks the pretensions of individual acumen and ingenuity. For it is a citadel guarded by thick walls of ignorance and of mistrust which do not fall before the trumpets' blast or the politicians' imprecations or even a general's baton. They are, my friends, walls that must be directly stormed by the hosts of courage, of morality and of vision, standing shoulder to shoulder, unafraid of ugly truth, contemptuous of lies, half truths, circuses and demagoguery.

The people are wise—wiser than the Republicans think. And the Democratic Party is the people's party, not the labor party, not the farmers' party, not the employers' party—it is the party of no one because it is the party of everyone.

That I think, is our ancient mission. Where we have deserted it we have failed. With your help there will be no desertion now. Better we lose the election than mislead the people; and better we lose than misgovern the people. Help me to do the job in this autumn of conflict and of campaign; help me to do the job in these years of darkness, doubt and of crisis which stretch beyond the horizon of tonight's happy vision, and we will justify our glorious past and the loyalty of silent millions who look to us for compassion, for understanding and for honest purpose. Thus we will serve our great tradition greatly.

I ask of you all you have; I will give to you all I have, even as he who came here tonight and honored me, as he has honored you—the Democratic Party—by a lifetime of service and bravery that will find him an imperishable page in the history of the Republic and of the Democratic Party—President Harry S. Truman.

And finally, my friends, in the staggering task you have assigned me, I shall always try "to do justly and to love mercy and to walk humbly with my God."

☆

ADLAI E. STEVENSON

Campaign Speech

ACADEMY OF MUSIC, BROOKLYN, NEW YORK

October 31, 1952

Brooklyn has meant good fortune for Franklin Roosevelt and good fortune for Harry Truman. In fact, it seems to have meant good fortune for practically everybody, except the Dodgers.

I will never forget the time during the war when I was driving through Brooklyn from the Navy Yard with the Secretary of the Navy behind a motorcycle escort; we slowed down at a crowded corner, and I overhead somebody in the curious crowd say, "It must be dem bums." I was never more flattered in my life.

Now, as usual, my friends, the pre-election thunder comes from the Republicans. They have most of the nation's newspapers and magazines. They have the slickest slogans and the shiniest posters. They win most of the pre-election polls, and sometimes they win them in a "Gallup." It is not a very good pun but it is the best I could do.

Then—then the people will vote on Tuesday. I understand that on Wednesday the newspapers plan to publish a 5-Star Final.

Many thousands of our votes will come from rank-and-file Republicans who will vote with us. No doubt some Democrats will vote for the Republican candidates. We have already, for example, traded a couple of Southern Governors for the Senator from Oregon and the Vice Chairman of the National Young Republicans. And I regard this as a profitable exchange for us. I would be happy to throw in a second baseman—but not Jackie Robinson.

But, let's not speak of the approaching Republican sorrow without compassion. You in Brooklyn, of all places, know how melancholy is the sound of the words, "wait till next year."

The choice next Tuesday is a fateful one. It is a choice of parties, between the party whose affirmative leadership for many years is written in the strength and the prosperity of our nation and in the widening opportunity and security of our lives, and the party whose only consistent record is one of opposition, obstruction and stubborn negation. It is also a choice of leadership. My opponent has been making a great effort—here in the East anyway, and especially in New York—to persuade the people to forget the last three months. His friends are suggesting that what he said in

Champaign, Illinois, doesn't count, that those words in Milwaukee really weren't uttered, that none of his Midwestern tour expressed the real Eisenhower. But those words were spoken, those speeches were made; the visits with Senator Jenner and Senator McCarthy were all too real. The General may forget, but those Senators won't, and if they should be returned to the Senate and the General sent to the White House, they won't forget and won't let the General forget either.

A man who has the confidence of the public has a public trust not to abuse that confidence for any ends, let alone his own.

In the field of foreign policy the obligation is even stronger. The issues are the relations of our country with our allies and our enemies, the issues of peace or war.

Deception cannot be condoned as campaign oratory. I thought for a time that the issues of foreign policy and of our future could be freely and honestly debated between us on a level worthy of the American people. But the Republicans have concentrated not on discussing, but on systematically disparaging the policies which, with all their defects, have brought the United States to a peak of world prestige and power and responsibility never before dreamed of. Confronted with the great achievements and potentialities of the Marshall Plan, the Truman Doctrine, the North Atlantic Pact, Point Four, the Trade Agreements Program, the Good Neighbor Policy, they have fallen back upon the parrot-like repetition of a monotonous charge. The Democratic foreign policy, they say, does not promise quick solutions; the answers are not all to be found in the back of the book.

As a result, they have now got their own candidates into a trap. For they feel, unless he can come up with the big answer, unless he can promise a quick and easy road to peace and world leadership, the American people will begin to find out how good our foreign policy really has been. The General's advisers seem to have assured him that the American people will buy any merchandise so long as you package it gaudily enough. But the public has rejected the General's merchandise, piece by piece as second-hand and deceptive.

Now, let us, if you will, review this dreary history because it is important in these last hours of this fateful campaign.

The General's experience in Europe and in working with Europeans should have made him unusually sensitive to the importance of guarding and strengthening our European alliances. Yet in his first major policy speech last August, what did he do? He said, speak "with cold finality," to the Soviet Union and prepare to roll back Soviet power and liberate the satellite states. How we were to accomplish this, he did not say; but these words, spoken on the General's eminent authority, raised momentary hopes among those Americans whose friends or relatives were trapped behind the Iron Curtain.

As the idea sank in, however, the effect was greatly different. It became apparent that the General's proposal would lead, not to the liberation of the captive peoples, but to their obliteration—not to release, but to war.

Caught out in this manner, the General explained that he didn't mean what he had said. Yet the damage in Europe had already been done—damage not only to the General himself—which you and I have all regretted—but, far more important, to that funded capital of confidence in American stability and judgment which we have so carefully built up in the postwar years.

And this was only the beginning.

I was surprised that the General should have recklessly gambled with the confidence of our European allies in view of his experience as the head of the North Atlantic Treaty Organization. I was even more surprised when he showed a willingness to undermine that organization itself. In May of 1952, the General had told the Congress that a cut of more than one billion dollars in the foreign-aid program would endanger the proposed military buildup which he said he considered essential in the interests of United States security.

As soon as he took off his uniform, however, he changed his tune.

What this country needed, he said, was a forty-billion-dollar budget cut and a major tax reduction. Pressed by his own astonished colleagues, he qualified this claim. He did not propose, he said, to cut the budget immediately by forty billion, but to work toward a reduction of that amount over a period of five years.

It was at this point that Senator Taft took the General firmly by the hand. The forty-billion figure, he apparently dismissed as a typographical error. In his Morningside Heights Manifesto he pledged the General to a mere ten-billion-dollar cut next year, and a twenty-five-billion cut the following year.

Again false hopes were raised—hopes that we could quickly reduce our taxes and still not reduce our safety. And once again the hopes were doomed to disappointment.

Before the Chicago Convention the General appeared willing to keep Korea out of the campaign. Last June, at Abilene, he denied that there was, and I quote him, "any clear-cut answer" to the Korean problem. He said he did not think it would be possible for our forces to carry through a decisive attack; he ruled out the alternative of retreat; and he ended with this candid conclusion: "We have got to stand firm and take every possible step we can to reduce our losses and stand right there and try to get a decent armistice."

But a few weeks as a political candidate began to alter his opinion. Where once he had sought to unite public sentiment behind our stand in Korea, he now sought out the possibilities of division and of mistrust, echoing the views of his Republican advisers who had even called this first, great, historic case of collective security under arms a "useless war" and "Truman's war."

He first began to speak of what he called the truly terrible blunders that led up to the Korean War, including the very decision to withdraw our troops from Korea, in which he had participated as Chief of Staff of the Army.

Then he reversed his position on the all-important question of bombing the Manchurian bases across the Yalu and expanding the war—a question which the nation had pondered through the weeks of the MacArthur hearings and had decided in the negative. On June 5th, at Abilene, the General declared that he was against bombing bases in Chinese territory on the other side of the Yalu. Yet in September, he could say that he had always stood behind MacArthur on bombing those bases.

And now, as this political campaign has grown in intensity, and as each day sees the increase in Democratic strength, the General is indulging in something far more insidious than self-contradiction. He is seeking one easy solution after another for the Korean War.

Early this month in Illinois, the General propounded the startling theory that the American forces could soon be withdrawn and replaced by South Korean troops. "If there must be a war there," he said, "let it be Asians against Asians."

Now, there are several things wrong with this proposal. In the first place, the General put it forward as though it were a brand-new idea, although he knew that it has been our policy since the start of the Korean conflict to arm and train South Korean forces as fast as possible. In the second place, he suggested that it would be relatively easy to replace our American boys with Koreans; yet our Commander on the spot immediately stated that no matter how much training and equipment we supplied, it would be impossible for the South Koreans to take over the entire front.

Apart from these military questions, however, the General's statement displayed an alarming disdain for the sensibilities of our allies both in Europe and in Asia. The General talked as if we had entered Korea to fight Asians; yet he must know that we entered Korea to resist communist aggression, and that in such a fight there can be no color line. And, as the former head of NATO, how could the General be unaware that such talk would undermine the confidence of all our allies in the sincerity of our world leadership?

"Let Asians fight Asians" is the authentic voice of a resurgent isolationist. In 1939 the Republican Old Guard, faced with the menace of the Nazi world, was content to say, "Let Europeans fight Europeans," ignoring completely the fact that the menace of Nazism was a menace to Americans as much as to Frenchmen and Englishmen. What a curious remark for a man who led the crusade against a Nazi tyranny!

Again the General raised false hopes of a quick solution, and again the false hopes were doomed to disappointment. Confronted with scathing comment for this proposal, even from members of his own party, such as Senator Smith of Maine, the General has now put forth a new proposal—a proposal suggested not by an experienced diplomat, or even by an experienced soldier, but rather by one of the General's new ghost writers, recruited from the staff of a slick magazine.

This new proposal is simplicity itself. "Elect me President," the General says, "and you can forget about Korea; I will go there personally." I don't think for a moment that the American people are taken in by a promise without a program. It is not enough to say, "I will fix it for you." The principle of blind leadership is alien to our tradition. And, unfortunately, the ghost writer who provided the proposal failed to give it content. The General was to go to Korea, but nobody indicated what he should do when he got there. The American people were quick to realize also that the conduct of a military campaign is the task of a field commander, whereas the making of peace requires negotiation with the central adversary—and in this case the central adversary is in Moscow, not in Korea.

And so, once again having raised the hopes of American families, he has been forced to beat a retreat from his first proposals. In a series of statements in the last two days he has abandoned his promise of making peace. At Kew Gardens he said that he was going out only to—and I quote him—"improve our plans." At Mineola he referred to his duty to go to Korea to see what our problems were and—I quote him—"how we can bring that situation under better control."

In the Bronx, on Wednesday, he referred to his Korean trip as an opportunity, "to see how we stand in organizing the forces of the Republic of Korea in order to prepare the Koreans to defend their own line."

And in New York City on the same day he again talked in terms of increasing the contribution of the Republic of Korea.

Now, these are admirable objectives, and such a trip would be informative. But, the label on the bottle was different, and the contents are misbranded.

If we are to bring about an honorable peace in Korea—which is what the General talked about in his Detroit speech—we must face the facts. There are only four possible courses open to us: Get out, or enlarge the war, or purchase a truce through the abandonment of our moral position, or continue the negotiations with all of the resource and self-discipline at our command.

Last summer the General excluded the alternatives of extending the war or retreating from it. I don't know what his position is now. Retreat can only mean the loss of the whole Far East to communism. And extending the war to China would tie up the bulk of our armed strength in Asia while the Red Army was left free for new adventures in the industrial heart of Europe.

But if he would neither enlarge the war nor abandon it, what would he do? Would he make new concessions in the truce negotiations, or has he forgotten the nature of the problem which has caused the deadlock?

Negotiations with communists are never easy, always exasperating, but not necessarily hopeless.

At the time we instituted the Berlin Airlift many impatient Americans said that we were undertaking a hopeless task; but we regained access to Berlin and our prestige in Europe was greater than ever.

The Korean truce negotiations have dragged on through many months, but they have not been without result. Most of the problems which first confronted us in reaching an agreement have now, one by one, been eliminated. Only one major issue remains, and this is not a military but a moral issue.

It is whether we and the other United Nations fighting in Korea should force thousands of Chinese and North Korean prisoners to return to communist territory and almost certain death.

We sent our troops into Korea two and one-half years ago because we knew that mobsters who get away with one crime are only encouraged to start on another. Korea was a crucial test in the struggle between the free world and communism.

The question of the forcible return of prisoners of war is an essential part of that test. Fifty thousand prisoners have stated that they would rather kill themselves than return to their homeland. Many of those prisoners surrendered in response to our own appeals. They surrendered to escape the communist world. They surrendered because in their eyes the United States stood for freedom from slavery. So far the United States *has* stood for freedom—and this is our greatest asset in our struggle against communism. How many of you suppose that we could retain that asset if we sent these men back to their death at the point of a bayonet?

This is the sole question remaining unresolved in the truce negotiations. Is this the question General Eisenhower intends to settle by going to Korea? I do not ask this idly. Quite recently at Richmond, Senator Capehart, one of the Republican Old Guard whom General Eisenhower has embraced, accused President Truman of prolonging the war by refusing to force these prisoners to return. The Senator's position with respect to these prisoners is identical with that of the communists. It is a position which no government in the world has taken except the Soviet Union and its satellites.

And I think it is worth noting that this was the same Senator Capehart who said on October 12th, "In another two weeks, General Eisenhower will be thinking and talking on foreign policy just like Senator Taft."

Now I think the General should answer one question. In embracing the Republican Old Guard has he embraced their contention that we should give up our moral position? And in asking the General this question, let me state my own views.

I have the profoundest sympathy for every mother and father in the United States who is affected by this tragic war. No one is more determined than I to see that it is brought to a conclusion. But that conclusion must be honorable, for if we do not maintain our moral position we have lost everything—our young men will have died in vain. If we give up on this point, if we send these 50,000 prisoners to their death, we will no longer lead the coalition of the free world. Today we stand in that position of leadership not merely because we are physically strong but because our cause is just. Once we commit a gross injustice, our allies will fall away like the leaves in autumn.

With patience and restraint and with the building up of our strength the communists will be compelled to yield, even as they yielded on the Berlin Airlift.

As of the moment we have a stalemate, and stalemates are abhorrent to Americans. But let us not deceive ourselves. A stalemate is better than surrender—and it is better than atomic war. And let us not forget that a stalemate exists for the enemy as well as for ourselves.

There is no greater cruelty, in my judgment, than the raising of false hopes—no greater arrogance than playing politics with peace and war. Rather than exploit human hopes and fears, rather than provide glib solutions and false assurances, I would gladly lose this Presidential election.

There is strength in freedom—strength far greater than we know. I have no fear that our present ordeal is without end. Working together, united in respect for human beings, and united in respect for ourselves, the free peoples can stop the communist conquest, save the peace, and move together to build a new and spacious and friendly world.

If we have the courage and the fortitude to walk through the valley of the shadow boldly and mercifully and justly, we shall yet emerge in the blazing dawn of a glorious new day.

☆

1956

——— ☆ ———

Perhaps the most important question surrounding the 1956 presidential election was whether or not Eisenhower would run for reelection,
for between September, 1955 and June, 1956, the President had suffered a heart attack and undergone a serious operation for an intes-
tinal obstruction. But in July, one month after his surgery and a
month before the Republican national convention was scheduled to
meet in San Francisco, Eisenhower announced that he would enter
the campaign.

During his first administration Eisenhower kept his pledge to go
to Korea. By July, 1953, the communists had agreed to an armistice.
Two years later Eisenhower met Khrushchev at Geneva to discuss
disarmament and the reunification of East and West Germany.

Domestically Eisenhower accepted the "welfare" legislation of
the New Deal and the Fair Deal, and in some areas, such as social
security, he even extended it. In addition, in 1953 he created a Department of Health, Education, and Welfare, and later supported federal
aid to school and highway construction projects.

One of the major lessons the general learned during his first
term in office was that a politician is a different brand of soldier: he
does not always march to the beat of his Commander-in-Chief, even
though he is a member of the President's party. When Eisenhower
entered office he was getting more support from the Democratic

minority (under the leadership of Sam Rayburn in the House and Lyndon Johnson in the Senate) than he was from his own party. This was particularly true in the area of foreign affairs. Following the recession of 1953 and the mid-term elections of 1954 the Democrats again took over the House and Senate, but they continued to work effectively with the Republican administration.

At the Democratic convention in Chicago, the party renominated Adlai Stevenson. In their party platform the Democrats attacked the Eisenhower administration, reiterated their 1952 pledges to labor and agriculture, and accepted the recent Supreme Court decisions on desegregation, although they opposed "all proposals for the use of force to interfere with the orderly determination of these matters by the courts." In his acceptance speech Stevenson charged that "the country is stalled on dead center." What was needed, he said, was the creation of a new society based upon the principles of the New Deal and the Fair Deal.

Certainly the most important feature of Eisenhower's acceptance speech was the President's statement that peaceful coexistence with the Russians was possible. But with relative prosperity in the country —the recession of 1957 was yet to come—Eisenhower chose to make peace, prosperity, and unity the key issues of the campaign. In an interesting speech delivered at Cleveland, Ike echoed these themes and voiced his criticism of large-scale government intervention in social and economic spheres.

Stevenson's major issues in 1956 were the hydrogen bomb and the draft. In a September 29th speech in Minneapolis Stevenson pledged to end hydrogen bomb testing and to replace the draft with a volunteer defense corps.

Shortly after Stevenson's Minneapolis address war erupted in the Middle East and the Hungarian revolt broke out in Budapest. By November 4th the communists had crushed the last pockets of resistance in Hungary, and on Election Day, November 6th, British Prime Minister Anthony Eden announced a cease-fire in Egypt. Bombs and armies were difficult subjects to discuss in 1956. On Election Day Eisenhower defeated Stevenson even more soundly than he did in 1952.

DWIGHT D. EISENHOWER

Acceptance Speech

SAN FRANCISCO, CALIFORNIA

August 23, 1956

Chairman Martin, delegates and alternates to this great convention, distinguished guests and my fellow Americans wherever they may be in this broad land.

I should first tell you that I have no words in which to express the gratitude that Mrs. Eisenhower and I feel for the warmth of your welcome, the cordiality you extended to us and to the members of our family —our son and daughter, my brothers and their wives—touches our hearts deeply. Thank you very much, indeed.

I thank you additionally and personally for the high honor you have accorded me in entrusting me once more with your nomination for the Presidency. And I should like to say that it is a great satisfaction to me that the team of individuals you selected in 1952 you've selected to keep intact for this campaign.

I am not here going to attempt a eulogy of Mr. Nixon. You have heard his qualifications described in the past several days. I merely want to say this: that whatever dedication to country, loyalty and patriotism and great ability can do for America, he will do—and that I know.

Ladies and gentlemen, when Abraham Lincoln was nominated in 1860, and a committee brought the news to him at his home in Springfield, Ill., his reply was two sentences long. Then, while his friends and neighbors waited in the street, and while bonfires lit up the May evening, he said simply, "And now I will not longer defer the pleasure of taking you, and each of you, by the hand."

I wish I could do the same—speak two sentences, and then take each of you by the hand, all of you who are in sound of my voice. If I could do so, I would first thank you individually for your confidence and your trust. Then, as I am sure Lincoln did as he moved among his friends in the light of the bonfires, we could pause and talk a while about the questions that are uppermost in your minds.

I am sure that one topic would dominate all the rest. That topic is: the future.

This is a good time to think about the future, for this convention is celebrating its one hundredth anniversary. And a centennial is an occasion not just for recalling the inspiring past, but even more for looking ahead to the demanding future.

Just as on New Year's Day we instinctively think, "I wonder where I will be a year from now," so it is quite natural for the Republican party to ask today, "What will happen, not just in the coming election, but even 100 years from now?"

My answer is this: If we and our successors are as courageous and forward-looking and as militantly determined, here under the Klieg lights of the twentieth century, as Abraham Lincoln and his associates were in the bonfire light of the nineteenth, the Republican party will continue to grow in the confidence and affection of the American people, not only to November next, but indeed to and beyond, its second centennial.

Now, of course, in this convention setting you and I are momentarily more interested in November, 1956, than in 2056. But the point is this: Our policies are right today only as they are designed to stand the test of tomorrow.

The great Norwegian, Henrik Ibsen, once wrote:

"I hold that man is in the right who is most clearly in league with the future."

Today I want to demonstrate the truth of a single proposition:

The Republican party is the party of the future.

I hold that the Republican party and platform are right in 1956, because they are "most closely in league with the future." And for this reason the Republican party and program are and will be decisively approved by the American people in 1956.

My friends, I have just made a very flat statement for victory for the Republican party in November. And I believe it from the bottom of my heart, but what I say is based upon certain assumptions and those assumptions must become true if the prediction I make is to be valid.

And that is this: that every American who believes as we do—the Republicans, the independents, the straight-thinking Democrats must carry the message of the record and the pledges that we have made and here make to all the people in the land.

We must see as we do our civic duty that not only do we vote but that everybody is qualified to vote—that everybody registers, then everybody goes to the polls in November.

Here is the task—not only for the Republican National Committee, for the women's organizations, for the citizen's organizations, for the so-called Youth For Eisenhower—everybody that bears this message in his heart must carry it to the country. In that way we will win.

And which reminds me, my friends, there are only a few days left for registering in a number of our states. That is one thing you cannot defer. The records show that our registration as compared to former years at this time is way down across the land—registration across the board.

Let's help the American Heritage, let's help the Boy Scouts, let's help everybody to get people out and registered to vote.

Now of special relevance, and to me particularly gratifying, is the fact that the country's young people show a consistent preference for this Administration. After all, let us not forget these young people are America's future. Parenthetically, may I say I shall never cease to hope that the several states will give them the voting privilege at a somewhat earlier age than is now generally the case.

Now, the first reason of the five I shall give you why the Republican party is the party of the future is this:

Because it is the party of long-range principle, not short-term expediency.

One of my predecessors is said to have observed that in making his decisions he had to operate like a football quarterback—he could not very well call the next play until he saw how the last play turned out. Well, that may be a good way to run a football team, but in these times it is no way to run a government.

Now why is it so important that great government programs be based upon principle rather than upon shifting political opportunism?

It is because what government does affects profoundly the daily lives and plans of every person in the country. If governmental action is without the solid guidelines of enduring principle, national policies flounder in confusion. And more than this, the millions of individuals, families and enterprises, whose risk-taking and planning for the future are our country's very life force, are paralyzed by uncertainty, diffidence and indecision.

Change based on principle is progress. Constant change without principle becomes chaos.

I shall give you several examples of rejecting expediency in favor of principle.

First, the farm issue.

Expediency said: "Let's do something in a hurry—anything—even multiply our price-depressing surpluses at the risk of making the problem twice as bad next year—just so we get through this year."

People who talk like that do not care about principle, and do not know farmers. The farmer deals every day in basic principles of growth and life. His product must be planned, and cultivated, and harvested over a long period. He has to figure not just a year at a time but over cycles and spans of years, as to his soil, his water, his equipment, the strains of his stock—and the strains on his income.

And so, for this man of principle, we have designed our program of principle. In it, we recognize that we have received from our forebears a rich legacy: our continent's basic resource of soil. We are determined that, through such measures as the soil bank and the great plains program, this legacy shall be handed on to our children even richer than we received it.

We are equally determined that farm prices and income, which were needlessly pushed down under surpluses—surpluses induced first by war and then by unwise political action that was stubbornly and recklessly prolonged, shall in the coming months and years get back on a genuinely healthy basis.

This improvement must continue until a rightful share of our prosperity is permanently enjoyed by agriculture—on which our very life depends.

A second example: labor relations.

Expediency said: "When a major labor dispute looms, the Government must do something—anything—to settle the dispute even before the parties have finished negotiating. Get an injunction. Seize the steel mills. Appoint a board. Knock their heads together."

Principle says: "Free collective bargaining without Government interference is the cornerstone of American philosophy of labor-management relations."

If the Government charges impatiently into every major dispute, the negotiations between parties will become a pointless preliminary farce, while everyone waits around to see what the Government will do. This Administration has faith in the rightness of the collective bargaining principle. It believes in the maturity of both labor and business leaders, and in their determination to do what is best not only for their own side but for the country as a whole.

The results: for the first time in our history a complete steel contract was negotiated and signed without direct Government intervention, and the last three and a half years have witnessed one of the most remarkable periods of labor peace on record.

Another example: concentration of power in Washington.

Expediency said: "We cannot allow our fine new ideas to be at the mercy of fifty-one separate state and territorial Legislatures. It is so much easier to plan, finance and direct all major projects from Washington."

Principle says: "Geographical balance of power is essential to our form of free society. If you take the centralization short-cut every time something is to be done, you will perhaps sometimes get quick action. But there is no perhaps about the price you will pay for your impatience: the growth of a swollen, bureaucratic, monster government in Washington, in whose shadow our state and local governments will ultimately wither and die."

And so we stemmed the heedless stampede to Washington. We made a special point to build up state activities, state finances, and state prestige.

Our founding fathers showed us how the Federal Government could exercise its undoubted responsibility for leadership, while still stopping short of the kind of interference that deadens local vigor, variety, initiative and imagination.

So today we say to our young people: the party of their future will pass along to you undamaged the unique system of division of authority which has proved so successful in reconciling our oldest ideas of personal freedom with the twentieth-century need for decisiveness in action.

My second reason for saying that the Republican party is the party of the future is this: it is the party which concentrates on the facts and issues of today and tomorrow, not the facts and issues of yesterday.

More than twenty years ago, our opponents found in the problems of the depression a battleground on which they scored many political victories. Now economic cycles have not been eliminated. Still, the world has moved on from the Nineteen Thirties: good times have supplanted depression; new techniques for checking serious recession have been learned and tested and a whole new array of problems has sprung up. But their obsession with the depression still blinds many of our opponents to the insistent demands of today.

The present and future are bringing new kinds of challenge to Federal and local governments: water supply, highways, health, housing, power development, and peaceful uses of atomic energy. With two-thirds of us living in big cities, questions of urban organization and redevelopment must be given high priority. Highest of all, perhaps, will be the priority of first-class education to meet the demands of our swiftly growing school-age population.

The party of the young and all ages says: Let us quit fighting the battles of the past and let us all turn our attention to these problems of the present and future, on which the long-term well-being of our people so urgently depends.

Third: The Republican party is the party of the future because it is the party that draws people together, not drives them apart.

Our party despises the technique of pitting group against group for cheap political advantage. Republicans view as a central principle of conduct—not just as a phrase on nickels and dimes—that old motto of ours: "E Pluribus Unum"—"Out of Many—One."

Our party as far back as 1856 began establishing a record of bringing together, as its largest element, the working people and small farmers, as well as the small business men. It attracted minority groups, scholars and writers, not to mention reformers of all kinds, free-soilers, independent Democrats, conscience Whigs, barn-burners, "soft hunkers," teetotallers, vegetarians and transcendentalists!

Now, 100 years later, the Republican party is again the rallying point for Americans of all callings, ages, races and incomes. They see in its broad, forward-moving, straight-down-the-road, fighting program the best promise for their own steady progress toward a bright future. Some opponents have tried to call this a "one-interest party." Indeed it is a one-interest party; and that one interest is the interest of every man, woman and child in America! And most surely as long as the Republican party continues to be this kind of a one-interest party—a one-universal-interest party—it will continue to be the party of the future.

And now the fourth reason: The Republican party is the party of the future because it is the party through which the many things that still need doing will soonest be done—and will be done by enlisting the fullest energies of free, creative, individual people.

Republicans have proved that it is possible for a government to have a warm, sensitive concern for the everyday needs of people, while steering clear of the paternalistic "big-brother-is-watching-you" kind of interference. The individual—and especially the idealistic young person—has no faith in a tight Federal monopoly on problem-solving. He seeks and deserves opportunity for himself and every other person who is burning to participate in putting right the wrongs of the world.

In our time of prosperity and progress, one thing we must always be on guard against is smugness. True, things are going well; but there are thousands of things still to be done. There are still enough needless sufferings to be cured, enough injustices to be erased to provide careers for all the young crusaders we can produce or find.

We want them all! Republicans, independents, discerning Democrats, come on in and help.

One hundred years ago the Republican party was created in a devout belief in equal justice and equal opportunity for all in a nation of free men and women.

What is more, the Republican party's record on social justice rests, not on words and promises, but on accomplishment. The record shows that a wide range of quietly effective actions, conceived in understanding and good will for all, has brought about more genuine—and often voluntary—progress toward equal justice and opportunity in the last three years than was accomplished in all the previous twenty put together.

Elimination of various kinds of discrimination in the armed services, the District of Columbia, and among the employes of government contractors provides specific examples of this progress. In this work, incidentally, no one has been more effective and more energetic than our Vice President, who is head of one of the great committees in this direction.

Now, in all existing kinds of discrimination there is much to do. We must insure a fair chance to such people as mature workers who have trouble getting jobs, older citizens with problems of health, housing, security and recreation, migratory farm laborers and physically-handicapped workers. We have with us, also, problems involving American Indians, low-income farmers and laborers, women who sometimes do not get equal pay for equal work, small businessmen, and employers and workers in areas which need special assistance for redevelopment.

Specific new programs of action are being pushed for all of these, the most recent being a new fourteen-point program for small businessmen which was announced early in August. And the everyday well-being of people is being advanced on many other fronts. This is being done, not by paternalistic regimentation. It is done by clear cut, aggressive Federal leadership and by releasing the illimitable resources and drives of our millions of self-reliant individuals and our thousands of private organizations of every conceivable kind and size—each of these is consecrated to the task of meeting some human need, curing some human evil, or enriching some human experience.

Finally, a party of the future must be completely dedicated to peace, as indeed must all Americans. For without peace there is no future.

It was in the light of this truth that the United States proposed its atoms-for-peace plan in 1953, and since then has done so much to make this new science universally available to friendly nations in order to promote human welfare. We have agreements with more than thirty nations for research reactors, and with seven for power reactors, while many others are under consideration. Twenty thousand kilograms of nuclear fuel have been set aside for the foreign programs.

In the same way, we have worked unceasingly for the promotion of effective steps in disarmament so that the labor of men could with confidence be devoted to their own improvement rather than wasted in the building of engines of destruction.

No one is more aware than I that it is the young who fight the wars, and it is the young who give up years of their lives to military training and service. It is not enough that their elders promise "peace in our time": it must be peace in their time too, and in their children's time; indeed, my friends, there is only one real peace now, and that is peace for all time.

Now there are three imperatives of peace—three requirements that the prudent man must face with unblinking realism.

The first imperative is the elementary necessity of maintaining our own national strength—moral, economic and military.

It is still my conviction, as I wrote in 1947:

"The compelling necessities of the moment leave us no alternative to the maintenance of real and respectable strength—not only in our moral rectitude and our economic power, but in terms of adequate military preparedness."

During the past three and one-half years, our military strength has been constantly augmented, soberly and intelligently. Our country has never before in peacetime been so well prepared militarily. So long as the world situation requires, our security must be vigorously sustained.

Our economic power, as everyone knows, is displaying a capacity for growth which is both rapid and sound, even while supporting record military budgets. We must keep it growing.

But moral strength is also essential. Today we are competing for men's hearts, and minds, and trust all over the world. In such a competition, what we are at home and what we do at home is even more important than what we say abroad. Here again, my friends, we find constructive work for each of us. What each of us does, how each of us acts has an influence on this question.

Now the second imperative of peace is collective security.

We live in a shrunken world, a world in which oceans are crossed in hours, a world in which a single-minded despotism menaces the scattered freedoms of scores of struggling independent nations. To insure the combined strength of friendly nations is for all of us an elementary matter of self-preservation—as elementary as having a stout militia in the days of the flintlock.

Again the strength I speak of is not military strength alone. The heart of the collective security principle is the idea of helping other nations to realize their own potentialities—political, economic and military. The strength of the free world lies not in cementing the free worlds into a second monolithic mass to compete with that of the Communists. It lies rather in the unity that comes of the voluntary association of nations which, however diverse, are developing their own capacities and asserting their own national destinies in a world of freedom and of mutual respect.

There can be no enduring peace for any nation while other nations suffer privation, oppression, and a sense of injustice and despair. In our modern world, it is madness to suppose that there could be an island of tranquillity and prosperity in a sea of wretchedness and frustration. For America's sake, as well as the world's, we must measure up to the challenge of the second imperative: the urgent need for mutual economic and military cooperation among the free nations, sufficient to deter or repel aggression wherever it may threaten.

But even this is no longer enough.

We are in the era of the thermonuclear bomb that can obliterate cities and can be delivered across continents. With such weapons, war has become, not just tragic, but preposterous. With such weapons, there can be no victory for anyone. Plainly the objective now must be to see that such a war does not occur at all.

And so the third imperative of peace is this: without for a moment relaxing our internal and collective defenses, we must actively try to bridge the great chasm that separates us from the people under Communist rule. In those regions are millions of individual human beings who have been our friends, and who themselves have sincerely wanted peace and freedom, throughout so much of our mutual history.

Now for years the Iron Curtain was impenetrable. Our people were unable to talk to these individuals behind the curtain, or travel among them, or share their arts or sports, or invite them to see what life is like in a free democracy, or even get acquainted in any way. What future was there in such a course, except greater misunderstanding and an ever deepening division in the world?

Of course, good will from our side can do little to reach these peoples unless there is some new spirit of conciliation on the part of the Governments controlling them. Now, at last, there appear to be signs that some small degree of friendly intercourse among peoples may be permitted. We are beginning to be able—cautiously and with our eyes open—to encourage some interchange of ideas, of books, magazines, students, tourists, artists, radio programs, technical experts, religious leaders and governmental officials. The hope is, little by little, mistrust based on falsehoods will give way to international understanding based on truth.

Now as this development gradually comes about, it will not seem futile for young people to dream of a brave and new and shining world, or for older people to feel that they can in fact bequeath to their children a better inheritance than that which was their own. Science and technology, labor-saving methods, management, labor organization, education, medicine—and not least, politics and government—all these have brought within our grasp a world in which backbreaking toil and longer hours will not be necessary.

Travel all over the world, to learn to know our brothers abroad, will be fast and cheap. The fear and pain of crippling disease will be greatly reduced. The material things that make life interesting and pleasant will be available to everyone. Leisure, together with educational and recreational facilities, will be abundant, so that all can develop the life of the spirit, of reflection, of religion, of the arts, of the full realization of the good things of the world. And political wisdom will ensure justice and harmony.

This picture of the future brings to mind a little story.

A Government worker, when he first arrived in Washington in 1953, was passing the National Archives Building in a taxi, where he saw this motto carved on one of its pedestals: "What is past is prologue." He had heard that Washington cab drivers were noted for knowing all the Washington answers, so he asked the driver about the motto. "Oh, that," said the driver. "That's just bureaucrat talk. What it really means is—you ain't seen nothing yet."

My fellow Americans, the kind of era I have described is possible. But it will not be attained by revolution. It will not be attained by the sordid politics of pitting group against group. It will be brought about by the ambitions and judgments and inspirations and darings of 168,000,000 free Americans working together and with friends abroad toward a common ideal in a peaceful world.

Lincoln, speaking to a Republican state convention in 1858, began with the biblical quotation: "A house divided against itself cannot stand."

Today the world is a house divided.

But—as is sometimes forgotten—Lincoln followed this quotation with a note of hope for his troubled country:

"I do not expect the house to fall," he said, "but I do expect it will cease to be divided."

A century later, we too must have the vision, the fighting spirit, and the deep religious faith in our Creator's destiny for us, to sound a similar note of promise for our divided world; that out of our time there can, with incessant work and with God's help, emerge a new era of good life, good will and good hope for all men.

One American put it this way: "Every tomorrow has two handles. We can take hold of it with the handle of anxiety or the handle of faith."

My friends, in firm faith, and in the conviction that the Republican purposes and principles are "in league" with this kind of future, the nomination that you have tendered me for the Presidency of the United States I now—humbly but confidently—accept.

☆

DWIGHT D. EISENHOWER

Campaign Speech

CLEVELAND, OHIO

October 1, 1956

Mr. Chairman, Secretary Humphrey, Senator Bricker, Senator Bender, members of the Ohio Republican contingent in the Congress, Republican candidates for State Office—let me pause here long enough to say I wish for each of them overwhelming success where they are standing for election this fall—and My fellow citizens in this great throng and over the Nation:

Almost two years have passed since I last visited Cleveland, but I find that even a few hours in this city provide a tremendous tonic for me, as an American. From my heart, I thank you for the warmth of your welcome.

This time I am here in the midst of a political campaign—a political campaign to determine what kind of government this country is going to have for the next four years.

Now let there be no mistake. There are deep and essential differences in the beliefs and convictions of the two major parties as established by the words of their candidates and by their records in office.

Speaking simply and directly to the problem: one of the most vital of these differences is that a dominant element in the other party believes primarily in big government and paternalistic direction by Washington bureaucrats of important activities of the entire nation. Those people have in the past sponsored the Brannan plan and price controls in time of peace. They have flirted with socialized medicine. In general, they preach continuous extension of political control over our economy.

On the other hand, we of this Administration and this Party believe that the great American potential can be realized only through the unfettered and free initiative, talents and energies of our entire people.

We believe that the government has the function of insuring the national security and domestic tranquillity, and beyond this, has to perform, in Lincoln's phrase—all those things which individuals cannot well do for themselves.

We believe that government must be alert—and this Administration has been alert—to every need of our people, especially in those things affecting their health and education and their human rights. A sound nation is built of individuals sound in body and mind and spirit. Government dares not ignore the individual citizen.

But we emphatically reject every unnecessary invasion into the daily lives of our people and into their occupations, both industrial and on the farm.

Let no one tell you that this difference is either merely doctrinal or fanciful. It is practical. It is real. It affects your lives, the life of the nation today and the life of the nation tomorrow.

Now naturally, the busy orators of the opposition deplore—and even attempt to deny—this faith of ours, in you, the people.

Daily I read about politicians—some of them candidates for high office—who go about the country expressing at length their worries about America and the American people. They profess to be alarmed, scared, and convinced that in all ways we are slipping badly. They cry that the country is going to pot and only they—prescribing for our ills from the seat of government in Washington—can save it.

Now I have a simple prescription for their worries and fears. It is this:

Let them forget themselves for awhile, and their partisan speeches. When they visit a city like Cleveland, let them look around at the hustle and bustle; talk to, and especially listen to, the people here. Let these politicians absorb some of the spirit that animates Clevelanders, all of them—whether they work in banks, in factories, in orchards and fields or in kitchens. Their worries and fears of the future of America should begin to sound foolish—even to them.

Now, my friends, despite this good advice, I am sure these men of fretting fear and worried doubt will reject my prescription instantly. They want too much to have you believe in the story of gloom they spread. For, you see, they assert that these fancied ills can be cured only if the government in Washington—with they themselves occupying its important posts—runs the entire country, including Cleveland.

Now, for a few years in the past, they, and men like them, almost succeeded in selling us this philosophy. But, now the shoe is on the other foot and they are extremely unhappy about it.

For Cleveland, and the rural areas in Ohio, and the citizens of all the other 47 States, are not only running their own jobs efficiently, but are doing their part to run Washington. The result is a better America, an America of increasing peace, security and progress.

Together, we Americans have moved along way forward in the last four years.

For, you see, Cleveland is not an island of prosperity in an ocean of stagnation. All America has advanced in the past four years.

Now that advance didn't happen just by accident. Your Government in Washington has adopted policies that have created a tremendous confidence in America's future.

And with that confidence, you people of Cleveland, your neighbors in Detroit and Toledo—yes, all the people of the United States—you have done the rest.

You here in this Square, the tens of millions like you all over the country, are the source of this tremendous advance—not a group of bureaucrats in Washington or a group of politicians bewailing the fix the country is in. And how did you do this? You accomplished this by hard work; by investing your money; by sticking to your job and doing a good job. You did it because you had faith in yourselves, in your community, and your country. You did it by using your Government as a servant, not turning to it as a kindly master who could parcel out to you—in its great wisdom—the measure of prosperity it believes you merit.

Now the results have been wonderful.

The cost of living has been remarkably stabilized—only about 2½ percent increase in 3½ years. During the final six years of the previous Administration the cost of living increase was twenty times as great as that.

Today, we have a stable dollar. One man who has powerfully helped restore its honesty and dependability is your own fellow citizen, your great Secretary of the Treasury, George Humphrey.

You have a right—a definite right—to be proud of him. With the late Senator Taft, he has added stature to the Republican Party in this generation.

Now, my friends, we have balanced the Federal Budget, and have even made some payment on our huge national debt.

We have record high employment—66.8 million jobs in August—and without war.

Just before I left Washington, one of the technicians gave me the latest figures on unemployment in the month of September, and it looks like it's down below three percent—almost a record in our entire history.

Working people have higher wages than ever—for the average factory worker, 12 percent more than when the prior Administration left office—and this worker has greatly increased his purchasing power.

Production of goods and services is at a rate exceeding 400 billion dollars a year.

In the first three years of this Administration there were more single-family homes built in America than in any prior three-year period.

A nation-wide highway construction program is now under way.

Those are the facts—that is where America is today. Now while Americans were accomplishing this—were making these tremendous advances—what has your Government been doing?

In virtually every area of human concern, it is moving forward.

Government has had a heart as well as a head.

Now, my friends, in telling you about some of the things this Administration has been doing, I hope you will not take it that I am boasting. There will never be room for boasting in this regard until there is not a single needy person left in the United States, when distress and disease have been eliminated. I am talking about progress—how far we have gone ahead.

Now here are some things the opposition would like you to forget:

Social Security has been extended to an additional 10 million Americans—unemployment compensation to an additional 4 million Americans.

Our health program has been greatly improved—research into the causes of crippling and killing diseases has been markedly stepped up.

The minimum wage has been increased, even though my recommendation for its wider coverage was not acted on in the Congress.

We have had a 7.4 billion dollar tax cut—the largest in our Nation's history. And despite opposition charges, two thirds of that cut was given to individuals.

Sympathetic understanding has been fostered and intelligent progress has been made in civil rights. Segregation has been ended in restaurants, theatres, hotels, and schools in the District of Columbia—ended in Government departments, the Armed Forces, veterans' hospitals.

And we have been vigilant and successful in preserving the nation's security—and peace.

Now let me say, this peace is not all that we could wish, and not all that—with God's help—it will one day be. Centuries of mutual hatreds and prejudices and quarrels cannot disappear in a few short years.

But why this anguished cry of some politicians that we have no peace?

Do they think they can make America's parents and wives believe that their sons and husbands are being shot at?

Do they think they can bring Americans to believe that our nation's powerful voice is not daily urging conciliation, mutual understanding and justice?

That is exactly what we are doing in the Suez problem.

Do they believe that Americans do not know how strong have been our efforts to dedicate the atom to constructive instead of destructive purposes?

Are they so deluded as to believe they can conceal from all our people the steady policies directed toward removing the causes of war?

Let them think of these names: Korea, Trieste, Austria, Guatemala, West Germany. If they so think of them, they will realize that they would be very wise to stop this effort of fooling all the people all the time.

Not only is this Administration dedicated to peace, but we have established a record in behalf of peace that all the world respects.

Now these are just some of the things this Administration has been doing.

Let us look for a moment at a simple question: Which Party, in these recent years, has done more to help all citizens meet the problems of their daily lives? Which Party has helped more—not with words, with deeds?

As an early demonstration of its concern for the human problems of health, education and welfare, the Administration raised that agency to Cabinet level. Now national health, the proper education of our children, and the human welfare of all Americans are discussed at the same table— and with the same exhaustive care—as such great subjects as foreign affairs and national security.

The men of the opposition know perfectly well that one of the main reasons they were thrown out of office four years ago was their tolerance of the thievery of inflation. Just in the final seven years of their tenure of office this economic fever had cut the value of the dollar by almost one-third, damaging the livelihood of the aged—the pensioned—all salaried workers. The opposition did nothing effectively to stop this economic thievery. And they know it.

Take the St. Lawrence Seaway. For twenty years the opposition talked about the Seaway. Yet it was repeatedly shelved, by-passed, and blocked. This Administration acted and got the Seaway going. As a result, two years from now, great ocean ships will dock here in Cleveland.

All the money the Federal government could spend for this purpose won't hold a candle to the increased prosperity the Seaway will bring to the Great Lakes—to the Middle West. This Administration made it a reality. And they—the opposition—know it.

Take agriculture. They—the opposition—had 20 long years to do something for the most needy families on our farms. At the end of those 20 years, they had done nothing—except to by-pass the small farmer as they made corporation and big area farming more profitable than ever before. And the Administration's new rural development program is the first—I repeat the first—full-scale and integrated Federal effort to help these lowest-income families. Another Administration program enables the small farmer—often a young veteran—to get full and comprehensive credit in financing his farm and buildings and equipment and seed. And he can refinance his existing debts in the same way as any other business or industry. That's another "first" for this administration. And the opposition knows it.

Now, let's take small business. Just 18 years ago small business people from all over America gathered in Washington at the request of the Administration then in power. They made 23 recommendations—appeals

—for action. Yet for the next 14 years—for all the years when the opposition held power—virtually nothing was done. This Administration is the first Administration that has made a major attack upon the problems of small business. And they—the opposition—know it.

Take labor. The opposition say that they alone truly care for the working men and women of America and that the Republican Party is really a vague kind of political conspiracy by big business to destroy organized labor and to bring hunger and torment to every worker in America.

This is more than political bunk. It is willful nonsense. It is wicked nonsense.

Let's see what the record shows about this:

The record shows: Organized labor is larger in numbers and greater in strength today—after these years of Republican Administration—than ever in our Nation's history.

The record shows: Not under the opposition's leadership, but under the leadership of this Administration, the workers of America have received the greatest rise in real wages—the kind of wages that buys groceries and cars and homes—the greatest rise in 30 years.

The record shows: We—not they—have made the most successful fight to stop inflation's robbery of every paycheck.

The record shows that this check upon inflation is most vital—not for the few who are rich—but for the millions who depend upon salaries or pensions, those who are old, those who are sick, those who are needy.

The record shows: We—not they—have brought a reduction in the cost of Federal Government and a reduction in taxes—a reduction benefiting, not a favored few, but every taxpayer in the land. In fact, 11 out 12 increases that have been made in the individual income tax since it started were made under our opponents, while 5 out of 7 reductions were made under Republican Administrations.

And now I want to add this simple fact. We have given to our Nation the kind of government that is a living witness to the basic virtues in a democracy—public morality, public service, and public trust. In this Administration you cannot find those ugly marks of the past: Special favoritism, cronyism, and laxity in administration.

You have here in Ohio a vigorous exponent of the Administration's program—George Bender.

Two years ago I came here to add my voice to his campaign for the United States Senate. He ran on one basic platform pledge—to support the President and his Administration in Washington. In this he has a splendid record.

He has done an effective job for this State and for all the States of the Union. He has served with vigor and forthrightness. He has shown us a great dedication.

And this Administration is dedicated to the welfare—the peace and the prosperity—of 168 million American citizens. This dedication is equal for all. It is equal for all regardless of race or color or creed—regardless of region or section or of occupation—and regardless of social or economic fortune.

This is the kind of government that we have been developing for the past four years.

Now the Republican Party does not base its appeal on sectionalism, on playing worker against manager, housewife against storekeeper, farmer against manufacturer.

The Republican Party believes that none of us can truly prosper unless all of us prosper. It believes we cannot be secure unless we are strong—that no nation can enjoy true peace unless all nations are free from war.

If the Republican Party were not this sort of Party, I would not belong to it. I would not belong to it and I would not be running as its candidate. What benefits America benefits farmers and industrial workers, the school children and the aged, the West and North and South—all of us. We are one people, one Nation.

And finally, let me say this to you. One of my chief objectives and my greatest hope prior to taking office was to restore the respect of the American people for the Government of the United States. I think you agree with me that honor and integrity have been the landmarks of all that we have done during the last four years. But much remains to be done in the cause of good government for the future of America.

I sincerely and devotedly want to continue the job. To be successful two things are necessary: time; and your help.

With your help between now and November, we can gain the time for the next four years in which we can permanently establish an understanding of these truths—in Washington and throughout the country. There will be restored the faith and belief of the American people in our national processes.

The confidence of the American people in our institutions and our leaders must be strong and secure, if we are to lead the peoples and the nations toward the lasting and just peace, which we all so devoutly seek.

Friends, again I thank you for your welcome and for your courtesy in listening to me so attentively. Thank you very much.

☆

ADLAI E. STEVENSON

Acceptance Speech

CHICAGO, ILLINOIS

August 17, 1956

I accept your nomination and your program. And I pledge to you every resource of mind and strength that I possess to make your deed today a good one for our country and for our party.

Four years ago I stood in this same place and uttered those same words to you. But four years ago we lost. This time we will win!

My heart is full tonight, as the scenes and faces and events of these busy years in between crowd my mind.

To you here tonight and across the country who have sustained me in this great undertaking for months and even years, I am deeply, humbly grateful; and to none more than the noble lady who is also the treasurer of a legacy of greatness—Mrs. Eleanor Roosevelt, who has reminded us so movingly that this is 1956 and not 1932, nor even 1952; that our problems alter as well as their solutions; that change is the law of life, and that political parties, no less than individuals, ignore it at their peril.

I salute also the distinguished American who has been more than equal to the hard test of disagreement and has now reaffirmed our common cause so graciously—President Harry Truman. I am glad to have you on my side again, sir!

I am sure that the country is as grateful to this convention as I am for its action of this afternoon. It has renewed and reaffirmed our faith in free democratic processes.

The office of the Vice-Presidency has been dignified by the manner of your selection as well as by the distinction of your choice, Senator Kefauver is a great Democrat and a great campaigner—as I have reason to know better than anybody!

If we are elected and it is God's will that I do not serve my full four years, the people will have a new President whom they can trust. He has dignity; he has convictions, and he will command the respect of the American people and the world.

Perhaps these are simple virtues, but there are times when simple virtues deserve comment. This is such a time. I am grateful to you for my running mate—an honorable and able American—Senator Estes Kefauver and may I add that I got as excited as any of you about that photo-finish between Senator Kefauver and that great young American Senator John Kennedy.

When I stood here before you that hot night four years ago we were at the end of an era—a great era of restless forward movement, an era of unparalleled social reform and of glorious triumph over depression and tyranny. It was a Democratic era.

Tonight, after an interval of marking time and aimless drifting, we are on the threshold of another great, decisive era. History's headlong course has brought us, I devoutly believe, to the threshold of a new America—to the America of the great ideals and noble visions which are the stuff our future must be made of.

I mean a new America where poverty is abolished and our abundance is used to enrich the lives of every family.

I mean a new America where freedom is made real for all without regard to race or belief or economic condition.

I mean a new America which everlastingly attacks the ancient idea that men can solve their differences by killing each other.

These are the things I believe in and will work for with every resource I possess. These are the things I know you believe in and will work for with everything you have. These are the terms on which I accept your nomination.

Our objectives are not for the timid. They are not for those who look backward, who are satisfied with things as they are, who think that this great nation can ever sleep or ever stand still.

The program you have written is, I think, more than a consensus of the strongly held convictions of strong men; it is a signpost toward that new America. It speaks of the issues of our time with passion for justice, with reverence for our history and character, with a long view of the American future, and with a sober, fervent dedication to the goal of peace on earth.

Nor has it evaded the current problems in the relations between the races who comprise America, problems which have so often tormented our national life. Of course there is disagreement in the Democratic party on desegregation. It could not be otherwise in the only party that must speak responsibly and responsively in both the North and the South. If all of us are not wholly satisfied with what we have said on this explosive subject it is because we have spoken the only way a truly national party can—by the understanding accommodation of conflicting views.

But in so doing, in substituting realism and persuasion for the extremes of force or nullification, our party has preserved its effectiveness, it has avoided a sectional crisis, and it has contributed to our national unity as only a national party could.

As President it would be my purpose to press on in accordance with our platform toward the fuller freedom for all our citizens which is at once our party's pledge and the old American promise.

I do not propose to make political capital out of the President's illness. His ability to personally fulfill the demands of his exacting office is a matter between him and the American people. So far as I am concerned that is where the matter rests. As we all do, I wish deeply for the President's health and well-being.

But if the condition of President Eisenhower is not an issue as far as I am concerned, the condition and the conduct of the President's office and of the Administration is very much an issue.

The men who run the Eisenhower Administration evidently believe that the minds of Americans can be manipulated by shows, slogans and and the arts of advertising. And that conviction will, I dare say, be backed up by the greatest torrent of money ever poured out to influence an American election—poured out by men who fear nothing so much as change and who want everything to stay as it is—only more so.

This idea that you can merchandise candidates for high office like breakfast cereal—that you can gather votes like box tops—is, I think, the ultimate indignity to the democratic process. And we Democrats must also face the fact that no administration has ever before enjoyed such an uncritical and unenthusiastic support from so much of the press as this one.

But let us ask the people of our country to what great purpose for the republic has the President's popularity and this unrivaled opportunity for leadership been put? Has the Eisenhower Administration used this opportunity to elevate us? To enlighten us? To inspire us? Did it, in a time of headlong, world-wide revolutionary change, prepare us for stern decisions and great risks? Did it, in short, give men and women a glimpse of the nobility and vision without which peoples and nations perish?

Or did it just reassure us that all is well, everything is all right, that everyone is prosperous and safe, that no great decisions are required of us, and that even the Presidency of the United States has somehow become an easy job?

I will have to confess that the Republican Administration has performed a minor miracle—after twenty years of incessant damnation of the New Deal they not only haven't repealed it but they have swallowed it, or most of it, and it looks as though they could keep it down at least until after the election.

I suppose we should be thankful that they have caught up with the New Deal at last, but what have they done to take advantage of the great opportunities of these times—a generation after the New Deal?

Well, I say they have smothered us in smiles and complacency while our social and economic advancement has ground to a halt and which our leadership and security in the world have been imperiled.

In spite of these unparalleled opportunities to lead at home and abroad, they have, I say, been wasting our opportunities and losing our world.

I say that what this country needs is not propaganda and a personality cult. What this country needs is leadership and truth. And that's what we mean to give it.

What is the truth?

The truth is that the Republican party is a house divided. The truth is that President Eisenhower, cynically coveted as a candidate but ignored as a leader, is largely indebted to Democrats in Congress for what accomplishments he can claim.

The truth is that everyone is not prosperous. The truth is that the farmer, especially the family farmer who matters most, has not had his fair share of the national income and the Republicans have done nothing to help him—until an election year.

The truth is that 30,000,000 Americans live today in families trying to make ends meet on less than $2,000 a year. The truth is that the small farmer, the small business man, the teacher, the white collar worker, and the retired citizen trying to pay today's prices on yesterday's pension—all these are in serious trouble.

The truth is that in this Government of big men—big financially—no one speaks for the little man.

The truth is that in this government policy abroad has the Communists on the run. The truth, unhappily, is not—in the Republican President's words—that our "prestige since the last world war has never been as high as it is this day." The truth is that it has probably never been lower.

The truth is that we are losing the military advantage, the economic initiative and the moral leadership.

The truth is not that we are winning the cold war. The truth is that we are losing the cold war.

Don't misunderstand me. I, for one, am ready to acknowledge the sincerity of the Republican President's desire for peace and happiness for all. But good intentions are not good enough and the country is stalled on dead center—stalled in the middle of the road—while the world goes whirling by. America, which has lifted man to his highest economic state, which has saved freedom in war and peace, which saved collective security, no longer sparks and flames and gives off new ideas and initiatives. Our lights are dimmed. We chat complacently of this and that while, in Carlyle's phrase, "death and eternity sit glaring." And I could add that opportunity, neglected opportunity, sits glaring too!

But you cannot surround the future with arms, you cannot dominate the racing world by standing still. And I say it is time to get up and get moving again. It is time for America to be herself again.

And that's what this election is all about!

Here at home we can make good the lost opportunities; we can recover the wasted years; we can cross the threshold to the new America.

What we need is a rebirth of leadership—leadership which will give us a glimpse of the nobility and vision without which peoples and nations perish. Woodrow Wilson said that "when America loses its ardor for mankind it is time to elect a Democratic President." There doesn't appear to be much ardor in America just now for anything, and it's time to elect a Democratic Administration and a Democratic Congress, yes, and a Democratic Government in every state and local office across the land.

In our hearts we know that the horizons of the new America are as endless, its promise as staggering in its richness as the unfolding miracle of human knowledge. America renews itself with every forward thrust of the human mind.

We live at a time when automation is ushering in a second industrial revolution, and the powers of the atom are about to be harnessed for ever greater production. We live at a time when even the ancient spectre of hunger is vanishing. This is the age of abundance. Never in history has there been such an opportunity to show what we can do to improve the equality of living now that the terrible, grinding anxieties of daily bread, of clothing and shelter, are disappearing.

With leadership, Democratic leadership, we can do justice to our children, we can repair the ravages of time and neglect in our schools. We can and we will!

With leadership, Democratic leadership, we can restore the vitality of the American family farm. We can preserve the position of small business without injury to the large. We can strengthen labor unions and collective bargaining as vital institutions in a free economy. We can and our party history proves that we will!

With leadership, Democratic leadership, we can conserve our resources of land and forest and water and develop them for the benefit of all. We can and the record shows that we will!

With leadership, Democratic leadership, we can rekindle the spirit of liberty emblazoned in the bill of rights; we can build this new America where the doors of opportunity are open equally to all, yes, the doors of our factories and the doors of our school rooms. We can make this a land where opportunity is founded only on responsibility and freedom on faith, and where nothing can smother the lonely defiant spirit of the free intelligence. We can, and by our traditions as a party we will!

All these things we can do and we will. But in the international field the timing is only partially our own. Here the "unrepentant minute" once missed, may be missed forever. Other forces, growing yearly in potency, dispute with us the direction of our times. Here more than anywhere guidance and illumination are needed in the terrifying century of the hydrogen bomb. Here more than anywhere we must move, and rapidly, to repair the ravages of the past four years to America's repute and influence abroad.

We must move with speed and confidence to reverse the spread of communism. We must strengthen the political and economic fabric of our alliances. We must launch new programs to meet the challenge of the vast social revolution that is sweeping the world and turn the violent forces of change to the side of freedom.

We must protect the new nations in the exercise of their full independence; and we must help other peoples out of Communist or colonial servitude along the hard road to freedom.

And we must place our nation where it belongs in the eyes of the world—at the head of the struggle for peace. For in this nuclear age peace is no longer a visionary ideal. It has become an absolute, imperative, practical necessity. Humanity's long struggle against war has to be won and won now. Yes, and I say it can be won.

It is time to listen again to our hearts, to speak again our ideals, to be again our own great selves.

There is a spiritual hunger in the world today and it cannot be satisfied by material things alone. Our forebears came here to worship God. We must not let our aspirations so diminish that our worship becomes rather of bigness—bigness of material achievement.

For a century and a half the Democratic party has been the party of respect for people, of reverence for life, of hope for each child's future, of belief that "the highest revelation is that God is in every man."

Once we were not ashamed in this country to be idealists. Once we were proud to confess that an American is a man who wants peace and believes in a better future and loves his fellow man. We must reclaim these great Christian and humane ideas. We must dare to say again that the American cause is the cause of all mankind.

If we are to make honest citizens of our hearts we must unite them again to the ideals in which they have always believed and give those ideals the courage of our tongues.

Standing as we do here tonight at this great fork of history, may we never be silenced, may we never lose our faith in freedom and the better destiny of man.

☆

ADLAI E. STEVENSON

Campaign Speech

MINNEAPOLIS, MINNESOTA

September 29, 1956

Minnesota is the great overarching bridge between the old Midwest and the new Northwest, where people breathe freer and look higher and, somehow, the blood is quickened in the clean North air, where men are not afraid to speak their minds or vote their deep convictions. Up here in Minnesota men are never satisfied that things can't be better than they are.

Minnesota has always led the great traditions of protest in the upper Midwest—the protest against things that could be better.

In recent years across your Eastern border the heirs of the Wisconsin Progressives have found a home in the Democratic party; today to the west in North Dakota the Nonpartisan League is moving in with us, too.

Here in Minnesota the heirs of that same great tradition have fused their strength in the Democratic-Farmer-Labor party.

And two men who have helped to write the Democratic-Farmer-Labor story are its great leaders today—Hubert Humphrey and Orville Freeman.

These men—and the national leaders of the Democratic party down the years—had several things in common. They were not afraid of new ideas. They were not content to leave well enough alone. They had a passion for human life—they cared and, they cared deeply about people. And they tackled the people's problems with an enthusiasm that was boundless and unbeatable.

I want to talk to you tonight about the need for enthusiasm and new ideas in our national life.

Of course today the Republicans would have us feel all the problems are solved, that what we need is not enthusiasm and new ideas but caution, complacency and a passion not for the people but for things as they are.

Well, here is how things are for some of our people unfortunately.

Farmers and their wives and children are being forced to pack up and leave the farm—a good farm—and uproot their whole lives.

Men are being forced to sell the store on Main Street that for years has provided for their family and served their community well.

Too many of our older citizens are spending what ought to be the golden years in want and neglect.

Too many children are going to school in crowded ramshackle buildings with teachers that are only half-trained.

Millions of sick people can't afford to call a doctor.

Hundreds of thousands of our mental patients are consigned to disgraceful medieval institutions.

One family out of five must get by on less than $2,000 in times like these.

Millions of American citizens are still barred from schools and jobs and an equal chance merely because of their color.

In the city slums children are roaming the alleys behind the tenement buildings, and in some parts of our country poverty is converting farmland into a rural slum.

I say this is not right. And I say that only the Democratic party has the passion for human justice, the enthusiasm and determination and the new ideas, to drive want and suffering from all American homes, not just some of them.

But beyond this lies another goal—the goal of peace, and I want to say something about that tonight.

Like most Americans, I've read some of what that wise New England philosopher, Ralph Waldo Emerson, wrote. I fear I've forgotten a lot of what he said, but I've remembered this:

"Nothing great," Emerson said, "was ever achieved without enthusiasm." How true that is. As we look back over the centuries, we can see that nearly all the glorious achievements of mankind, nearly all the best things that characterize our society, sprang from the uncrushable enthusiasm of those who believed in the genius of man, and who believed in the possibility of doing the seemingly impossible. To these enthusiasts, whose optimism often exposed them to scorn and ridicule, we chiefly owe all the good things of our civilization.

This thought of Emerson's—this tribute to the power of man's ability to master his destiny—came to me again only recently when I heard the President's recent expression of views on war and peace—the area above all others where we need fresh and positive thinking.

I was distressed to see that the President not only had nothing new to suggest for the future but he seemed resentful over the efforts of others —including myself—to find some new and more hopeful answers to the problems of life and death that now confront us.

To be more specific, I have said before and I'll say it again that I, for one, am not content to accept the idea that there can be no end to compulsory military service. While I, like most others who have had intimate experience with our armed forces in war and peace, have felt that it was and is necessary, at the same time I have felt, and many others likewise, that the draft is a wasteful, inefficient, and often unfair way of maintaining our armed forces, and now it is fast becoming an obsolete way.

Let me make it perfectly clear that as long as danger confronts us, I believe we should have stronger, not weaker, defenses than we have now. Ever since Mr. Eisenhower became President we Democrats have fought hard to prevent the Administration from putting dollars ahead of defense. The Democrats in Congress forced the Administration to reverse itself and restore deep cuts in the strategic Air Force even during this last session of Congress.

But my point is that the draft does not necessarily mean a strong defense. Conditions change, and no conditions have changed more in our time than the conditions of warfare. Nothing is more hazardous in military policy than rigid adherence to obsolete ideas. France learned this in 1939; she crouched behind the Maginot Line, which was designed for an earlier war, and German panzers overran France. The Maginot Line gave France a false—and fatal sense of security. We must not let Selective Service become our Maginot Line.

What I am suggesting is that we ought to take a fresh and open-minded look at the weapons revolution and the whole problem of recruiting and training military manpower. We may very well find that in the not far distant future we can abolish the draft and at the same time have a stronger defense and at lower cost.

Defense is now so complex, its demand for highly skilled and specialized manpower so great, that the old fashioned conscript army, in which many men serve short terms of duty, is becoming less and less suited to the needs of modern arms. And it is becoming more and more expensive.

Let me say right here in all frankness that I have no special pride, no conceit, in the suggestions that I have tried to advance. No one will be happier than I if others find better solutions.

Once we start exploring this possibility seriously many new ideas will be forthcoming; that is always the case when men turn their creative energies full time upon a problem. Right now I had hoped to do no more than get this kind of creative thinking started.

I am distressed that President Eisenhower should dismiss this objective out of hand. If anyone had proposed the abolition of the draft right now, today, the President's attitude would be understandable; indeed, I would share it. But I don't see how we can ever get anywhere against the rigid, negative position that we cannot even discuss the matter, or even look forward to a time when we can do away with compulsory military service. I say it's time we stopped frowning and started thinking about them.

I am even more distressed that this attitude on the part of Mr. Eisenhower carries over into the all-important problem of controlling the hydrogen bomb, for here we are talking about the actual survival of the human race itself.

The testing alone of these super bombs is considered by scientists to be dangerous to man; they speak of the danger of poisoning the atmosphere; they tell us that radioactive fall-out may do genetic damage with effects on unborn children which they are unable to estimate.

I think almost everyone will agree that some measure of universal disarmament—some means of taming the nuclear weapons—is the first order of business in the world today.

It is not enough to say, well, we have tried and failed to reach agreement with the Russians. It is not enough to throw up our hands and say it's no use to try this or that new approach. This is one time we cannot take no for an answer, for life itself depends on our ultimately finding the right yes.

Again, I have no foolish pride in my own ideas on this subject. But there must be a beginning, a starting point, a way to get off the dead center of disagreement. I have proposed a moratorium on the testing of more super H-bombs. If the Russians don't go along, well then at least the world will know we tried. And we will know if they don't because we can detect H-bomb explosions without inspection.

It may be that others will come forward with other ideas; indeed, I hope they do. But I say to you that in this field, as in many others, fresh and openminded thinking is needed as never before—and in this field we may not have unlimited time to get the answers. We'd better start thinking now.

Furthermore, I do not see how we can ever hope to get the answers if fresh ideas, new proposals, new solutions, are not encouraged.

I was shocked when Mr. Eisenhower the other night brushed off my suggestion as a theatrical gesture. I don't believe that was worthy of the President of the United States. I have never questioned his sincerity on a matter that I am sure means more to both of us than anything else in the world—the matter of permanent peace—and I do not think he should have questioned mine.

All decent men and women everywhere hate war. We don't want our boys to be drafted and we don't want to live forever in the shadow of a radioactive mushroom cloud. And when I say "we," I mean Democrats and Republicans alike—I mean mankind everywhere.

Peace is not a partisan issue. Every American, Democrat and Republican alike, wants peace. There is no war party in this country; there is no peace party.

And the way to get started on the difficult road to disarmament and peace is not, I repeat, to scorn new ideas.

Just because this Administration has not been able to make any progress toward safe disarmament or even toward controlling H-bomb development, does not mean that such agreements are forever impossible. No matter which party wins in November, another supreme effort must be undertaken, and, if that fails, then another and another, for leaders must lead, and the conquest of this scourge is a more imperative goal of mankind than the conquest of the black plague in the Middle Ages.

I shall continue to concentrate my own attention on this problem, and I shall also do everything I can to encourage others to do likewise, for, as I have said, I know in my heart that Emerson was right when he said that "nothing great was ever achieved without enthusiasm."

And we saw it proved in our own time. For many years, you will recall, the world had dreamed of splitting the atom and releasing its boundless energy.

But most men despaired of ever making this dream come true. Had it not been for Franklin D. Roosevelt and his determination, the so-called impossible might still seem impossible. Then, as now, there were the skeptic, the defeatists, the non-enthusiasts who thought Roosevelt was off on a wild goose chase, who dubbed Oakridge his billion dollar folly. But he was not deterred.

He would not take no for an answer. Nuclear energy was finally placed at the disposal of man, and if we, who survived Franklin Roosevelt, show the will to control this energy that he showed in creating it, then it still may prove to be one of the greatest blessings of all time.

Franklin Roosevelt was not a physicist. He knew nothing about the hidden secrets of uranium. But he had to a supreme degree the first attributes of political leadership—that is, he had the enthusiastic will to act, and the genius for organizing great undertakings.

I, too, know little or nothing about the mechanics of the H-bomb. But I do know this: if man is capable of creating it, he also is capable of taming it. And nothing—including Presidential frowns—can make me believe otherwise.

My friends, this is not the first time the Republicans have dismissed or scorned Democratic efforts to make this a better world.

When Woodrow Wilson had his immortal dream of a League of Nations, the Republicans called it worse names than a "theatrical gesture"—yet American participation might have prevented a second World War.

Franklin Roosevelt proposed the United Nations. Yet even today many Republican leaders, even Senator Knowland, are still suspicious of it or positively hostile. The U.N. isn't perfect. Like most human institutions it probably never will be, and certainly not without the wholehearted support of America's leaders.

This negative, defeatist attitude among Republican leaders comes in an unbroken line down to the present. President Hoover's Fortress America concept is familiar. Senator Taft's negative, isolationist views are still shared by many of his followers.

And the fact is that the Republican party has been so divided since the first war and the League of Nations fight that even to this day it cannot conduct a coherent, consistent foreign policy, and the purpose of foreign policy for the United States is peace. Time and again in the past four years we have seen allied unity abroad sacrificed to Republican unity at home.

This is not to suggest for a second that the Republican party is, therefore, the war party, or that the Democratic party is the party of peace. I have no patience with such blanket charges.

Both parties are dedicated to peace, but historically they differ on how to realize this great objective. I think it is fair to say that, generally speaking, the Republican way has been the narrow, nationalistic one of the low, limited horizon, while the Democratic way has been that of the wide horizon, dotted with the ships and sails of beckoning hope.

One way, of course, is just as patriotic as the other. But in my opinion the Democratic way has usually been more attuned to the changes, the challenge and surprise, of this everchanging world. And I think this is just as true today as it has ever been.

And I think our Democratic enthusiasm for new ideas can better solve our problems here at home, too. For on the record it is the Democratic party that has always made new gains for the good of all the people.

Ours is the party that stopped child labor and started the nation on an eight-hour day, invented Social Security and built the T.V.A. It was the Democratic party that rescued the farmer with the Triple-A in the great depression, curbed the excesses of the stock promoters, built housing for the people, and wrote the G.I. Bill of Rights, I could go on and on.

I spoke a few minutes ago of the Democratic-Farmer-Labor story written here in Minnesota. We're going to tell a larger story, too, this year. Woodrow Wilson restrained the excesses of a new industrialism and met the challenge of the Kaiser; Franklin Roosevelt lifted the people from the slough of depression and beat down totalitarianism; Harry Truman made the great decision that lifted prostrate Europe and gave our nation leadership of the free in the world—and that is our story, written in the Twentieth Century here in blessed America.

I say there is yet much to be done. Great work lies ahead. I believe with all my heart and soul that this nation is about to enter a richer age than man has ever known. The question is: Shall we use our riches for all the people, or just for some of them? And, can we master the new machines, or must we serve them? And, can we put the atom to our peaceful use, or will it destroy us?

These are great questions, they require great answers, and those answers can come only from the strength and wisdom of you, the American people. And they will not be drawn forth by leadership that fails to lead, that frowns on new ideas. They will be drawn forth only by leadership that dares to try the new, that meets the crises of our time with unbeatable enthusiasm.

"Nothing great," I repeat, "was ever achieved without enthusiasm." Let us go forward in the spirit of you of Minnesota, never satisfied with things as they are, daring always to try the new, daring nobly and doing greatly, and so building a New America.

It is in this spirit that I come to you tonight. It is in this spirit that we will win in November.

☆

1960

———— ☆ ————

In 1960, 87 percent of the homes in the United States had at least one television set. This statistic takes on a deeper significance when it is placed alongside another fact: 1960 was a presidential election year. By that year, moreover, television had replaced the radio and the newspaper as the most important political medium.

The Democratic convention opened in Los Angeles on July 11th. The delegates' choice was Senator John F. Kennedy of Massachusetts. The scion of a well-to-do family, Kennedy was also a World War II hero and a Pulitzer Prize winner. Kennedy had worked hard for the nomination, traveling some 65,000 miles in the air and visiting twenty-four states. His efforts were rewarded with important primary victories in Wisconsin and West Virginia. The victory in West Virginia was particularly significant, for Kennedy was a Catholic and West Virginia's population was 95 percent Protestant. His victory there proved that he was a viable candidate.

In his acceptance speech Kennedy broadcast the theme of his campaign: the future of America. The world was changing, he stated, and it was important for Americans to employ new methods to meet the challenges of the "new frontier."

Ten days after Kennedy's address in Los Angeles, the Republicans opened their convention in Chicago. There the delegates entrusted Vice President Richard M. Nixon with their party's platform, which alerted the nation to the threat of communist imperialism and accented the need for experienced leadership to combat that threat.

Clearly, Nixon's most dramatic statement in his acceptance address was his pledge to campaign in all fifty states. Furthermore, in addition to praising the accomplishments of the Eisenhower administration, he reiterated another one of his perennial themes: that his career was testimony to the opportunities afforded by the American system.

Yet the peace and prosperity that Nixon referred to in his acceptance address were not that obvious in 1960. Eisenhower's second term had not been an overwhelming success, either in domestic or foreign affairs. By way of example, the United States had undergone its third recession in eight years (1957–58), Russia's launching of the Sputnik satellite (1957) caused many Americans to feel uneasy, and the downing of an American U–2 reconnaissance plane over Russian territory led to the collapse of a scheduled U.S.–Soviet summit meeting in Paris (1960).

Kennedy's campaign strategy was to canvas the northeast while his running mate, Senator Lyndon Johnson of Texas, secured the South. At the same time that Kennedy toured the country, his campaign workers tried to register as many nonregistered voters as possible.

Although Kennedy tried to center his campaign around such issues as the Republican party's failure to stimulate economic growth and to enhance America's prestige abroad, his religion loomed as a major issue. In early September a group of prominent Protestant clergymen accused the Catholic Church of, among other things, openly intervening in the election on behalf of Kennedy. On September 12th Kennedy laid the religious issue to rest in a speech before the Greater Houston Ministerial Association. So effective was this television address that the Democrats replayed segments of it for the duration of the campaign.

The highlight of the campaign was the four nationally televised "Nixon-Kennedy debates." Of these four debates, the first was the most important. It drew the largest crowd, some seventy million people as compared to fifty million for the other debates, and it had the most profound impact on the undecided voters. The general impressions the viewers came away with were more important than the issues that were debated.

After seeing the first debate, there was a general consensus among the American electorate that Kennedy *looked* better than his opponent. Whereas Kennedy appeared tan, vigorous, and well dressed, Nixon looked haggard (he had lost weight while recuperating from a knee injury), had a very pale complexion (this was the result of makeup which tried to cover his beard growth), showed poor posture, and wore clothes that did not fit properly.

Nixon recovered in the next debate and continued his campaign by returning to his basic issues: Kennedy's inexperience, Republican achievements at home, and Eisenhower's initiatives toward world peace. One of these initiatives was the President's attempt to conclude a nuclear test ban treaty with the Russians. Nixon's views on these efforts were the subject of a major address at Toledo, Ohio on October 26th.

JOHN F. KENNEDY

Acceptance Speech

LOS ANGELES, CALIFORNIA

July 15, 1960

With a deep sense of duty and high resolve, I accept your nomination. I accept it with a full and grateful heart—without reservation—and with only one obligation—the obligation to devote every effort of body, mind and spirit to lead our party back to victory and our nation back to greatness.

I am grateful, too, that you have provided me with such an eloquent statement of our party's platform. Pledges which are made so eloquently are made to be kept. "The rights of man"—the civil and economic rights essential to the human dignity of all men—are indeed our goal and our first principles. This is a platform on which I can run with enthusiasm and conviction.

And I am grateful, finally, that I can rely in the coming months on so many others—on a distinguished running-mate who brings unity to our ticket and strength to our platform, Lyndon Johnson—on one of the most articulate statesmen of our time, Adlai Stevenson—on a great spokesman for our needs as a nation and a people, Stuart Symington—and on that fighting campaigner whose support I welcome, President Harry S. Truman.

I feel a lot safer now that they are on my side again. And I am proud of the contrast with our Republican competitors. For their ranks are apparently so thin that not one challenger has come forth with both the competence and the courage to make theirs an open convention.

I am fully aware of the fact that the Democratic party, by nominating someone of my faith, has taken on what many regard as a new and hazardous risk—new, at least, since 1928. But I look at it this way:

The Democratic Party has once again placed its confidence in the American people, and in their ability to render a free, fair judgment.

And you have, at the same time, placed your confidence in me, and in my ability to render a free, fair judgment—to uphold the Constitution and my oath of office—and to reject any kind of religious pressure or obligation that might directly or indirectly interfere with my conduct of the Presidency in the national interest.

My record of fourteen years supporting public education—supporting complete separation of church and state—and resisting pressures from any source on any issue should be clear by now to everyone.

I hope that no American, considering the really critical issues facing this country, will waste his franchise by voting either for me or against me solely on account of my religious affiliation. It is not relevant, I want to stress, what some other political or religious leader may have said on this subject. It is not relevant what abuses may have existed in other countries or in other times. It is not relevant what pressures, if any, might conceivably be brought to bear on me.

I am telling you now what you are entitled to know:

That my decisions on every public policy will be my own—as an American, a Democrat and a free man.

Under any circumstances, however, the victory we seek in November will not be easy. We all know that in our hearts. We recognize the power of the forces that will be aligned against us. We know they will invoke the name of Abraham Lincoln on behalf of their candidate—despite the fact that his political career has often seemed to show charity toward none and malice for all.

We know that it will not be easy to campaign against a man who has spoken or voted on every known side of every known issue. Mr. Nixon may feel it is his turn now, after the New Deal and the Fair Deal—but before he deals, someone had better cut the cards.

That "someone" may be the millions of Americans who voted for President Eisenhower but balk at his would-be, self-appointed successor. For just as historians tell us that Richard I was not fit to fill the shoes of bold Henry II—and that Richard Cromwell was not fit to wear the mantle of his uncle—they might add in future years that Richard Nixon did not measure to the footsteps of Dwight D. Eisenhower.

Perhaps he could carry on the party policies—the policies of Nixon, Benson, Dirksen and Goldwater. But this nation cannot afford such a luxury. Perhaps we could afford a Coolidge following Harding. And perhaps we could afford a Pierce following Fillmore.

But after Buchanan this nation needed a Lincoln—after Taft, we needed a Wilson—after Hoover we needed Franklin Roosevelt—and after eight years of drugged and fitful sleep, this nation needs strong, creative Democratic leadership in the White House.

But we are not merely running against Mr. Nixon. Our task is not merely one of itemizing Republican failures. Nor is that wholly necessary. For the families forced from the farm will know how to vote without our telling them. The unemployed miners and textile workers will know how to vote. The old people without medical care—the families without a decent home—the parents of children without adequate food or schools—they all know that it's time for a change.

But I think the American people expect more from us than cries of indignation and attack. The times are too grave, the challenge too urgent, and the stakes too high—to permit the customary passions of political debate. We are not here to curse the darkness, but to light the candle that can guide us through that darkness to a safe and sane future. As Winston Churchill said on taking office some twenty years ago:

"If we open a quarrel between the present and the past, we shall be in danger of losing the future."

Today our concern must be with that future. For the world is changing. The old era is ending. The old ways will not do.

Abroad, the balance of power is shifting. There are new and more terrible weapons—new and uncertain nations—new pressures of population and deprivation. One-third of the world, it has been said, may be free—but one-third is the victim of cruel repression—and the other one-third is rocked by the pangs of poverty, hunger and envy. More energy is released by the awakening of these new nations than by the fission of the atom itself.

Meanwhile, Communist influence has penetrated further into Asia, stood astride the Middle East and now festers some ninety miles off the coast of Florida. Friends have slipped into neutrality—and neutrals into hostility. As our keynoter reminded us, the President who began his career by going to Korea ends it by staying away from Japan.

The world has been close to war before—but now man, who has survived all previous threats to his existence, has taken into his mortal hands the power to exterminate the entire species some seven times over.

Here at home, the changing fact of the future is equally revolutionary. The New Deal and the Fair Deal were bold measures for their generations—but this is a new generation.

A technological revolution on the farm has led to an output explosion—but we have not yet learned to harness that explosion usefully, while protecting our farmers' right to full parity income.

An urban population revolution has overcrowded our schools, cluttered up our suburbs, and increased the squalor of our slums.

A peaceful revolution for human rights—demanding an end to racial discrimination in all parts of our community life—has strained at the leashes imposed by timid Executive leadership.

A medical revolution has extended the life of our elder citizens without providing the dignity and security those later years deserve. And a revolution of automation finds machines replacing men in the mines and mills of America, without replacing their income or their training or their need to pay the family doctor, grocer and landlord.

There has also been a change—a slippage—in our intellectual and moral strength. Seven lean years of drouth and famine have withered the field of ideas. Blight has descended on our regulatory agencies—and a dry rot, beginning in Washington, is seeping into every corner of America—in the payola mentality, the expense account way of life, the confusion between what is legal and what is right. Too many Americans have lost their way, their will and their sense of historic purpose.

It is time, in short, for a new generation of leadership—new men to cope with new problems and new opportunities.

All over the world, particularly in the newer nations, young men are coming to power—men who are not bound by the traditions of the past— men who are not blinded by the old fears and hates and rivalries—young men who can cast off the old slogans and delusions and suspicions.

The Republican nominee-to-be, of course is also a young man. But his approach is as old as McKinley. His party is the party of the past. His speeches are generalities from Poor Richard's Almanac. Their platform, made up of left-over Democratic planks, has the courage of our old convictions. Their pledge is a pledge to the status quo—and today there can be no status quo.

For I stand tonight facing west on what was once the last frontier. From the lands that stretch 3,000 miles behind me, the pioneers of old gave up their safety, their comfort and sometimes their lives to build a new world here in the West.

They were not the captives of their own doubts, the prisoners of their own price tags. Their motto was not "every man for himself"—but "all for the common cause." They were determined to make that new world strong and free, to overcome its hazards and its hardships, to conquer the enemies that threatened from without and within.

Today some would say that those struggles are all over—that all the horizons have been explored—that all the battles have been won—that there is no longer an American frontier.

But I trust that no one in this vast assemblage will agree with those sentiments. For the problems are not all solved and the battles are not all won—and we stand today on the edge of a new frontier—the frontier of the 1960's—a frontier of unknown opportunities and perils—a frontier of unfulfilled hopes and threats.

Woodrow Wilson's New Freedom promised our nation a new political and economic framework. Franklin Roosevelt's New Deal promised security and succor to those in need. But the New Frontier of which I speak is not a set of promises—it is a set of challenges. It sums up not what I intend to offer the American people, but what I intend to ask of them. It appeals to their pride, not their pocketbook—it holds out the promise of more sacrifice instead of more security.

But I tell you the New Frontier is here, whether we seek it or not. Beyond that frontier are uncharted areas of science and space, unsolved problems of peace and war, unconquered pockets of ignorance and prejudice, unanswered questions of poverty and surplus.

It would be easier to shrink back from that frontier, to look to the safe mediocrity of the past, to be lulled by good intentions and high rhetoric—and those who prefer that course should not cast their votes for me, regardless of party.

But I believe the times demand invention, innovation, imagination, decision. I am asking each of you to be new pioneers on that New Frontier. My call is to the young in heart, regardless of age—to the stout in spirit, regardless of party—to all who respond to the scriptural call:

"Be strong and of good courage; be not afraid, neither be thou dismayed."

For courage—not complacency—is our need today—leadership—not salesmanship. And the only valid test of leadership is the ability to lead, and lead vigorously. A tired nation, said David Lloyd George, is a tory nation—and the United States today cannot afford to be either tired or tory.

There may be those who wish to hear more—more promises to this group or that—more harsh rhetoric about the men in the Kremlin—more assurances of a golden future, where taxes are always low and subsidies ever high. But my promises are in the platform you have adopted. Our ends will not be won by rhetoric and we can have faith in the future only if we have faith in ourselves.

For the harsh facts of the matter are that we stand on this frontier at a turning-point in history. We must prove all over again whether this nation—or any nation so conceived—can long endure—whether our society—with its freedom of choice, its breadth of opportunity, its range of alternatives—can compete with the single-minded advance of the Communist system.

Can a nation organized and governed such as ours endure? That is the real question. Have we the nerve and the will? Can we carry through in an age where we will witness not only new breakthroughs in weapons of destruction—but also a race for mastery of the sky and the rain, the ocean and the tides, the far side of space and the inside of men's minds?

Are we up to the task? Are we equal to the challenge? Are we willing to match the Russian sacrifice of the present for the future? Or must we sacrifice our future in order to enjoy the present?

That is the question of the New Frontier. That is the choice our nation must make—a choice that lies not merely between two men or two parties, but between the public interest and private comfort—between national greatness and national decline—between the fresh air of progress and the stale, dank atmosphere of "normalcy"—between determined dedication and creeping mediocrity.

All mankind waits upon our decision. A whole world looks to see what we will do. We cannot fail their trust; we cannot fail to try.

It has been a long road from that first snowy day in New Hampshire to this crowded convention city. Now begins another long journey, taking me into your cities and homes all over America. Give me your help, your hand, your voice, your vote. Recall with me the words of Isaiah:

"They that wait upon the Lord shall renew their strength; they shall mount up with wings as eagles; they shall run, and not be weary."

As we face the coming challenge, we too, shall wait upon the Lord and ask that He renew our strength. Then shall we be equal to the test. Then we shall not be weary. And then we shall prevail.

JOHN F. KENNEDY

Campaign Speech

HOUSTON, TEXAS

September 12, 1960

I am grateful for your generous invitation to state my views.

While the so-called religious issue is necessarily and properly the chief topic here tonight, I want to emphasize from the outset that I believe that we have far more critical issues in the 1960 election: the spread of Communist influence, until it now festers only ninety miles off the coast of Florida—the humiliating treatment of our President and Vice-President by those who no longer respect our power—the hungry children I saw in West Virginia, the old people who cannot pay their doctor's bills, the families forced to give up their farms—an America with too many slums, with too few schools, and too late to the moon and outer space.

These are the real issues which should decide this campaign. And they are not religious issues—for war and hunger and ignorance and despair know no religious barrier.

But because I am a Catholic, and no Catholic has ever been elected President, the real issues in this campaign have been obscured—perhaps deliberately, in some quarters less responsible than this. So it is apparently necessary for me to state once again—not what kind of church I believe in, for that should be important only to me, but what kind of America I believe in.

I believe in an America where the separation of church and state is absolute—where no Catholic prelate would tell the President (should he be a Catholic) how to act and no Protestant minister would tell his parishioners for whom to vote—where no church or church school is granted any public funds or political preference—and where no man is denied public office merely because his religion differs from the President who might appoint him or the people who might elect him.

I believe in an America that is officially neither Catholic, Protestant nor Jewish—where no public official either requests or accepts instructions on public policy from the Pope, the National Council of Churches or any other ecclesiastical source—where no religious body seeks to impose its will directly or indirectly upon the general populace or the public acts of its officials—and where religious liberty is so indivisible that an act against one church is treated as an act against all.

For while this year it may be a Catholic against whom the finger of suspicion is pointed, in other years it has been, and may someday be again, a Jew—or a Quaker—or a Unitarian—or a Baptist. It was Virginia's harassment of Baptist preachers, for example, that led to Jefferson's statute of religious freedom. Today, I may be the victim—but tomorrow it may be you—until the whole fabric of our harmonious society is ripped apart at a time of great national peril.

Finally, I believe in an America where religious intolerance will someday end—where all men and all churches are treated as equal—where every man has the same right to attend or not to attend the church of his choice—where there is no Catholic vote, no antiCatholic vote, no bloc voting of any kind—and where Catholics, Protestants and Jews, both the lay and the pastoral level, will refrain from those attitudes of disdain and division which have so often marred their works in the past, and promote instead the American ideal of brotherhood.

That is the kind of America in which I believe. And it represents the kind of Presidency in which I believe—a great office that must be neither humbled by making it the instrument of any religious group, nor tarnished by arbitrarily withholding it, its occupancy, from the members of any religious group. I believe in a President whose views on religion are his own private affair, neither imposed upon him by the nation or imposed by the nation upon him as a condition to holding that office.

I would not look with favor upon a President working to subvert the First Amendment's guarantees of religious liberty (nor would our system of checks and balances permit him to do so). And neither do I look with favor upon those who would work to subvert Article VI of the Constitution by requiring a religious test—even by indirection—for if they disagree with that safeguard, they should be openly working to repeal it.

I want a Chief Executive whose public acts are responsible to all and obligated to none—who can attend any ceremony, service or dinner his office may appropriately require him to fulfill and whose fulfillment of his Presidential office is not limited or conditioned by any religious oath, ritual or obligation.

This is the kind of America I believe in—and this is the kind of America I fought for in the South Pacific and the kind my brother died for in Europe. No one suggested than that we might have a "divided loyalty," that we did "not believe in liberty" or that we belonged to a disloyal group that threatened "the freedoms from which our forefathers died."

And in fact this is the kind of America for which our forefathers did die when they fled here to escape religious test oaths, that denied office to members of less favored churches, when they fought for the Constitution, the Bill of Rights, the Virginia Statute of Religious Freedom—and when they fought at the shrine I visited today—the Alamo. For side by side with Bowie and Crocket died Fuentes and McCafferty and Bailey and Bedillio and Carey—but no one knows whether they were Catholics or not. For there was no religious test there.

I ask you tonight to follow in that tradition, to judge me on the basis of fourteen years in the congress—on my declared stands against an ambassador to the Vatican, against unconstitutional aid to parochial schools, and against any boycott of the public schools (which I attended myself)—instead of judging me on the basis of these pamphlets and publications we have all seen that carefully select quotations out of context from the statements of Catholic Church leaders, usually in other countries, frequently in other centuries, and rarely relevant to any situation here—and always omitting, of course, that statement of the American bishops in 1948 which strongly endorsed church-state separation.

I do not consider these other quotations binding upon my public acts—why should you? But let me say, with respect to other countries, that I am wholly opposed to the state being used by any religious group, Catholic or Protestant, to compel, prohibit or persecute the free exercise of any other religion. And that goes for any persecution at any time, by anyone, in any country.

And I hope that you and I condemn with equal fervor those nations which deny their Presidency to Protestants and those which deny it to Catholics. And rather than cite the misdeeds of those who differ, I would also cite the record of the Catholic Church in such nations as France and Ireland—and the independence of such statesmen as de Gaulle and Adenauer.

But let me stress again that these are my views—for, contrary to common newspaper usage, I am not the Catholic candidate for President. I am the Democratic Party's candidate for President, who happens also to be a Catholic.

I do not speak for my church on public matters—and the church does not speak for me.

Whatever issues may come before me as President, if I should be elected—on birth control, divorce, censorship, gambling, or any other subject—I will make my decision in accordance with these views, in accordance with what my conscience tells me to be in the national interest, and without regard to outside religious pressure or dictate. And no power or threat of punishment could cause me to decide otherwise.

But if the time should ever come—and I do not concede any conflict to be remotely possible—when my office would require me to either violate my conscience, or violate the national interest, then I would resign the office, and I hope any other conscientious public servant would do likewise.

But I do not intend to apologize for these views to my critics of either Catholic or Protestant faith, nor do I intend to disavow either my views or my church in order to win this election. If I should lose on the real issues, I shall return to my seat in the Senate, satisfied that I tried my best and was fairly judged.

But if this election is decided on the basis that 40,000,000 Americans lost their chance of being President on the day they were baptized, then it is the whole nation that will be the loser in the eyes of Catholics and non-Catholics around the world, in the eyes of history, and in the eyes of our own people.

But if, on the other hand, I should win this election, I shall devote every effort of mind and spirit to fulfilling the oath of the Presidency— practically identical, I might add, with the oath I have taken for fourteen years in the Congress. For, without reservation, I can, and I quote, "solemnly swear that I will faithfully execute the office of President of the United States and will to the best of my ability preserve, protect and defend the Constitution, so help me God."

☆

RICHARD M. NIXON

Acceptance Speech

CHICAGO, ILLINOIS

July 28, 1960

Mr. Chairman, delegates to this convention, my fellow Americans:

I have made many speeches in my life and never have I found it more difficult to find the words adequate to express what I feel as I find them tonight.

To stand here before this great convention, to hear your expression of affection for me, for Pat, for our daughters, for my mother, for all of us who are representing our party is, of course, the greatest moment of my life.

And I just want you to know that my only prayer as I stand here is that in the months ahead I may be in some way worthy of the affection and the trust which you have presented to me on this occasion in everything that I say, everything that I do, everything that I think in this campaign and afterwards.

May I say also that I have been wanting to come to this convention, but because of the protocol that makes it necessary for a candidate not to attend the convention until the nominations are over, I've had to look in on it on television. But I want all of you to know that I have never been so proud of my party as I have been in these last three days, and as I have compared this convention, the conduct of our delegates and our speakers with what went on in my native state of California just two weeks ago.

And I congratulate Chairman Halleck and Chairman Morton and all of those who have helped to make this convention one that will stand in the annals of our party forever as one of the finest we have ever held.

Have you ever stopped to think of the memories you will take away from this convention?

The things that run through my mind are these: that first day with the magnificent speech by Mr. Hoover with his great lesson for the American people, Walter Judd with one of the most outstanding keynote addresses in either party in the history and last night our beloved fighting President making the greatest speech that I have ever heard him make before this convention.

Your platform and its magnificent presentation by Chuck Percy, the chairman. For these and for so many other things, I want to congratulate you tonight and to thank you from the bottom of my heart and on behalf of Americans—not just Republicans—Americans everywhere for making us proud of our country and of our two-party system for what you have done.

And tonight, too, I particularly want to thank this convention for nominating as my running mate, a world statesman of the first rank, my friend and colleague, Henry Cabot Lodge of Massachusetts.

In refreshing contrast to what happened in Los Angeles you nominated a man who shares my views on the great issues and who will work with me and not against me in carrying out our magnificent platform.

And may I say that during this week we Republicans who feel our convictions strongly about our party and about our country have had our differences but as the speech by Senator Goldwater indicated yesterday and the eloquent and gracious remarks of my friend Nelson Rockefeller indicated tonight, we Republicans know that the differences that divide us are infinitesimal compared to the gulf beween us and what the Democrats would put upon us from what they did at Los Angeles at their convention two weeks ago.

It was only eight years ago that I stood in this very place after you had nominated as our candidate for the President one of the great men of our century, and I say to you tonight that for generations to come Americans, regardless of party, will gratefully remember Dwight Eisenhower as the man who brought peace to America, as the man under whose leadership Americans enjoyed the greatest progress and prosperity in history, but above all they will remember him as the man who restored honesty, integrity and dignity to the conduct of government in the highest office of this land.

My fellow Americans, I know now that you will understand what I next say because the next President of the United States will have his great example to follow; because the next President will have new and challenging problems in the world of utmost gravity this truly is the time for greatness in America's leadership.

I am sure you will understand why I do not say tonight that I alone am the man who can furnish that leadership. That question is not for me but for you to decide. And I only ask that the thousands in this hall and the millions listening to me on television, I only ask that you make that decision in the most thoughtful way that you possibly can because what you decide this November will not only affect your lives, and your future, it will affect the future of millions throughout the world.

And I urge you study the records of the candidates, listen to my speeches and that of my opponent and that of Mr. Lodge and that of his opponent and then after you have studied our records and listened to our speeches decide—decide on the basis of what we say and what we believe which is best qualified to lead America and the free world in this critical period.

And to help you make this decision I would like to discuss tonight some of the great problems which will confront the next President of the United States and the policies I believe that should be adopted to meet them.

One hundred years ago in this city Abraham Lincoln was nominated for President of the United States. The problems which will confront our next President will be even greater than those that confronted him.

The question then was freedom for the slaves and survival of the nation. The question now is freedom for all mankind and the survival of civilization and the choice you make—each of you listening to me makes this November—can affect the answer to that question.

What should your choice be and what is it?

Well, let's first examine what our opponents offered in Los Angeles two weeks ago.

They claim theirs was a new program but you know what it was? It was simply the same old proposition that a political party should be all things to all men and nothing more than that.

And they promised—everything to everybody with one exception. They didn't promise to pay the bill. And I say tonight that with their convention, their platform and their ticket they composed a symphony of political cynicism which is out of harmony with our times today.

Now we come to the key question: what should our answer be? And some might say, why, do as they do. Out-promise them, because that's the only way to win.

And I want to tell you my answer. I happen to believe that their program would be disastrous for America. It would wreck our economy; it would dash our people's high hopes for a better life.

And I serve notice here and now that whatever the political consequences, we are not going to try to out-promise our opponents in this campaign.

We are not going to make promises we cannot and should not keep and we are not going to try to buy the people's votes with their own money.

And to those who say that this position will mean political defeat, my answer is this: We have more faith than that in the good sense of the American people, provided the people know the facts, and that's where we come in.

And I pledge to you tonight that we will bring the facts home to the American people, and we will do it with a campaign such as this country has never seen before.

I have been asked by the newsmen sitting on my right and my left all week long, when is this campaign going to begin, Mr. Vice President, on the day after Labor Day or one of the other traditional starting dates? And this is my answer: This campaign begins tonight, here and now, and it goes on.

And this campaign will continue from now until Nov. 8 without any let up.

And I've also been asked by my friends in the press on either side here. They say, "Mr. Vice President, where are you going to concentrate. What states are you going to visit?" And this is my answer: In this campaign, we are going to take no states for granted and we aren't going to concede any states to the opposition!

And I announce to you tonight and I pledge to you that I, personally, will carry this campaign into every one of the fifty states of this nation between now and Nov. 8.

And in this campaign I make a prediction. I say that just as in 1952 and 1956, millions of Democrats will join us not because they are deserting their party but because their party deserted them at Los Angeles two weeks ago.

Now I have suggested to you what our friends of the opposition offered to the American people. What do we offer?

First, we are proud to offer the best eight-year record of any Administration in the history of this country.

But, my fellow Americans, that isn't all, and that isn't enough, because we happen to believe that a record is not something to stand on but something to build on, and building on the great record of this Administration we shall build a better America. We shall build an America in which we shall see the realization of the dreams, the dreams of millions of people not only in America but throughout the world for a fuller, freer, richer life than men have ever known in the history of mankind.

Let me tell you something of the goal of this better America towards which we will strive.

In this America, our older citizens shall not only have adequate protection against the hazards of ill-health but a greater opportunity to lead a useful and productive life by participating to the extent they are able in the nation's exciting work rather than sitting on the sidelines.

And in this better America, young Americans shall not only have the best basic education in America but every boy and girl of ability regardless of his financial circumstances shall have the opportunity to develop his intellectual capabilities to the full.

Our wage-earners shall enjoy increasingly higher wages in honest dollars with better protection against the hazards of unemployment and old age and for those millions of Americans who are still denied equality of rights and opportunity, I say there shall be the greatest progress in human rights since the days of Lincoln, 100 years ago.

And America's farmers—America's farmers—to whose hard work and almost incredible efficiency we owe the fact that we are the best fed, best clothed people in the world, I say American farmers must and will receive what they do not have today and what they deserve—a fair share of America's ever-increasing prosperity.

And to accomplish these things, we will develop to the full the untapped natural resources our water, our minerals, our power with which we are so fortunate to be blessed in this rich land of ours.

And we shall provide for our scientists, the support they need for the research that will open exciting new highways into the future—new highways in which we shall have progress which we cannot even dream of today. And above all, in this decade of the Sixties, this decade of decision and progress, we will witness the continued revitalization of America's moral and spiritual strength with the renewed faith in the eternal ideals of freedom and justice under God which are our priceless heritage as a people.

And now I am sure that many of you in this hall and many of you on television might well ask, "but Mr. Nixon, don't our opponents favor just such goals as these?" And my answer is yes, of course. All Americans regardless of party want a better life for our people. What's the difference then? And I'll tell you what it is. The difference is in the way we propose to reach these goals, and the record shows that our way works and theirs doesn't. And we're going to prove it in this campaign.

We produce on the promises that they make. We succeed where they fail. Do you know why? Because we put, as Governor Rockefeller said in his remarks, we put our primary reliance not upon government but upon people for progress in America. That is why we will succeed.

And we must never forget that the strength of America is not in its government but in its people. And we say tonight that there is no limit to the goals America can reach provided we stay true to the great American tradition.

A government has a role and a very important one but the role of government is not to take responsibility from people but to put responsibility on them. It is not to dictate to people but to encourage and stimulate the creative productivity of 180,000,000 free Americans. That's the way to progress in America.

In other words, we have faith in the people and because our programs for progress are based on that faith, we shall succeed where our opponents will fail in building the better America that I've described.

But if these goals are to be reached, the next President of the United States must have the wisdom to choose between the things government should and should not do. He must have the courage to stand against the pressures of the few for the good of the many, and he must have the vision to press forward on all fronts for the better life our people want.

I have spoken to you of the responsibilities of our next President at home. Those which he will face abroad will be infinitely greater. But before I look to the future, let me say a word about the past.

At Los Angeles two weeks ago, we heard the United States—our Government—blamed for Mr. Khrushchev's sabotage of the Paris conference. We heard the United States blamed for the actions of communist-led mobs in Caracas and Tokyo. We heard that American education and American scientists are inferior. We heard that America militarily and economically is a second-rate country. We heard that America's prestige is at an all-time low.

This is my answer: I say that at a time the Communists are running us down abroad it's time to speak up. And my friends, let us recognize America has its weaknesses, and constructive criticism of those weaknesses is essential, essential so that we can correct our weaknesses in the best traditions of our democratic process.

But let us also recognize that while it is dangerous to see nothing wrong in America, it is just as wrong to refuse to recognize what is right about America.

And tonight I say to you: no criticism—no criticism—should be allowed to obscure the truth either at home or abroad that today America is the strongest nation militarily, economically and ideologically in the world and we have the will and the stamina, the resources to maintain that strength in the years ahead.

And now, if we may turn to the future. We must recognize that the foreign policy problems of the Sixties will be different and they will be vastly more difficult than those of the Fifties through which we have just passed.

We are in a race tonight, my fellow Americans, in a race for survival in which our lives, our fortunes, our liberties are at stake. We are ahead now. But the only way to stay ahead in a race is to move ahead and the next President will make decisions which will determine whether we win or whether we lose this race.

What must we do?

These things, I believe:

He must resolve first and above all that the United States must never settle for second-best in anything.

Let's look at the specifics:

Militarily the security of the United States must be put before all other consideration. Why? Not only because this is necessary to deter aggression but because we must make sure that we are never in a position at the conference table so Mr. Khrushchev or his successor is able to coerce an American President because of his strength and our weakness.

Diplomatically, let's look at what this problem is. Diplomatically, our next President must be firm, firm on principle. But he must never be belligerent. He must never engage in a war of words which might heat up the international climate to the igniting point of nuclear catastrophe. But, while he must never answer insults in kind, he must leave no doubt at any time that whether it is in Berlin or in Cuba or anywhere else in the world, America will not tolerate being pushed around by anybody, any place.

Because we have already paid a terrible price in lives and resources to learn that appeasement leads not to peace but to war.

It will indeed take great leadership to steer us through these years, and avoiding the extremes of belligerency on the one hand and appeasement on the other.

Now, Mr. Kennedy has suggested that what the world needs is young leadership, and understandably this has great appeal. Because it is true, true, that youth does bring boldness and imagination, and drive to leadership, and we need all these things.

But I think most people will agree with me tonight when I say that President de Gaulle, Prime Minister Macmillan, Chancellor Adenauer, are not young men.

But we are indeed fortunate that we have their wisdom and their experience, and their courage on our side in the struggle for freedom today in the world.

And I might suggest that as we consider the relative merits of youth and age, it's only fair to point out that it was not Mr. de Gaulle, or Mr. Macmillan, or Mr. Adenauer, but Mr. Kennedy who made the rash and impulsive suggestion that President Eisenhower should have apologized and sent regrets to Mr. Khrushchev for the U-2 flight which the President had ordered to save our country from surprise attack.

But formidable as will be the diplomatic and military problems confronting the next President, far more difficult and critical will be the decisions he must make to meet and defeat the enemies of freedom in an entirely different kind of struggle.

And now, I want to speak to you of another kind of aggression—

aggression without war, for the aggressor comes not as a conqueror but as a champion of peace, of freedom, offering progress and plenty and hope to the unfortunates of the earth.

And I say tonight that the major problem—the biggest problem—confronting the next President of the United States will be to inform the people of the character of this kind of aggression, to arouse the people to the mortal danger it presents and to inspire the people to meet that danger.

And he must develop a brand new strategy which will win the battle for freedom for all men and women without a war. That is the great task of the next President of the United States.

And this will be a difficult task. Difficult because at times our next President must tell the people not what they want to hear but what they need to hear. Why, for example, it may be just as essential to the national interest to build a dam in India as in California. It will be difficult, too, because we Americans have always been able to see and understand the danger presented by missiles and airplanes and bombs, but we found it hard to recognize the even more deadly danger of the propaganda that warps the mind, the economic offensive that softens the nation, the subversion that destroys the will of a people to resist tyranny.

And yet may I say tonight that the fact that this threat is as I believe it to be the greatest danger we have ever confronted this is no reason for lack of confidence in the outcome.

You know why?

Because there is one great theme that runs through our history as a nation. Americans are always at their best when the challenge is greatest.

And I say tonight that we Americans shall rise to our greatest heights in this Decade of the Sixties as we mount the offensive to meet those forces which threaten peace and the rights of free men everywhere.

But there are some things we can do and things we must do, and I would like to list them for you tonight.

First, we must take the necessary steps which will assure that the American economy grows at a maximum rate so that we can maintain our present massive lead over the Communist bloc.

How do we do this? There isn't any magic formula by which government in a free nation can bring this about. The way to insure maximum growth in America is not by expanding the functions of government but by increasing the opportunities for investment and creative enterprise for millions of individual Americans.

And at a time when the Communists have found it necessary to turn to decentralization of their economy and to turn to the use of individual incentive to increase productivity, at a time, in other words when they are turning our way, I say we must and we will not make the mistake of turning their way.

There is another step that we must take—a second one. Our government activity must be reorganized—reorganized to take the initiative from the Communists and to develop and carry out a world-wide strategy, an offensive for peace and freedom.

The complex of agencies which has grown up through the years for exchange of persons, for technical assistance, for information, for loans and for grants, all these must be welded together into one powerful economic and ideological striking force under the direct supervision and leadership of the President of the United States.

Because what we must do you see is to wage the battles for peace and freedom with the same unified direction and dedication with which we wage battles in wars.

And if these activities are to succeed, we must develop a better training program for the men and women who will represent our country at home and abroad.

And what we need are men with broad knowledge of the intricacies and techniques of the strategy of communism, with a keen knowledge of the great principles for which free people stand and above all men who with zeal and dedication which the Communists cannot match will outthink and outwork and outlast the enemies of freedom wherever they meet them anyplace in the world.

This is the kind of men we must train.

And we must recognize something else. Government can't do this job alone. The most effective proponents of freedom are not governments but free people.

And this means that every American, every one of you listening tonight who works or travels abroad must represent his country at its best in everything that he does.

And the United States, the United States, big as it is, strong as it is, we can't do this job alone.

The best brains, the fullest resources of other free nations which have as great a stake in freedom as we have must be mobilized to participate with us in this task to the extent they are able.

But do you know what is most important of all—above all—we must recognize that the greatest economic strength that we can imagine, the finest of government organizations—all this will fail if we are not united and inspired by a great idea—an idea which will be a battle cry for a grand offensive to win the minds and the hearts and the souls of men.

Do we have such an idea?

The Communists proclaim over and over again that their aim is the victory of communism throughout the world. It is not enough for us to reply that our aim is to contain communism, to defend the free world against communism, to hold the line against communism. The only answer to a strategy of victory for the communist world is a strategy of victory for the free world.

But let the victory we seek be not victory over any other nation or any other people. Let it be the victory of freedom over tyranny, of plenty over hunger, of health over disease in every country of the world.

When Mr. Khrushchev says our grandchildren will live under communism, let us say his grandchildren will live in freedom.

When Mr. Khrushchev says the Monroe Doctrine is dead in the Americas, we say the doctrine of freedom applies everywhere in the world.

And I say tonight let us welcome Mr. Khrushchev's challenge to peaceful competition of our system. But let us reply, let us compete in the Communist world as well as in the free world, because the Communist dictators must not be allowed the privileged sanctuary from which to launch their guerrilla attacks on the citadels of freedom.

And we say further, extend this competition—extend it to include not only food and factories as he has suggested but extend it to include the great spiritual and moral values which characterize our civilization.

And further, let us welcome, my friends, let us welcome the challenge, not be disconcerted by it, not fail to meet it. The challenge, presented by the revolution of peaceful peoples' aspirations in South America, in Asia, in Africa. We can't fail in this mission. We can't fail to assist them in finding a way to progress with freedom, so that they will be faced with the terrible alternative of turning to communism with its promise of progress at the cost of freedom.

Let us make it clear to them that our aim in helping them is not merely to stop communism but that in the great American tradition of concern for those less fortunate than we are, that we welcome the opportunity to work with people everywhere in helping them to achieve their aspirations for a life of human dignity.

And this means that our primary aim must be not to help government but to help people—to help people attain the life they deserve.

In essence, what I am saying tonight is that our answer to the threat of Communist revolution is renewed devotion to the great ideals of the American Revolution—ideals that caught the imagination of the world 180 years ago and it still lives in the minds and hearts of people everywhere.

I could tell you tonight that all you need to do to bring all these things about that I have described is to elect the right man as President of this country and leave these tasks to him. But my fellow Americans, America demands more than that of me and of you.

When I visited the Soviet Union, in every factory there was a huge sign which read: "Work for the victory of communism."

And what America needs today is not just a President, not just a few leaders, but millions of Americans working for the victory of freedom.

Each American must make a personal and total commitment to the cause of freedom and all it stands for. It means wage earners and employers making an extra effort to increase the productivity of our factories. It means our students in schools striving for excellence rather than adjusting to mediocrity.

It means supporting, encouraging our scientists to explore the unknown, not for just what we can get but for what we can learn. And it means on the part of each American assuming personal responsibility to make this country which we love a proud example of freedom for all the world. Each of us for example doing our part in ending the prejudice which 100 years after Lincoln, to our shame, still embarrasses us abroad and saps our strength at home. Each of us participating in this or other political campaigns, not just by going to the polls and voting but working with the candidate of your choice.

And it means, my fellow Americans, it means sacrifice. But not the grim sacrifice of desperation but the rewarding sacrifice of choice which lifts us out of the humdrum life in which we live and gives us the supreme satisfaction which comes from working together in a cause greater than ourselves, greater than our nation, as great as the whole world itself.

What I proposed tonight is not new. It is as old as America and as young as America because America will never grow old.

You will remember. Listen, Thomas Jefferson said "We act not for ourselves alone but for the whole human race." Lincoln said, "In giving freedom to the slaves we assure freedom to the free. We shall nobly save or meanly lose the last best hope of earth." And Teddy Roosevelt said, "Our first duty as citizens of the nation is owed to the United States but if we are true to our principles we must also think of serving the interests of mankind at large."

And Woodrow Wilson said, "A patriotic American is never so proud of the flag under which he lives as when it comes to mean to others as well as to himself a symbol of hope and liberty."

And we say—we say today—that a young America shall fulfill her destiny by helping to build a new world in which men can live together in peace and justice and freedom with each other.

But there is a difference today, an exciting difference. And the difference is because of the dramatic breakthroughs in science for the first time in human history we have the resources—the resources to wage a winning war against poverty, misery and disease wherever it exists in the world, and upon the next President of the United States will rest the responsibility to inspire and to lead the forces of freedom toward this goal.

I am sure now that you understand why I said at the beginning that it would be difficult for any man to say that he was qualified to provide this kind of leadership.

I can only say tonight to you that I believe in the American dream because I have seen it come true to my own life.

I know something of the threat which confronts us, and I know something of the effort which will be needed to meet it.

I have seen hate for America, not only in the Kremlin, but in the eyes of Communists in our own country, and on the ugly face of a mob in Caracas.

I have heard doubts about America, expressed not just by Communists but by sincere students and labor leaders in other countries, searching for the way to a better life and wondering if we had lost the way.

And I have seen love for America in countries throughout the world, in a crowd in Jakarta, in Bogota; in the heart of Siberia, in Warsaw— 250,000 people on the streets on a Sunday afternoon singing, crying with tears running down their cheeks and shouting: "Nacheea! Nacheea!" "Long live the United States."

And I know, my fellow Americans, I know tonight that we must resist the hate. We must remove the doubts, but above all we must be worthy of the love and the trust of millions on this earth for whom America is the hope of the world.

A hundred years ago Abraham Lincoln was asked during the dark days of the tragic war between the states whether he thought God was on his side. His answer was "my concern is not whether God is on our side, but whether we are on God's side."

My fellow Americans, may that ever be our prayer for our country, and in that spirit with faith in America, with faith in her ideals and in her people I accept your nomination for President of the United States.

☆

RICHARD M. NIXON

Campaign Speech

TOLEDO, OHIO

October 27, 1960

Tonite I want to talk about a question of major significance, both to our survival as a nation and our progress as a society—our atomic policy both as it affects peaceful uses and weapons.

We are not a warlike people. We yearn as deeply as any nation to convert our wealth, energy, and science into the pursuit of peaceful progress.

Unfortunately for all men, there are others in the world who boldly assert, by word and deed, that force and violence are justified to accomplish their political ambitions. War and threats of war are to them just as worthy tactics of basic policy as words of peace. They have repeatedly used the sword to deprive people of their freedom and compel them to serve the purposes of a tyrannical state.

Because of this continuing menace, America must stay powerfully armed and vigilant. But we have hoped, and we continue to hope, that the Communists would fully comprehend that a thermonuclear war can only destroy attacker and defender alike. Thus, two years ago we sat down with the Soviets in Geneva to negotiate on control of nuclear weapons testing.

Both sides agreed that control was desirable but the obstacle was Soviet refusal to accept adequate inspection. The Soviets have remained intent upon keeping their society walled off from the rest of mankind. They have insisted that we simply take their word that they would adhere to any agreed controls. This has been unacceptable to ourselves and our allies as we earnestly seek the way to world peace. Years of the big and little lie, ignored pledges, broken promises, and violated agreements, make obvious the necessity of a foolproof inspection system. Until now, the Soviet atomic negotiators have stalled in implementing Chairman Khrushchev's letters of April 23, 1959, to President Eisenhower and Prime Minister Macmillan, when he stated that "we are quite able to find a solution to the problem of discontinuing tests . . . and to establish such controls as would guarantee strict observance of the treaty."

In an open society like ours, a ban on atom testing is self-policing, in that any activities of this nature are widely reported immediately. The

Soviets, by contrast, simply do not permit people, even their own people, to move freely about the country and speak or write what they see. The limited inspection system which they are willing to accept would permit them to cheat and allow the cheating to go undetected.

During these two years of negotiations, we have not detonated any nuclear devices and the Soviets know that we have not. However, during the same period, the Soviets have fired at least one large underground explosion and several smaller ones. They state that these have not been nuclear shots, simply high explosives. We have no way of knowing whether this is the fact. Nor will the Soviets permit us, or the United Nations, or neutral nations, to make an inspection.

Only a few days ago, the new seismic station at Fort Sill, Oklahoma, recorded a disturbance in the Soviet Union. It might have been an earthquake. Or it might have been a large underground nuclear explosion. We have no way of knowing.

The seriousness of this great uncertainty becomes clear when we consider where we are in point of time as it concerns weapons development. Originally, the moratorium on testing was fixed for one year; then, in a carefully calculated risk, the President decided to extend the moratorium, a risk which he accepted for the purpose of going the second mile, and beyond, to reach agreement with the Soviets.

Now consider the situation. For two years we have not tested our nuclear technology. And the history of weapons development is such that it requires only between three and four years to complete a new breakthrough. Two years of this time has run, as the United States has worked earnestly for this positive step toward eliminating the war threat to all humanity.

Where has this left us? We have no agreement, There is reason to believe that the Soviets may have used the time to attempt to overtake us. We cannot prolong the risk much longer without seriously jeopardizing the very objective toward which we hoped the Geneva negotiations would point—peace and human survival.

Recently my opponent made a campaign statement on the question of atomic testing, in the form of a reply to an open letter to us both from former Atomic Energy Commissioner Thomas E. Murray. He stated that "this subject like all other public issues is properly a matter for critical discussion and debate." Then he outlined his course of action.

I will deal briefly with Senator Kennedy's proposals because of the fact that one or the other of us is going to have the responsibility for resolving this question bearing on our very survival. I will deal with them because his approach is different from the one which I believe this nation must follow if we are to keep our vital military and technological superiority over the Soviets in the crucial years ahead.

My opponent said that he did not believe that underground nuclear weapons tests " should be resumed at this time." He would want, he said, even at this late date, to continue or reopen negotiations with the Soviets with new negotiators and new instructions. Noting specifically that the present negotiators "are not representatives chosen by me," he added that he would "direct vigorous negotiation, in accordance with my personal instructions on policy."

He is saying, in effect, that the negotiations of the past two years by the United States representatives have not been sufficiently vigorous and that their instructions have not been adequate to the task. He is proposing a course of action which would delay any possible resolution of this vital matter for much too long—far beyond any margin of safety—since he is proposing to handle the matter with new men and new instructions. And he is suggesting nothing more concrete toward resolving the issue than to imply that his "personal instructions" must be more effective than President Eisenhower's have been during the past two years.

The delay, and Senator Kennedy's reasons for it, are both unacceptable. I say to him that it is impossible to imply in truth that these negotiations could have been pursued with greator vigor or sincerity on the part of Ambassador [James J.] Wadsworth and our career negotiators and our top scientists. I say to him no instruction would have produced agreement to date, except and unless we had been willing to sacrifice the principles of adequate inspection.

The only major obstacle to an atomic test agreement has been, and is now, the Soviet refusal to accept adequate inspection. Clearly, then, the only "new policy instructions" through which the United States could remove this obstacle would entail surrender on this point. The security of the United States, and of the entire free world, simply will not permit either such a surrender or the indefinite continuation of the present moratorium, entirely without inspection.

And I say that we cannot and should not blame ourselves, our policies, our negotiators, their scientific advisers, or their instructions for the unyielding refusal of the Soviets to make an agreement at Geneva. The time and patience which we have already expended to explore this way out of the disarmament dilemma have been fulsome proof of our own intentions and of the Soviets'. The blame rests squarely on them. We cannot permit further delay.

This is exactly what Mr. Khrushchev and his intransigent negotiators are seeking to accomplish. They are trying to buy critical time, critical time designed to arrest our atomic development, both military and peaceful, while they are free to proceed with their own. Another delay, of the length indicated in Senator Kennedy's proposals, could be decisive in the struggle for peace and freedom.

We must resolve the issue now. We must never allow the Soviets, by deceit, to make America second in nuclear technology. This outcome could defeat us without even the direct horror of atomic war.

As President Eisenhower already has for the present Administration, I will make the settlement of the atomic-test negotiations a question of the highest priority of American policy.

We must act now to break this Soviet filibuster against peace and the security of the free nations.

To allow this Soviet filibuster against a test agreement to continue would dangerously increase the risk of war, the risk of war in the most frightful form in human history, an annihilating atomic war.

It has become one of the grim facts of our times that whatever increases Soviet strength relative to our own thereby increases the risk of war. Hearing Mr. Khrushchev bluster and threaten to launch his rockets from his present position of significant military inferiority leaves us small room for doubt about what he would be tempted to do if he ever gained the overall advantage.

The peace of the world, the very survival of the human race, demands that we break this fateful filibuster. We must and will take the necessary steps to maintain the peace. If I am elected, I will on November 9 ask the President to designate Ambassador Lodge to go to Geneva personally to participate in the present negotiations with a view to resolving this question by February 1. There is no conceivable, no honest reason why this cannot be accomplished if the Soviets have any intention of ever coming to an agreement. After two years they are still haggling over matters that can only be construed as naked attempts to further obstruct and delay.

I would have Mr. Khrushchev know that if Amabassador Lodge and the Soviet negotiator are able to bring an agreement in sight in this eighty-day period, I would be prepared to meet with Prime Minister Macmillan and—so important do I hold this question to be—with Mr. Khrushchev to make the final agreement at the summit.

But I would have him understand that, if at the end of the eighty-day period—by February 1—there is no progress, the United States will be prepared to detonate atomic devices necessary to advance our peaceful technology. Such devices already are prepared for underground use in such a way as to guarantee no contamination.

Further, I would have him understand that the United States is willing to continue negotiations for a nuclear weapons test ban as long as the Soviet representatives will sit, but not under an uninspected moratorium of indefinite duration. I would have Mr. Khrushchev understand that if an agreement is not signed within a reasonable period after February 1, the United States will have no alternative but resume underground testing of atomic weapons.

I say underground testing because there is no question of resuming tests in the atmosphere, where some still undetermined danger of contamination exists. The United States has abandoned such testing, certainly until more knowledge is available as to the exact consequences.

We must not, and will not, continue the present moratorium on weapons testing without adequate safeguards of inspection for an extended period of time such as implicit in Senator Kennedy's position.

On the other hand, if before then an agreement can be negotiated, the United States will proceed, in concert with all nations, to realize the enormous potential which nuclear energy holds for the human race. It must, of course, be an integral part of such an atomic agreement that the nations will continue—with proper safeguards—to experiment for peaceful purposes.

As things now stand, we face a fateful alternative. We can and must go forward with our atomic technology in one of these two ways:

1. With an agreement guaranteeing that nuclear energy will not further be developed into still greater weapons of annihilation, but for the benefit of humanity, or—

2. With no agreement, each nation insuring its own survival and maintaining its technological progress, military and peaceful, as it sees fit.

We are on the threshold of developing major peaceful uses of the atom. Large power reactors are coming into being, next year we will witness the sea trials of the Savannah—the world's first atomic merchant ship. By 1965 we will have from Project Rover a nuclear-fueled space engine that will be capable of propelling space probes.

However, without exploding atomic devices we cannot achieve many peaceful benefits of our nuclear technology. This is particularly true of a new and imaginative peaceful use of the atom which has tremendous potential—the use of explosive power for great engineering projects which would otherwise not be practical or economical. Our plan to develop peaceful constructive uses of nuclear explosives has been given the name of Project Plowshare because it literally is an attempt to convert the most destructive weapon in history into a tool for human betterment. Through Project Plowshare, we now have a great opportunity to turn our atomic armory into a tool for peace.

From the study on the very few subsurface shots that were conducted prior to the Geneva talks, we have gained tantalizing glimpses of great new vistas of future achievement. In Project Plowshare, scientists and engineers already know of some things they expect to find and some hints as to what else they may find. Exciting as these factors may be, the other still unknown findings may outshine all the rest.

In numerous private and official discussions with our scientists and our leaders in this exciting new field, I have full reports on both the progress and the promise of this development. I will discuss them briefly tonite.

First a word about safety from atomic radiation. I am assured by all scientists familiar with Project Plowshare that the underground projects can go forward without fear of the consequences of radiation. Eventually, with further development and more knowledge, ways can be found to explore all of the promising areas which the Plowshare researchers now suggest. It would be my firm policy that projects of this character would only be undertaken after the most thorough consideration and with the utmost regard for public health and safety.

In small underground explosions, the scientists advise, the fireball is small—only a few feet in diameter—and it transmits its heat through the ground for a radius of sixty to 150 feet. Everything immediately around the fireball is vaporized. A few feet beyond everything is melted. As the intense heat of the fireball diminishes, all this molten material cools and forms a glasslike shell. A major portion of the radioactivity produced by the explosion is permanently trapped inside the shell.

And in this underground shell and the broken rock formations around it—between 100,000 and 100,000,000 tons of broken and crushed rock—is enormous potential to be extracted for man's benefit. First the scientists believe the heat which is trapped may be trapped for a long enough time to produce steam for the economical generation of electric power.

Think of the implications for a moment—the energy unit of an atomic power plant to be available wherever engineers want to place it. Think of the vast mineral riches in remote areas of Alaska, Canada, South America, Africa, Asia, which lie untapped because there presently is no way to bring in electricity or any other conventional form of energy to mine and extract the ores. Any of these areas would be vastly benefited and enriched if they sought to avail themselves of such scientific development.

Moreover, we have in this country, in our Rocky Mountain states, oil deposits that equal the reserves of the entire Middle East, oil deposits that are denied to us because they are tightly locked in shale rock. At present we know of no economical way to get oil out of the shale. Plowshare offers a solution.

There is another great potential of enormous significance to millions of Americans, particularly in the presently depressed coal-mining regions. For some time the coal industry has searched for cheap and reasonable methods to accomplish coal "gasification," to convert this resource, not presently in great enough demand, into one that is. The Plowshare scientists have been led to believe from results of previous underground tests that an answer may lie in their researches.

The versatility of Project Plowshare goes on and on. Of immediate and far-reaching importance to the peoples of all the world is the use of atomic energy in this form for massive engineering projects, the costs of which heretofore have been prohibitive. Plowshare scientists anticipate that, with further research and testing, nuclear explosions will make it possible to build harbors where none now exist, thus accelerating by many times the economic development of such areas as Alaska and many other areas of the world. They are already drawing plans and designing devices to adapt the "nuclear dynamite" of Plowshare to cut sea-level canals between the oceans and other navigable bodies, dredge rivers, literally to lift the face of the earth to the benefit of all mankind.

Our determination to proceed with these works of great general benefit to humanity is fully in accord with the great American tradition. I repeat that, with or without a trustworthy agreement with the Soviets in the next few months, we must get on with our work.

Significantly, this kind of effort has been a discernible part of the American character and the American purpose from the beginnings of our century. Early in the nineteenth century the French observer de Tocqueville noted this difference between the American character and the Russian:

"The American struggles against the obstacles that nature opposes to him.

"The adversaries of the Russian are men. The conquests of the American are therefore gained by the plowshare; those of the Russian by the sword."

We will continue to gain our conquests by the plowshare, in the modern context of the atomic plowshares. At the same time we will maintain our military superiority so that the Soviets can never again gain new conquests by the sword.

And ultimately we will realize the vision of the prophet Isaiah for the community of man: ". . . and they shall beat their swords into plowshares, and their spears into pruning hooks; nation shall not lift up sword against nation. Neither shall they learn war any more."

☆

1964

———— ☆ ————

On November 22, 1963, the "Thousand Days" of the Kennedy administration came to a tragic end, when an assassin's bullet killed the President in Dallas, Texas.

Most of Kennedy's domestic programs, such as his civil rights legislation, medical care for the aged program, support of federal aid to education, and his January, 1963, "radical" proposal to reduce taxes by $10 billion without a concomitant reduction in government spending as a vehicle for stimulating economic growth, were resisted by a coalition of Republicans and conservative Southern Democrats.

It remained for Lyndon Johnson to push through Kennedy's tax reduction and civil rights legislation—legislation that ended discrimination in public accommodations. In 1964 Johnson was prepared to be elected in his own right.

The 1964 Republican national convention was held in San Francisco. Before a particularly vocal gathering the party nominated Senator Barry Goldwater of Arizona as their candidate. An ardent conservative, Goldwater had voted against censuring Senator Joseph McCarthy, and, in 1957, he broke with the Republican administration over fiscal policy, calling Eisenhower's record "a betrayal of the people's trust."

The Republican platform was vintage Goldwater: an attack against the expanding role of the national government in economic and social affairs, and a call for a foreign policy that would produce victory over communism in "every place on earth." In his acceptance speech he asserted that foreign policy was the key issue and that "violence in our streets" would be the number two issue of his campaign. Toward the close of his address he uttered these famous lines: "I would remind you that extremism in the defense of liberty is no vice. And let me remind you that moderation in the pursuit of justice is no virtue."

Yet the same convention that unanimously selected Goldwater on the first ballot also sealed the Republican candidate's defeat. After watching the zealous Goldwater forces boo and hiss such liberal Republicans as Governor Nelson Rockefeller of New York, other liberals began to disassociate themselves from the conservative faction of the party. Governor George Romney of Michigan, for example, refused to appear on the same platform with Goldwater.

The Democratic convention opened in Atlantic City, New Jersey, on August 23rd. The Democrats were confident of victory as Lyndon Johnson (on the occasion of his fifty-sixth birthday) recited the accomplishments and goals of his administration and called on the American people to unite to "build a great society."

There was a wave of prosperity in 1964, and the President had the full support of the Congress. This latter fact was crystallized in August by the passage of the Gulf of Tonkin Resolution, which gave the President a free hand to resist aggression in Southeast Asia.

The dramatic confrontation of ideologies that many expected to see in this campaign never materialized. Johnson, in fact, did not begin to campaign actively until October. In an October 7th address Johnson struck the basic themes of his campaign: that the prosperity of the country was the result of Democratic policies, that this election offered the people a "basic choice," and that Goldwater's program represented a "radical departure."

Goldwater continued to focus on foreign policy. On October 21st he warned the American people of an impending Sino-Soviet rapprochement and emphasized that all "communism is our enemy."

But much of what Goldwater had to say was erased by events abroad. Just a few days before Goldwater's speech Khrushchev fell from power and Communist China exploded its first nuclear bomb on the remote central Asian province of Sinkiang. (In addition, the Conservative government in England was voted out of power.)

Although there had been some thaws in the Cold War, Americans still remembered the 1962 Cuban missile crisis and refused to entrust their nuclear weapons to someone who was personified as an impulsive ideologue rather than as a statesman. On Election Day the American electorate gave Johnson a landslide victory. Once again the American people had affirmed their acceptance of big government.

LYNDON B. JOHNSON

Acceptance Speech

ATLANTIC CITY, NEW JERSEY

August 27, 1964

Chairman McCormack. My fellow Americans:

I accept your nomination.

I accept the duty of leading this party to victory this year.

And I thank you, I thank you from the bottom of my heart for placing at my side the man that last night you so wisely selected to be the next Vice President of the United States.

I know I speak for each of you and all of you when I say we—he proved himself tonight in that great acceptance speech.

And I speak for both of us when I tell you that from Monday on he's going to be available for such speeches in all 50 states.

We will try to lead you as we were led by that great champion of freedom, the man from Independence, Harry S. Truman.

But the, but the gladness of his high occasion cannot mask the sorrow which shares our hearts. So let us here tonight, each of us, all of us, rededicate ourselves to keeping burning the golden torch of promise which John Fitzgerald Kennedy set aflame.

And let none of us stop to rest until we have written into the law of the land all the suggestions that made up the John Fitzgerald Kennedy program and then let us continue to supplement that program with the kind of laws that he would have us write.

Tonight we offer ourselves on our records and by our platform as a party for all Americans, an all-American party for all Americans!

This prosperous people, this land of reasonable men, has no place for petty partisanship or peevish prejudice.

The needs of all can never be met by parties of the few.

The needs of all cannot be met by a business party, or a labor party, not a war party or a peace party; not by a Southern party or a Northern party.

Our deeds will meet our needs only if we are served by a party which serves all our people.

We are members together of such a party—the Democratic party of 1964.

We have written a proud record of accomplishments for all Americans. If any ask what we have done, just let them look at what we promised to do.

For those promises have become our deeds; and the promises of tonight, I can assure you, will become the deeds of tomorrow.

We are in the midst of the largest and the longest period of peace-time prosperity in our history.

And almost every American listening to us tonight has seen the results in his own life. But prosperity for most has not brought prosperity to all.

And those who have received the bounty of this land, who sit tonight secure in affluence and safe in power, must not now turn from the needs of their neighbors.

Our party and our nation will continue to extend the hand of compassion and extend the hand of affection and love, to the old and the sick and the hungry.

For who among us dares betray the command: Thou shalt open thy hand unto thy Brother, to thy poor and to thy needy in the Land?

The needs that we seek to fill, the hopes that we seek to realize, are not our needs, our hopes alone. They are the needs and hopes of most of the people.

Most Americans want medical care for older citizens, and so do I.

Most Americans want fair and stable prices and decent income for our farmers, and so do I.

Most Americans want a decent home in a decent neighborhood for all, and so do I.

Most Americans want an education for every child to the limit of his ability, and so do I.

Most Americans want a job for every man who wants to work, and so do I.

Most Americans want victory in our war against poverty, and so do I.

Most Americans want continually expanding and growing prosperity, and so do I.

These are your goals; these are our goals; these are the goals and will be the achievements of the Democratic party.

These are the goals of this great, rich nation; these are the goals toward which I will lead if the American people choose to follow.

For 30 years, year by year, step by step, vote by vote, men of both parties have built a solid foundation for our present prosperity.

Too many have worked too long and too hard to see this threatened now by policies which promise to undo all that we have done together over these years.

I believe most of the men and women in this hall tonight and I believe most Americans understand that to reach our goals in our own land we must work for peace among all lands.

America's cause is still the cause of all mankind. Over the last four years, the world has begun to respond to a simple American belief—the belief that strength and courage and responsibility are the keys to peace.

Since 1961, under the leadership of that great President, John F. Kennedy, we have carried out the greatest peacetime build-up of national strength of any nation, at any time in the history of the world.

And I report tonight that we have spent $30 billions more on preparing this nation in the four years of the Kennedy Administration than would have been spent if we had followed the appropriations of the last of the previous Administration.

I report tonight as President of the United States and as Commander in Chief of the Armed Forces on the strength of your country and I tell you that it is greater than any adversary's.

I assure you that it is greater than the combined might of all the nations in all the wars in all the history of this planet.

And I report our superiority is growing.

Weapons do not make peace; men make peace. And peace comes not through strength alone, but through wisdom and patience and restraint.

And these qualities under the leadership of President Kennedy brought a treaty banning nuclear tests in the atmosphere and a hundred other nations in the world joined us.

Other agreements were reached and other steps were taken. And their single guide was to lessen the danger to men without increasing the danger of freedom.

Their single purpose was peace in the world. And as a result of these policies, the world tonight knows where we stand and our allies know where we stand, too.

And our adversaries have learned again that we will never waver in the defense of freedom.

The true courage of this nuclear age lies in the quest for peace. There is no place in today's world for recklessness.

We cannot act rashly with the nuclear weapons that could destroy us all. The only course is to press with all our minds and all our will to make sure, doubly sure, that these weapons are never really used at all.

This is a dangerous and a difficult world in which we live tonight. I promise no easy answers. But I do promise this: I pledge the firmness to defend freedom; the strength to support that firmness, and a constant, patient effort to move the world toward peace instead of war.

And here, at home, one of our greatest responsibilities is to assure fair play for all of our people.

Every American has the right to be treated as a person. He should be able to find a job. He should be able to educate his children. He should be able to vote in elections.

And he should be judged on his merits as a person.

Well, this is the fixed policy and the fixed determination of the Democratic party and the United States of America.

So long as I am your President, I intend to carry out what the Constitution demands and justice requires. Equal justice under law for all Americans.

We cannot and we will not allow this great purpose to be endangered by reckless acts of violence.

Those who break the law, those who create disorder, whether in the North or the South, must be caught and must be brought to justice.

And I believe that every man and woman in this room tonight joins me in saying that in every part of this country the law must be respected and violence must be stopped.

And wherever local officers seek help or Federal law is broken, I have pledged and I will use the full resources of the Federal Government.

Let no one tell you that he can hold back progress and at the same time keep the peace. This is a false and empty promise. So to stand in the way of orderly progress is to encourage violence.

And I say tonight to those who wish us well and to those who wish us ill the growing forces in this country are the forces of common human decency and not the forces of bigotry and fear and smears.

Our problems are many and are great. But our opportunities are even greater. And let me make this clear. I ask the American people for a mandate, not to preside over a finished program, not just to keep things going. I ask the American people for a mandate to begin.

This nation, this generation, in this hour has man's first chance to build a great society, a place where the meaning of man's life matches the marvels of man's labor.

We seek a nation where every man can find reward in work and satisfaction in the use of his talents. We seek a nation where every man can seek knowledge and touch beauty and rejoice in the closeness of family and community.

We seek a nation where every man can work—follow the pursuit of happiness—not just security, but achievement and excellence and fulfillment of the spirit. So let us join together in this great task. Will you join me tonight in starting, in rebuilding our cities to make them a decent place for our children to live in?

Will you join me tonight in starting a program that will protect the beauty of our land and the air that we breathe?

Won't you join me tonight in starting a program that will give every child education of the highest quality that he can take?

So let us, let us join together in giving every American the fullest life which he can hope for, for the ultimate test of our civilization, the ultimate test of our faithfulness to our past has not been our goods and has not been our guns. It is in the quality—the quality of our people's lives and in the men and women that we produce.

This goal can be ours. We have the resources; we have the knowledge. But tonight we must seek the courage.

Because tonight the contest is the same that we have faced at every turning point in history. It is not between liberals and conservatives, it is not between party and party or platform and platform. It is between courage and timidity.

It is between those who have visions and those who see what can be and those who want only to maintain the status quo.

It is between those who welcome the future and those who turn away from its promise. This is the true cause of freedom. The man who is hungry, who cannot find work or educate his children, who is bowed by want—that man is not fully free. For more than 30 years, from Social Security to the war against poverty, we have diligently worked to enlarge the freedom of man, and as a result Americans tonight are freer to live as they want to live, to pursue their ambitions to meet their desires, to raise their families than in any time in all of our glorious history.

And every American knows in his heart that this is right!

I am determined in all the time that is mine to use all the talents that I have for bringing this great lovable land, this great nation, for ours together, together in greater unity in pursuit of this common purpose.

I truly believe that some day we will see an America that knows no North or South, no East nor West, an America, an America that is undivided by creed or color and untorn by suspicion or class.

The Founding Fathers dreamed America before it was. The pioneers dreamed of great cities on the wilderness that they had crossed. Our tomorrow is on its way. It can be a shape of darkness or it can be a thing of beauty. The choice is ours—is yours. For it will be the dream that we dare to dream.

I know what kind of a dream Franklin Delano Roosevelt and Harry S. Truman and John F. Kennedy would dream if they were here tonight.

And I think that I know what kind of a dream you want to dream.

Tonight we of the Democratic party confidently go before the people offering answers, not retreats; offering unity, not division; offering hope, not fear or smear.

We do offer the people a choice. A choice of continuing on the courageous and the compassionate course that has made this nation the strongest and the freest and the most prosperous and the most peaceful nation in history of mankind.

To those who have sought to divide us, they have only helped to unite us.

To those who would provoke us, we have turned the other cheek.

So as we conclude our labors, let us tomorrow turn to our new task. Let us be on our way.

LYNDON B. JOHNSON

Campaign Speech

WASHINGTON, D. C.

October 7, 1964

My fellow Americans:

I have been in this office for almost a year—ever since that black and unforgetttable day when America lost one of its greatest leaders—cut down in the fullness of his manhood and promise.

I have drawn much of my strength in this task from loyal and dedicated public servants. Most of all I have drawn strength from the warm support and understanding of the American people.

I will always be grateful to you for that.

I am now on a tour that will take me to every section of the country—to discuss with you the important issues of this campaign.

Few presidential elections in our entire history have presented—as this one does—a basic choice that involves the fundamental principles of American life.

We must decide whether we will move ahead by building on the solid structure created by forward-looking men of both parties over the past 30 years. Or whether we will begin to tear down this structure and move in a radically different, and—I believe—a deeply dangerous direction.

Most of you listening to me have felt the steady progress of American prosperity in your own life and the life of your family. Most of you, more than ever before, can look forward, with confidence, to a steadily improving life for your children.

Our prosperity is not just good luck. It rests on basic beliefs which a generation of leaders has carefully woven into the fabric of American life.

Our prosperity rests on the basic belief that the work of free individuals makes a nation—and it is the job of Government to help them do the best they can.

Our prosperity rests on the basic belief that our greatest resource is the health and skills and knowledge of our people. We have backed up this belief with public and private investment in education and training, and many other programs.

Our prosperity rests on the basic belief that older Americans—those who have fought our wars and built our Nation—are entitled to live out ther lives in dignity. We have backed up this belief, for over 30 years, with the social security system—supported by every President of both parties.

Our prosperity rests on the basic belief that individual farmers and individual workers have a right to some protection against those forces which might deprive them of a decent income from the fruits of their labor. We have backed up this belief with a system of fair collective bargaining. We have backed it with agricultural programs which have kept the farmer from suffering the neglect and despair of only a few decades ago.

Today our whole approach to these problems is under attack.

We are now told that we the people acting through Government should withdraw from education, from public power, from agriculture, from urban renewal, and from a host of other vital programs.

We are now told that we should end social security as we know it, sell TVA, strip labor unions of many of their gains, and terminate all farm subsidies.

We are told that the object of leadership is not to pass laws but to repeal them.

And these views have been supported by a consistent record of opposition in the Congress to every progressive proposal of both parties—Democratic and Republican.

This is a radical departure from the historic and basic current of American thought and action. It would shatter the foundation on which our hopes for the future rest.

Too many have worked too hard and too long to let this happen now.

I propose to build on the basic beliefs of the past, to innovate where necessary, to work to bring us closer to a growing abundance in which all Americans can seek to share.

The choice is yours.

For 20 years our country has been the guardian at the gate of freedom. Our cause has been the cause of all mankind.

The strength of that leadership has come from the fact that every President, and the leaders of both parties, have followed the same basic principles of foreign policy. They have built our strength—so that today America is the greatest military power on earth.

They have moved with courage and firmness to the defense of freedom. President Truman met Communist aggression in Greece and Turkey. President Eisenhower met Communist aggression in the Formosa Strait. President Kennedy met Communist aggression in Cuba.

And, when our destroyers were attacked, we met Communist aggression in the waters around Viet-Nam.

But each of these Presidents has known that guns and rockets alone do not bring peace. Only men can bring peace.

They have used great power with restraint—never once taking a reckless risk which might plunge us into large-scale war.

They have patiently tried to build bridges of understanding between people and nations. They have used all their efforts to settle disputes peacefully—working with the United Nations. They have never been afraid to sit down at the council table to work out agreements which might lessen the danger of war without increasing the danger to freedom.

But today these established policies are under the severest attack.

We are told we should consider using atomic weapons in Viet-Nam, even in Eastern Europe should there be an uprising.

We are told we should break off relations with Russia—and with it any hope of lasting agreement. We are urged to withdraw from the United Nations and stop our help to other countries.

We have heard the test ban treaty denounced. This is the treaty that has halted the radioactive poisoning of the air we breathe.

We are urged to threaten others with force if they don't do as we say.

We are told, in effect, to withdraw into an armed camp—with a few carefully selected friends—and try to intimidate our adversaries into submission.

This kind of attack contradicts the entire course of America in the postwar period.

If we should follow this course—if we should discard the tested policies of the last 20 years—the peace of the world will be in grave danger.

I will not discard them. I will continue them. I will match firmness to strength. And I will continue, with all the skill at my command, the patient search for lasting peace.

Here, again, the choice is yours.

I will discuss these issues in the next few weeks. They are among the most important questions ever presented to the American people.

It is you who will decide these questions. And you will decide them on November 3 in polling booths across the Nation. No person can afford to sit comfortably at home, confident that others will take care of the job. You must work, and register, and vote.

For this is a turning point in the history of our Nation. At stake is all that we have so carefully built, and all the hopes that rest upon it.

I will do all I can.

I need your help.

Then we can turn to our work. Together we will build the Great Society—a place where every one of us has the chance to seek happiness and fulfillment to the limit of his abilities.

And we will work together to make the world a place where free men can live in peace.

BARRY M. GOLDWATER

Acceptance Speech

SAN FRANCISCO, CALIFORNIA

July 17, 1964

My good friend and great Republican, Dick Nixon and your charming wife, Pat; my running mate—that wonderful Republican who has served us so well for so long—Bill Miller and his wife, Stephanie; to Thurston Morton, who's done such a commendable job in chairmaning this convention; to Mr. Herbert Hoover who I hope is watching, and to that great American and his wife, General and Mrs. Eisenhower. To my own wife, fellow Republicans here assembled, and Americans across this great nation:

From this moment, united and determined, we will go forward together dedicated to the ultimate and undeniable greatness of the whole man.

Together we will win.

I accept your nomination with a deep sense of humility. I accept, too, the responsibility that goes with it, and I seek your continued help and your continued guidance. My fellow Republicans, our cause is too great for any man to feel worthy of it. Our task would be too great for any man did he not have with him the heart and the hands of this great Republican party.

And I promise you tonight that every fibre of my being is consecrated to our cause, that nothing shall be lacking from the struggle that can be brought to it by enthusiasm, by devotion and plain hard work.

In this world no person, no party can guarantee anything, but what we can do and what we shall do is to deserve victory and victory will be ours. The Good Lord raised this mighty Republican—Republic to be a home for the Brave and to flourish as the land of the free—not to stagnate in the swampland of collectivism, not to cringe before the bully of Communism.

Now my fellow Americans, the tide has been running against freedom. Our people have followed false prophets. We must, and we shall, return to proven ways—not because they are old, but because they are true.

We must, and we shall, set the tide running again in the cause of freedom. And this party, with its every action, every word, every breath and every heart beat, has but a single resolve, and that is freedom.

Freedom made orderly for this nation by our constitutional government. Freedom under a government limited by laws of nature and of nature's God. Freedom balanced so that order lacking liberty will not become the slavery of the prison cell; balanced so that liberty lacking order will not become the license of the mob and of the jungle.

Now, we Americans understand freedom, we have earned it; we have lived for it, and we have died for it. This nation and its people are freedom's models in a searching world. We can be freedom's missionaries in a doubting world.

But, ladies and gentlemen, first we must renew freedom's mission in our own hearts and in our own homes.

During four futile years the Administration which we shall replace has distorted and lost that faith. It has talked and talked and talked and talked the words of freedom but it has failed and failed and failed in the works of freedom.

Now failure cements the wall of shame in Berlin; failures blot the sands of shame at the Bay of Pigs; failures marked the slow death of freedom in Laos; failures infest the jungles of Vietnam, and failures haunt the houses of our once great alliances and undermine the greatest bulwark ever erected by free nations, the NATO community.

Failures proclaim lost leadership, obscure purpose, weakening wills and the risk of inciting our sworn enemies to new aggressions and to new excesses.

And because of this Administration we are tonight a world divided. We are a nation becalmed. We have lost the brisk pace of diversity and the genius of individual creativity. We are plodding along at a pace set by centralized planning, red tape, rules without responsibility and regimentation without recourse.

Rather than useful jobs in our country, people have been offered bureaucratic makework; rather than moral leadership, they have been given bread and circuses; they have been given spectacles, and, yes, they've even been given scandals.

Tonight there is violence in our streets, corruption in our highest offices, aimlessness among our youth, anxiety among our elderly, and there's a virtual despair among the many who look beyond material success toward the inner meaning of their lives. And where examples of morality should be set, the opposite is seen. Small men seeking great wealth or power have too often and too long turned even the highest levels of public service into mere personal opportunity.

Now, certainly simple honesty is not too much to demand of men in government. We find it in most. Republicans demand it from everyone.

They demand it from everyone no matter how exalted or protected his position might be.

The growing menace in our country tonight, to personal safety, to life, to limb and property, in homes, in churches, on the playgrounds and places of business, particularly in our great cities, is the mounting concern or should be of every thoughtful citizen in the United States. Security from domestic violence, no less than from foreign aggression, is the most elementary and fundamental purpose of any government, and a government that cannot fulfill this purpose is one that cannot long command the loyalty of its citizens.

History shows us, demonstrates that nothing, nothing prepares the way for tyranny more than the failure of public officials to keep the streets safe from bullies and marauders.

Now we Republicans see all this as more—much more—than the result of mere political differences, or mere political mistakes. We see this as the result of a fundamentally and absolutely wrong view of man, his nature and his destiny.

Those who seek to live your lives for you, to take your liberty in return for relieving you of yours; those who elevate the state and downgrade the citizen, must see ultimately a world in which earthly power can be substituted for Divine Will. And this nation was founded upon the rejection of that notion and upon the acceptance of God as the author of freedom.

Now those who seek absolute power, even though they seek it to do what they regard as good, are simply demanding the right to enforce their own version of heaven on earth, and let me remind you they are the very ones who always create the most hellish tyranny.

Absolute power does corrupt, and those who seek it must be suspect and must be opposed. Their mistaken course stems from false notions, ladies and gentlemen, of equality. Equality, rightly understood as our founding fathers understood it, leads to liberty and to the emancipation of creative differences; wrongly understood, as it has been so tragically in our time, it leads first to conformity and then to despotism.

Fellow Republicans, it is the cause of Republicanism to resist concentrations of power, private or public, which enforce such conformity and inflict such despotism.

It is the cause of Republicanism to insure that power remains in the hands of the people—and, so help us God, that is exactly what a Republican President will do with the help of a Republican Congress.

It is further the cause of Republicanism to restore a clear understanding of the tyranny of man over man in the world at large. It is our cause to dispel the foggy thinking which avoids hard decisions in the delusion that a world of conflict will somehow resolve itself into a world of harmony, if we just don't rock the boat or irritate the forces of aggression—and this is hogwash.

It is, further, the cause of Republicanism to remind ourselves, and the world, that only the strong can remain free; that only the strong can keep the peace.

Now, I needn't remind you, or my fellow Americans regardless of party, that Republicans have shouldered this hard responsibility and marched in this cause before. It was Republican leadership under Dwight Eisenhower that kept the peace, and passed along to this Administration the mightiest arsenal for defense the world has ever known.

And I needn't remind you that it was the strength and the believable will of the Eisenhower years that kept the peace by using our strength, by using it in the Formosa Strait, and in Lebanon, and by showing it courageously at all times.

It was during those Republican years that the thrust of Communist imperialism was blunted. It was during those years of Republican leadership that this world moved closer not to war but closer to peace than at any other time in the last three decades.

And I needn't remind you, but I will, that it's been during Democratic years that our strength to deter war has been stilled and even gone into a planned decline. It has been during Democratic years that we have weakly stumbled into conflicts, timidly refusing to draw our own lines against aggression, deceitfully refusing to tell even our own people of our full participation and tragically letting our finest men die on battlefields unmarked by purpose, unmarked by pride or the prospect of victory.

Yesterday it was Korea: tonight it is Vietnam. Make no bones of this. Don't try to sweep this under the rug. We are at war in Vietnam. And yet the President, who is the Commander in Chief of our forces, refuses to say, refuses to say mind you, whether or not the objective over there is victory, and his Secretary of Defense continues to mislead and misinform the American people, and enough of it has gone by.

And I needn't remind you, but I will, it has been during Democratic years that a billion persons were cast into Communist captivity and their fate cynically sealed.

Today—today in our beloved country we have an Administration which seems eager to deal with Communism in every coin known—from gold to wheat; from consulates to confidence, and even human freedom itself.

Now the Republican cause demands that we brand communism as the principal disturber of peace in the world today. Indeed, we should brand it as the only significant disturber of the peace. And we must make clear that until its goals of conquest are absolutely renounced, and its relations with all nations tempered, Communism and the governments it now controls are enemies, of every man on earth who is or wants to be free.

Now, we here in America can keep the peace only if we remain vigilant, and only if we remain strong. Only if we keep our eyes open and keep our guard up can we prevent war.

And I want to make this abundantly clear—I don't intend to let peace or freedom be torn from our grasp because of lack of strength, or lack of will—and that I promise you Americans.

I believe that we must look beyond the defense of freedom today to its extension tomorrow. I believe that the Communism which boasts it will bury us will instead give way to the forces of freedom. And I can see in the distant and yet recognizable future the outlines of a world worthy of our dedication, our every risk, our every effort, our every sacrifice along the way. Yes, a world that will redeem the suffering of those who will be liberated from tyranny.

I can see, and I suggest that all thoughtful men must contemplate, the flowering of an Atlantic civilization, the whole world of Europe reunified and free, trading openly across its borders, communicating openly across the world.

This is a goal far, far more meaningful than a moon shot.

It's a truly inspiring goal for all free men to set for themselves during the latter half of the twentieth century. I can see and all free men must thrill to the events of this Atlantic civilization joined by a straight ocean highway to the United States. What a destiny! What a destiny can be ours to stand as a great central pillar linking Europe, the Americas and the venerable and vital peoples and cultures of the Pacific.

I can see a day when all the Americas—North and South—will be linked in a mighty system—a system in which the errors and misunderstandings of the past will be submerged one by one in a rising tide of prosperity and interdependence.

We know that the misunderstandings of centuries are not to be wiped away in a day or wiped in an hour. But we pledge, we pledge, that human sympathy—what our neighbors to the South call an attitude of sympatico —no less than enlightened self-interest will be our guide.

And I can see this Atlantic civilization galvanizing and guiding emergent nations everywhere. Now I know this freedom is not the fruit of every soil. I know that our own freedom was achieved through centuries of unremitting efforts by brave and wise men. And I know that the road to freedom is a long and a challenging road, and I know that some men may walk away from it, that some men resist challenge, accepting the false security of governmental paternalism.

And I pledge that the America I envision in the years ahead will extend its hand in help in teaching and in cultivation so that all new nations will be at least encouraged to go our way; so that they will not wander down the dark alleys of tyranny or to the dead-end streets of collectivism.

My fellow Republicans, we do no man a service by hiding freedom's light under a bushel of mistaken humility.

I seek an America proud of its past, proud of its ways, proud of its dreams and determined actively to proclaim them. But our examples to the world must, like charity, begin at home.

In our vision of a good and decent future, free and peaceful, there must be room, room for the liberation of the energy and the talent of the individual, otherwise our vision is blind at the outset.

We must assure a society here which while never abandoning the needy, or forsaking the helpless, nurtures incentives and opportunity for the creative and the productive.

We must know the whole good is the product of many single contributions. And I cherish the day when our children once again will restore as heroes the sort of men and women who, unafraid and undaunted, pursue the truth, strive to cure disease, subdue and make fruitful our natural environment, and produce the inventive engines of production, science and technology.

This nation, whose creative people have enhanced this entire span of history, should again thrive upon the greatness of all those things which we—we as individual citizens—can and should do.

During Republican years, this again will be a nation of men and women, of families proud of their role, jealous of their responsibilities, unlimited in their aspirations—a nation where all who can will be self-reliant.

We Republicans see in our constitutional form of government the great framework which assures the orderly but dynamic fulfillment of the whole man, and we see the whole man as the great reason for instituting orderly government in the first place.

We see in private property and in economy based upon and fostering private property the one way to make government a durable ally of the whole man rather than his determined enemy.

We see in the sanctity of private property the only durable foundation for constitutional government in a free society.

And beyond that we see and cherish diversity of ways, diversity of thoughts, of motives, and accomplishments. We don't seek to live anyone's life for him. We only seek to secure his rights, guarantee him opportunity, guarantee him opportunity to strive with government performing only those needed and constitutionally sanctioned tasks which cannot otherwise be performed.

We, Republicans, seek a government that attends to its inherent responsibilities of maintaining a stable monetary and fiscal climate, encouraging a free and competitive economy and enforcing law and order.

Thus do we seek inventiveness, diversity and creative difference within a stable order, for we Republicans define government's role where needed at many, many levels, preferably through the one closest to the people involved: our towns and our cities, then our counties, then our states then our regional contacts and only then the national government.

That, let me remind you, is the land of liberty built by decentralized power. On it also we must have balance between the branches of government at every level.

Balance, diversity, creative difference—these are the elements of Republican equation. Republicans agree, Republicans agree heartily, to disagree on many, many of their applications. But we have never disagreed on the basic fundamental issues of why you and I are Republicans.

This is a party—this Republican party is a party for free men. Not for blind followers and not for conformists.

Back in 1858 Abraham Lincoln said this of the Republican party, and

I quote him because he probably could have said it during the last week or so: It was composed of strained, discordant, and even hostile elements. End of the quote, in 1958 [sic].

Yet all of these elements agreed on one paramount objective: to arrest the progress of slavery, and place it in the course of ultimate extinction.

Today, as then, but more urgently and more broadly than then, the task of preserving and enlarging freedom at home and of safeguarding it from the forces of tyranny abroad is great enough to challenge all our resources and to require all our strength.

Anyone who joins us in all sincerity we welcome. Those, those who do not care for our cause, we don't expect to enter our ranks in any case. And let our Republicanism so focused and so dedicated not be made fuzzy and futile by unthinking and stupid labels.

I would remind you that extremism in the defense of liberty is no vice!

And let me remind you also that moderation in the pursuit of justice is no virtue!

By the—the beauty of the very system we Republicans are pledged to restore and revitalize, the beauty of this Federal system of ours is in its reconciliation of diversity with unity. We must not see malace in honest differences of opinion, and no matter how great, so long as they are not inconsistent with the pledges we have given to each other in and through our Constitution.

Our Republican cause is not to level out the world or make its people conform in computer-regimented sameness. Our Republican cause is to free our people and light the way for liberty throughout the world. Ours is a very human cause for very humane goals. This party, its good people, and its unquestionable devotion to freedom will not fulfill the purposes of this campaign which we launch here now until our cause has won the day, inspired the world, and shown the way to a tomorrow worthy of all our yesteryears.

I repeat, I accept your nomination with humbleness, with pride and you and I are going to fight for the goodness of our land. Thank you.

☆

BARRY M. GOLDWATER

Campaign Speech

WASHINGTON, D. C.

October 21, 1964

Good evening, my fellow Americans. Before doing anything else I want to call your attention to two headlines in this week's news.

"Kremlin shift hints harder line."

"Brezhnev hints at improved links with Peking."

These tell a story which seems to contradict the story you heard from President Johnson last Sunday evening. That is why I am here tonight.

I come before you this evening to discuss two events of great importance to the security of this nation and the free world.

As you all know, Khrushchev has been thrown out of the Government of the Soviet Union and the dictatorship of that country has been put into the hands of new leaders.

As you also know, a nuclear explosion took place in Red China within hours of this change of government.

These are momentous events. They present both a challenge and an opportunity to this country. You deserve a straight and honest explanation from each candidate for the Presidency on how he proposes to meet this challenge and exploit this opportunity.

I have said many times, and I repeat it again tonight, that every President owes it to the American people to take them into his full confidence when critical decisions confront the nation. This is particularly true when national security is at stake. We cannot afford—and let me stress that—we simply cannot afford any security risks.

Now what is the significance of these events in the Communist world?

First, the Communist threat to our security has become grave. The dissension in Communist ranks brought on by a clash of personalities is being repaired. Red China and the Soviet Union seem to be patching up their differences, and we must look forward to being faced by a more unified Communist movement.

Second, the foreign policy of the present Administration—based on a belief that there are "good" and "bad" Communists—has been an utter failure. It has failed to halt the march of Communism and the testing of nuclear weapons and the spread of nuclear power through the Communist world. This policy, if I may call it that, has instead helped the

Communist world through a time of troubles and allowed it to emerge as a greater threat than ever to the freedom of the West.

Third, these events have laid bare—for all to see—the real meaning of "peaceful coexistence." By this slogan the Communists simply mean, "We won't hurt you if you peacefully surrender to us."

Now let's see why these conclusions are so clear. Over the last several years we have all read about the troubles besetting the Communist world. There were grave economic difficulties everywhere—in the Soviet Union, in its European satellites, in Red China and its satellites, in Cuba—everywhere. Beyond that, Mao Tse-tung, the dictator of Red China, was quarreling with Khrushchev, the dictator of the Soviet Union. They were quarreling over who would be the big boss of the entire Communist movement and what would be the best way to bury us.

Meanwhile, the Communist countries of Eastern Europe were becoming restless and were demanding more independence.

Khrushchev decided that the best way to get out of trouble and to stay on top was to get the West to bail him out. And so he dusted off the old slogan of "peaceful coexistence" and worked it on the leaders of the present Administration with a soft sell. And they fell for it.

Khrushchev, we were being told, was a "good" Communist—one who was concerned, as we were, with finding a peaceful resolution of the conflict between Communist aggression and Western resistance. Only last Sunday Lyndon Johnson paid tribute to him as a man of "good sense and sober judgment."

We were also being told that standing against Khrushchev were the "bad" Communists—namely, his personal enemies in Red China. Why were they "bad"? Because they openly admitted that Communism could not conquer the world without fighting wars against the free nations.

Never mind that Khrushchev vowed to bury us. Never mind that the only difference between "good" and "bad" Communists is a disagreement on how to bury us. Khrushchev thought we would simply surrender without putting up a fight, while the Chinese and some other Communists thought some fighting would be necessary.

But never mind those things. This Administration embarked on the dangerous policy of being nice to the "good" Communists. If their economy fails, sell them wheat at bargain prices. If they are short of cash, give them credit. If they promise not to blow up any more nuclear bombs, sign a treaty giving our solemn and faithful word not to do the same. If they object to our armaments program, cut it back unilaterally. If our pursuit of national interest in Cuba makes them nervous, promise never to rock the boat as long as Communism reigns.

In these and other ways we actively helped Khrushchev over his difficult times. We helped this man who did not hesitate to remind us that he intended to bury us. Listen, for example, to what he said last July:

"Of course, when I say that we are against war, I mean aggressive, predatory wars. But there are other wars, wars of national liberation; such wars are just and sacred. We support the peoples who take up arms and uphold their independence and freedom, and we support them not only in words but by concrete deeds."

In other words, it's all right to kill our boys in Vietnam, or Cuba, or the Congo, or anywhere people are being "liberated" by Communism. Do you think for a moment that the United States is not also marked for Communist "liberation"?

And let's just see what the Communists really mean by "peaceful coexistence." Here's what an official journal of the international Communist movement says:

"Peaceful coexistence being a form of the class struggle between capitalism and Socialism, provides, as the events of recent years have shown, a favorable climate for the revolutionary struggle of all peoples. It is in the conditions of peaceful coexistence that the colonial system of imperialism has disintegrated, that the Socialist revolution has triumphed in Cuba, and that the working class and democratic movements have grown in the capitalist countries. Peaceful coexistence, then, does not signify 'accommodation' with imperialism, 'reconciliation' between the oppressed and the oppressors, or 'coexistence of ideologies' but the future development of the class struggle economic, political and ideological."

Mark these words well. This is what the Communists really mean by "peaceful coexistence." They do not mean "peace." "Peaceful coexistence" is simply the Communist strategy for world conquest. Communists may sometimes disagree about the best tactics for carrying out this strategy, but they all agree on the strategy.

Now the only thing any reasonable man can conclude is that the present Administration has made the mistake of thinking that "peaceful coexistence" is the same as "peace." And it has made the mistake of trying to distinguish different kinds of Communism and of supporting some and not others. It has ignored the fact that all Communists agree on the same goal—a Communist-dominated world. And so this Administration chose Khrushchev as the "good" Communist who should be supported. But some months ago it began to be clear that Khrushchev was not doing so well, even with help from the United States.

Khrushchev pushed his tactical differences with the Chinese leaders too far last summer. His call for a conference of all Communist parties gave those parties an opportunity to disapprove of him and his tactics. Such objections came out in the open in the testament supposedly left by

Togliatti, the leader of the Italian Communist party, who died during a
visit to the Soviet Union last July. Finally—just a little over a week ago
—the French Communist party flatly refused to attend the conference
and declared its support for the greater independence of parties.

While this opposition was growing outside the Soviet Union, interesting changes in party and government were taking place inside as well.
Khrushchev's self-appointed successor, Frol Kozlov, disappeared. They
said only that he had suffered a stroke. A man named Brezhnev gradually
took his place in the party organization, moving from his ceremonial post
as head of state. Some old Communists, such as Suslov, who prosecuted
the case against Khrushchev, remained in power. Men little known in the
West, such as Panomorov, seemed to have increasing influence. Mikoyan,
the hardy perennial of the Soviet scene, and Kosygin, a relative newcomer
who was to take Khrushchev's place in the Government, shifted about in
their positions. New men rose up in the party and Government structure
—men like Ustinov, who has been connected with the armament industry.
There were other organizational changes and counter-changes.

Soviet and Chinese party emissaries met in a conference in East
Germany. Rumors flew of an imminent nuclear explosion in Red China,
and these were given credence by our own Secretary of State.

In short, there were many signs that something was afoot.

Yet this Administration was caught completely by surprise when
Khrushchev was deposed. Last Sunday on television, the Secretary of State
confirmed the fact that the Administration was caught flat-footed by
Khrushchev's fall.

The Administration was undoubtedly caught even more by surprise
when the leaders of Red China immediately congratulated the new rulers
of the Soviet Union and forecast a new era of friendly relations between
the two countries. Here is what their message said:

"On learning that Comrade Brezhnev has been elected first secretary
of the Central Committee of the Communist party of the Soviet Union and
that Comrade Kosygin has been appointed chairman of the Council of
Ministers, we extend you our warm greetings.

"It is our sincere wish that the fraternal Soviet people will achieve
new successes in their constructive work in all fields and in the struggle
for the defense of world peace.

"The Chinese Communist party, the Chinese Government, and the
Chinese people rejoice at every progress made by the great Soviet Union,
the Communist party of the Soviet Union, and the Soviet people on their
road of advance.

"The recent successful launching and landing of the Soviet spaceship
represented another great achievement of the working people of the

Soviet Union. We wish to avail ourselves of this opportunity to convey our sincere congratulations to you, and through you to the great Soviet people.

"The Chinese and Soviet parties and the two countries unite on the basis of Marxism-Leninism and proletarian internationalism.

"May the fraternal, unbreakable friendship between the Chinese and Soviet peoples continuously develop.

"May the Chinese and Soviet peoples win one victory after another in their common struggle against imperialism headed by the United States and for the defense of world peace."

Can you imagine a stronger message of friendship and declaration of unity? And remember this was sent by the four top leaders of Red China —the chairman of the party, the President, the head of the armed forces, and the Prime Minister. And here is the response given this week by Brezhnev, the new Communist leader.

"Our party will strive for the strengthening of the unity of the great community of the fraternal Socialist countries on a fully equal footing and on the basis of correct combination of the common interests of the Socialist community with the interests of the people of each country, the development of an all-sided cooperation between the Socialist states, in our common struggle for peace and socialism."

Where is the Chinese-Soviet rift today? Can we even be sure that the Soviet Union did not take a hand in the nuclear explosion? What does the test ban treaty mean now—if it ever meant anything? You may recall that I warned of the possibility, when the test-ban treaty was before the Senate, that the Soviets might easily evade the treaty by conducting their tests in Red China. Surely nothing prevents them from doing so.

So where do we stand?

Every sign before us now says that our policy toward the Communists has been a failure. It was bad enough to make a fatal mistake about Nikita Khrushchev. It was bad enough to have a foreign policy—if we may call it that—based on a choice between "good" and "bad" Communists. It was bad enough to count on personal diplomacy to solve the problems of a clash of systems.

But worst of all was the insane policy of strengthening an enemy who has sworn to bury us.

We are now brought face to face with reality. We must now confront an enemy reunified and strengthened by our policy of aid.

This Administration once faced an enemy plagued with disunity and trouble, and it followed a policy that brought back unity and greater strength.

This Administration once had friends in the free world who were unified in purpose and strength, and it followed a policy that tore them asunder. This Administration has lived in the world of empty wishes and slogans.

It is now time for this nation to move forward into the world of reality and good sense. And I pledge to you that I will lead you back to sanity in our foreign relations.

Here are the three things we must do immediately in establishing a sensible policy toward Communism.

First, we must rebuild our once grand alliance. And we must start with the North Atlantic Treaty Organization. Here in these 15 countries rests more than two-thirds of the world's productive capacity. Here live 470 million intelligent and able people. The economic power of our North Atlantic allies, taken together, equals our own.

Here are the elements of power in the free world. Here are all the elements we need, already in being—just waiting to be put to use in ending the Communist threat.

Only one thing is missing, but it means everything. That one thing is unity—unity in cause, unity in purpose and unity in action. In its place we have disunity and disarray, brought to the free world by four years of drift, deception, defeat.

How can we create unity out of chaos? It will not be easy, but it can be done by a bold and joint attack on the roots of the problem.

I have already pledged that one of my first acts as President will be to initiate a call for a North Atlantic conclave. That conclave will have a single purpose—to create a North Atlantic community unified in spirit, purpose and action.

As the first move, I will name a blue ribbon delegation of American citizens to meet with the delegates from other NATO nations to plan the conclave. Those great statesmen of this nation who helped build NATO should join in leading the American delegation.

Only through such a bold venture can we create a climate of true friendship and partnersship. We must reclaim our friends and reassure them of our own friendship through concrete deeds. We must treat them as genuine partners in the pursuit of freedom.

The second thing we must do is to recognize that Communism is our enemy—the whole of Communism, not just some faction of the movement. After all, we spend $50 billion a year to defend ourselves against the "good" Communists—so-called by this Administration. We must understand the nature, aim, and strategy of the international Communist movement. We must never let the zigs and zags in tactics take our eyes off the ultimate strategy, which is plainly and simply a blueprint for world revolution and world conquest.

The third thing to do is to confront Communism with a firm policy of resistance. We must move as quickly as possible to rebuild a policy of strength and resolution with the overriding goal of promoting our national interests. This is the only policy Communist leaders understand and respect. We will keep the peace if—and only if—we take a firm stand against Communist aggression: if—and only if—we insist on concrete concessions and safeguards every step of the way toward a lasting peace.

Of course we must act prudently and cautiously. Of course we must make responsible use of our great power.

But let us never again fall into the trap of thinking that weakness means prudence, or that inaction means caution. These are the truly irresponsible policies. These are the policies that have led this Administration down the road to failure and our nation to the brink of disaster.

We face a challenge and an opportunity. Before us lies a new team in control of the Soviet Union. There will be days and months and perhaps even years of jockeying for power. We cannot see the final outcome.

But what we do now—in the immediate future—will play a major role in shaping the future of freedom throughout the world. If we have the will and wisdom to show the Communist leaders that we firmly intend to protect and promote our interests, we will blunt the thrust of Communist aggression. We will deny success to their ambitions for expansion. We will cause the Communist leaders to look inward to their own internal problems and to work out solutions—solutions that can be found only through relaxing the totalitarian despotism that now reigns in the Communist world. Then we can have a real hope for lasting peace.

My fellow Americans, you have a clear choice to make. You may continue the bankrupt policy of this Administration—a policy of drift and deception. This can only lead to defeat, to an ultimate choice between total war or total surrender.

Or you can strike out once again on the path of peace through strength and resolution. This is the only responsible course, the only course to peace and freedom.

I have faith in the choice you will make. And with your help and with God's blessing, I will take up the task of leadership.

☆

1968

———— ☆ ————

Despite protestations to the contrary, America has a long history of violence. Perhaps at no time in American history did this violent "spirit" manifest itself more dramatically or more persistently than during the 1960s. Whether it was caused by a general disaffection with the Vietnam War, or by American society's inability to eradicate poverty, racism, and slums, or by a general disillusionment with America's political and cultural institutions, confrontation was one of the hallmarks of the 1960s.

In his 1966 State of the Union message President Johnson announced that Americans "can continue the Great Society while we fight in Vietnam." Accordingly, he recommended a $113 billion budget without a concurrent tax increase. So began the inflation that is still plaguing the American economy.

Nor were Americans satisfied to learn that they could have guns and butter simultaneously. Beginning with the February, 1965, bombing raids over North Vietnam, and the August, 1965, troop movements into Vietnam (movements that would eventually send over half-a-million men to Vietnam), Americans began dividing themselves into "hawks" and "doves."

In November of 1967, one month after a massive antiwar march on the Pentagon, Senator Eugene McCarthy of Minnesota announced that he would enter the Democratic presidential primaries to challenge Johnson's "continued escalation and intensification of the war in Vietnam." In the March 12th New Hampshire primary the Democrats repudiated their party leader.

On March 16th Senator Robert Kennedy of New York announced his candidacy. Then, in a nationally televised address on March 31st, Johnson announced that there would be a cutback in the bombing of North Vietnam and that he would call on the Hanoi government to enter into peace talks. The President then delivered the heart of his message: "I shall not seek and I will not accept the nomination of my party for another term as President."

Following this message McCarthy and Kennedy became the two leading contenders for the Democratic nomination. (Democrat George Wallace, the ex-governor of Alabama, ran on the American Independent party ticket.) On May 7th Kennedy defeated McCarthy in the Indiana primary; one week later he defeated McCarthy in Nebraska. But on May 28th McCarthy beat Kennedy in Oregon.

Thus California was to be the site of their important showdown. Kennedy won the primary, but was fatally shot after delivering a victory address. (Two months earlier another important figure, Martin Luther King, Jr., was fatally shot in Memphis, Tennessee.)

In the meantime, Richard Nixon had been out campaigning for the Republican nomination. Although he announced that he was retiring from politics after he lost the 1962 California gubernatorial race, Nixon was back on the Republican campaign trail in 1964 and 1966. In 1964 he covered 36 states on behalf of Republican candidates; in 1966 he toured 35 states on behalf of 86 candidates, two-thirds of whom won their elections.

On August 5th Nixon collected his IOU's as the Republican convention in Miami Beach gave him their party's nomination on the first ballot. In a forty-minute acceptance speech aimed at the "forgotten Americans," Nixon promised that his administration would offer opportunity for all and that his "new leadership" would bring "an honorable end to the war in Vietnam," and "reestablish freedom from fear in America and freedom from fear in the world."

At their August convention in Chicago, the Democrats nominated Vice President Hubert Humphrey for the presidency on the first ballot. But to many Americans the confrontations outside the convention center were more significant than the events within the amphitheatre. Again violence was making the headlines, as Chicago's police force battled students and newsmen in the streets.

In his acceptance speech Humphrey mentioned the Vietnam War and his support of an end to the arms race, but he focused his attention on domestic affairs, stressing such issues as justice, national unity, and urban renewal.

Because he was Johnson's vice president and had supported the administration's role in Vietnam, Humphrey had great difficulty in winning over the McCarthy-Kennedy forces of his party. It was not until he disassociated himself from the Johnson administration and presented himself as a peace candidate that his campaign began gaining momentum. In an important September 30th television address from Salt Lake City, Utah, Humphrey stated that if elected "he would stop the bombing of the North as an acceptable risk for peace." In addition, he asserted that he would move toward a "de-Americanization of the war."

Throughout his campaign Nixon tried to etch one thought indelibly into the minds of the American people: that he would end the war in Vietnam honorably. But in a September 19th radio message, he addressed himself to a question that is "seldom dealt with directly in a Presidential campaign: The nature of the Presidency itself."

RICHARD M. NIXON

Acceptance Speech

MIAMI BEACH, FLORIDA

August 8, 1968

Mr. Chairman, delegates to this convention, my fellow Americans.

Sixteen years ago I stood before this convention to accept your nomination as the running mate of one of the greatest Americans of our time or of any time—Dwight D. Eisenhower.

Eight years ago I had the highest honor of accepting your nomination for President of the United States.

Tonight I again proudly accept that nomination for President of the United States.

But I have news for you. This time there's a difference—this time we're going to win.

We're going to win for a number of reasons. First a personal one.

General Eisenhower, as you know, lies critically ill in the Walter Reed Hospital tonight. I have talked, however, with Mrs. Eisenhower on the telephone.

She tells me that his heart is with us. She says that there is nothing that he lives more for, and there is nothing that would lift him more than for us to win in November.

And I say let's win this one for Ike.

We're going to win because this great convention has demonstrated to the nation that Republican party has the leadership, the platform and the purpose that America needs.

We're going to win because you have nominated as my running mate a statesman of the first rank who will be a great campaigner, and one who is fully qualified to undertake the new responsibilities that I shall give to the next Vice President of the United States.

And he is a man who fully shares my conviction and yours that after a period of 40 years when power has gone from the cities and the states to the Government in Washington, D. C., it's time to have power go back from Washington to the states and to the cities of this country all over America.

We're going to win because at a time that America cries out for the unity that this Administration has destroyed, the Republican party, after a spirited contest for its nomination for President and Vice President, stands united before the nation tonight.

And I congratulate Governor Reagan, I congratulate Governor Rockefeller, I congratulate Governor Romney, I congratulate all those who have made the hard fight that they have for this nomination, and I know that you will all fight even harder for the great victory our party is going to win in November because we're going to be together in that election campaign.

And a party that can unite itself will unite America.

My fellow Americans, most important we're going to win because our cause is right. We make history tonight, not for ourselves but for the ages. The choice we make in 1968 will determine not only the future of America but the future of peace and freedom in the world for the last third of the 20th century, and the question that we answer tonight: can America meet this great challenge?

Let us listen to America to find the answer to that question.

As we look at America, we see cities enveloped in smoke and flame. We hear sirens in the night. We see Americans dying on distant battle-fields abroad. We see Americans hating each other; fighting each other; killing each other at home.

And as we see and hear these things, millions of Americans cry out in anguish: Did we come all this way for this? Did American boys die in Normandy and Korea and in Valley Forge for this?

Listen to the answers to these questions.

It is another voice, it is a quiet voice in the tumult of the shouting. It is the voice of the great majority of Americans, the forgotten Americans, the non-shouters, the non-demonstrators. They're not racists or sick; they're not guilty of the crime that plagues the land; they are black, they are white; they're native born and foreign born; they're young and they're old.

They work in American factories, they run American businesses. They serve in government; they provide most of the soldiers who die to keep it free. They give drive to the spirit of America. They give lift to the American dream. They give steel to the backbone of America.

They're good people. They're decent people; they work and they save and they pay their taxes and they care.

Like Theodore Roosevelt, they know that this country will not be a good place for any of us to live in unless it's a good place for all of us to live in.

And this I say, this I say to you tonight, is the real voice of America. In this year 1968, this is the message it will broadcast to America and to the world.

Let's never forget that despite her faults, America is a great nation. And America is great because her people are great.

With Winston Churchill we say, we have not journeyed all this way, across the centuries, across the oceans, across the mountains, across the prairies because we are made of sugar candy.

America's in trouble today not because her people have failed, but because her leaders have failed. And what America needs are leaders to match the greatness of her people.

And this great group of Americans—the forgotten Americans and others—know that the great question Americans must answer by their votes in November is this: Whether we shall continue for four more years the policies of the last five years.

And this is their answer, and this is my answer to that question: When the strongest nation in the world can be tied down for four years in a war in Vietnam with no end in sight, when the richest nation in the world can't manage its own economy, when the nation with the greatest tradition of the rule of law is plagued by unprecedented lawlessness, when a nation has been known for a century for equality of opportunity is torn by unprecedented racial violence, and when the President of the United States cannot travel abroad or to any major city at home without fear of a hostile demonstration—then it's time for new leadership for the United States of America.

Thank you. My fellow Americans, tonight I accept the challenge and the commitment to provide that new leadership for America and I ask you to accept it with me.

And let us accept this challenge not as a grim duty but as an exciting adventure in which we are privileged to help a great nation realize its destiny and let us begin by committing ourselves to the truth, to see it like it is and tell it like it is, to find the truth, to speak the truth and to live the truth. That's what we will do.

We've had enough of big promises and little action. The time has come for an honest government in the United States of America.

And so tonight I do not promise the millenium in the morning. I don't promise that we can eradicate poverty and end discrimination and eliminate all dangers of wars in the space of four, or even eight years. But I do promise action. A new policy for peace abroad, a new policy for peace and progress and justice at home.

Look at our problems abroad. Do you realize that we face the stark truth that we are worse off in every area of the world tonight than we were when President Eisenhower left office eight years ago? That's the record.

And there is only one answer to such a record of failure, and that is the complete house cleaning of those responsible for the failures and that record.

The answer is the complete reappraisal of America's policies in every section of the world. We shall begin with Vietnam.

We all hope in this room that there's a chance that current negotiations may bring an honorable end to that war. And we will say nothing during this campaign that might destroy that chance.

But if the war is not ended when the people choose in November, the choice will be clear. Here it is: For four years this Administration has had at its disposal the greatest military and economic advantage that one nation has ever had over another in a war in history. For four years America's fighting men have set a record for courage and sacrifice unsurpassed in our history. For four years this Administration has had the support of the loyal opposition for the objective of seeking an honorable end to the struggle.

Never has so much military and economic and diplomatic power been used so ineffectively. And if after all of this time, and all of this sacrifice, and all of this support, there is still no end in sight, then I say the time has come for the American people to turn to new leadership not tied to the mistakes and policies of the past. That is what we offer to America.

And I pledge to you tonight that the first priority foreign policy objective of our next Administration will be to bring an honorable end to the war in Vietnam.

We shall not stop there. We need a policy to prevent more Vietnams. All of America's peace-keeping institutions and all of America's foreign commitments must be reappraised.

Over the past 25 years, America has provided more than $150-billion in foreign aid to nations abroad. In Korea, and now again in Vietnam, the United States furnished most of the money, most of the arms, most of the men to help the people of those countries defend themselves against aggression. Now we're a rich country, we're a strong nation, we're a populous nation but there are 200 million Americans and there are two billion people that live in the free world, and I say the time has come for other nations in the free world to bear their fair share of the burden of defending peace and freedom around this world.

What I call for is not a new isolationism. It is a new internationalism in which America enlists its allies and its friends around the world in those struggles in which their interest is as great as ours.

And now to the leaders of the Communist world we say, after an era of confrontations, the time has come for an era of negotiations.

Where the world superpowers are concerned there is no acceptable alternative to peaceful negotiation. Because this will be a period of negotiations we shall restore the strength of America so that we shall always negotiate from strength and never from weakness.

And as we seek through negotiations let our goals be made clear. We do not seek domination over any other country. We believe deeply in our ideas but we believe they should travel on their own power and not on the power of our arms. We shall never be belligerent. But we shall be as firm in defending our system as they are in expanding theirs.

We believe this should be an era of peaceful competition not only in the productivity of our factories but in the quality of our ideas. We extend the hand of friendship to all people. To the Russian people. To the Chinese people. To all people in the world. And we shall work toward the goal of an open world, open sky, open cities, open heart, open minds. The next eight years my friends. . . .

This period in which we're entering—I think we will have the greatest opportunity for world peace, but also face the greatest danger of world war of anytime in our history.

I believe we must have peace. I believe that we can have peace. But I do not underestimate the difficulty of this task.

Because, you see, the art of preserving peace is greater than that of waging war, and much more demanding.

But I am proud to have served in an Administration which ended one war and kept the nation out of other wars for eight years afterward.

And it is that kind of experience, and it is that kind of leadership, that America needs today and that we will give to America, with your help.

And as we commit the new policies for America tonight, let me make one further pledge—For five years hardly a day has gone by when we haven't read or heard a report of the American flag being spit on, and our embassy being stoned, a library being burned, or an ambassador being insulted some place in the world, and each incident reduced respect for the United States until the ultimate insult inevitably occurred.

And I say to you tonight that when respect for the United States of

America falls so low that a fourth-rate military power like Korea will seize an American naval vessel in the high seas, it's time for new leadership to restore respect for the United States of America.

Thank you very much. My friends, America is a great nation. It is time we started to act like a great nation around the world.

It's ironic to note, when we were a small nation, weak militarily and poor economically, America was respected. And the reason was that America stood for something more powerful than military strength or economic wealth.

The American Revolution was a shining example of freedom in action which caught the imagination of the world, and today, too often, America is an example to be avoided and not followed.

A nation that can't keep the peace at home won't be trusted to keep the peace abroad. A president who isn't treated with respect at home will not be treated with respect abroad. A nation which can't manage its own economy can't tell others how to manage theirs.

If we are to restore prestige and respect for America abroad, the place to begin is at home—in the United States of America.

My friends, we live in an age of revolution in America and in the world. And to find the answers to our problems, let us turn to a revolution—a revolution that will never grow old, the world's greatest continuing revolution, the American Revolution.

The American Revolution was and is dedicated to progress. But our founders recognized that the first requisite of progress is order.

Now there is no quarrel between progress and order because neither can exist without the other.

So let us have order in America, not the order that suppresses dissent and discourages change but the order which guarantees the right to dissent and provides the basis for peaceful change.

And tonight it's time for some honest talk about the problem of order in the United States. Let us always respect, as I do, our courts and those who serve on them, but let us also recognize that some of our courts in their decisions have gone too far in weakening the peace forces as against the criminal forces in this country.

Let those who have the responsibility to enforce our laws, and our judges who have the responsibility to interpret them, be dedicated to the great principles of civil rights. But let them also recognize that the first civil right of every American is to be free from domestic violence. And that right must be guaranteed in this country.

And if we are to restore order and respect for law in this country, there's one place we're going to begin: We're going to have a new Attorney General of the United States of America.

I pledge to you that our new Attorney General will be directed by the President of the United States to launch a war against organized crime in this country.

I pledge to you that the new Attorney General of the United States will be an active belligerent against the loan sharks and the numbers racketeers that rob the urban poor in our cities.

I pledge to you that the new Attorney General will open a new front against the pill peddlers and the narcotics peddlers who are corrupting the lives of the children of this country.

Because, my friends, let this message come through clear from what I say tonight. Time is running out for the merchants of crime and corruption in American society. The wave of crime is not going to be the wave of the future in the United States of America.

We shall re-establish freedom from fear in America so that America can take the lead of re-establishing freedom from fear in the world.

And to those who say that law and order is the code word for racism, here is a reply: Our goal is justice—justice for every American. If we are to have respect for law in America, we must have laws that deserve respect. Just as we cannot have progress without order, we cannot have order without progress.

And so as we commit to order tonight, let us commit to progress.

And this brings me to the clearest choice among the great issues of this campaign.

For the past five years we have been deluged by Government programs for the unemployed, programs for the cities, programs for the poor, and we have reaped from these programs an ugly harvest of frustrations, violence and failure across the land. And now our opponents will be offering more of the same—more billions for Government jobs, Government housing, Government welfare. I say it's time to quit pouring billions of dollars into programs that have failed in the United States of America.

To put it bluntly, we're on the wrong road and it's time to take a new road to progress.

Again we turn to the American Revolution for our answers. The war on poverty didn't begin five years ago in this country; it began when this country began. It's been the most successful war on poverty in the history of nations. There's more wealth in America today, more broadly shared than in any nation in the world.

We are a great nation. And we must never forget how we became great. America is a great nation today, not because of what government did for people, but because of what people did for themselves over 190 years in this country.

And so it is time to apply the lessons of the American Revolution to our present problems.

Let us increase the wealth of America so we can provide more generously for the aged and for the needy and for all those who cannot help themselves.

But for those who are able to help themselves, what we need are not more millions on welfare rolls but more millions on payrolls in the United States of America.

Instead of Government jobs and Government housing let Government use its tax and credit policies to enlist in this battle the greatest engine of progress ever developed in the history of man—American private enterprise.

Let us enlist in this great cause the millions of Americans in volunteer organizations who will bring a dedication to this task that no amount of money can ever buy.

And let us build bridges, my friends, build bridges to human dignity across the gulf that separates black America from white America.

Black Americans—no more than white Americans—do not want more Government programs which perpetuate dependency. They don't want to be a colony in a nation. They want the pride and the self-respect and the dignity that can only come if they have an equal chance to own their own homes, to own their own businesses, to be managers and executives as well as workers, to have a piece of the action in the exciting ventures of private enterprise.

I pledge to you tonight that we shall have new programs which will provide that equal chance. We make great history tonight. We do not fire a shot heard round the world, but we shall light the lamp of hope in millions of homes across this land in which there is no hope today.

And that great light shining out from America will again become a beacon of hope for all those in the world who seek freedom and opportunity.

My fellow Americans, I believe that historians will recall that 1968 marked the beginning of the American generation in world history. Just to be alive in America, just to be alive at this time is an experience unparalleled in history. Here's where the action is.

Think: Thirty-two years from now most of Americans living today will celebrate a New Year that comes once in a thousand years.

Eight years from now, in the second term of the next President, we will celebrate the 200th anniversary of the American Revolution.

And by our decision in this we—all of us here, all of you listening on television and radio—we will determine what kind of nation America will be on its 200th birthday. We will determine what kind of a world America will live in in the year 2000.

This is the kind of a day I see for America on that glorious Fourth eight years from now: I see a day when Americans are once again proud of their flag; when once again at home and abroad it is honored as the world's greatest symbol of liberty and justice.

I see a day when the President of the United States is respected and his office is honored because it is worthy of respect and worthy of honor. I see a day when every child in this land, regardless of his background, has a chance for the best education that our wisdom and schools can provide, and an equal chance to go just as high as his talents will take him.

I see a day when life in rural America attracts people to the country rather than driving them away.

I see a day when we can look back on massive breakthroughs in solving the problems of slums and pollution and traffic which are choking our cities to death.

I see a day when our senior citizens and millions of others can plan for the future with the assurance that their government is not going to rob them of their savings by destroying the value of their dollar.

I see a day when we will again have freedom from fear in America and freedom from fear in the world. I see a day when our nation is at peace and the world is at peace and everyone on earth—those who hope, those who aspire, those who crave liberty will look to America as the shining example of hopes realized and dreams achieved.

My fellow Americans, this is the cause I ask you to vote for. This is the cause I ask you to work for. This is the cause I ask you to commit to not just for victory in November but beyond that to a new Administration because the time when one man or a few leaders could save America is gone. We need tonight nothing less than the total commitment and the total mobilization of the American people if we are to succeed.

Government can pass laws but respect for law can come only from people who take the law into their hearts and their minds and not into their hands.

Government can provide opportunity, but opportunity means nothing unless people are prepared to seize it.

A president can ask for reconciliation in the racial conflict that divides Americans, but reconciliation comes only from the hearts of people.

And tonight, therefore, as we make this commitment, let us look into our hearts, and let us look down into the faces of our children.

Is there anything in the world that should stand in their way? None of the old hatreds mean anything when you look down into the faces of our children. In their faces is our hope, our love and our courage.

Tonight, I see the face of a child. He lives in a great city, he's black or he's white, he's Mexican, Italian, Polish, none of that matters. What matters he's an American child.

That child in that great city is more important than any politician's promise. He is America, he is a poet, he is a scientist, he's a great teacher, he's a proud craftsman, he's everything we've ever hoped to be in everything we dare to dream about.

He sleeps the sleep of a child, and he dreams the dreams of a child. And yet when he awakens, he awakens to a living nightmare of poverty, neglect and despair.

He fails in school, he ends up on welfare. For him the American system is one that feeds his stomach and starves his soul. It breaks his heart. And in the end it may take his life on some distant battlefield.

To millions of children in this rich land this is their prospect, but this is only part of what I see in America.

I see another child tonight. He hears a train go by. At night he dreams of faraway places where he'd like to go. It seems like an impossible dream. But he is helped on his journey through life. A father who had to go to work before he finished the sixth grade sacrificed everything he had so that his sons could go to college.

A gentle Quaker mother with a passionate concern for peace, quietly wept when he went to war but she understood why he had to go.

A great teacher, a remarkable football coach, an inspirational minister encouraged him on his way. A courageous wife and loyal children stood by him in victory and also in defeat.

And in his chosen profession of politics, first there was scores, then hundreds, then thousands, and finally millions who worked for his success.

And tonight he stands before you, nominated for President of the United States of America.

You can see why I believe so deeply in the American dream.

For most of us the American revolution has been won, the American dream has come true. What I ask of you tonight is to help me make that dream come true for millions to whom it's an impossible dream today.

One hundred and eight years ago the newly elected President of the United States, Abraham Lincoln, left Springfield, Ill., never to return again.

He spoke to his friends gathered at the railroad station. Listen to his words:

"Today I leave you. I go to assume a greater task than devolved on General Washington. The Great God which helped him must help me. Without that great assistance I will surely fail. With it, I cannot fail."

Abraham Lincoln lost his life but he did not fail.

The next President of the United States will face challenges which in some ways will be greater than those of Washington or Lincoln, because for the first time in our nation's history an American President will face not only the problem of restoring peace abroad, but of restoring peace at home.

Without God's help, and your help, we will surely fail.

But with God's help and your help, we shall surely succeed.

My fellow Americans, the dark long night for America is about to end.

The time has come for us to leave the valley of despair and climb the mountain so that we may see the glory of the dawn, a new day for America, a new dawn for peace and freedom to the world.

RICHARD M. NIXON

Campaign Speech

RADIO BROADCAST

September 19, 1968

During the course of this campaign, I have discussed many issues with the American people. Tonight, I would like to talk with you about a subject often debated by scholars and the public, but seldom dealt with directly in the Presidential campaign: The nature of the Presidency itself.

What *kind* of leadership should a President give? Is the office too strong, or not strong enough? How can it be made more responsive? Should a President lead public opinion, or follow it? What are the priorities for Presidential attention, and the range of Presidential responsibilities?

Perhaps the best way to begin my own answer is with another question, one I am often asked as I travel around the country: "Why do you seek the office? With all the troubles that we have, why would *anyone* want to be President today?"

The answer is not one of glory, or fame; today the burdens of the office outweigh its privileges. It's not because the Presidency offers a chance to *be* somebody, but because it offers a chance to *do* something.

Today, it offers a greater opportunity to help shape the future than ever before in the nation's history—and if America is to meet its challenges, the next President must seize that opportunity.

We stand at a great turning point—when the nation is groping for a new direction, unsure of its role and its purposes, caught in a tumult of change. And for the first time, we face serious, simultaneous threats to the peace both at home and abroad.

In the watershed year of 1968, therefore, America needs Presidential leadership that can establish a firm focus, and offer a way out of a time of towering uncertainties. Only the President can hold out a vision of the future and really the people behind it.

The next President must unite America. He must calm its angers, ease its terrible frictions, and bring its people together once again in peace and mutual respect. He has to take *hold* of America before he can move it forward.

This requires leadership that believes in law, and has the courage to enforce it; leadership that believes in justice, and is determined to promote it; leadership that believes in progress, and knows how to inspire it.

The days of a passive Presidency belong to a simpler past. Let me be very clear about this: The next President must take an activist view of his office. He must articulate the nation's values, define its goals and marshal its will. Under a Nixon Administration, the presidency will be deeply involved in the entire sweep of America's public concerns.

The first responsibility of leadership is to gain mastery over events, and to shape the future in the image of our hopes.

The President today cannot stand aside from crisis; he cannot ignore division; he cannot simply paper over disunity. He must lead.

But he must bear in mind the distinction between forceful leadership and stubborn willfulness. And he should not delude himself into thinking that he can do everything himself. America today cannot afford vest-pocket government, no matter who wears the vest.

In considering the kind of leadership the next President should give, let us first consider the special relationship—the special trust—that has developed between President and people.

The President is trusted, not to follow the fluctuations of the public-opinion polls, but to bring his own best judgment to bear on the best *ideas* his administration can muster.

There are occasions on which a President must take unpopular measures.

But his responsibility does not stop there. The President has a duty to decide, but the people have a right to know why. The President has a responsibility to tell them—to lay out all the facts, and to explain not only why he chose as he did but also what it means for the future. Only through an open, candid dialogue with the people can a President maintain his trust and his leadership.

It's time we once again had an open administration—open to ideas *from* the people, and open in its communication *with* the people—an administration of open doors, open eyes and open minds.

When we debate American commitments abroad, for example, if we expect a decent hearing from those who now take to the streets in protest, we must recognize that neither the Department of State nor of Defense has a monopoly on all wisdom. We should bring dissenters into policy discussions, not freeze them out; we should invite constructive criticism, not only because the critics have a right to be heard, but also because they often have something worth hearing.

And this brings me to another, related point: The President cannot isolate himself from the great intellectual ferments of his time. On the contrary, he must consciously and deliberately place himself at their center. The lamps of enlightenment are lit by the spark of controversy; their flame can be snuffed out by the blanket of consensus.

This is one reason why I don't want a government of yesmen. It's why I do want a government drawn from the broadest possible base—an administration made up of Republicans, Democrats and independents, and drawn from politics, from career government service, from universities, from business, from the professions—one including not only executives and administrators, but scholars and thinkers.

While the President is a leader of thought, he is also a user of thought, and he must be a catalyst of thought. The thinking that he draws upon must be the best in America—and not only in government. What's happening today in America and the world is happening not only in politics and diplomacy, but in science, education, the arts—and in all areas a President needs a constant exposure to ideas that stretch the mind.

Only if we have an Administration broadly enough based philosophically to ensure a true ferment of ideas, and to invite in interplay of the best minds in America, can we be sure of getting the best and most penetrating ideas.

We cannot content ourselves with complacency, with an attitude that because something worked once before, it must be good enough for us now. The world is changing, America is changing, and so must our ideas and our policies change—and our pursuit of the new must be an unremitting pursuit of excellence.

When we think of leadership, we commonly think of persuasion. But the coin of leadership has another side.

In order to lead, a President today must listen. And in this time of searching and uncertainty, government must learn to listen in new ways.

A President has to hear not only the clamorous voices of the organized, but also the quiet voices, the *inner voices*—the voices that speak through the silences, and that speak from the heart and the conscience.

These are the voices that carry the real meaning and the real message of America.

He's got to articulate these voices so that they can be heard, rather than being lost in the wail and bellow of what too often passes today for public discourse. He must be, in the words of Woodrow Wilson, "the spokesman for the real sentiment and purpose of the country."

The President is the one official who represents every American—rich and poor, privileged and underprivileged. He represents those whose misfortunes stand in dramatic focus, and also the great, quiet forgotten majority—the non-shouters and the non-demonstrators, the millions who ask principally to go their own way in decency and dignity, and to have their own rights accorded the same respect they accord the rights of others. Only if he listens to the quiet voices can he be true to this trust.

This I pledge, that in a Nixon Administration, America's citizens will not have to break the law to be heard, they will not have to shout or resort to violence. We can restore peace only if we make government attentive to the quiet as well as the strident, and this I intend to do.

But what of the burdens of the Presidency? Have they, as some maintain, grown beyond the capacity of any one man?

The Presidency has been called an impossible office.

If I thought it were, I would not be seeking it. But its functions have become cluttered, the President's time drained away in trivia, the channels of authority confused.

When questions of human survival may turn on the judgments of one man, he must have time to concentrate on those great decisions that only he can make.

One means of achieving this is by expanding the role of the Vice President—which I will do.

I also plan a re-organized and strengthened Cabinet, and a stronger White House staff than any yet put together.

The people are served not only by a President, but by an Administration, and not only by an Administration, but by a government.

The President's chief function is to lead, not to administer; it is not to oversee every detail, but to put the right people in charge, to provide them with basic guidance and direction, and to let them do the job. As Theodore Roosevelt once put it, "the best executive is the one who has enough sense to pick good men to do what he wants done, and self-restraint enough to keep from meddling with them while they do it."

This requires surrounding the President with men of stature, including young men, and giving them responsibilities commensurate with that stature. It requires a Cabinet made up of the ablest men in America, leaders in their own right and not merely by virtue of appointment—men who will command the public's respect and the President's attention by the power of their intellect and the force of their ideas.

Such men are not attracted to an Administration in which all credit is gathered to the White House and blame parceled out to scapegoats, or in which high officials are asked to dance like puppets on a Presidential string. I believe in a system in which the appropriate Cabinet officer gets credit for what goes right, and the President takes the blame for what goes wrong.

Officials of a new Administration will not have to check their consciences at the door, or leave their powers of independent judgment at home.

Another change I believe necessary stems directly from my basic concept of government. For years now, the trend has been to sweep more and more authority toward Washington. Too many of the decisions that would better have been made in Seattle or St. Louis have wound up on the President's desk.

I plan a streamlined Federal system, with a return to the states, cities and communities of decision-making powers rightfully theirs.

The purpose of this is not only to make government more effective and more responsive, but also to concentrate Federal attention on those functions that can only be handled on the Federal level.

The Presidency is a place where priorities are set, and goals determined.

We need a new attention to priorities, and a new realism about goals.

We are living today in a time of great promise—but also of too much wishful imagining that all the ills of man could be set right overnight, merely by making a national "commitment."

A President must tell the people what cannot be done immediately, as well as what can. Hope is fragile, and too easily shattered by the disappointment that follows inevitably on promises unkept and unkeepable. America needs charts of the possible, not excursions into the impossible.

Our cause today is not a nation, but a planet—for never have the fates of all the peoples of the earth been so bound up together.

The tasks confronting the next President abroad are among the most complex and difficult ever faced. And, as Professor Clinton Rossiter has observed, "Leadership in foreign affairs flows today from the President— or it does not flow at all."

The whole structure of power in the world has been undergoing far-reaching changes. While these pose what may be our period of greatest danger, they open what also may be our greatest opportunity. This is a time when miscalculation could prove fatal; a time when the destructive power amassed by the world's great nations threatens the planet. But it is also a time when leaders both East and West are developing a new, sobering awareness of the terrible potential of that power and the need to restrain it.

The judgments of history can bestow no honor greater than the title of peacemaker. It is this honor—this destiny—that beckons America, the chance to lead the world at last out of turmoil and onto that plateau of peace man has dreamed of since the dawn of time. This is our summons to greatness. If we answer the call, generations yet unborn will say of this generation of Americans that we truly mastered our moment, that we at last made the world safe for mankind.

The President cannot stand alone. Today, more than ever in modern times, he must reach out and draw upon the strength of the people.

Theodore Roosevelt called the Presidency "a bully pulpit;" Franklin Roosevelt called it pre-eminently "a place of moral leadership." And surely one of a President's greatest resources is the moral authority of his office. It's time we restored that authority—and time we used it once again, to its fullest potential—to rally the people, to define those moral imperatives which are the cement of a civilized society, to point the ways in which the *energies* of the people can be enlisted to serve the *ideals* of the people.

What has to be done, has to be done by President and people together, or it won't be done at all.

In asking you to join this great effort, I am asking not that you give something *to* your country, but that you do something *with* your country; I am asking not for your gifts, but for your hands. Together, we can hardly fail, for there is no force on earth to match the will and the spirit of the people of America, if that will and that spirit are mobilized in the service of a common aim.

Let me add a personal note. I made a point of conducting my campaign for the nomination in a way that would make it possible to unite the party after the convention. That was successful. I intend now to conduct my election campaign in a way that will make it possible to unite the nation after November. It is not my intention to preside over the disintegration of America or the dissolution of America's force for good in the world. Rather, I want the Presidency to be a force for pulling our people back together once again, and for making our nation whole by making our people one. We have had enough of discord and division, and what we need now is a time of healing of renewal, and of realistic hope.

No one who has been close to the Presidency would approach its powers lightly, or indifferently, or without a profound sense of the awesome responsibility these powers carry.

Nor should the American people approach this time of challenge without a sense of the majesty of the moment.

Greatness comes from stepping up to events, not from sitting on the sidelines while history is made by others.

History will be made in these years just ahead—history that can change the world for generations to come. So let us seize the moment, and accept the challenge—not as a burden, and not in fear—but in the full confidence that no people have ever had such resources to meet its challenge. Ours is the chance to see the American dream fulfilled at last in the destiny of man. This is the role that history offers; this is the hope that summons us; this is our generation's call to greatness as a nation. This, today, is America's opportunity.

HUBERT H. HUMPHREY

Acceptance Speech

CHICAGO, ILLINOIS

August 29, 1968

Mr. Chairman, my fellow Americans, my fellow Democrats—

I proudly accept the nomination of our party. This moment—this moment is one of personal pride and gratification. Yet one cannot help but reflect the deep sadness that we feel over the troubles and the violence which have erupted, regrettably and tragically, in the streets of this great city, and for the personal injuries which have occurred.

Surely we have now learned the lesson that violence breeds counter-violence and it cannot be condoned, whatever the source.

I know that every delegate to this convention shares tonight my sorrow and my distress over these incidents. And for just one moment, in sober reflection and serious purpose, may we just quietly and silently, each in our own way, pray for our country. And may we just share for a moment a few of those immortal words of the prayer of St. Francis of Assisi, words which I think may help heal the wounds, ease the pain and lift our hearts.

Listen to this immortal saint: "Where there is hatred, let me know love. Where there is injury, pardon. Where there is doubt, faith. Where there is despair, hope. Where there is darkness, light."

Those are the words of a saint. And may those of us of less purity listen to them well and may America tonight resolve that never, never again shall we see what we have seen.

Yes, I accept your nomination in this spirit and I have spoken knowing that the months and the years ahead will severely test our America. And might I say that as this America is tested, that once again we give our testament to America. And I do not think it is sentimental nor it is cheap, but I think it is true that each and everyone of us in our own way should once again reaffirm to ourselves and our posterity that we love this nation, we love America!

But take heart my fellow Americans. This is not the first time that our nation has faced a challenge to its life and its purpose. And each time that we've had to face these challenges we have emerged with new greatness and with new strength.

We must make this moment of crisis—we must make it a moment of creation.

As it has been said, in the worst of times a great people must do the best of things—and let us do it.

We stand at such a moment now in the affairs of this Nation, because, my fellow Americans, something new, something different has happened. There is an end of an era, and there is the beginning of a new day.

And it is the special genius of the Democratic party that it welcomes change—not as an enemy but as an ally—not as a force to be suppressed but as an instrument of progress to be encouraged.

This week our party has debated the great issues before America in this very hall, and had we not raised these issues—troublesome as they were—we would have ignored the reality of change.

Had we just papered over the differences of frank, hard debate, we would deserve the contempt of our fellow citizens and the condemnation of history.

Yes, we dare to speak out and we have heard hard and sometimes bitter debate. But I submit that this is the debate, and this is the work of a free people, the work of an open convention and the work of a political party responsive to the needs of this nation.

Democracy affords debate, discussion and dissent. But, my fellow Americans, it also requires decision. And we have decided here, not by edict, but by vote; not by force, but by ballot.

Majority rule has prevailed but minority rights are preserved.

There is always the temptation, always the temptation to leave the scene of battle in anger and despair, but those who know the true meaning of democracy accept the decision of today but never relinquishing their right to change it tomorrow.

In the space of but a week this convention has literally made the foundations of a new Democratic party structure in America. From precinct level to the floor of this convention, we have revolutionized our rules and procedures.

And that revolution is in the proud tradition of our party. It is in the tradition of Franklin Roosevelt, who knew that America had nothing to fear but fear itself!

And it is in the tradition of that one and only Harry Truman, who let 'em have it and told it like it was.

And that's the way we're going to do it from here on out.

And it is in the tradition of that beloved man, Adlai Stevenson, who talked sense to the American people—and oh, tonight, how we miss this great, good and gentle man of peace in America—

And my fellow Americans, all that we do and all that we ever hope to do, must be in the tradition of John F. Kennedy, who said to us: Ask not what your country can do for you, but what can you do for your country.

And, my fellow Democrats and fellow Americans, in that spirit of that great man let us ask what together we can do for the freedom of man.

And what we are doing is in the tradition of Lyndon B. Johnson, who rallied a grief-stricken nation when our leader was stricken by the assassin's bullet and said to you and said to me, and said to all the world—let us continue.

And in the space, and in the space of five years since that tragic moment, President Johnson has accomplished more of the unfinished business of America than any of his modern predecessors.

And I truly believe that history will surely record the greatness of his contribution to the people of this land.

And tonight to you, Mr. President, I say thank you. Thank you, Mr. President.

Yes, my fellow Democrats, we have recognized and indeed we must recognize the end of an era and the beginning of a new day—and that new day, and that new day belongs to the people—to all the people, everywhere in this land of the people, to every man, woman and child that is a citizen of this Republic.

And within that new day lies nothing less than the promise seen a generation ago by that poet Thomas Wolfe—to every man his chance, to every man regardless of his birth his shining golden opportunity, to every man the right to live and to work and be himself, and to become whatever thing his manhood and his vision can combine to make him—this is the promise of America.

Yes, the new day is here across America. Throughout the entire world forces of emancipation are at work. We hear freedom's rising course—"Let me live my own life, let me live in peace, let me be free," say the people.

And that cry is heard today in our slums, on our farms and in our cities. It is heard from the old as well as from the young. It is heard in Eastern Europe and it is heard in Vietnam. And it will be answered by us, in how we face the three realities that confront this nation.

The first reality is the necessity for peace in Vietnam and in the world.

The second reality, the second reality is the necessity for peace and justice in our cities and in our nation.

And the third reality is the paramount necessity for unity—unity in our country.

Let me speak first, then, about Vietnam.

There are differences of course, serious differences within our party on this vexing and painful issue of Vietnam, and these differences are found even within the ranks of all of the Democratic Presidential candidates.

But I might say to my fellow Americans that once you have examined the differences I hope you will also recognize the much larger areas of agreement.

Let those who believe that our cause in Vietnam has been right, or those who believe that it has been wrong, agree here and now, agree here and now, that neither vindication nor repudiation will bring peace or be worthy of this country!

The question is not the yesterdays but the question is what do we do now? No one knows what the situation in Vietnam will be when the next President of the United States takes that oath of office on Jan. 20, 1969.

But every heart in America prays that by then we shall have reached a cease-fire in all Vietnam and be in serious negotiation toward a durable peace.

Meanwhile, as a citizen, a candidate and Vice President, I pledge to you and to my fellow Americans that I will do everything within my power, within the limits of my capacity and ability to aid the negotiations and to bring a prompt end to this war!

May I remind you of the words of a truly great citizen of the world, Winston Churchill. It was he who said—and we should heed his words well—"those who use today and the present to stand in judgment of the past may well lose the future."

And if there is any one lesson that we should have learned, it is that the policies of tomorrow need not be limited by the policies of yesterday.

My fellow Americans, if it comes my high honor to serve as President of these states and people, I shall apply that lesson to the search for peace in Vietnam as to all other areas of national policy.

Now let me ask you, do you remember these words at another time, in a different place: Peace and freedom do not come cheap. And we are destined—all of us here today—to live out most if not all of our lives in uncertainty and challenge and peril. The words of a prophet—yes, the words of a President—yes, the words of the challenge of today—yes. And the words of John Kennedy to you, and to me, and to posterity!

Last week we witnessed once again in Czechoslovakia the desperate attempt of tyranny to crush out the forces of liberalism by force and brutal power, to hold back change.

But in Eastern Europe as elsewhere the old era will surely end, and there, as here, a new day will dawn.

And to speed this day we must go far beyond where we've been— beyond containment to communication; beyond the emphasis of differences to dialogue; beyond fear to hope.

We must cross those remaining barriers of suspicion and despair. We must halt the arms race before it halts humanity.

And is this, is this a vain hope, is it but a dream? I say the record says no.

Within the last few years we have made progress, we have negotiated a nuclear test ban treaty, we have laid the groundwork for a nuclear nonproliferation treaty.

We have reached agreement on banning weapons in outer space. We have been building patiently—stone by stone, each in our own way—the cathedral of peace.

And now we must take new initiative, new initiative with prudence and caution but with perseverance. We must find the way and the means to control and reduce offensive and defensive nuclear missile systems. The world cannot indefinitely hope to avoid nuclear war which one last act, one erring judgment, one failure in communication could unleash upon all humanity and destroy all of mankind.

But the search for peace is not for the timid or the weak, it must come from a nation of high purpose—firm without being belligerent, resolute without being bellicose, strong without being arrogant. And that's the kind of America that will help build the peace of this world.

But the task of slowing down the arms race, of halting the nuclear escalation—there is no more urgent task than ending this threat to the very survival of our planet, and if I am elected as your President, I commit myself body, mind and soul to this task.

Now our second reality is the necessity for peace at home. There is, my friends, let's see it as it is—there is trouble in America. But it does not come from a lack of faith. But it comes from the kindling of hope.

When the homeless can find a home, they do not give up the search for a better home. When the hopeless find hope, they seek higher hopes. And in 1960 and again in 1964, you, the American people, gave us a mandate to awaken America. You asked us to get America moving again, and we have—and America is on the move.

And we have, we have awakened expectations. We have aroused new voices and new voices that must and will be heard.

We have inspired new hope in millions of men and women, and they are impatient—and rightfully so, impatient now to see their hopes and their aspirations fulfilled.

We have raised a new standard of life in our America, not just for the poor but for every American—wage earner, businessman, farmer, school child and housewife. A standard by which the future progress must be judged.

Our most urgent challenge is in urban America, where most of our people live. Some 70 percent of our people live on 2 percent of our land, and within 25 years 100 million more will join our national family.

I ask you tonight—where shall they live? How shall they live? What shall be their future? We're going to decide in the next four years those questions. The next President of the United States will establish policies not only for this generation but for children yet unborn. Our task is tremendous and I need your help.

The simple solution of the frustrated and the frightened to our complex urban problems is to lash out against society. But we know—and they must know—that this is no answer.

Violence breeds more violence: disorder destroys, and only in order can we build. Riot makes for ruin; reason makes for solution.

So from the White House to the court house to the city hall, every official has the solemn responsibility of guaranteeing to every American— black and white, rich and poor—the right to personal security—life.

Every American, black or white, rich or poor, has the right in this land of ours to a safe and a decent neighborhood, and on this there can be no compromise.

I put it very bluntly—rioting, burning, sniping, mugging, traffic in narcotics, and disregard for law are the advance guard of anarchy, and they must and they will be stopped.

But may I say most respectfully, particularly to some who have spoken before, the answer lies in reasoned, effective action by state, local and Federal authority. The answer does not lie in an attack on our courts, our laws or our Attorney General.

We do not want a police state. But we need a state of law and order.

We do not want a police state but we need a state of law and order, and neither mob violence nor police brutality have any place in America.

And I pledge to use every resource that is available to the Presidency, every resource available to the President, to end once and for all the fear that is in our cities.

Now let me speak of other rights. Nor can there be any compromise with the right of every American who is able and who is willing to work to have a job—that's an American right, too.

Who is willing to be a good neighbor, to be able to live in a decent home in the neighborhood of his own choice.

Nor can there be any compromise with the right of every American who is anxious and willing to learn, to have a good education.

And it is to these rights—the rights of law and order, the rights of life, the rights of liberty, the right of a job, the right of a home in a decent neighborhood, and the right of an education—it is to these rights that I pledge my life and whatever capacity and ability I have.

And now the third reality, essential if the other two are to be achieved, is the necessity, my fellow Americans, for unity in our country, for tolerance and forbearance for holding together as a family, and we must make a great decision. Are we to be one nation, or are we to be a nation divided, divided between black and white, between rich and poor, between north and south, between young and old? I take my stand—we are and we must be one nation, united by liberty and justice for all, one nation under God, indivisible with liberty and justice for all. This is our America.

Just as I said to you there can be no compromise on the right of personal security, there can be no compromise on securing of human rights.

If America is to make a crucial judgment of leadership in this coming election, then let that selection be made without either candidate hedging or equivocating.

Winning the Presidency, for me, is not worth the price of silence or evasion on the issue of human rights.

And winning the Presidency—and listen well—winning the Presidency is not worth a compact with extremism.

I choose not simply to run for President. I seek to lead a great nation.

And either we achieve through justice in our land or we shall doom ourselves to a terrible exhaustion of body and spirit.

I base my entire candidacy on the belief which comes from the very depths of my soul—which comes from basic religious conviction that the American people will stand up, that they will stand up for justice and fair play, and that they will respond to the call of one citizenship—one citizenship open to all for all Americans!

So this is the message that I shall take to the people, and I ask you to stand with me.

To all of my fellow Democrats now who have labored hard and openly this week, at the difficult and sometimes frustrating work of democracy, I pledge myself to that task of leading the Democratic Party to victory in November.

And may I say to those who have differed with their neighbor, or those who have differed with fellow Democrats, may I say to you that all of your goals, that all of your high hopes, that all of your dreams, all of them will come to naught if we lose this election and many of them can be realized with the victory that can come to us.

And now a word to two good friends. To my friends—and they are my friends—and they're your friends—and they're fellow Democrats.

To my friends Gene McCarthy and George McGovern—to my friends Gene McCarthy and George McGovern, who have given new hope to a new generation of Americans that there can be greater meaning in their lives, that America can respond to men of moral concern, to these two good Americans: I ask your help for our America, and I ask you to help me in this difficult campaign that lies ahead.

And now I appeal, I appeal to those thousands—yea millions—of young Americans to join us, not simply as campaigners but to continue as vocal, creative and even critical participants in the politics of our time. Never were you needed so much, and never could you do so much if you want to help now.

Martin Luther King, Jr. had a dream. Robert F. Kennedy as you saw tonight had a great vision. If Americans will respond to that dream and that vision, if Americans will respond to that dream and that vision, their deaths will not mark the moment when America lost its way. But it will mark the time when America found its conscience.

These men, these men have given us inspiration and direction, and I pledge from this platform tonight we shall not abandon their purpose—we shall honor their dreams by our deeds now in the days to come.

I am keenly aware of the fears and the frustrations of the world in which we live. It is all too easy, isn't it, to play on these emotions. But I do not intend to do so. I do not intend to appeal to fear, but rather to hope. I do not intend to appeal to frustration, but rather to your faith.

I shall appeal to reason and to your good judgment.

The American Presidency, the American Presidency is a great and powerful office, but it is not all-powerful. It depends most of all upon the will and the faith and the dedication and the wisdom of the American people.

So I call you forth—I call forth that basic goodness that is there—I call you to risk the hard path of greatness.

And I say to America. Put aside recrimination and dissension. Turn away from violence and hatred. Believe—believe in what America can do, and believe in what America can be, and with the vast—with the help of that vast, unfrightened, dedicated, faithful majority of Americans, I say to this great convention tonight, and to this great nation of ours, I am ready to lead our country!

☆

HUBERT H. HUMPHREY

Campaign Speech

SALT LAKE CITY, UTAH

September 30, 1968

Tonight I want to share with you my thoughts as a citizen and a candidate for President of the United States. I want to tell you what I think about great issues which I believe face this nation.

I want to talk with you about Vietnam, and about another great issue in the search for peace in the world—the issue of stopping the threat of nuclear war.

After I have told you what I think, I want you to think.

And if you agree with me, I want you to help me.

For the past several weeks, I have tried to tell you what was in my heart and on my mind.

But sometimes that message has been drowned out by the voices of protesters and demonstrators.

I shall not let the violence and disorder of a noisy few deny me the right to speak or to destroy the orderly democratic process.

I have paid for this television time this evening to tell you my story uninterrupted by noise . . . by protest . . . or by second-hand interpretation.

When I accepted the Democratic party's nomination and platform, I said that the first reality that confronted this nation was the need for peace in Vietnam.

I have pledged that my first priority as President shall be to end the war and obtain an honorable peace.

For the past four years I have spoken my mind about Vietnam, frankly and without reservation, in the Cabinet and in the National Security Council—and directly to the President.

When the President has made his decisions, I have supported them.

He has been the Commander in Chief. It has been his job to decide. And the choices have not been simple or easy.

President Johnson will continue—until Jan. 20, 1969—to make the decisions in Vietnam. The voice at the negotiating table must be his. I shall not compete with that voice. I shall cooperate and help.

We all pray that his efforts to find peace will succeed.

But, 112 days from now, there will be a President . . . a new Administration . . . and new advisers.

If there is no peace by then, it must be their responsibility to make a complete reassessment of the situation in Vietnam—to see where we stand and to judge what we must do.

As I said in my acceptance speech: The policies of tomorrow need not be limited by the policies of yesterday.

We must look to the future. For neither vindication nor repudiation of our role in Vietnam will bring peace or be worthy of our country.

The American people have a right to know what I would do—if I am President—after Jan. 20, 1969, to keep my pledge to honorably end the war in Vietnam.

What are the chances for peace?

The end of the war is not yet in sight. But our chances for peace are far better today than they were a year or even a month ago.

On March 31, the war took on an entirely new dimension.

On that date President Johnson by one courageous act removed the threat of bombing from 90 percent of the people, and 78 percent of the land area, of North Vietnam.

On that date President Johnson sacrificed his own political career in order to bring negotiations that could lead to peace.

Until that time, the struggle was only on the battlefield.

Now our negotiators are face to face across the table with negotiators from North Vietnam.

A process has been set in course. And lest that process be set back, our perseverance at the conference table must be great as our courage has been in the war.

There have been other changes during these past few months.

The original Vietnam decision—made by President Eisenhower— was made for one basic reason.

President Eisenhower believed it was in our national interest that Communist subversion and aggression should not succeed in Vietnam.

It was his judgment—and the judgment of President Kennedy and President Johnson since then—that if aggression did succeed in Vietnam, there was a danger that we would become involved on a more dangerous scale in a wider area of Southeast Asia.

While we have stood with our allies in Vietnam, several things have happened.

Other nations of Southeast Asia—given the time we have bought for them—have strengthened themselves . . . have begun to work together . . . and are far more able to protect themselves against any future subversion or aggression.

In South Vietnam itself, a constitution has been written . . . elections have been stepped up . . . and the South Vietnamese Army has increased its size and capacity, and improved its equipment, training and performance—just as the Korean Army did during the latter stages of the Korean War.

So—in sharp contrast to a few months ago—we see peace negotiations going on.

We see a stronger Southeast Asia.

We see a stronger South Vietnam.

Those are the new circumstances which a new President will face in January.

In light of those circumstances—and assuming no marked change in the present situation—how would I proceed as President?

Let me first make clear what I would not do.

I would not undertake a unilateral withdrawal.

To withdraw would not only jeopardize the independence of South Vietnam and the safety of other Southeast Asian nations. It would make meaningless the sacrifices we have already made.

It would be an open invitation to more violence . . . more aggression . . . more instability.

It would, at this time of tension in Europe, cast doubt on the integrity of our word under treaty and alliance.

Peace would not be served by weakness or withdrawal.

Nor would I escalate the level of violence in either North or South Vietnam. We must seek to de-escalate.

The platform of my party says that the President should take reasonable risks to find peace in Vietnam. I shall do so.

North Vietnam, according to its own statements and those of others, has said it will proceed to prompt and good faith negotiations, if we stop the present limited bombing of the North.

We must always think of the protection of our troops.

As President, I would stop the bombing of the North as an acceptable risk for peace because I believe it could lead to success in the negotiations and thereby shorten the war. This would be the best protection for our troops. . . . In weighing that risk—and before taking action—I would place key importance on evidence—direct or indirect—by deed or word—of Communist willingness to restore the demilitarized zone between North and South Vietnam.

Now if the Government of North Vietnam were to show bad faith, I would reserve the right to resume the bombing.

Now secondly, I would take the risk that South Vietnamese would meet the responsibilities they say they are now ready to assume in their own self-defense.

I would move, in other words, toward de-Americanization of the war.

I would sit down with the leaders of South Vietnam to set a specific timetable by which American forces could be systematically reduced while South Vietnamese forces took over more and more of the burden.

The schedule must be a realistic one—one that would not weaken the over-all Allied defense posture. I am convinced such action would be as much in South Vietnam's interest as in ours.

What I am proposing is that it should be basic to our policy in Vietnam that the South Vietnamese take over more and more of the defense of their own country.

That would be an immediate objective of the Humphrey-Muskie Administration as I sought to end the war.

If the South Vietnamese Army maintains its present rate of improvement, I believe this will be possible next year—without endangering either our remaining troops or the safety of South Vietnam.

I do not say this lightly. I have studied this matter carefully.

Third, I would propose once more an immediate cease-fire—with United Nations or other international supervision and supervised withdrawal of all foreign forces from South Vietnam.

American troops are fighting in numbers in South Vietnam today only because North Vietnamese forces were sent to impose Hanoi's will on the South Vietnamese people by aggression.

We can agree to bring home our forces from South Vietnam, if the North Vietnamese agree to bring theirs home at the same time.

External forces assisting both sides could and should leave at the same time, and should not be replaced.

The ultimate key to an honorable solution must be free elections in South Vietnam—with all people, including members of the National Liberation Front and other dissident groups, able to participate in those elections if they were willing to abide by peaceful processes.

That, too, would mean some risk.

But I have never feared the risk of one man, one vote. I say: let the people speak. And accept their judgment, whatever it is.

The Government of South Vietnam should not be imposed by force from Hanoi or by pressure from Washington. It should be freely chosen by all the South Vietnamese people.

A stopping of the bombing of the North—taking account of Hanoi's actions and assurances of prompt good faith negotiations and keeping the option of resuming that bombing if the Communists show bad faith.

Careful, systematic reduction of American troops in South Vietnam— a de-Americanization of the war—turning over to the South Vietnamese Army a greater share of the defense of its own country.

An internationally supervised cease-fire—and supervised withdrawal of all foreign forces from South Vietnam.

Free elections, including all people in South Vietnam willing to follow the peaceful process.

Those are risks I would take for peace.

I do not believe any of these risks would jeopardize our security or be contrary to our national interest.

There is, of course, no guarantee that all these things could be successfully done.

Certainly, none of them could be done if North Vietnam were to show bad faith.

But I believe there is a good chance these steps could be undertaken with safety for our men in Vietnam.

As President, I would be dedicated to carrying them out—as I would be dedicated to urging the Government of South Vietnam to expedite all political, economic and social reforms essential to broadening popular participation including high priority to land reform . . . more attention to the suffering of refugees . . . and constant Government pressure against inflation and corruption.

I believe all of these steps could lead to an honorable and lasting settlement, serving both our own national interest and the interests of the independent nations of Southeast Asia.

We have learned a lesson from Vietnam.

The lesson is not that we should turn our backs on Southeast Asia, or on other nations or people in less familiar parts of the world neighborhood.

The lesson is, rather, that we should carefully define our goals and priorities. And within those goals and priorities, that we should formulate policies which will fit new American guidelines.

Applying the lesson of Vietnam, I would insist as President that we review other commitments made in other times, that we carefully decide what is and is not in our national interest.

I do not condemn any past commitment.

I do not judge the decisions of past Presidents when, in good conscience, they made those decisions in what they thought were the interests of the American people.

But I do say, if I am President, I owe it to this nation to bring our men and resources in Vietnam back to America where we need them so badly, and to be sure we put first things first in the future.

Let me be clear: I do not counsel withdrawal from the world.

I do not swerve from international responsibility.

I only say that, as President, I would undertake a new strategy for peace in this world, based not on American omnipotence, but on American leadership, not only military and economic but moral.

That new strategy for peace would emphasize working through the United Nations . . . strengthening and maintaining our key alliances for mutual security, particularly including NATO . . . supporting international peacekeeping machinery . . . and working with other nations to build new institutions and instruments for cooperation.

In a troubled and dangerous world we should seek not to march alone, but to lead in such a way that others will wish to join us.

Even as we seek peace in Vietnam, we must for our own security and well-being seek to halt and turn back the costly and even more dangerous arms race.

Five nations now have nuclear bombs.

The United States and the Soviet Union already possess enough weapons to burn and destroy every human being on this earth.

Unless we stop the arms race . . . unless we stop 15 to 20 more nations from getting nuclear bombs and nuclear bomb technology within the next few years, this generation may be the last.

For 20 years we have lived under the constant threat that some irresponsible action or even some great miscalculation could blow us all up in the wink of an eye.

There is danger that we have become so used to the idea that we no longer think it abnormal—forgetting that our whole world structure depends for its stability on the precarious architecture of what Winston Churchill called the "balance of terror." This is no longer an adequate safeguard for peace.

There is a treaty now before the Senate which would stop the spread of nuclear weapons. That treaty must be ratified now.

If this nation cannot muster the courage to ratify this treaty—a treaty which in no way endangers our national security, but adds to it by keeping these weapons out of the hands of a Nassar, a Castro . . . and many others —then there can be little hope for our future in this world. We must ratify this treaty.

I also believe that we must have the courage—while keeping our guard up and fulfilling our commitments to NATO—to talk with the Soviet Union as soon as possible about a freeze and a reduction of offensive and defensive nuclear missiles systems.

To escalate the nuclear missile arms race is to raise the level of danger and total destruction. It is costly, menacing, fearsome and offers no genuine defense.

Beyond that, if I am President, I shall take the initiative to find the way—under carefully safeguarded, mutually acceptable international inspection—to reduce arms budgets and military expenditures systematically among all countries of the world.

Our country's military budget this year is $80-billion.

It is an investment we have to make under existing circumstances. It protects our freedom.

But if we can work with other nations so that we can all reduce our military expenditures together, with proper safeguards and inspection, then it will be a great day for humanity.

All of us will have moved further away from self-destruction. And all of us will have billions of dollars with which to help people live better lives.

The American people must choose the one man they believe can best face these great issues.

I would hope that Mr. Nixon, Mr. Wallace and I could express our views on Vietnam not only individually, but on the same public platform.

I call for this because—on the basis of our past records and past careers—there are great differences between our policies and programs.

Those views of Governor Wallace which I have seen reported indicate that he would sharply escalate the war.

Mr. Nixon's past record reveals his probable future policies.

In 1954—at the time of the French defeat at Dienbienphu—he advocated American armed intervention in Vietnam in aid of French colonialism. It was necessary for President Eisenhower to repudiate his proposal.

Since then, he has taken a line on Vietnam policy which I believe could lead to greater escalation of the war.

In January of this year, Mr. Nixon described as "bunk" the idea that free elections in South Vietnam were of importance.

In February of this year, when questioned about the use of nuclear weapons in Vietnam, Mr. Nixon said that a general "has to take the position that he cannot rule out the use of nuclear-weapons in extreme situations that might develop."

Since then, he has indicated he has a plan to end the war in Vietnam but will not disclose it until he becomes President.

If he has such a plan, he has an obligation to so inform President Johnson and the American people.

A few days ago the Republican Vice-Presidential nominee said there is not now and never has been a Nixon-Agnew plan for peace in Vietnam. It was, he said, a ploy "to maintain suspense."

And then he said: "Isn't that the way campaigns are run?"

I think we need some answers about this from Mr. Nixon.

Mr. Nixon's public record shows, also, consistent opposition to measures for nuclear arms controls.

He attacked Adlai Stevenson and myself for advocating a nuclear test ban treaty—a treaty to stop radioactive fallout from poisoning and crippling people the world over. He called our plan "a cruel hoax." We can be thankful that President Kennedy and the Congress did not follow his advice.

Today, he is asking for delay of ratification of a treaty carefully negotiated over several years and signed by 80 nations—the nuclear nonproliferation treaty designed to stop the spread of nuclear weapons.

I speak plainly: I do not believe the American Presidency can afford a return to leadership which would increase tension in the world; which would, on the basis of past statements, escalate the Vietnam war; and which would turn the clock back on progress that has been made at a great sacrifice to bring the great powers of the world into a saner relationship in this nuclear age.

On the great issues of Vietnam, of the arms race and of human rights in America, I have clear differences with Mr. Nixon and Mr. Wallace.

I call on both of these men to join me in open debate before the American people.

Let us put our ideas before the people. Let us offer ourselves for their judgment—as men and as leaders.

Let us appear together—in front of the same audiences or on the same television screens, and at the same time—to give the people a choice.

We must not let a President be elected by the size of his advertising budget.

We cannot let a President be elected without having met the issues before the people.

I am willing to put myself, my programs, my capacity for leadership, before the American people for their judgment.

I ask the Republican nominee and the third-party candidate to do the same.

I ask, before Election Day, that we be heard together as you have heard me alone tonight.

I appeal to the people—as citizens of a nation whose compassion and sense of decency and fair play have made it what Lincoln called "the last best hope on earth."

I appeal to you as a person who wants his children to grow up in that kind of country.

I appeal to you to express and vote your hopes and not your hates.

I intend, in these five weeks, to wage a vigorous, tireless and forthright campaign for the Presidency. I shall not spare myself, or those who will stand with me.

I have prepared myself. I know the problems facing this nation. I do not shrink from these problems. I challenge them. They were made by men. I believe they can be solved by men.

If you will give me your confidence and support, together we shall build a better America.

☆

1972

— ☆ —

In addition to inheriting the Vietnam War from the Johnson administration, Nixon also succeeded to an inflationary economy. Partly this inflation was the result of large military expenditures on the war. Partly it was due to the monetary policy of the Johnson administration.

Although Nixon was able to balance the 1969 budget, he was unable to check the inflationary spiral; nor was he able to halt the nation's mounting unemployment. In an effort to restore economic stability Nixon decided to implement a 1970 law which empowered the President to control prices and wages. In the summer of 1971 he instituted a ninety-day freeze on all wages, rents, and prices. This initiative was followed up by the creation of a Pay Board and a Price Commission to oversee wage and price increases once the freeze was over.

For Nixon, however, the settlement of the Vietnam War was still first on his agenda of priorities. Beginning in June, 1969, he began withdrawing American troops from Vietnam. The promise of staggered withdrawals did little to appease the American public. On October 15, 1969 students across the country organized the first Moratorium Day to protest the administration's actions. The administration's response to this event was expressed by Vice President Spiro Agnew, who called the student leaders "an effete corps of impudent snobs who characterize themselves as intellectuals."

Nor did troop withdrawals halt the bombing of North Vietnam; in fact, the bombing was intensified. And on April 30, 1970, the administration launched a joint U.S.-South Vietnam invasion of neutral Cambodia to ferret out communist sanctuaries. While Nixon terminated the bombing of Cambodia, new communist assaults in March, 1972, led the President not only to resume bombing of the North, but to begin the mining of Haiphong and other northern ports in order to cut off supplies that the communists were receiving.

Concurrently, Nixon had sent his chief foreign policy adviser, Dr. Henry Kissinger, to arrange summit meetings in China and Russia. In February, 1972, Nixon travelled to China to confer with Premier Chou En-Lai. By meeting Chou, Nixon was acknowledging an event that had occurred more than a generation before their conference: the Chinese Communist Revolution. Before leaving China Nixon signed a declaration stating that Taiwan was part of mainland China, that American forces would eventually evacuate Taiwan, and that the future of Taiwan would be left in Chinese hands.

In May the President visited Moscow. His major achievement at the Kremlin was the conclusion of two treaties: one freezing offensive strategic missiles and another limiting each superpower to two antiballistic missile deployments. That the two leading communist nations were receptive to Nixon's initiatives during this period was one of the first signals of an abatement in the Cold War.

When the Democrats met in Miami Beach in July, they nominated Senator George McGovern of South Dakota as their candidate. One of the nation's most outspoken critics of the war, McGovern advocated an immediate withdrawal from Vietnam. That the "brutal war" in Vietnam must be ended and that military spending must be channeled into domestic programs were among the major themes of McGovern's acceptance speech.

McGovern, however, was forced to halt his campaign almost before it got underway. Unbeknown to McGovern, his running mate, Senator Thomas Eagleton of Missouri, had in the past undergone psychiatric treatment, a fact that Eagleton never revealed to McGovern. After some vacillation, McGovern asked Eagleton to withdraw and replaced him with Sargent Shriver, the former head of the Peace Corps. McGovern recommended Shriver for the position in an August 5th television address—an address in which the candidate also reiterated his position on the issues of the day: the war, military spending, tax reform, welfare reform, urban renewal.

With the return of prosperity in the summer of 1972, the Republicans were particularly confident of victory as they met at Miami Beach to renominate Nixon. In his acceptance speech Nixon stated that the people had a clear choice in 1972: McGovern paternalism or Republican economic and political individualism. Above all, he asked to be allowed to continue his efforts at world peace. Nixon repeated these basic themes in a November 2nd campaign address from the White House.

RICHARD M. NIXON

Acceptance Speech

MIAMI BEACH, FLORIDA

August 23, 1972

Mr. Chairman, delegates to this convention, my fellow Americans:

Four years ago, standing in this very place, I proudly accepted your nomination for President of the United States.

With your help and with the votes of millions of Americans, we won a great victory in 1968.

Tonight, I again proudly accept your nomination for President of the United States.

Let us pledge ourselves to win an even greater victory this November in 1972.

I congratulate Chairman Ford. I congratulate Chairman Dole, Anne Armstrong, and the hundreds of others who have laid the foundation for that victory by their work at this great convention.

Our platform is a dynamic program for progress for America and for peace in the world.

Speaking in a very personal sense, I express my deep gratitude to this convention for the tribute you have paid to the best campaigner in the Nixon family—my wife Pat. In honoring her, you have honored millions of women in America who have contributed in the past and will contribute in the future so very much to better government in this country.

Again, as I did last night, when I was not at the convention, I express the appreciation of all of the delegates and of all America for letting us see young America at its best at our convention. As I express my appreciation to you, I want to say that you have inspired us with your enthusiasm, with your intelligence, with your dedication at this convention. You have made us realize that this is a year when we can prove the experts' predictions wrong, because we can set as our goal winning a majority of the new voters for *our* ticket this November.

I pledge to you, all of the new voters in America who are listening on television and listening here in this convention hall, that I will do everything that I can over these next 4 years to make your support be one that you can be proud of because, as I said to you last night, and I feel it very deeply in my heart: Years from now I want you to look back and be able to say that your first vote was one of the best votes you ever cast in your life.

Mr. Chairman, I congratulate the delegates to this convention for renominating as my running-mate the man who has just so eloquently and graciously introduced me, Vice President Ted Agnew.

I thought he was the best man for the job 4 years ago.

I think he is the best man for the job today.

And I am not going to change my mind tomorrow.

Finally, as the Vice President has indicated, you have demonstrated to the Nation that we can have an open convention without dividing Americans into quotas.

Let us commit ourselves to rule out every vestige of discrimination in this country of ours. But my fellow Americans, the way to end discrimination against some is not to begin discrimination against others.

Dividing Americans into quotas is totally alien to the American traditions.

Americans don't want to be part of a quota. They want to be part of America. This Nation proudly calls itself the United States of America. Let us reject any philosophy that would make us the divided people of America.

In that spirit, I address you tonight, my fellow Americans, not as a partisan of party, which would divide us, but as a partisan of principles which can unite us.

Six weeks ago our opponents at their convention rejected many of the great principles of the Democratic Party. To those millions who have been driven out of their home in the Democratic Party, we say come home. We say come home not to another party, but we say come home to the great principles we Americans believe in together.

And I ask you, my fellow Americans, tonight to join us not in a coalition held together only by a desire to gain power. I ask you to join us as members of a new American majority bound together by our common ideals.

I ask everyone listening to me tonight—Democrats, Republicans,

Independents, to join our new majority—not on the basis of the party label you wear in your lapel, but on the basis of what you believe in your hearts.

In asking for your support I shall not dwell on the record of our Administration which has been praised perhaps too generously by others at this convention.

We have made great progress in these past 4 years.

It can truly be said that we have changed America and that America has changed the world. As a result of what we have done, America today is a better place and the world is a safer place to live in than was the case 4 years ago.

We can be proud of that record, but we shall never be satisfied. A record is not something to stand on; it is something to build on.

Tonight I do not ask you to join our new majority because of what we have done in the past. I ask your support of the principles I believe should determine America's future.

The choice in this election is not between radical change and no change. The choice in this election is between change that works and change that won't work.

I begin with an article of faith.

It has become fashionable in recent years to point up what is wrong with what is called the American system. The critics contend it is so unfair, so corrupt, so unjust, that we should tear it down and substitute something else in its place.

I totally disagree. I believe in the American system.

I have traveled to 80 countries in the past 25 years, and I have seen Communist systems, I have seen Socialist systems, I have seen systems that are half Socialist and half free.

Every time I come home to America, I realize how fortunate we are to live in this great and good country.

Every time I am reminded that we have more freedom, more opportunity, more prosperity than any people in the world; that we have the highest rate of growth of any industrial nation; that Americans have more jobs at higher wages than in any country in the world; that our rate of inflation is less than that of any industrial nation; that the incomparable productivity of America's farmers has made it possible for us to launch a winning war against hunger in the United States; and that the productivity of our farmers also makes us the best fed people in the world with the lowest percentage of the family budget going to food of any country in the world.

We can be very grateful in this country that the people on welfare in America would be rich in most of the nations of the world today.

Now, my fellow Americans, in pointing up those things, we do not overlook the fact that our system has its problems.

Our Administration, as you know, has provided the biggest tax cut in history, but taxes are still too high.

That is why one of the goals of our next Administration is to reduce the property tax which is such an unfair and heavy burden on the poor, the elderly, the wage earner, the farmer, and those on fixed incomes.

As all of you know, we have cut inflation in half in this Administration, but we have got to cut it further. We must cut it further so that we can continue to expand on the greatest accomplishment of our new economic policy: For the first time in 5 years wage increases in America are not being eaten up by price increases.

As a result of the millions of new jobs created by our new economic policies, unemployment today in America is less than the peacetime average of the sixties, but we must continue the unparalleled increase in new jobs so that we can achieve the great goal of our new prosperity—a job for every American who wants to work, without war and without inflation. The way to reach this goal is to stay on the new road we have charted to move America forward and not to take a sharp detour to the left, which would lead to a dead end for the hopes of the American people.

This points up one of the clearest choices in this campaign. Our opponents believe in a different philosophy.

Theirs is the politics of paternalism, where master planners in Washington make decisions for people.

Ours is the politics of people—where people make decisions for themselves.

The proposal that they have made to pay $1,000 to every person in America insults the intelligence of the American voters.

Because you know that every politician's promise has a price—the taxpayer pays the bill.

The American people are not going to be taken in by any scheme where Government gives money with one hand and then takes it away with the other.

Their platform promises everything to everybody, but at an increased net in the budget of $144 billion, but listen to what it means to you, the taxpayers of the country. That would mean an increase of 50 percent in what the taxpayers of America pay. I oppose any new spending programs which will increase the tax burden on the already overburdened American taxpayer.

And they have proposed legislation which would add 82 million people to the welfare rolls.

I say that instead of providing incentives for millions of more Americans to go on welfare, we need a program which will provide incentives for people to get off of welfare and to get to work.

We believe that it is wrong for anyone to receive more on welfare than for someone who works. Let us be generous to those who can't work without increasing the tax burden of those who do work.

And while we are talking about welfare, let us quit treating our senior citizens in this country like welfare recipients. They have worked hard all their lives to build America. And as the builders of America, they have not asked for a handout. What they ask for is what they have earned—and that is retirement in dignity and self-respect. Let's give that to our senior citizens.

Now, when you add up the cost of all of the programs our opponents have proposed, you reach only one conclusion: They would destroy the system which has made America number one in the world economically.

Listen to these facts: Americans today pay one-third of all of their income in taxes. If their programs were adopted, Americans would pay over one-half of what they earn in taxes. This means that if their programs are adopted, American wage earners would be working more for the government than they would for themselves.

Once we cross this line, we cannot turn back because the incentive which makes the American economic system the most productive in the world would be destroyed.

Theirs is not a new approach. It has been tried before in countries abroad, and I can tell you that those who have tried it have lived to regret it.

We cannot and we will not let them do this to America.

Let us always be true to the principle that has made America the world's most prosperous nation—that here in America a person should get what he works for and work for what he gets.

Let me illustrate the difference in our philosophies. Because of our free economic system, what we have done is to build a great building of economic wealth and money in America. It is by the far the tallest building in the world and we are still adding to it. Now because some of the windows are broken, they say tear it down and start again. We say, replace the windows and keep building. That is the difference.

Let me turn now to a second area where my beliefs are totally different from those of our opponents.

Four years ago crime was rising all over America at an unprecedented rate. Even our Nation's Capital was called the crime capital of the world. I pledged to stop the rise in crime. In order to keep that pledge, I promised in the election campaign that I would appoint judges to the Federal courts, and particularly to the Supreme Court, who would recognize that the first civil right of every American is to be free from domestic violence.

I have kept that promise. I am proud of the appointments I have made to the courts, and particularly proud of those I have made to the Supreme Court of the United States. And I pledge again tonight, as I did 4 years ago, that whenever I have the opportunity to make more appointments to the courts, I shall continue to appoint judges who share my philosophy that we must strengthen the peace forces as against the criminal forces in the United States.

We have launched an all-out offensive against crime, against narcotics, against permissiveness in our country.

I want the peace officers across America to know that they have the total backing of their President in their fight against crime.

My fellow Americans, as we move toward peace abroad, I ask you to support our programs which will keep the peace at home.

Now, I turn to an issue of overriding importance not only to this election, but for generations to come—the progress we have made in building a new structure of peace in the world.

Peace is too important for partisanship. There have been five Presidents in my political lifetime—Franklin D. Roosevelt, Harry Truman, Dwight Eisenhower, John F. Kennedy, and Lyndon Johnson.

They had differences on some issues, but they were united in their belief that where the security of America or the peace of the world is involved we are not Republicans, we are not Democrats. We are Americans, first, last, and always.

These five Presidents were united in their total opposition to isolation for America and in their belief that the interests of the United States and the interests of world peace require that America be strong enough and intelligent enough to assume the responsibilities of leadership in the world.

They were united in the conviction that the United States should have a defense second to none in the world.

They were all men who hated war and were dedicated to peace.

But not one of these five men and no President in our history believed that America should ask an enemy for peace on terms that would betray our allies and destroy respect for the United States all over the world.

As your President, I pledge that I shall always uphold that proud bipartisan tradition. Standing in this Convention Hall 4 years ago, I pledged to seek an honorable end to the war in Vietnam. We have made great progres toward that end. We have brought over half a million men home and more will be coming home. We have ended America's ground combat role. No draftees are being sent to Vietnam. We have reduced our casualties by 98 percent. We have gone the extra mile, in fact, we have gone tens of thousands of miles trying to seek a negotiated settlement of the war. We have offered a cease-fire, a total withdrawal of all American forces, an exchange of all prisoners of war, internationally supervised free elections with the Communists participating in the elections and in the supervision.

There are three things, however, that we have not and that we will not offer.

We will never abandon our prisoners of war.

Second, we will not join our enemies in imposing a Communist government on our allies—the 17 million people of South Vietnam.

And we will never stain the honor of the United States of America.

Now I realize that many, particularly in this political year, wonder why we insist on an honorable peace in Vietnam. From a political standpoint they suggest that since I was not in office when over a half million American men were sent there, that I should end the war by agreeing to impose a Communist government on the people of South Vietnam and just blame the whole catastrophe on my predecessors.

This might be good politics, but it would be disastrous to the cause of peace in the world. If, at this time, we betray our allies, it will discourage our friends abroad and it will encourage our enemies to engage in aggression.

In areas like the Mideast, which are danger areas, small nations who rely on the friendship and support of the United States would be in deadly jeopardy.

To our friends and allies in Europe, Asia, the Mideast, and Latin America, I say the United States will continue its great bipartisan tradition—to stand by our friends and never to desert them.

Now in discussing Vietnam, I have noted that in this election year there has been a great deal of talk about providing amnesty for those few hundred Americans who chose to desert their country rather than to serve it in Vietnam. I think it is time that we put the emphasis where it belongs. The real heroes are two and one-half million young Americans who chose to serve their country rather than desert it. I say to you tonight, in these times when there is so much of a tendency to run down those who have served America in the past and who serve it today, let us give those who serve in our Armed Forces and those who have served in Vietnam the honor and the respect that they deserve and that they have earned.

Finally, in this connection, let one thing be clearly understood in this election campaign: The American people will not tolerate any attempt by our enemies to interfere in the cherished right of the American voter to make his own decision with regard to what is best for America without outside intervention.

Now it is understandable that Vietnam has been a major concern in foreign policy. But we have not allowed the war in Vietnam to paralyze our capacity to initiate historic new policies to construct a lasting and just peace in the world.

When the history of this period is written, I believe it will be recorded that our most significant contributions to peace resulted from our trips to Peking and to Moscow.

The dialogue that we have begun with the People's Republic of China has reduced the danger of war and has increased the chance for peaceful cooperation between two great peoples.

Within the space of 4 years in our relations with the Soviet Union we have moved from confrontation to negotiation, and then to cooperation in the interest of peace.

We have taken the first step in limiting the nuclear arms race.

We have laid the foundation for further limitations on nuclear weapons and eventually of reducing the armaments in the nuclear area.

We can thereby not only reduce the enormous costs of arms for both our countries, but we can increase the chances for peace.

More than on any other single issue, I ask you, my fellow Americans, to give us the chance to continue these great initiatives that can contribute so much to the future of peace in the world.

It can truly be said that as a result of our initiatives, the danger of war is less today than it was; the chances for peace are greater.

But a note of warning needs to be sounded. We cannot be complacent. Our opponents have proposed massive cuts in our defense budget which would have the inevitable effect of making the United States the second strongest nation in the world.

For the United States unilaterally to reduce its strength with the naive hope that other nations would do likewise would increase the danger of war in the world.

It would completely remove any incentive of other nations to agree to a mutual limitation or reduction of arms.

The promising initiatives we have undertaken to limit arms would be destroyed.

The security of the United States and all the nations in the world who depend upon our friendship and support would be threatened.

Let's look at the record on defense expenditures. We have cut spending in our Administration. It now takes the lowest percentage of our national product in 20 years. We should not spend more on defense than we need. But we must never spend less than we need.

What we must understand is, spending what we need on defense will cost us money. Spending less than we need could cost us our lives or our freedom.

So tonight, my fellow Americans, I say, let us take risks for peace, but let us never risk the security of the United States of America.

It is for that reason that I pledge that we will continue to seek peace and the mutual reduction of arms. The United States, during this period, however, will always have a defense second to none.

There are those who believe that we can entrust the security of America to the good will of our adversaries.

Those who hold this view do not know the real world. We can negotiate limitation of arms and we have done so. We can make agreements to reduce the danger of war, and we have done so.

But one unchangeable rule of international diplomacy that I have learned over many, many years is that, in negotiations between great powers, you can only get something if you have something to give in return.

That is why I say tonight: Let us always be sure that when the President of the United States goes to the conference table, he never has to negotiate from weakness.

There is no such thing as a retreat to peace.

My fellow Americans, we stand today on the threshold of one of the most exciting and challenging eras in the history of relations between nations.

We have the opportunity in our time to be the peacemakers of the world, because the world trusts and respects us, and because the world knows that we shall only use our power to defend freedom, never to destroy it; to keep the peace, never to break it.

A strong America is not the enemy of peace; it is the guardian of peace.

The initiatives that we have begun can result in reducing the danger of arms, as well as the danger of war which hangs over the world today.

Even more important, it means that the enormous creative energies of the Russian people and the Chinese people and the American people and all the great peoples of the world can be turned away from production of war and turned toward production for peace.

In America it means that we can undertake programs for progress at home that will be just as exciting as the great initiatives we have undertaken in building a new structure of peace abroad.

My fellow Americans, the peace dividend that we hear so much about has too often been described solely in monetary terms—how much money we could take out of the arms budget and apply to our domestic needs. By far the biggest dividend, however, is that achieving our goal of a lasting peace in the world would reflect the deepest hopes and ideals of all of the American people.

Speaking on behalf of the American people, I was proud to be able to say in my television address to the Russian people in May: "We covet no one else's territory. We seek no dominion over any other nation. We seek peace not only for ourselves, but for all the people of the world."

This dedication to idealism runs through America's history.

During the tragic War Between the States, Abraham Lincoln was asked whether God was on his side. He replied, "My concern is not whether God is on our side, but whether we are on God's side."

May that always be our prayer for America.

We hold the future of peace in the world and our own future in our hands. Let us reject therefore the policies of those who whine and whimper about our frustrations and call on us to turn inward.

Let us not turn away from greatness.

The chance America now has to lead the way to a lasting peace in the world may never come again.

With faith in God and faith in ourselves and faith in our country, let us have the vision and the courage to seize the moment and meet the challenge before it slips away.

On your television screen last night, you saw the cemetery in Leningrad I visited on my trip to the Soviet Union—where 300,000 people died in the siege of that city during World War II.

At the cemetery I saw the picture of a 12-year-old girl. She was a beautiful child. Her name was Tanya.

I read her diary. It tells the terrible story of war. In the simple words of a child she wrote of the deaths of the members of her family. Zhenya in December. Grannie in January. Then Leka. Then Uncle Vasya. Then Uncle Lyosha. Then Mama in May. And finally—these were the last words in her diary: "All are dead. Only Tanya is left."

Let us think of Tanya and of the other Tanyas and their brothers and sisters everywhere in Russia, in China, in America, as we proudly meet our responsibilities for leadership in the world in a way worthy of a great people.

I ask you, my fellow Americans, to join our new majority not just in the cause of winning an election, but in achieving a hope that mankind has had since the beginning of civilization. Let us build a peace that our children and all the children of the world can enjoy for generations to come.

☆

RICHARD M. NIXON

Campaign Speech

WHITE HOUSE, WASHINGTON, D. C.

November 2, 1972

Good evening:

I am speaking to you tonight from the Library of the White House. This room, like all the rooms in this great house, is rich in history.

Often late at night I sit here thinking of the crises other Presidents have known—and of the trials that other generations of Americans have come through.

I think, too, of the Presidents who will be sitting here a generation from now, and how they will look back on these years. And I think of what I want to accomplish in these years. I would like to share some of those thoughts with you this evening.

Above all, I want to complete the foundations for a world at peace— so that the next generation can be the first in this century to live without war and without the fear of war.

Beyond this, I want Americans—all Americans—to see more clearly and to feel more deeply what it is that makes this Nation of ours unique in history, unique in the world, a nation in which the soul and spirit are free, in which each person is respected, in which the individual human being, each precious, each different, can dare to dream and can live his dreams.

I want progress toward a better life for all Americans—not only in terms of better schools, greater abundance, a cleaner environment, better homes, more attractive communities, but also in a spiritual sense, in terms of greater satisfaction, more kindness in our relations with each other, more fulfillment.

I want each American—all Americans—to find a new zest in the pursuit of excellence, in striving to do their best and to be their best, in learning the supreme satisfaction of setting a seemingly impossible goal, and meeting or surpassing that goal, of finding in themselves that extra reserve of energy or talent or creativity that they had not known was there.

These are goals of a free people, in a free nation, a nation that lives not by handout, not by dependence on others or in hostage to the whims of others, but proud and independent—a nation of individuals with self-respect and with the right and capacity to make their own choices, to chart their own lives.

That is why I want us to turn away from a demeaning, demoralizing dependence on someone else to make our decisions and to guide the course of our lives.

That is why I want us to turn toward a renaissance of the individual spirit, toward a new vitality of those governments closest to the people, toward a new pride of place for the family and the community, toward a new sense of responsibility in all that we do, responsibility for ourselves and to ourselves, for our communities and to our communities, knowing that each of us, in every act of his daily life, determines what kind of community and what kind of a country we all will live in.

If, together, we can restore this spirit, than 4 years from now America can enter its third century buoyant and vital and young, with all the purpose that marked its beginning two centuries ago.

In these past 4 years, we have moved America significantly toward this goal. We have restored peace at home, and we are restoring peace abroad.

As you know, we have now made a major breakthrough toward achieving our goal of peace with honor in Vietnam. We have reached substantial agreement on most of the terms of a settlement. The settlement we are ready to conclude would accomplish the basic objectives that I laid down in my television speech to the Nation on May 8 of this year:

—the return of all of our prisoners of war, and an accounting for all of those missing in action;

—a cease-fire throughout Indochina; and

—for the 17 million people of South Vietnam, the right to determine their own future without having a Communist government or a coalition government imposed upon them against their will.

However, there are still some issues to be resolved. There are still some provisions of the agreement which must be clarified so that all ambiguities will be removed. I have insisted that these be settled before we sign the final agreement. That is why we refused to be stampeded into meeting the arbitrary deadline of October 31.

Now, there are some who say: "Why worry about the details? Just get the war over!"

Well, my answer is this. My study of history convinces me that the details can make the difference between an agreement that collapses and an agreement that lasts—and equally crucial is a clear understanding by all of the parties of what those details are.

We are not going to repeat the mistake of 1968, when the bombing halt agreement was rushed into just before an election without pinning down the details.

We want peace—peace with honor—a peace fair to all and a peace that will last. That is way I am insisting that the central points be clearly settled, so that there will be no misunderstandings which could lead to a breakdown of the settlement and a resumption of the war.

I am confident that we will soon achieve that goal.

But we are not going to allow an election deadline or any other kind of deadline to force us into an agreement which would be only a temporary truce and not a lasting peace. We are going to sign the agreement when the agreement is right, not one day before. And when the agreement is right, we are going to sign, without one day's delay.

Not only in America, but all around the world, people will be watching the results of our election. The leaders in Hanoi will be watching. They will be watching for the answer of the American people—for your answer —to this question: Shall we have peace with honor or peace with surrender?

Always in the past you have answered "Peace with honor." By giving that same answer once again on November 7 you can help make certain that peace with honor can now be achieved.

In these past 4 years, we have also been moving toward lasting peace in the world at large.

We have signed more agreements with the Soviet Union than were negotiated in all the previous years since World War II. We have established the basis for a new relationship with the People's Republic of China, where one-fourth of all the people in this world live. Our vigorous diplomacy has advanced the prospects for a stable peace in the Middle East. All around the world, we are opening doors to peace, doors that were previously closed. We are developing areas of common interest where there have been previously only antagonisms. All this is a beginning. It can be the beginning of a generation of peace—of a world in which our children can be the first generation in this century to escape the scourge of war.

These next 4 years will set the course on which we begin our third century as a nation. What will that course be? Will it have us turning inward, retreating from the responsibilities not only of a great power but of a great people—of a nation that embodies the ideals man has dreamed of and fought for through the centuries?

We cannot retreat from those responsibilities. If we did America would cease to be a great nation, and peace and freedom would be in deadly jeopardy throughout the world.

Ours is a great and a free nation today because past generations of Americans met their responsibilities. And we shall meet ours.

We have made progress toward peace in the world, toward a new relationship with the Soviet Union and the People's Republic of China, not through naive sentimental assumptions that good will is all that matters, or that we can reduce our military strength because we have no intention of making war and we therefore assume other nations would have no such intention. We have achieved progress through peace for precisely the opposite reasons: because we demonstrated that we would not let ourselves be surpassed in military strength and because we bargained with other nations on the basis of their national interest and ours.

As we look at the real world, it is clear that we will not in our lifetimes have a world free of danger. Anyone who reads history knows that danger has always been part of the common lot of mankind. Anyone who knows the world today knows that nations have not all been suddenly overtaken by some new and unprecedented wave of pure good will and benign intentions. But we can lessen the danger. We can contain it. We can forge a network of relationships and of interdependencies that restrain aggression and that take the profit out of war.

We cannot make all nations the same, and it would be wrong to try. We cannot make all of the world's people love each other. But we can establish conditions in which they will be more likely to live in peace with one another. Tonight I ask for your support as we continue to work toward that great goal.

Here at home, as we look at the progress we have made, we find that we are reaching new levels of prosperity.

We have cut inflation almost in half. The average worker has scored his best gains in 8 years in real spendable earnings. We are creating record numbers of new jobs. We are well on the way to achieving what America has not had since President Eisenhower lived here in the White House: prosperity with full employment, without inflation and without war.

We have lowered the level of violence, and we are finally turning the tide against crime.

I could go on with what we have done—for the environment, for the consumer, for the aging, for the farmer, for the worker, for all Americans —but now we must not look backward to what we have done in the past, but forward to what we will do in the future.

It is traditional for a candidate for election to make all sorts of promises about bold new programs he intends to introduce if elected. This year's Presidential campaign has probably established an all-time record for promises of huge new spending programs for just about anything and everything for everybody imaginable. I have not made such promises in this campaign. And I am not going to do so tonight. Let me tell you why.

In the first place, the sort of bold new programs traditionally promised by candidates are all programs that you—the taxpayer—pay for. The programs proposed by our opponents in this campaign would require a 50-percent increase in Federal taxes in your taxes. I think your taxes are already too high. That is why I oppose any new program which would add to your tax burden.

In the second place, too many campaign promises are just that—campaign promises. I believe in keeping the promises I make, and making only those promises I am confident I can keep. I have promised that I will do all in my power to avoid the need for new taxes. I am not going to promise anything else in the way of new programs that would violate that pledge.

In the third place, my own philosophy of government is not one that looks to new Federal dollars—your dollars—as the solution of every social problem.

I have often said that America became great not because of what government did for people, but because of what people did for themselves. I believe government should free the energies of people to build for themselves and their communities. It should open opportunities, provide incentives, encourage initiative—not stifle initiative by trying to direct everything from Washington.

This does not mean that the Federal Government will abdicate its responsibilities where only it can solve a problem.

It does mean that after 40 years of unprecedented expansion of the Federal Government, the time has come to redress the balance—to shift more people and more responsibility and power back to the States and localities and, most important, to the people, all across America.

In the past 40 years, the size of the Federal budget has grown from $4.6 billion to $250 billion. In that same period, the number of civilian employees of the Federal Government has increased from 600,000 to 2,800,000. And in just the past 10 years the number of Federal grant-in-aid programs has increased from 160 to more than 1,000.

If this kind of growth were projected indefinitely into the future, the result would be catastrophic. We would have an America topheavy with bureaucratic meddling, weighted down by big government, suffocated by taxes, robbed of its soul.

We must not and we will not let this happen to America. That is why I oppose the unrestrained growth of big government in Washington. That is why one of my first priorities in the next 4 years will be to encourage a rebirth and renewal of State and local government. That is why I believe in giving the people in every community a greater say in those decisions that most directly affect the course of their daily lives.

Now, there will be those who will call this negative, who call it a retreat from Federal responsibilities.

I call it affirmative—an affirmation of faith in the people, faith in the individual, faith in each person's ability to choose wisely for himself and for his community.

I call it an affirmation of faith in those principles that made America great, that tamed a continent, that transformed a wilderness into the greatest and strongest and freest nation in the world.

We have not changed. The American people have not grown weak. What has grown weak is government's faith in people. I am determined to see that faith restored.

I am also determined to see another kind of faith restored and strenghtened in America. I speak of the religious faith, the moral and spiritual values that have been so basically a part of our American experience. Man does not live for himself alone, and the strength of our character, the strength of our faith, and the strength of our ideals—these have been the strength of America.

When I think of what America means, I think of all the hope that lies in a vast continent—of great cities and small towns, of factories and farms, of a greater abundance, more widely shared, than the world has ever known, of a constant striving to set right the wrongs that still persist—and I think of 210 million people, of all ages, all persuasions, all races, all stations in life.

More particularly, I think of one person, one child—any child. That child many be black or brown or white, rich or poor, a boy whose family came here in steerage in 1920, or a girl whose ancestors came on the Mayflower in 1620. That one child is America, with a life still ahead, with his eyes filled with dreams, and with the birthright of every American child to a full and equal opportunity to pursue those dreams.

It is for that one child that I want a world of peace and a chance to achieve all that peace makes possible. It is for that one child that I want opportunity, and freedom, and abundance. It is for that one child that I want a land of justice, and order, and a decent respect for the rights and feelings of others.

It is for that one child that I want it said, a generation from now, a century from now, that America in the 1970's had the courage and the vision to meet its responsibilities and to face up to its challenges—to build peace, not merely for our generation but for the next generation; to restore the land, to marshal our resources, not merely for our generation but for the next generation; to guard our values and renew our spirit, not merely for our generation but for the next generation,

It is for that one child that I want these next 4 years to be the best 4 years in the whole history of America.

The glory of this time in our history is that we can do more than ever before—we have the means, we have the skills, we have an increasing understanding of how the great goals that we seek can be achieved.

These are not partisan goals. They are America's goals. That is why I ask you tonight, regardless of party, to join the new American majority next Tuesday in voting for candidates who stand for these goals. That is why I ask for your support—after the election—in helping to move forward toward these goals over the next 4 years.

If we succeed in this task, then that one child—all of our children—can look forward to a life more full of hope, promise, than any generation, in any land, in the whole history of mankind.

Thank you, and good evening.

☆

GEORGE S. McGOVERN

Acceptance Speech

MIAMI BEACH, FLORIDA

July 14, 1972

With a full heart, I accept your nomination. And this afternoon, I crossed the wide Missouri to recommend a running mate of wide vision and deep compassion—Tom Eagleton.

My nomination is all the more precious in that it is the gift of the most open political process in our national history. It is the sweet harvest cultivated by tens of thousands of tireless volunteers—old and young—and funded by literally hundreds of thousands of small contributors. Those who lingered on the edge of despair a brief time ago had been brought into this campaign—heart, hand, head and soul.

I have been the beneficiary of the most remarkable political organization in American history—an organization that gives dramatic proof to the power of love and to a faith that can move mountains.

As Yeats put it: "Count where man's glory most begins and ends, and say, my glory was I had such friends."

This is a nomination of the people, and I hereby dedicate this campaign to the people.

And next January we will restore the government to the people. American politics will never be the same again.

We are entering a new period of important, hopeful change in America comparable to the political ferment released in the eras of Jefferson, Jackson and Roosevelt.

I treasure this nomination especially because it comes after vigorous competition with the ablest men and women our party can offer.

In the months ahead, I covet the help of every Democrat and every Republican and independent who wants America to be the great and good land it can be.

This is going to be a national campaign carried to every part of the nation—North, South, East and West. We are not conceding a single state to Richard Nixon. I want to say to my friend, Frank King, that Ohio may have passed a few times at this convention, but I'm not going to pass Ohio. Governor Gilligan, Ohio may be a little slow counting the votes, but when they come in this November, they are going to show a Democratic victory.

To anyone in this hall or beyond who doubts the ability of Democrats to join together in common cause, I say never underestimate the power of Richard Nixon to bring harmony to Democratic ranks. He is our unwitting unifier and the fundamental issue of this campaign. And all of us together are going to help him recede the pledge he made ten years ago. Next year you won't have Richard Nixon to kick around any more.

We have had our fury and our frustrations in these past months and at this convention.

My old and treasured friend and neighbor, Hubert Humphrey; that gracious and good man from Maine, Ed Muskie; a tough fighter for his beliefs, Scoop Jackson; a brave and spirited woman, Shirley Chisholm; a wise and powerful lawmaker from Arkansas, Wilbur Mills; the man from North Carolina who opened new vistas in education and public excellence, Terry Sanford; the leader who in 1968 combined the travail and the hope of the American spirit, Gene McCarthy.

I was as moved as all of you by the appearance at this convention of the Governor of Alabama, George Wallace, whose votes in the primary showed the depths of discontent in this country, and whose courage in the face of pain and adversity is the mark of a man of boundless will. We all despise the senseless act that disrupted his campaign. Governor, we pray for your speedy and full recovery, so you can stand up and speak out forcefully for all those who see you as their champion.

Well, I frankly welcome the contrast with the smug, dull, and empty event which will take place here in Miami next month. We chose this struggle. We reformed our party and let the people in.

And we stand today not as a collection of backroom strategists, not as a tool of I.T.T. or any other special interest, but as a direct reflection of the public will.

So let our opponents stand on the status quo, while we seek to refresh the American spirit.

Let the opposition collect their $10-million in secret money from the privileged. And let us find one million ordinary Americans who will contribute $25 to this campaign—a McGovern "million-member club" with members who will expect not special favors for themselves but a better land for us all.

In Scripture and in the music of our children we are told: "To everything there is a season, and a time to every purpose under heaven."

And for America, the time has come at last.

This is the time for truth, not falsehood.

In a democratic nation, no one likes to say that his inspiration came from secret arrangements behind closed doors. But in a sense that is how my candidacy began. I am here as your candidate tonight in large part because during four administrations of both parties, a terrible war has been charted behind closed doors.

I want those doors opened, and I want that war closed. And I make these pledges above all others—the doors of government will be open, and that brutal war will be closed.

Truth is a habit of integrity, not a strategy of politics. And if we nurture the habit of candor in this campaign, we will continue to be candid once we are in the White House. Let us say to Americans, as Woodrow Wilson said in his first campaign: "Let me inside [the government] and I will tell you everything that is going on in there."

And this is a time not for death, but for life.

In 1968, Americans voted to bring our sons home from Vietnam in peace—and since then, 20,000 have come home in coffins.

I have no secret plan for peace. I have a public plan.

As one whose heart has ached for 10 years over the agony of Vietnam, I will halt the senseless bombing of Indochina on Inauguration Day.

There will be no more Asian children running ablaze from bombed-out schools.

There will be no more talk of bombing the dikes or the cities of the North.

Within 90 days of my inauguration, every American soldier and every American prisoner will be out of the jungle and out of their cells and back home in America where they belong.

And then let us resolve that never again will we shed the precious young blood of this nation to perpetuate an unrepresentative client abroad.

Let us choose life, not death, this is the time.

This is also the time to turn away from excessive preoccupation overseas to rebuilding our own nation.

American must be restored to her proper role in the world. But we can do that only through the recovery of confidence in ourselves. The greatest contribution America can make to our fellow mortals is to heal our own great but deeply troubled land. We must respond to that ancient command: "Physician, heal thyself."

It is necessary in an age of nuclear power and hostile ideology that we be militarily strong. America must never become a second-rate nation. As one who has tasted the bitter fruits of our weakness before Pearl Harbor, 1941, I give you my sacred pledge that if I become President of the United States, America will keep its defenses alert and fully sufficient to meet any danger. We will do that not only for ourselves, but for those who deserve and need the shield of our strength—our old allies in Europe, and elsewhere, including the people of Israel, who will always have our help to hold their promised land.

Yet we know that for 30 years we have been so absorbed with fear and danger from abroad that we have permitted our own house to fall into disarray. We must now show that peace and prosperity can exist side by side—indeed, each now depends on the other.

National strength includes the credibility of our system in the eyes of our own people as well as the credibility of our deterrent in the eyes of others abroad.

National security includes schools for our children as well as silos for our missiles, the health of our families as much as the size of our bombs, the safety of our streets and the condition of our cities and not just the engines of war.

And if we some day choke on the pollution of our own air, there will be little consolation in leaving behind a dying continent ringed with steel.

Let us protect ourselves abroad and perfect ourselves at home.

This is the time.

And we must make this a time of justice and jobs for all.

For more than three years, we have tolerated stagnation and a rising level of joblessness, with more than five million of our best workers unemployed. Surely this is the most false and wasteful economics.

Our deep need is not for idleness but for new housing and hospitals, for facilities to combat pollution and take us home from work, for products better able to compete on vigorous world markets.

The highest domestic priority of my Administration will be to insure that every American able to work has a job to do. This job guarantee will and must depend upon a reinvigorated private economy, freed at last from the uncertainties and burdens of war.

But it is our commitment that whatever employment the private sector does not provide, the Federal Government will either stimulate, or provide itself. Whatever it takes, this country is going back to work.

America cannot exist with most of our people working and paying taxes to support too many others mired in the demeaning, bureaucratic welfare system. Therefore, we intend to begin by putting millions back to work; and after that is done, we will assure those unable to work an income sufficient to assure a decent life.

Beyond this, a program to put America back to work demands that work be properly rewarded. That means the end of a system of economic controls in which labor is depressed, but prices and corporate profits are the highest in history. It means a system of national health insurance, so that a worker can afford decent health care for himself and his family. It means real enforcement of the laws so that the drug racketeers are put behind bars for good and our streets are once again safe for our families.

Above all, honest work must be rewarded by a fair and just tax system. The tax system today does not reward hard work—it penalizes it. Inherited or invested wealth frequently multiplies itself while paying no taxes at all. But wages earned on the assembly line, or laying bricks, or picking fruit—these hard earned dollars are taxed to the last penny. There is a depletion allowance for oil wells, but no allowance for the depletion of a man's body in years of toil.

The Administration tells us that we should not discuss tax reform in an election year. They would prefer to keep all discussion of the tax code in closed committee rooms, where the Administration, its powerful friends and their paid lobbyists can turn every effort at reform into a new loophole for the rich. But an election year is the people's year to speak—and this year, the people are going to insure that the tax system is changed so that work is rewarded and so that those who derive the highest benefits will pay their fair share, rather than slipping through the loopholes at the expense of the rest of us.

So let us stand for justice and jobs, and against special privilege. This is the time.

We are not content with things as they are. We reject the view of those who say: "America—love it or leave it." We reply: "Let us change it so we can love it the more."

And this is the time. It is the time for this land to become again a witness to the world for what is noble and just in human affairs. It is the time to live more with faith and less with fear—with an abiding confidence that can sweep away the strongest barriers between us and teach us that we truly are brothers and sisters.

So join with me in this campaign, lend me your strength and your support, give me your voice—and together, we will call America home to the founding ideals that nourished us in the beginning.

From secrecy and deception in high places, come home, America.

From a conflict in Indochina which maims our ideals as well as our soldiers, come home, America.

From the entrenchment of special privilege and tax favoritism, come home, America.

From military spending so wasteful that it weakens our nation, come home, America.

From the waste of idle hands to the joy of useful labor, come home, America.

From the prejudice of race and sex, come home, America.

From the loneliness of the aging poor and the despair of the neglected sick, come home, America.

Come home to the affirmation that we have a dream.

Come home to the conviction that we can move our country forward.

Come home to the belief that we can seek a newer world.

For:

    This land is your land,

    This land is my land,

    From California to the New York Island,

    From the Redwood Forest

    To the Gulfstream waters,

    This land was made for you and me.

May God grant us the wisdom to cherish this good land to meet the challenge that beckons us home.

GEORGE S. McGOVERN

Campaign Speech

WASHINGTON, D. C.

August 5, 1972

My fellow citizens:

Last week, as most of you know, Senator Thomas Eagleton withdrew as the Democratic Vice-Presidential nominee. When I learned of his treatment for mental distress, I hoped that his past afflictions would not be allowed to obscure and dominate the public dialogue.

After all, the purpose of psychiatric treatment is to restore the individual to the fullness of his powers. For millions of Americans such treatment has permanently eliminated barriers to a successful life, and who among us has not known the suffering of temporary depression—the feelings which lead many to seek professional help are often similar to these—merely more intense? They can be resolved and overcome and permanently laid to rest.

Senator Eagleton has done this, and his has been no secret victory.

Yet it soon became apparent that a disclosure of psychiatric treatment stirred a powerful sense of uneasiness among many Americans, that this question might obscure and confuse the real choices of this Presidential year, and that could not be permitted.

The scales of judgment did not contain just the careers and ambitions of a few. The issue could not be the medical history of a single man, but whether the American people will turn from the policies of the Nixon Administration to a new leadership whose capacity for thoughtful and constructive change would have their fullest confidence. That is the central issue.

With that decision in the balance and so much more, so many human hopes and so much human anguish, I felt it necessary to pursue my public responsibilities as best I saw them rather than follow the inclinations of my heart. On Tuesday the Democratic National Committee will meet to select a candidate for Vice President. At that time I will recommend the selection of Sargent Shriver as my Presidential running mate.

Mr. Shriver has served with great distinction in a number of high and difficult positions. President Kennedy chose him to organize and direct the Peace Corps, while under President Johnson he was the first director of the Office of Economic Opportunity. He later served as Ambassador to France under both President Johnson and President Nixon. A distinguished business leader, his life has been marked by a special dedication to the needs of the poor and to those who suffer from racial injustice.

I am fully confident of his ability to serve as Vice President of the United States.

And now we can move toward what President Nixon has called the the clearest political choice of the century. I agree with that analysis. It is a choice—this choice of the century between your hopes on one hand and your fears on the other, between today's America and the one you want for your children, between those who believe we must abandon our ideals to present realities and those who wish to shape reality to American ideals.

Four years ago the present Republican Administration assumed the responsibilities of national leaders. They can now be judged, not by their attacks on others but by their own actions. You elected a President who promised to end the war in Vietnam and to halt inflation, an Administration which offered to restore prosperity and replace a welfare system which is unfair both to those it serves and to those who pay for it, and Administration which pledged to make your streets safe, your air cleaner and to reunify a divided and troubled people.

Now they offer four more years of the same men and the same policies which have presided over a continued deterioration of American life.

How can they imagine that this is what you want? Perhaps they think you will accept the claims of success which flow from an election year White House. But they cannot deceive you about the experiences of your own daily lives.

You need no economist to tell you what happens to a week's wages at the supermarket checkout counter, or to the savings of a lifetime when illness strikes. The pronouncements of bureaucratic experts have not removed the fear from your streets or made it easier to send your children to decent schools.

Despite the slogans and pieties of the White House, we are a divided people still. The poor remain still, the jobless remain jobless and we seem to be losing our confidence that difficulties however great can be solved.

Men who must run on such a record are driven to conceal their own failures by trying to awaken your fears. Indeed, they have already begun. This, too, is in the tradition of a party whose nominee predicted that if Franklin Roosevelt were elected, grass would grow in the streets of a hundred cities, the weeds will overrun the fields of millions of farms, their churches and school houses will decay.

But we need not go back that far. In 1960, the Republican nominee said that John Kennedy's domestic policies could only produce cruel inflation, Government interference with every aspect of our economic life, recession or even worse.

But President Nixon did not see his warning fulfilled until his own Administration.

They could not scare the country then, and they will not scare the American people now, for the policies of the Democratic party are a danger only to those who seek power or selfish gain at the expense of the nation's strength and the well-being of its citizens.

And first among those policies that we must pursue is an end to the war in Vietnam. Like President Eisenhower, President Nixon pledged to end the war which he inherited.

Unlike President Eisenhower, he has not kept that pledge in four years. And there is no reason to believe that the President who could not bring peace in four years will be able to produce it in eight years.

After a decade of effort, after spending hundreds of billions of dollars, losing tens of thousand of lives, it is now time to come home.

We have done more than we promised. The rest is up to the people of Southeast Asia.

I will no longer deprive this nation of the honor of bringing peace in order to save the prestige of the warmakers.

I fully understand the dangers of war and the needs of security and adequate defense, but the desire for more money and for new weapons seems to have no limit at all.

.We reduce our involvement in Vietnam, and military spending goes on.

We sign an arms control agreement with the Russians, and military spending goes on.

We open up new relations with China, and military spending goes up.

I call for an end to military waste in the defense budget.

My proposed defense budget is actually larger than that of President Eisenhower at the height of the cold war. It is designed like his to satisfy the needs of security rather than the appetites of the military-industrial complex.

It will produce only one white flag when a handful for professionals and industries surrender their claim to money which has wiser and more urgent uses.

And even President Nixon may find it difficult to call us the party of war and the party of surrender in the same campaign.

Our tax reform rests on the simple principle that all citizens should be equally responsible for the burden of taxation. The tax code now fills hundreds of pages. It is riddled with loopholes, special exemptions and shelters, available to those with access to wealth or to legal talent.

Income which is earned on an assembly line or in an office should no longer be more heavily taxed than profits from oil or securities.

Tax reform endangers only those whose ability to avoid taxes has made it necessary for the rest of you to pay more.

Most of us can also agree that our present welfare system must be abolished. Those who can work should have jobs, even if the government must provide them, and all our citizens, those who work and those who cannot, should be assured an adequate income, one which will let them feed and clothe and house their families.

President Nixon himself has proposed an annual guaranteed income. We do not disagree on that principle. But poverty cannot be ended by providing less than people need even for the barest necessities of life. Every worker, and every merchant will do better when poverty gives way to new purchasing power.

These proposals and others will of course be opposed. To the extent opposition is based on misunderstanding or on honest difference of opinion, I will try to clarify the one and debate the other. As for those who attack us in defense of their own power and unjust special privilege, I welcome the struggle. Once we expose the false issues we can perhaps debate more fundamental problems.

We have built the most productive nation in all the history of the world, inhabited by a people of unequal skill and energy. And yet this enormous triumph, this peerless society, is not leading to the rapid enrichment of human life. Factories produce, new buildings go up, technology advances and yet for many Americans life is getting emptier and harder. Work is drained of its real satisfaction while the products of that labor lack the quantities, the qualities which come from pride in their production and concern for the person that will use those products.

Our land is being ravaged while our cities become more painful and more dangerous. Our native impulses toward justice for the unfortunate, the poor and the oppressed seem subdued. It is almost as though we had turned our own creation against ourselves, had forgotten that the purpose of wealth and power is not to increase itself but to enlarge the happiness and well-being of the individual.

It is our task—even our obligation to our children—to seek understanding of these problems and to begin to solve them.

A native poet wrote that, to the pioneers, America was not a place or a way of life but a journey. It was, he said, the stream uncrossed, the promise still untried, the metal sleeping in the mountainside. Now the tracks are cold and the land subdued.

But the chronicle of America, like some great river, sweeps into the future. It cannot be mastered by clinging to threatened banks but only by those who, unafraid and desiring, set out upon powerful and uncertain currents, transforming shifting dangers and change into a trail for a new American journey. This time, not a journey to a distant coast but inward, toward the most powerful aspirations of the human heart.

To make this society, its factories, its institutions, its schools, its government, to serve each person's right to extend all the powers of his humanity to the limits of possibility—that is what Thomas Jefferson meant when he wrote of the pursuit of happiness.

Neither I nor any President can give you this but you can. I do not ask you to believe in me but to believe in yourselves. Yours will be the choice between America's present and those American possibilities between what we are and what we could be.

If those of us seeking positions of leadership can make that choice clear, if we can sweep away illusions and lies and false threats, I have no doubt what will be your answer. It is one Americans have always giv before.

For myself, as this campaign begins, I ask only, in the words of mon, give me now wisdom and knowledge that I may go out and before this people, for who can judge this thy people that is so

☆